# MUZZLELOADER MAGAZINE'S

# THE BOOK OF
# BUCKSKINNING V

Edited by
## WILLIAM H. SCURLOCK

REBEL PUBLISHING COMPANY, INC./TEXARKANA, TEXAS

# EDITORIAL STAFF

**EDITOR:**
William H. Scurlock

**ASSOCIATE EDITORS:**
Linda Cook Scurlock
Becky J. Rodgers

**GRAPHIC DESIGN:**
William H. Scurlock

**COVER PHOTOGRAPHY**
Athi Mara Magadi (Front)
David Wright (Back)

**PUBLISHER:**
Oran Scurlock, Jr.

# ABOUT THE COVERS

*FRONT:*
*Cathy Smith, author of "Fur Trade Indian Dresses" in this book and "Quillworking" in the Book of Buckskinning III, models an Upper Missouri style two-hide dress of her own making. Cathy is the proprietor of Medicine Mountain Trading Company, P.O. Box 6342, Santa Fe, New Mexico 87502.*

*BACK:*
*During a break in a late-season squirrel hunt, longhunters Steve Davis, Bruce Hering and Wally Fuller survey the landscape of Tennessee's Chestnut Mountain area. These longtime buckskinners from Tennessee, Illinois and Alabama, respectively, are active in 18th century events throughout the Southeast.*

*INSIDE FRONT:*
*"Virginia Soldier" by Lee Teter (courtesy of Fort Ligonier Association). This soldier of the First Virginia Regiment is attired in "Indian dress" for the Forbes campaign against Fort Duquesne. He wears a black or red silk handkerchief on his head, a linen shirt, a blue stroud "matchcoat" or mantle, a stroud breechcloth and leggings, garters and moccasins.*

*INSIDE BACK:*
*"The Arrowhead" by Lee Teter. An Eastern American Indian of the mid-18th century reflects upon the work of days gone by. The skills and life style of his forefathers are gradually dying out as evidenced by the clothing and tools he depends on now. Limited edition prints are available from Lee Teter, 1023 Shades Lane, Cumberland, MD 21502.*

First Printing: August 1989
Second Printing: March 1992

ISBN #0-9605666-6-X Library of Congress Catalog Card #89-060770

# Contents

# Fur Trade Indian Dresses

## by Cathy Smith with Jerry Fahrenthold

CATHY SMITH IS A SPECIALIST in the material culture of the northern Plains native peoples with technical expertise in the field of porcupine quillwork. A native of western South Dakota, her orientation derives from a lifelong association with the Lakota Sioux. Cathy's interests have led her to years of study and production of 19th century North American Indian art forms. She is well-known in the field of artifact restoration and her own contemporary work can be seen in galleries and collections across the country. Cathy has recently moved her business, Medicine Mountain, to Santa Fe, New Mexico.

Cathy is a historian and living history interpreter of the fur trade era as well. She has spoken at each of the Annual Fur Trade Symposiums, lectured at universities and galleries and is a promoter of cross-cultural interpretation.

Selected publications by Cathy Smith are: "Rendezvous & Religion: A Commentary on Contemporary Ceremonialism" (1986); "Silent Partners: Women in the Fur Trade, 1670-1987" (1987); "Quillworking" in *The Book of Buckskinning III* (1985). In addition, her work was featured in *Crafts of America: A Guide to the Finest Traditional Crafts Made in the United States,* edited by Constance Stapleton.

Cathy may be contacted by mail at Medicine Mountain, Box 6342, Santa Fe, New Mexico 87502, or by phone at (505) 894-0710.

JERRY FAHRENTOLD, AGE 39, has been an avid student of American Indian art since he was 12 years old. Originally from Poth, Texas, near San Antonio, his interest began with the Order of the Arrow in the Boy Scouts and moved on to the Hunka Indian Dancers and the Texas Indian Hobbyist Association. Continuing interest in a Western "cowboy club" in Munich, West Germany, and the desire to go powwow dancing in the Rocky Mountains near traditional northern Plains tribes led him to move to Red Lodge, Montana, where he has lived for 12 years.

Jerry has produced brain tanned and commercial deer hides for 15 years. He has been a student of the fur trade era since 1980 and has attended many rendezvous since. A gradute of the University of Texas, Jerry spends his time in glacier travel, dealing in and making Indian art, backpacking, building his own log home, canoe and horse trips, running, and folk dancing. He has spoken on parfleche manufacture at the Buffalo Bill Historical Center in Cody, Wyoming, and demonstrated brain tanning at the first Annual Fur Trade Symposium at Fort Laramie National Historic Site.

We know that there were few white women involved in the Western fur trade. Josiah Gregg, in his *Commerce of the Prairies,* speaks of a Spanish family with female members traveling with his Santa Fe Trail caravan in 1831. He also states that other women ''have crossed the prairies to Santa Fe at different times, among whom I have known two respectable French ladies, who now reside in Chihuahua'' (36). In 1836, Narcissa Whitman and Eliza Spaulding accompanied their missionary husbands to Oregon. They traveled with the rendezvous supply train of Thomas Fitzpatrick as far as the Green River Rendezvous and from there continued on to Walla Walla with the Hudson's Bay caravan of John McLeod and Thomas McKay (Gowans 130-143). There was also Susan Magoffin, who accompanied her husband Samuel, a Santa Fe trader, down the Santa Fe Trail into Mexico in 1846.

What we have is a half-dozen or so documented white women in the West at the time of the fur trade, none of which were really involved in the activity of the trade. Therefore, in writing this article on women's fur trade fashions, we must focus our attention on the women of the West that were truly involved in this historical epoch: the thousands of Native American women who were at home in the West before the first white man ever set out to explore its treasures.

Documentation of the Indian women of the West is scarce; descriptions of their clothing prior to 1850 are almost negligible, as are the existing artifacts themselves. Because of this unfortunate circumstance, drawings will have to take the place of photographs in many instances.

Our study will be divided into two main groups: one consisting of the northern plains, mountains and plateaus; and the other of the southern plains. These groups are divided mainly by factors of climate, resource availability and culture adaptation resulting from Indian-White contact (Ewers, ''Climate'' 63-82). Women's clothing consisted of five main pieces: the dress, robe or blanket, leggings, moccasins, and belt. Dress styles will be our major consideration.

# THE NORTHERN
# PLAINS DRESS

The northern plains area in the early 19th century contained a diverse mixture of ethnic subcultures. Some had been plains dwellers for generations (the Mandan, Hidatsa, Arikara and Crow) while a few such as the Teton Sioux and Cheyenne were relative newcomers to the plains, having migrated from the Great Lakes and upper Mississippi area. For our purposes we will include the plateau peoples (Nez Perce, Flathead, Blackfeet, Cree and Assiniboin) and the mountain Ute and Shoshoni in this section. The central plains east of the Missouri River and south to the South Platte ap-

Upper Missouri dress with quilled shoulder strips and deep crescent plugs on the bottom contour. Accessories include quilled "keyhole" moccasins and quilled bag. Made by Cathy Smith. Also pictured on page V of the color section.

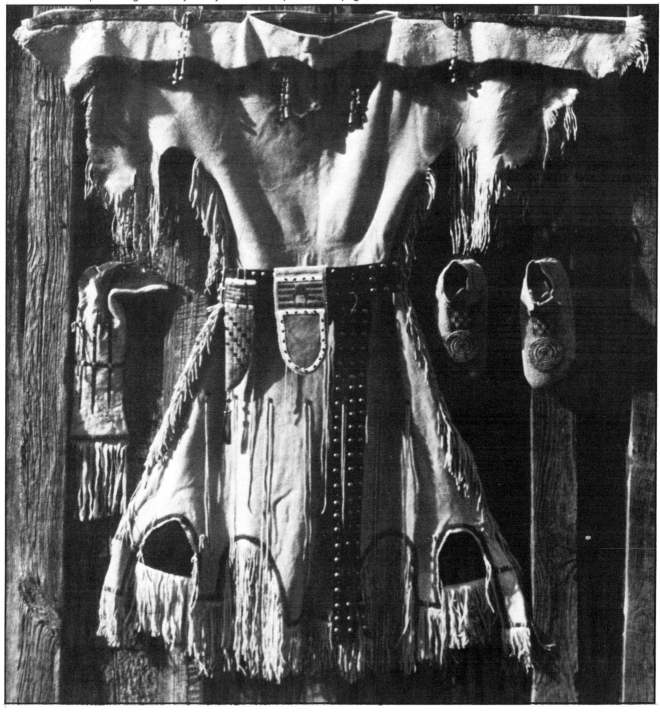

proaching the Arkansas River complete our sketch of the northern plains.

Clothing styles of the people within this culture area were interrelated due largely to an extensive native trade network that existed before the time of Lewis and Clark. The Assiniboin and Cree traded with the Mandan-Hidatsa as well as the English of Hudson's Bay and the Northwest Companies. The Crow traded with Shoshonis, Flatheads, Nez Perce and Mandan, while the Shoshonis in turn traded with the Spaniards through the Utes. The northern Cheyenne traded with the southern tribes through the Arapahoe for Spanish horses and with the Teton for English trade goods acquired through the eastern Sioux (Ewers, "Climate" 17-33). Through this contact gifts and ideas were exchanged and fashion styles were influenced and spread.

Three types of dresses have been documented on the northern plains in the early historic period. These are the strap or slip dress with detachable sleeves, the side-fold dress and the two-hide dress (Wissler 65-90).

The information we have on women's dresses prior to 1850 is often confusing in regard to tribal identification and incomplete as to construction detail. We will attempt to clarify these issues and offer some instruction tailored to those readers wishing to create authentic fur trade clothing. This article will consider the strap dress and the side-fold dress, but will focus primarily on the two-hide dress prevalent on the upper Missouri during the height of the American fur trade in the 1830s.

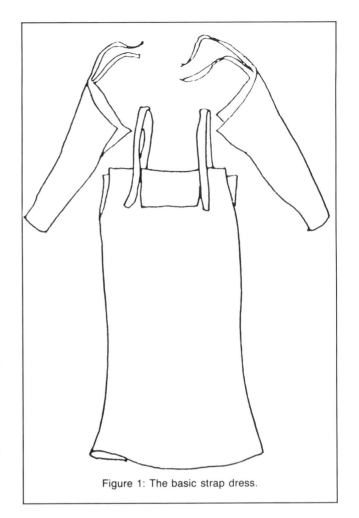

Figure 1: The basic strap dress.

## THE STRAP DRESS

This early style of dress is generally associated with the Ojibwa and plains Cree but was also documented among the Blackfeet in the 1790s (Henry and Thompson 514-515), the Sioux (Lessard 70), the Cheyenne, the Pawnee and the Assiniboin (Wissler 70-79).

The strap dress, as shown in Figure 1, is made of two large skins trimmed into rectangles, sewn together along the sides and held up with shoulder straps. The tops of the hides were folded down to form flaps over the chest and upper back. The dress is supported by two straps which leave the shoulders bare. Separate sleeves are usually attached to each other by a strap or tie and are worn in cold weather.

Daniel Harmon in his journal gives the following account:

*The shirt or coat, which is so long as to reach the middle of the leg, is tied at the neck, is fringed around the bottom, and fancifully painted, as high as the knee. Being very loose, it is girded around the waist with a stiff belt, ornamented with tassels, and fastened behind. The arms are covered as low as the wrists with sleeves, which are sewed up, as far as the bend of the arm, having the seam on the under side; and extend to the shoulders, becoming broader toward the upper end, so that the corners hang down as low as the waist. They are connected together, and kept on, by a cord, extending from one to the other, across the shoulders."* (53)

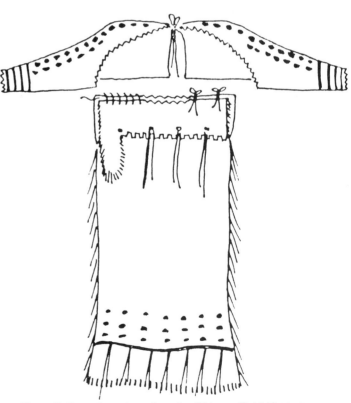

Figure 2: Cree strap dress from the Chicago Field Museum.

4

Figure 3: Cree strap dress from the Chicago Field Museum. Made from smoked buckskin and painted with red ochre.

Strap dresses were fashioned from wool stroud or trade cloth as well as hides. James Isham observed that Cree women near the Hudson's Bay posts were making their dresses of trade cloth as early as 1743 (109-110). Rudolph Kurz, in his Ft. Union journal of 1850, reports that Salteur (Ojibwa and Chippewa) women dressed in blue wool strap dresses with elaborate beaded girdles and straps. He further comments that Cree dress, like Salteur, is a skirt held up by straps, but in cold weather they put on sleeves leaving the right arm free and they wear shirt-like skirts that, instead of being held in place by straps, are made to extend over the shoulders. This later description seems to be of a side-fold dress, the second of our three types (84, 157).

Before we discuss the side-fold dress, mention should be made of a dress in the collections of the Chicago Field Museum that seems to be a transition between the strap and side-fold. It is a Cree dress, pictured in Figures 2, 3 and 4, made of heavy buckskin with two pieces sewn and fringed down the sides and a top fold with one non-functional strap extension. It is painted red along the top of the detachable sleeves and along the bottom hem.

In 1833, when Prince Maximilian zu Wied visited the upper Missouri, the strap dress was no longer in fashion. The Cree and Salteur women documented by Kurz seem to be the only ones still dressed in this fashion by the mid-1800s.

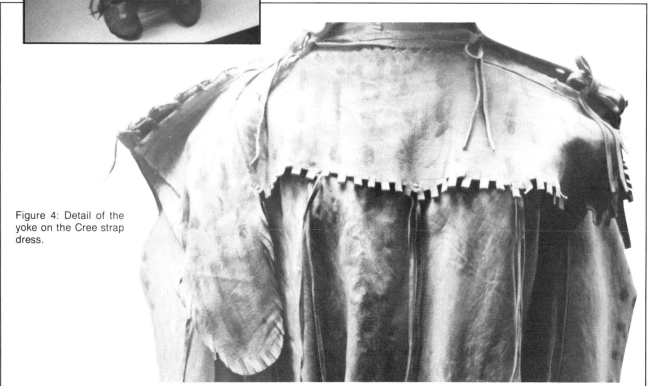

Figure 4: Detail of the yoke on the Cree strap dress.

5

## THE SIDE-FOLD DRESS

The side-fold dress is made from one large hide, possibly moose or buffalo cow. The skin must be large enough to wrap around the entire body, so that there is a seam on only one side. The top is folded down to produce a straight top edge and a flap that usually hangs down to about the waist. More often than not this flap is cut on the fold and resewn to the dress body so the texture of the hide is the same on body and yoke. This horizontal seam is usually hidden by the top fold (Feder, ''Side Fold'' 55). A vertical cut is then made in the side fold edge to form an armhole for the right arm and a strap is sewn in place to fit over the right shoulder. The left side of the dress is sewn together and hangs down lower than the right side. Other variations define tribal differences. The layout and construction of this dress is shown in Figure 5.

According to Norman Feder in his informative article on side-fold dresses, there are ten such dresses in existing collections (48-55). Three are documented as Cree, two as Sioux and five are undocumented, but they may be Sioux, Cheyenne, Assiniboin or Cree. Lewis and Clark brought two of these dresses back in 1804, Maximilian collected one in 1833 and his artist Bodmer painted a Teton Sioux woman wearing such a dress in that same year (Thomas and Ronnefeldt 47). Dr. Nathan Sturges Jarvis collected a Yankton Sioux dress at Fort Snelling between 1833 and 1836 (Brooklyn Museum), Paul Kane painted a Cree girl in a side-fold dress at Edmonton in 1847 (Manitoba Museum of Man & Nature) and Kurz sketched a Cree dress with attached sleeves in 1850 (Feder, ''Side Fold'' 56).

It seems that this type of dress was typical among the Cree much later into the 19th century than it was among other plains women. The Cree dress was distinct in that it usually had a rectangular panel of quill-wrapped fringe across the breast and the left shoulder, as well as quill-wrapped fringe on the bottom edge. These dresses were often painted or smudged with spots of vermilion across the yoke and bottom third. See Figure 6 and Figure 7.

The Sioux side-fold dress has been likened to the buffalo robe outer garment worn by most northern plains women. If one folded down the top quarter of a quilled robe, wrapped it around a woman and sewed up the open side, the process would produce a garment similar to a side-fold dress (Lessard 71). All of the known Sioux dresses are decorated with quilled horizontal stripes across the skirt, a row of metal cone tinklers across the bottom edge and additional pony-beaded strips across the top fold or along the bottom hem.

George Bird Grinnell substantiated the use of the side-fold dress among the early Cheyenne:

*'In the time of our grandmothers,' old women say, 'perhaps a hundred years ago [1800], the dresses worn by the women were longer on the right side than on the left. The right arm had a short sleeve, there was a strap over the left shoulder, and the hide was double back, hanging from the upper chest in a loose flap, ending in an edge which ran diagonally from the right shoulder in front around the body to below the left shoulder blade.'* (57)

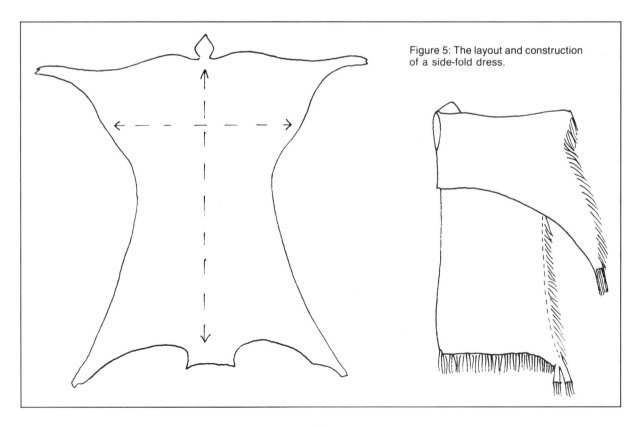

Figure 5: The layout and construction of a side-fold dress.

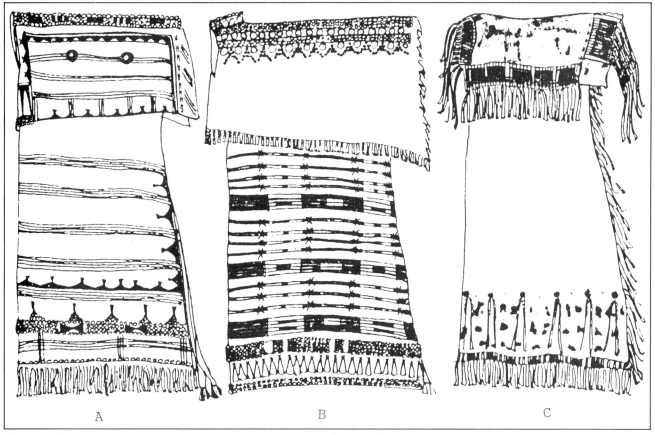

Figure 6: Three side-fold dresses. A: Sioux-type dress collected by Lewis & Clark with painted stripes and pony-beaded shoulder and bottom edge. B: Second Sioux-type dress collected by Lewis & Clark with "pony-trader blue" pony beaded yoke and hem and horizontal quilled stripes across the skirt. C: Cree-type dress with quill-wrapped fringe on yoke, sleeve and hem. Also smudged with red paint.

Feder maintains that in spite of the above information, the strap hung over the right shoulder and the open seam, which hung down further, was on the left side. The Bodmer painting noted above is shown this way, as is Kurz's sketch. Wearing the dress in this way would leave the right arm free and uncovered for work, which makes sense (Feder, "George" 51). It is also reasonable to assume that detachable sleeves were worn with these side-fold dresses in cold weather.

Ornamentation on all existing specimens consists of quillwork or pony beadwork. Many of the dresses are painted on the yokes and lower border as well. One of the Lewis and Clark dresses has painted stripes instead of quilled stripes as its main decoration, with a narrow band of pony beadwork on the top fold and bottom edge. This Sioux-type dress is illustrated in Figure 6A. The other Lewis and Clark dress, Figure 6B, is beaded in three sizes of "pony trader blue" pony beads; has numerous horizontal quilled stripes in white, orange-red, and blue; flat brass buttons on one side and cowrie shells on the other (below the beaded stripe on the yoke); copper cones across the bottom; and horizontal stripes across the bodice painted with clear sizing. This is also a Sioux-type dress. The Cree dresses, in contrast, have panels across the yoke and left sleeve of intricate quill-wrapped fringe. The bottom fringe is also quill-wrapped. One has a pony beaded stripe in black and white across the lower third, the other has a quilled

stripe, and both are smudged with red paint between this stripe and the hem. This is shown in Figure 6C.

Cheyenne dresses were originally quilled and painted, but after beads arrived "it is said they were decorated with two rows of blue beads running across above the belt . . . ornaments of porcupine quills, in the form of loops, hung down from them. Across her bare arm a woman might paint a red stripe for every coup her husband had counted" (Powell 43).

The side-fold dress, then, was fashionable at approximately the same time as the strap dress. Perhaps Kurz's speculation that the side-fold dress was winter wear while the strap dress was worn in summer is a reasonable assumption.

Figure 7: (Facing page) A Cree side-fold dress from the Ottawa National Museum of Man. Intricate bands of quill-wrapped fringe decorate the yoke and sleeve, as well as the bottom. This dress is also pictured on page II of the color section.

## THE TWO-HIDE DRESS

The two-hide dress was the established style when Prince Maximilian zu Wied explored the upper Missouri in 1833-34. Maximilian's journal, illustrated with the paintings of Karl Bodmer, gives us numerous descriptions of this dress:

June 18, 1833: At Ft. Clark — Crow women were described in dresses of bighorn leather embroidered with dyed quills, as were their buffalo robes (Thomas and Ronnefeldt 36).

June 24, 1833: At Ft. Union — Bodmer painted a Cree woman wearing an undecorated two-hide dress with the deer tail retained on the yoke. Her chin was tatooed and her face painted with vermilion (Thomas and Ronnefeldt 69).

August 1833: At Ft. McKenzie — Bodmer painted a Piegan Blackfeet in a two-hide dress ornamented with blue and white pony beaded shoulder strips and a similarly beaded belt. A Shoshone woman was depicted as well, in a similar dress with pony trader blue and white pony beadwork (Thomas and Ronnefeldt 126-127).

George Catlin visited the Upper Missouri the year before Maximilian. He recorded in his paintings many two-hide dresses as well. Catlin's paintings cannot, however, be accepted with the photographic literacy of Bodmer's, for he was known to assume some artistic license (Feder, ''George'' 72-75). From Catlin we have:

*An Assiniboin woman and girl, wearing respectively a two-hide dress with a quilled or pony beaded shoulder strip, wrapped in a robe or cape having a quilled star on the shoulder, and the girl's dress ornamented with elk teeth. (Quimby 26)*

*A Mandan girl with gray hair, Sha-ko-ka, in a classic two-hide dress with saved hair and deer tail on the edge of the yoke, pony beaded shoulder and breast bands, as well as a row of elk teeth. (Quimby 48) See Figure 8E.*

Catlin also depicts a Blackfeet and a Sioux woman in this style of dress (62, 32). Look at Figure 8D for illustration of this Sioux dress yoke covered in brass buttons, with pony beaded shoulder strips.

According to Clark Wissler in his *Costumes of the Plains Indians,* the origin of the two-hide dress is clearly restricted to the Nez Perce, Crow, Mandan, Hidatsa, Arapaho, Kiowa and some of the Shoshoni (Wissler 85).

Figure 8: A cross section of two-hide dress yokes. A: Canadian Blackfeet from the Museum of the American Indian. B: Blackfeet from the Museum of the American Indian. C: Upper Missouri from the American Museum of Natural History. D: Sioux painted by George Catlin (pony-beaded shoulders and brass buttons). E: Mandan painted by George Catlin in 1832 (pony beads and elk teeth). F: Shoshone painted by Bodmer in 1833.

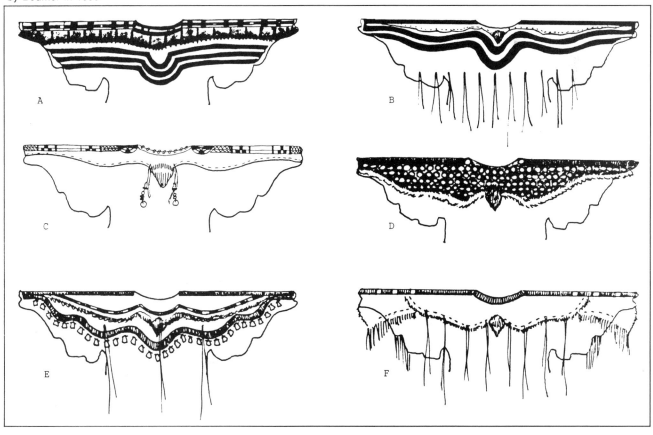

A Ute two-hide dress from the Chicago Field Museum.

A Klamath two-hide dress from the Chicago Field Museum. The wide rows of pony beads are green, red, pony-trader blue and white.

## CONSTRUCTION

Many specimens are constructed of big horn sheep hides, but deer hides are also common. This is easily determined by observing the hair that is most often left on the hides at the tail and legs. The complete female hide is left intact. This includes features such as mammaries, legs (sometimes including dewclaws), the tail with the hair remaining (this often includes hair remaining on the edge of the buttocks) and frequently the entire face (including the nose). To brain tan such a hide requires rare skill. Generally, the plateau hides are wet beamed to removed the hair, which produces a beautiful texture on the grain side of the hide, while plains hides are sometimes dry scraped. Dry scraping leaves ''chatter marks'' on the grain.

A basic feature of construction involves the method in which the yoke is put together using the butt end of the hide. This method of construction is pictured in Figure 9. With the flesh side facing upwards, approximately five inches of the butt end is folded back over itself causing the grain side of this section to now face upwards. You should use the center of the hide at the tail end. The tail is centered and this new top is evenly overlapped across the surface of the flesh side. This will cause the top part of the dress, especially near the sleeves, to form a crescent-shaped curve. Note that the 5-inch fold must be tapered down along the legs to about one inch on the end (See Figure 9A). This top is then pinned down all the way across the hide. The edge of the butt side is then laced to its underside using a running stitch with a very fine buckskin thong all the way across the hide. The lacing stitches must be as small and close as strength allows. This means that holes punched by the awl are about ¼-inch apart. This procedure has now given us a hide with a closed cylinder at the butt end.

Now, right next to the butt end of the stitching, cut the bottom or back side of this cylinder all the way across the hide, following the line of your stitches as shown in Figure 9B. Fold out the bottom side of the cylinder and we have created a new butt side or top for the dress (Figure 9C). This gives us the unique shape of the dress with the grain side and the tail showing on the yoke. This procedure is repeated with the other hide to form the opposite side of the dress.

Place the yoke or top edge of one hide next to that of the other hide with the right sides together. There will be a natural curve in the center of each, which will become the slit for the head. Trim this evenly to form a neck slot of about 12 inches or whatever fits well. Trim the remainder of what will become the shoulder seam so that both hides will fit evenly and symmetrically (Figure 9D). Lace the two hides together with buckskin thongs in a whip stitch from the edge of the neck slot to the bottom edge of the leg. There should be about 6 or 7 inches remaining at the end of each leg. Three or four inches of this should be fringed. See Figure 9E. Note that all fringe and lacing on the dress should be about ⅛-inch wide. Fine fringe is a must! About ½ to 1 inch of red wool tradecloth is bound around the neck opening with buckskin lacing applied in a wide whip stitch over the wool, producing a decorative effect.

A Blackfoot two-hide dress from the Chicago Field Museum. It features blue and white pony beads on the yoke, red and white around the neck and black and white bordering the bottom.

11

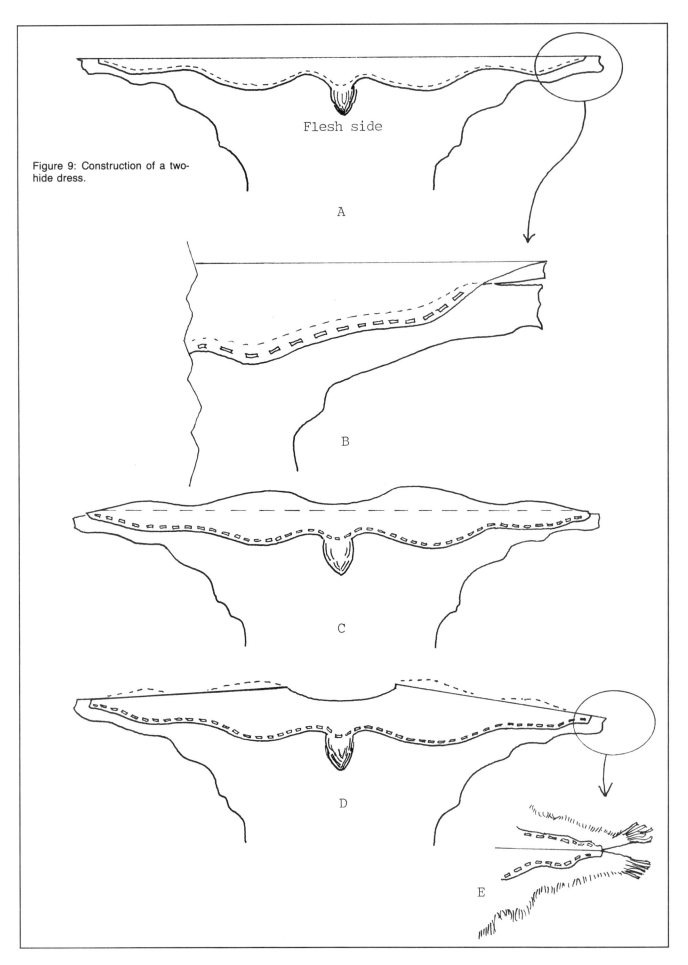

Figure 9: Construction of a two-hide dress.

Flesh side

A

B

C

D

E

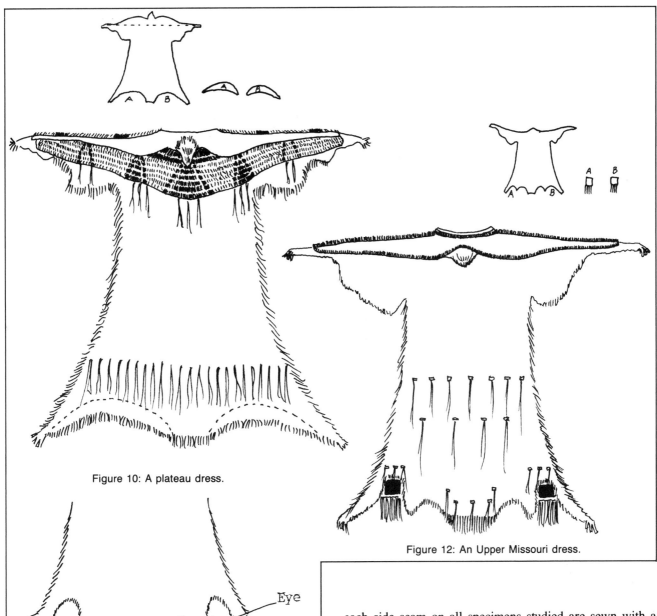

Figure 10: A plateau dress.

Figure 12: An Upper Missouri dress.

Figure 11: The bottom contour of a Sioux dress with a deer face used as the plugs.

Eye

Nose

Very little trimming is needed to shape the sides of the skirt (Wissler 65). To sew the sides, find the point below the mammaries where the flank goes farthest into the hide. Turn the dress inside out and place these sides together. Here we will need buckskin from an extra hide to cut out fringe welts. (If the hides are large enough, they may be cut from the same area where they will be replaced as fringe.) Place two fringe welts about 2½ to 3 inches wide between each hide, running the entire length of the dress. We will leave about 4 or 5 inches of unlaced hide at the end of the forelegs. Lace the two sides containing the two fringe welts between them with fine, long buckskin thonging. Examination of collection pieces has shown that the bottom 7 inches or so of

each side seam on all specimens studied are sewn with a whip stitch using sinew. This was perhaps done because this area of the hide is thinner and more delicate. It is also subject to a lot of rough wear. Repeat this process with the other side and cut and stretch the fringe. You may also elect to wet and twist the fringe.

The contour of the lower portion of the dress basically follows the natural shape of the hide, as it does with the rest of the garment. Regional variations, though, are obvious. Plateau dresses, such as the one shown in Figure 10, are distinct with their gentle, bottom curves that smooth out the basic trifurcate contour created by the neck flap and the forelegs. A smooth, crescent-shaped plug is added on each side of the neck flap. Note that many dresses require the addition of plugs in order to acquire the desired bottom contour. Examination of a Sioux dress in a private collection revealed the use of the deer's face as the plug. The nose and eye holes were apparent on the plugs, half of the face used on each side. This is pictured in Figure 11. No portion of the hides was wasted.

Upper Missouri dresses have an extra deep, yet more narrow crescent-shaped cutout next to each foreleg on the

dress bottom. These dresses have much more sharply defined lines along the bottom, often containing the entire face of the animal as well. They also have the characteristic red and blue wool plugs attached under the deeper cutouts next to the forelegs. See Figure 12.

Many specimens examined have up to 10 inches of attached fringe laced onto the neck flap and adjacent cutouts, while the Sioux dress described above has a 1½-inch unfringed border along the upper side, which is laced onto the lower section of the dress. This is laced with a long, narrow buckskin thong in a whip stitch. The awl-punched holes are about ¼-inch apart. The crescent cutouts under which the plugs are attached are usually cut into short, 1-inch fringe along their edge. Sometimes this feature may be omitted if the bottom of the dress has a row of beadwork along the edge.

Upper Missouri two-hide dress made by Cathy Smith. It has blue and white pony beadwork on the shoulders. Note the deep crescent cutouts with wool plugs. Also pictured on page IV of the color section.

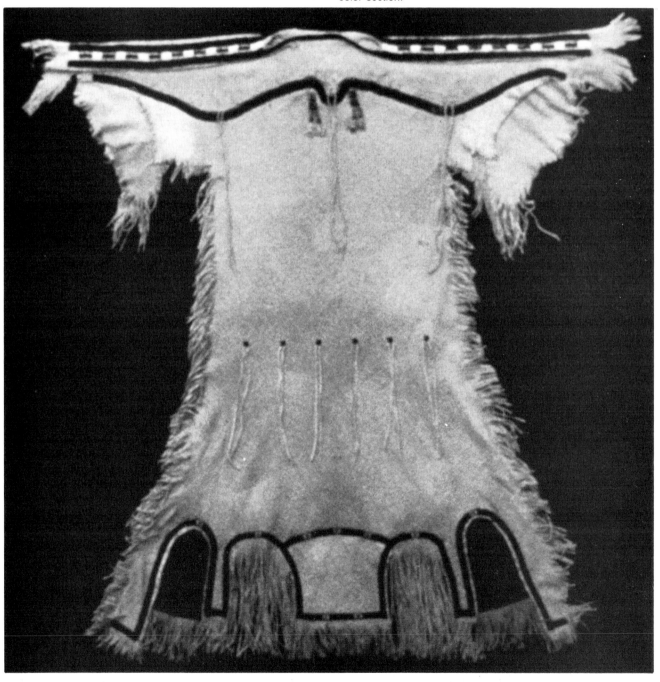

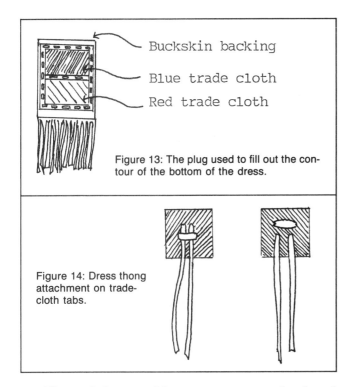

Buckskin backing

Blue trade cloth

Red trade cloth

Figure 13: The plug used to fill out the contour of the bottom of the dress.

Figure 14: Dress thong attachment on trade-cloth tabs.

sisting of approximately 20 sets of thongs in each row. Thongs are also attached just below the yoke seam. These are also arranged in various symmetrical patterns.

The ends of all the legs are fringed about 4 inches, cutting into the remaining hair. The sleeves beneath the hind legs extending to the side seams are fringed out of the edges of the hide. This cuts into the mammary area, which also contains some hair. The sleeve pattern sometimes varies in the cut, especially with later evolution. The early Sioux dress described above cuts in at a right angle just above the mammaries. However, this may have more to do with the shape of the original hide than a specific pattern procedure. A Crow specimen is also trimmed narrowly along the hind leg, further above the mammary area (Wissler 64). We suggest leaving as much of the original hide intact as possible. The front and back sides of the dress should be identical.

Ornamentation on pre-1850 dresses is limited to the use of quillwork or pony beads (Lyford 56). Many plateau specimens use several sizes of pony beads in the same field. We recommend using the smaller sizes of pony beads. Colors used in this period are also extremely limited. Upper Missouri dresses rarely contain more than two colors. Many use black and white, but blue and white is a more desirable combination. A pumpkin color was sometimes used with black or white. A few deep buff, light and dark red, and dark blue pony beads have also been noted (Lyford 56). We have observed at least six different shades of the pony trader blue on various specimens and several shades are sometimes used within the same field. Some beads currently available may

The wool plugs are either square or rectangular shaped and approximately 4 inches wide, the upper half usually blue wool and the lower half red. Sometimes the patches of wool are divided vertically. These are attached to a larger buckskin plug by lacing and the edges of the wool are bound to the buckskin plug within a ¼-inch wide strip of buckskin binding. The lower portion of the buckskin backing extends

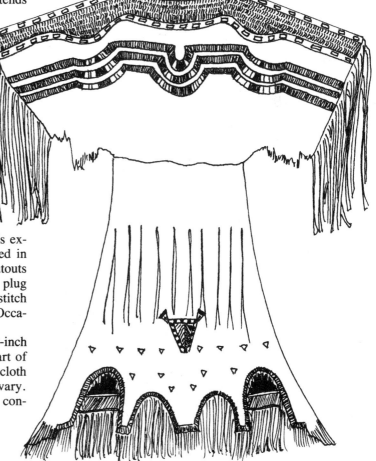

Figure 15: A Sioux (?) dress from the Twiss Collection.

approximately 4 or more inches below the wool. This extension is then fringed. The complete plug, illustrated in Figure 13, is attached just underneath the crescent cutouts next to the forelegs by sewing the upper edge of the plug to the dress hide with sinew, using a whip stitch. The stitch does not penetrate all the way through the dress hide. Occasionally the plugs are decorated with beadwork.

Two or three rows of approximately 16- to 30-inch doubled buckskin thongs are attached to the lower part of the dress using a ½-inch square red or blue wool tradecloth tab, as shown in Figure 14. Quantity and arrangement vary. Plateau dresses often have two rows near the bottom con-

A Yakima two-hide dress from the Chicago Field Museum. Note the wide lanes of blue and white pony beads characteristic of the plateau style.

An unusual Crow two-hide dress from the Chicago Field Museum. The buckskin is rubbed with ochre and decorated with hundreds of "eye" beads.

16

tern flows with the natural contour of the butt end of the hide which also curves downward on each side of the tail. Here we can clearly see the beginning of the evolution of contemporary fully beaded Sioux yokes.

Many Blackfeet dresses also have a single row of lazy stitch running along the bottom hem contour above the fringe. Bodmer shows a similar row along the bottom foreleg portion of a dress on a Teton Sioux woman. A triangular ornament usually placed about mid-way on the skirt portion of the dress is common on Blackfeet dresses. It is similar to that found on some buffalo robes, Red Cloud's shirt and later period panel leggings. The triangular patch is usually split vertically: half red wool and half blue or black wool bordered by a single row of lazy stitch beadwork. This is illustrated in Figure 16. Blackfeet informants have said that this ornament could only be used by special women who lived in a tipi painted in a way indicative of owning a buffalo calling stone (Razka).

It is interesting to note the evolution of dresses from the two-hide to the three-hide style. One particular specimen in the Heye Foundation (Twiss Collection circa 1855), depicted in Figure 15, exhibits this change. It is labeled Blackfeet and is highly stylized in both hide tailoring and beadwork design. It has a third hide added as the yoke and the sleeves are cut square with much fringe added. While it has the classic Blackfeet beaded strips across the yoke with the usual curve under the now-absent tail, it also has the fully beaded upper yoke typical of early Sioux dresses. The bottom of the dress has a lot of long added fringe and very deeply cut crescent curves to show a new creativity that is accented with a single row of lazy stitch. Also notable are small beaded triangles above each set of decorative thongs hanging from the body of the skirt. The dress has been cut around the waist and an extra piece added, perhaps to adjust in size for a new owner. This would easily be covered by a belt.

Another dress at Heye labeled Blackfeet exhibits the fully beaded yoke of the Sioux style with the tail absent but replaced by a beaded representation. The beadwork on the yoke contains more intricate design elements than earlier dresses. Again the sleeves are cut straight and the bottom of the dress is heavily fringed with the stylish, exaggerated crescent-shaped cutouts. We suggest that these two dresses are excellent examples of the transition that took place circa 1850. Both examples are pictured on page 45 of *Blackfoot Craftworkers Book* by Adoph and Beverly Hungry Wolf. We also suggest that they may indeed be Sioux instead of Blackfeet because of the Sioux-style yokes. Additional evidence to support this conclusion comes from the fact that the first dress was part of the Twiss Collection. Twiss was an agent at Ft. Laramie in 1855 and married an Oglala woman.

It appears to be simple enough to identify a plateau dress from an upper Missouri specimen, but to give a specific tribal designation becomes much more academic. Records on the origin of specimens from this period are much too obscure. We can see a great similarity in most pre-1850 upper Missouri dresses by their simplicity in adapting the complete shape of the hide to the human form. The specifics of this regional style are also predominant in the lower cutouts around the animal's head and foreleg area, with further insight coming from any beadwork style that may be present. Hopefully, we have provided some clarification on the construction of these elegant garments of the fur trade era.

Figure 16: A Blackfoot dress from the Ottawa National Museum of Man. Note the triangular motif in the center of the skirt. This dress is also pictured on page III of the color section.

be treated with hydrofluoric acid to produce shades closer to that of beads on original pieces.

Many dresses lack beadwork, but the design elements of those specimens that are beaded give us more insight as to tribal origin. Blackfeet dresses usually are identified by their classic striped bands of alternating, contrasting colors (often black or blue and white) with the U-shaped curve below the tail (Conn, ''Blackfeet'' 115). These are accompanied by a row of lazy stitch along the shoulder seam. See Figure 8A and B. Many dresses from various tribes have only this beaded shoulder seam. See Karl Bodmer's painted examples of this shoulder seam on Piegan Blackfeet, Shoshoni and Cree women. Plateau beadwork is distinguishable by wide rows of large pony heads and the use of more colors on the same piece. Sioux examples generally show more rows of beadwork parallel to the shoulder strip, as shown in Figure 15.

On Sioux dresses, this fully beaded field curves downward below each side of the neck opening. This pat-

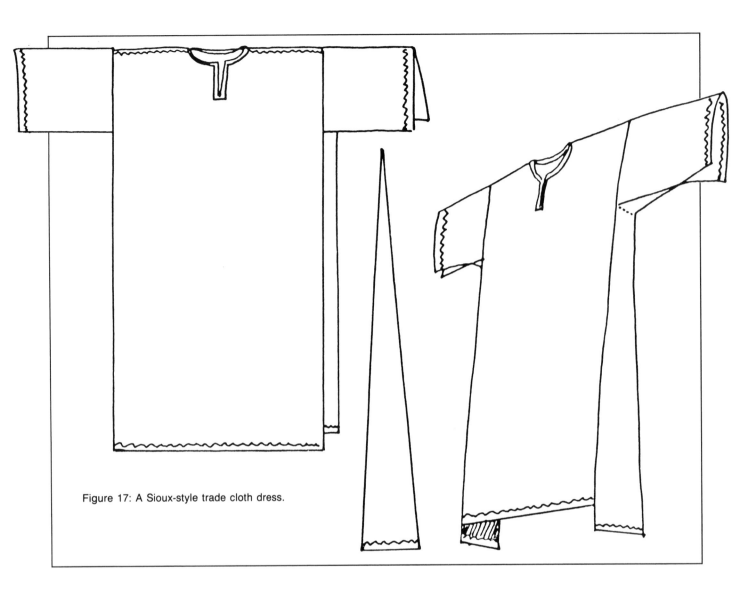

Figure 17: A Sioux-style trade cloth dress.

## THE NORTHERN PLAINS TRADE CLOTH DRESS

European trade brought wool stroud cloth to the northern plains and "from the very first was substituted for skins in making the garments" (Wissler 66). Because of cloth's tendency to stretch and ravel, cloth dresses could not be made exactly like the earlier skin dresses. They were, however, made in the same general style (Conn. "Cheyenne" 120).

Blackfeet and Sioux cloth dresses were first made as nearly like a two-hide skin dress as possible. The basic change was the addition of a gusset at the sides to fill out the required width. An early Blackfeet specimen has skin pieces used for this purpose, as well as skin fringes around the hem and sleeve edges (Conn, "Cheyenne" 120). The Sioux-type trade cloth dress is shown in Figure 17 and described in the southern plains section.

These dresses were generally made of red or dark blue tradecloth with the white selvage edge of the cloth retained as a decorative stripe. Less often they were made in green stroud or other cloths of the trade. Blackfeet dresses were often pony beaded in the U-shaped, undulating stripe pattern common to the two-hide dress. Sioux and northern Cheyenne dresses sometimes had additions of elk teeth or cowrie shells.

Crow tradecloth dresses with hundreds of elk teeth and the V-shaped insert of contrasting cloth below the neck can be seen in many museum collections today. These dresses have sleeves which are sewn closed in contrast to the Sioux-type, open, wing-like sleeves. It is doubtful, however, that these Crow dresses were the style worn in the fur trade era. Gary Johnson brought our attention to an 1872 photograph of a Crow delegation that pictured cloth elk-tooth dresses with open sleeves, which leads us to speculate that this was the earlier style. How early, though, is another question. We have not found any documentation of this cloth dress prior to 1850. Edwin Denig, a factor at Ft. Union, wrote in 1856 that Crow "women have scarlet or blue cloth dresses, others white cotillions made of the dressed skins of the bighorn sheep, which are covered across the breast and back with rows of elk teeth and sea shells...the price of the elk teeth alone is 100 teeth for a good horse or in money the value of $50.00. A frock is not complete unless it has 300 elk teeth, which with the other shells, skin, etc. could not be bought for less than $200" (*Of the Crow* 36).

Kurz, also at Ft. Union in 1850, reported the Hidatsa wearing a traditional deerskin dress or a dress of blue and white ticking made in the old style (80).

Denig also states that in the case of the Assiniboin, Crow

18

and Sioux: "Articles of European manufacture have been substituted for their skins as far as the cold weather will allow." The buffalo robe was still indispensable for durability and warmth. In the summer clothing traded from whites was preferred, "but in their usual occupations, in winter, at war, in the chase, or any public ceremonies amoung themselves," they preferred their native garb. In fact their own elaborately decorated dresses were more highly prized than anything of white manufacture (Denig, *Assiniboin* 584-592).

At the end of this chapter is a tabulation compiled by Denig in 1856 of summer and winter dress and its comparative value in terms of buffalo robes. It gives some interesting insight into clothing of that time. Keep in mind that 1856 is virtually past the peak of the fur trade, so we can only hopefully infer that some of this data reflects that earlier time. Denig adds that there were many other dresses worn, some more or less costly. As a rule, most of the Indians renewed their white man's clothing every spring, cutting up the discarded parts for leggings, breech cloths, caps and gun wadding (*Assiniboin* 588).

As we can see, clothing was dear even in the fur trade era, and heavily ornamented dresses were valued at quite a high price. This should encourage contemporary women to pursue those great fur trade outfits!

# THE SOUTHERN PLAINS DRESS

The clothing style of the southern plains Indian women was distinct from that of the northern groups. For the purpose of this discussion, the Arkansas River will be considered the line of demarcation on the great plains. South of the Arkansas, the Comanche, Wichita, Tonkawa, Apache, Lipan Apache, Caddo and Kiowa roamed. The Kiowas and Kiowa-Apache, originally residents of the northern plains, began migrating southward by the end of the 18th century. Both of these latter peoples originated in the drainages of the upper Mississippi (mid-1600s) but migrated to the Missouri River, Black Hills and North and South Platte River areas when they were forced west by the Sioux. By 1820, they were scattered from the Missouri to the Arkansas. The Arapahoe and southern Cheyenne brought northern clothing influences with them, which they adapted to the climate of the southern plains (Berthrong 22).

John Ewers, in his extensive studies of the plains Indian, stated that the clothing of southern plains women was "Quite unlike that worn by Indian women of the northern plains at the time of first white contact or at any other time of which we have record" ("Climate" 63). Three main styles of garment prevailed among the southern women: the skirt and poncho, the trade cloth dress, and the three-hide buckskin dress.

## THE SKIRT AND PONCHO

The earliest known garment among the people of this region was a sort of skirt comprised of two skins, shown in Figure 18. This skirt was either used as the sole article of clothing or it was coupled with a poncho-like upper garment made of one skin with a transverse slit or neck opening in the middle.

In 1820, Major Stephan H. Long's exploring expedition on the Arkansas encountered a combined encampment of Arapahoe, Cheyenne, Kiowa and Kiowa-Apache. Long's account reads:

*Their costume is very simple, that of the female consisting of a leathern petticoat, reaching the calf of the leg, destitute of a seam and often exposing a well-formed thigh...the leg and foot are often naked, but usually invested by gaiters and mockasins. A kind of sleeveless short gown, composed of a single piece of the same material, loosely clothes the body,*

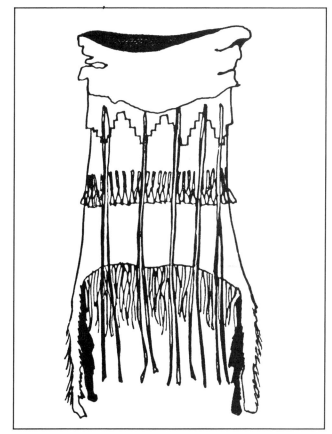

Figure 18: An Apache skirt.

*hanging upon the shoulders, readily thrown off, without any sense of indelicacy, when suckling their children or under the influence of a heated atmosphere, displaying loose and pendant mammae.* (James 180-181)

The French naturalist Jean Louis Berlandier made detailed observations of the southern plains people between 1828 and 1851, which were illustrated by the drawings of Lino Sanchez y Tapia. Comanche women, he says, "wear only a shirt (camisole) without any ornamentation, and a skin fastened around their bodies to hide their nakedness" (51). They were

"ordinarily drab" in appearance, with clothing limited to the dictates of the weather. In later historic times (after the fur trade), stimulated by frequent white contact, these skirts and ponchos were heavily decorated with beads, tinklers and fringe, as shown in Figure 19A.

Comanche women's hair was usually cut or "hacked off" bluntly and left loose, but their faces were carefully painted. "Eyes accented with red or yellow lines above and below the lids and sometimes crossing at the corners. Her ears were painted red inside and both cheeks were daubed with a solid red-orange circle or triangle" (Wallace and Hoebel 86).

The Tonkawas were a marginal plains people, living in central Texas from approximately 1687 to the 19th cen-

Figure 19: Examples of southern plains clothing from the watercolors of Lino Sanchez y Tapia. A: Commanche. B: Karankawa. C: Tonkawa. D: Lipan Apache.

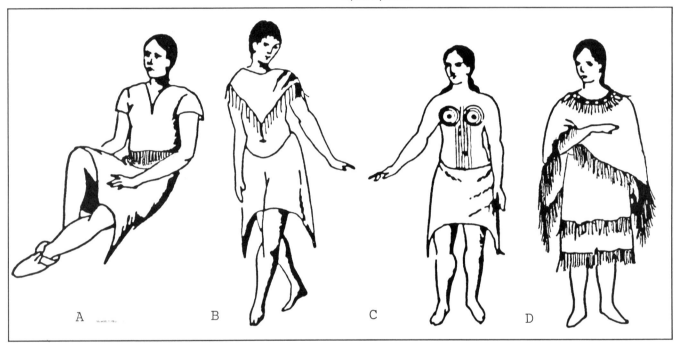

A          B          C          D

tury. Their clothing, shown in Figure 19C, consisted of a very short skirt tied in a point at each side, making a sort of curved apron in front and back. The women tattooed their bare abdomens and inscribed concentric circles around their nipples. They wore high-topped moccasins (Berlandier 147).

The Lipan Apache women that Berlandier saw at Laredo in 1828 were hard to distinguish from the men "save from their longer leggings ended in slippers, while most of the men wore sandals" (Berlandier 129). These leggings have been further described as snug-fitting and attached to a belt around their waists, much like men's leggings. Further, they wore a deerskin skirt of knee length and high moccasins. By the 19th century, their costume was topped by a poncho-like doe skin with the deer's tail (hair left on) hanging down the back (Newcomb 110). See Figure 19D.

The Wichita's striking features were their dark skin and extensive tatoos. Women's tatoos commonly ran down the bridge of their nose to the upper lip, then encircled the mouth and ran down the chin. A chin-line tatoo ran from ear to ear, and a row of solid triangles was tatooed above. There were other triangles on the neck and upper breast and a series of zig-zag lines up and down the arms. Breasts, including nip-

ples, were tatooed with several short lines surrounded by three concentric circles. This was said to prevent pendulous breasts in old age (Dorsey 2-3). Catlin and Josiah Gregg both noted the Wichita as wearing only a deerskin skirt, their upper half covered by tatoos.

The Caddoes of the Red River region in east Texas were also given to tatoos. Faces, torsos and basically anything from the waist up was fair game. Socially prominent women wore skirts of cloth woven from nettles or bulberry bark (Newcomb 290-293). Tanned deerskin was used for most of their clothing, and they were known for tanning a lustrous black leather. Their garments were often fringed and decorated with small white seeds, pierced and sewn on (Newcomb 291). An interesting sideline about the Caddoes is that in La Salle's time their chief was a woman (Newcomb 291).

The skirt and poncho, pictured in Figure 20, continued in favor among both eastern and western Apache until after the Civil War. During the 1890s, the wearing of the long-fringed skin poncho and skirt became a status symbol among young women of prominent families (Ewers, "Climate" 71).

The poncho and skirt then seem to be the aboriginal gar-

20

ment of the women of the southern plains. According to Ewers, climate was an important factor in defining the northern limit of this costume. Nearly all the wearers of the skirt and poncho lived south of the limit of 180 frost-free days, shown on the accompanying map, where winters were shorter and milder than they were on the northern plains. The short poncho could easily be thrown off in the heat of summer. Deer and antelope skins were also available in this area and this three-piece outfit could easily be made from these smaller southern hides (Ewers, "Climate" 72).

Figure 20: A southern plains poncho and skirt made by Cathy Smith. This outfit is also pictured on page VI of the color section.

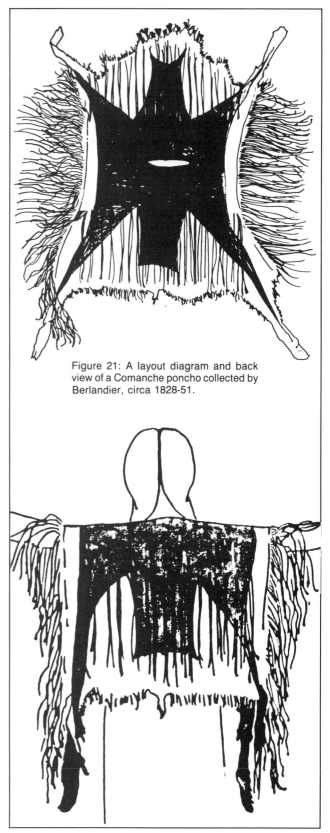

Figure 21: A layout diagram and back view of a Comanche poncho collected by Berlandier, circa 1828-51.

21

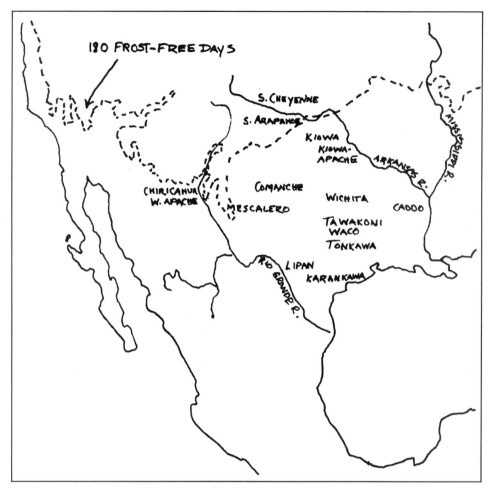

Map showing the 180 frost-free days line.

The poncho, shown in Figure 21, was an ingenious use of a single deerskin. The basic shape of the hide was little altered, preserving the legs and tail. A transverse slit in the center of the hide provided the neck opening. The hide drapped over the shoulders with the head of the skin in front and tail portion behind. It was commonly decorated by painting with red and yellow ochre. Shoulder fringes were cut long and sometimes rubbed green with verdigris. The lower edges had short fringes cut into the body of the hide. Other additions were brass tacks, buckskin thong pendants and metal cone jinglers.

## THE SOUTHERN TRADE CLOTH DRESS

The first use of trade cloth (wool stroud supplied by traders) was probably the substitution of cloth for skins in making the traditional skirt and poncho. Long's previously cited record of an encounter with the combined Kiowa, Kiowa-Apache, Arapahoe and Cheyenne encampment in 1820 described a few women who were:

*Covered by the more costly attire of coarse red or blue cloth, ornamented with a profusion of blue and white beads; the short gown of this dress has the addition of wide sleeves descending below the elbow. Its body is of square form with*

*a transverse slit in the upper edge for the head to pass through; around this aperture and on the upper side of the sleeves is a continuous stripe, the breadth of the hand, of blue and white beads, tastefully arranged in contact with each other, and adding considerable weight, as well as ornament to this part of the dress; around the petticoat, and on a line with the knees, is an even row of oblong conic bells, made of sheet copper, each about an inch and a half in length suspended vertically by short leathern thongs as near to each other as possible, so that when the person is in motion they strike upon each other and produce a tinkling sound. (James 181)*

This dress was probably the attire of the wives and daughters of the most affluent Indians in 1820. Kiowa women sometimes wore skin ponchos in combination with striped cloth skirts (Ewers, "Climate" 75).

The earliest documented reference to a true dress of trade cloth that we have found is Ewers reference to a watercolor done by Richard Petri (Fredericksburg, Texas 1852-57). An Indian girl, possibly Comanche or Lipan Apache, is depicted wearing a full dress of blue cloth. The short, elbow length kimona sleeves are of red cloth, as is the side gusset from armpit to hem. Ewers indicates that this style of dress may have been quite new in the middle 1850s, as Petri's other illustrations from the time show skin ponchos and knee length skirts (Ewers, "Climate" 75).

22

We do know that the trade cloth dress was in vogue among the Comanche, southern Cheyenne, Arapahoe and Kiowa from 1867 to 1876 (Ewers, "Climate" 75-85). It is our speculation that the dress was adopted earlier, as women readily accepted cloth as a substitute for skins. The labor of tanning was done away with, it was cooler in summer, warmer when wet, came in beautiful colors and was washable. Cheyenne and Arapahoe women with northern dress styles still fresh in their minds might have easily transposed the northern plains two-hide dress into one of cloth, since the wing-like sleeves were similar to the sleeves of the traditional hide dress and the gusset which hung below the hemline could be an imitation of the deer foreleg that hung below the hem on a hide dress. See Figure 17. These cloth dresses were often decorated similarly to their northern counterparts, with the addition of bands of pony beadwork, elk teeth and metal tinklers. Red or blue wool was most commonly used, though green was available and sometimes used. Any cloth available from traders at the time could have feasibly been used for dresses: corduroy, calico, cotton ticking, etc. These fabrics were distributed following the Medicine Lodge Treaties of 1867, but whether they were obtainable by many women prior to this is speculation.

## THE THREE-HIDE BUCKSKIN DRESS

The pictorial record suggests that the three-hide buckskin dress replaced the trade-cloth dress by the 1890s. Buckskin, harder to obtain in the reservation economy, became a status symbol (Ewers, "Climate" 77). We have been able to document this dress at least as far back as 1845. Lt. James W. Abert painted the Cheyenne wife of William Bent at Bent's Fort wearing what appears to be a three-hide dress decorated with panels of blue, white and black pony beads. The beadwork strips are on the shoulders from neck to sleeve bottom and across the chest and presumably the back of the yoke. The simple, bold geometric pattern of the beading indicates the use of pony beads. Abert writes: *"She put on her handsomest dress in order to sit for me...her beautiful leggings, which extended only to the knee, were so nicely joined with the moccasin that the connection could not be perceived..."* (28). This description suggests that the moccasins were the classic southern plains high-top boot style. See Figure 22 for a drawing of this dress and Figure 23 for a diagram of moccasin style.

Abert also painted the daughter of the Cheyenne warrior Winged Bear wearing a similar dress and high moccasins, with a brass-studded belt as well. He notes:

*She is very rich, possessing several complete suits of buckskin, all most tastefully ornamented. She wears a singular girdle, the portion around the waist covered with scarlet cloth and the whole studded with large flat gilt buttons.* (40)

Figure 22: The construction layout of a three-hide dress and Cheyenne three-hide dress worn by the wife of William Bent (drawn from a painting by Abert).

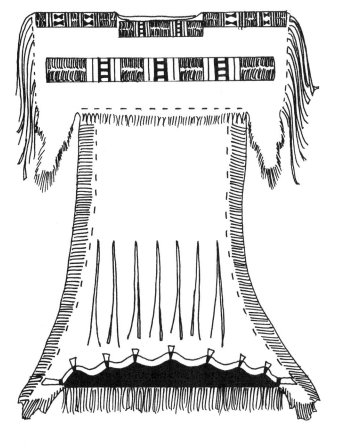

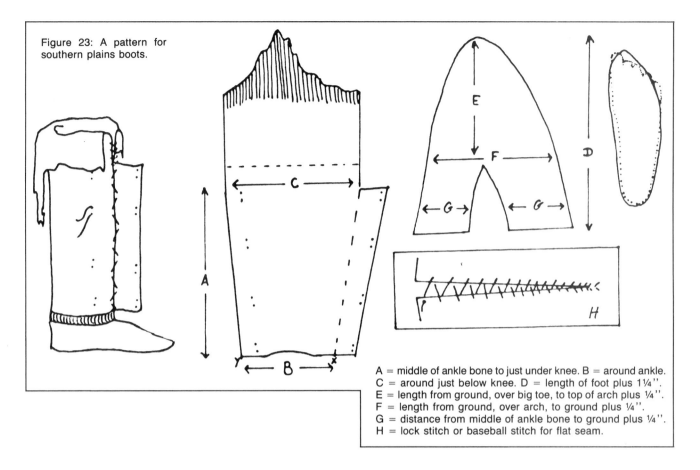

Figure 23: A pattern for southern plains boots.

A = middle of ankle bone to just under knee. B = around ankle.
C = around just below knee. D = length of foot plus 1¼''.
E = length from ground, over big toe, to top of arch plus ¼''.
F = length from ground, over arch, to ground plus ¼''.
G = distance from middle of ankle bone to ground plus ¼''.
H = lock stitch or baseball stitch for flat seam.

## CONSTRUCTION

The three-hide dress was formed from three large hides. The yoke was made from a single large hide folded and sewn on at a 90° angle to the two other skins, forming the body of the dress. The hide shapes were retained as much as possible, with the animal legs extending below the sleeve portion of the yoke. One or two smaller skins were often needed for extra fringe on the edges of the sleeves. Two large hides were used for the front and back of the skirt body of the dress. In contrast to northern two-hide dresses, the tail end of these hides was often placed at the hem of the dress to gain the extra width necessary for mounting a horse. The hindlegs of the animal were left intact to create extensions at the outside corners of the hemline. If the tanned hide was without the legs, pieces of hide were often sewn on to simulate these legs in the proper position. These pieces were often sewn almost invisibly with sinew, while the yoke was attached to the body with fine buckskin lacing using a visible running stitch. The construction layout of this dress is shown in Figure 22.

According to Peter Powell, noted Cheyenne authority, two traditions of decorating this three-hide dress have been handed down by the Cheyenne elders. Both traditions agree that there are three bands of quill embroidery (northern Cheyenne) or beadwork used on the yoke: one shoulder strip, one across the breast, and one across the back of the yoke extending its full width. The neck opening, a simple slit, was trimmed with red quillwork and later red tradecloth was substituted. The three strips were usually made of beads or quills applied directly to yoke, but occasionally separate strips were appliqued on. Below these bands, pairs of buckskin thongs with quill-wrapped tops were attached. The yoke was

often painted yellow, the color of the sun. For a beloved woman, rows of elk teeth might be added between the beaded strips. At the bottom outside edges of the skirt hung the animals legs with dewclaws. The bottom hem between these leg extensions was often painted red, solidly quilled or beaded red. Sometimes a separate piece of red-painted skin was stitched to the bottom of the dress to form this curved or zig-zagged pattern (Powell 43). See Figures 22 and 24.

The second tradition concerning ornamentation was recalled by members of the Southern Cheyenne Beadworkers Guild in the late 1930s. This tradition described the dress yoke as being painted blue. Blue was the old sacred earth color obained from paint pots in Yellowstone Park before the Cheyenne split into northern and southern groups. The blue yoke represented the sky. As in all Cheyenne dresses, there were three quilled, beaded or painted strips on the yoke. However, "at the center of the front strip, breaking the strip design, there was a separate loop-shaped design in the form of a quarter ellipse...about 6 inches long and 3 inches wide, it rested between the woman's breasts" (Powell 44). This was the symbol for the turtle, the same used on Lakota Sioux dresses. This dress design is pictured in Figure 25. The skirt of these dresses was mostly unornamented, with the exception of a narrow band of red or green paint above the hem.

24

Figure 24 (facing page): A Cheyenne three-hide dress made by Cathy Smith. This dress is also pictured on page VII of the color section.

Figure 26 (below): A Taos Pueblo dress of two-hide construction.

Figure 25: A Sioux, fully-beaded-yoke dress which illustrates Powell's description of early dresses with yokes painted blue with a center stripe and turtle design. Made by Cathy Smith, this dress carries these symbols into the 1870s, interpreting them in seedbeads. This is NOT a fur trade era dress.

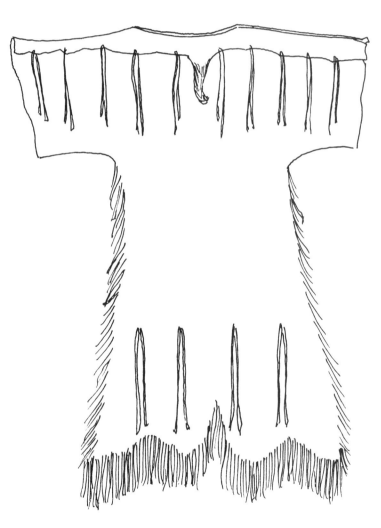

This three-hide dress was worn by the southern Cheyenne and Arapahoe, and by the end of the 19th century, it was photographed on Kiowa and Comanche women as well. When these women adopted this style is speculation. The poncho and skirt has remained the traditional ceremonial dress for the Comanche and Apache to this day.

Two exceptions exist to our classification of northern and southern traditions in dress. One is the northern Cheyenne, who also wore the three-hide dress, and the other is the Taos Pueblo. Taos is included in our delineation of the southern plains, but these women wore a two-hide dress reminiscent of the northern style, presumably acquired from neighboring Jicarilla Apache and Ute. Taos dresses were trimmed to make square-cut sleeves and rubbed with yellow paint, having a lower contour similar to the plateau style dress. Taos women were wearing this style regularly by the late 18th century (Conn, *Robes* 60). A drawing of a Taos Pueblo dress is shown in Figure 26.

# LEGGINGS

Leggings were a necessary part of every dressed woman's outfit, summer and winter, though bare feet and legs were probably very common on summer workdays. Leggings can be very simple and unornamented, such as a basic rectangle or trapezoid of hide wrapped around the leg and laced or sewn together, extending high enough to be tied under the knee with a garter of buckskin. The top of the legging was often folded down over the tie. Early northern and plateau leggings were practically undecorated, of skin or trade cloth, tight-fitted and sewn closed so that they tucked inside the moccasin flaps. Crow and Blackfeet leggings of this sort have been documented (Conn, "Blackfeet" 122). Other, probably later, leggings were a skin or cloth tube with a beaded panel at the bottom. The panel is closed with tie strings after the legging is on. See Figure 27.

Whether these Crow and Blackfeet leggings can be dated to the time of the fur trade is unknown. To be safe we sug-

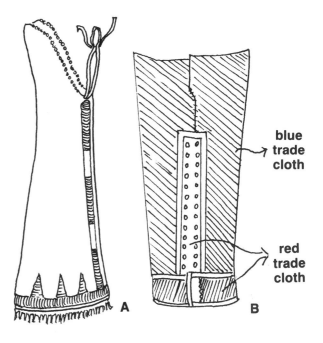

blue trade cloth

red trade cloth

Figure 28: (Left) Upper Missouri leggings painted by Bodmer in 1833. Made from buckskin with blue and white pony beads. (Right) Early Crow (?) leggings from the collection of Western Heritage Center in Billings, Montana. Made from trade cloth with a white selvedge and flat brass buttons.

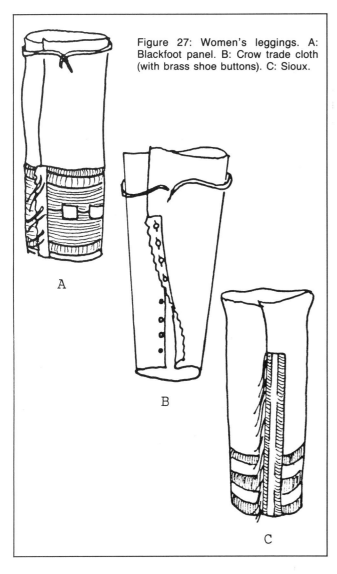

Figure 27: Women's leggings. A: Blackfoot panel. B: Crow trade cloth (with brass shoe buttons). C: Sioux.

A

B

C

gest an upper Missouri pair painted by Bodmer in 1833, illustrated in Figure 28. These are essentially a tube sewn closed, with a lazy stitch row of pony beadwork covering the seam and extending around the bottom edge, fringed along the bottom and below the beadwork (Thomas and Ronnefeldt 232). An early pair of Sioux quilled leggings is shown in Figure 29. Early Sioux, Arapahoe and Northern Cheyenne leggings were similar in layout: a row or more of bead or quillwork running horizontally around the bottom of the skin tube, and a second, usually narrower lane or group of lanes running vertically up the center front of the legging. These were looser fitting than the plateau style, laced together on the bottom two-thirds and then sewn from here to the top or tied together all the way up (Conn, "Cheyenne" 50).

Figure 30 shows a sketch of a pair of pony beaded leggings in the collections of the State Historic Society of Wisconsin. These are a very simple, probably Sioux, pair of leggings beaded in black and white.

Figure 30 also illustrates a pair of early southern Cheyenne boots from a private collection. They are made of heavy buffalo hide and sewn with an external welted seam. Pony beaded in white, black and blue with small amounts of pink and yellow, they also have two rows of metal buttons up the side. The earliest Cheyenne leggings were not beaded but painted, often yellow with blacks stripes horizontally around. These represented coups, the woman's own or her husband's. After the introduction of beads, these stripes

Figure 29: Oglala quilled leggings from the American Museum of Natural History. Also pictured on page VII of the color section.

began to be designated with beaded stripes (Powell 43). It is probable that many of the northern plains tribes used some version of this simple painted legging. We know that it was common on the southern plains and was sewn to the moccasin, creating a one-piece, high-top boot among the Cheyenne, Kiowa and Commanche. These were often painted yellow or green with blue coup stripes. See Figure 31.

Figure 31: Southern plains boots made by Cathy Smith. Also pictured on page IV of the color section.

Figure 30: (Left) Sioux-type leggings decorated with black and white pony beads. (Right) Southern Cheyenne boots with black, white and blue pony beads. Note the external seam on the sole.

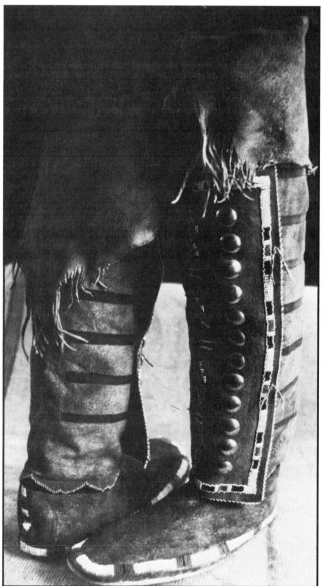

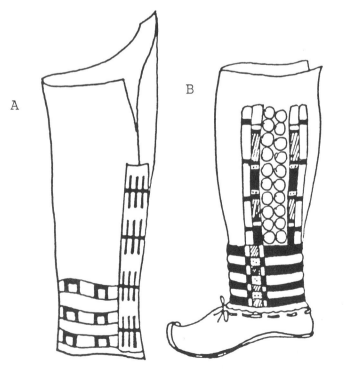

28

Two pairs of Kiowa boots from the collection of Cathy Smith.
One is painted yellow and the other green.

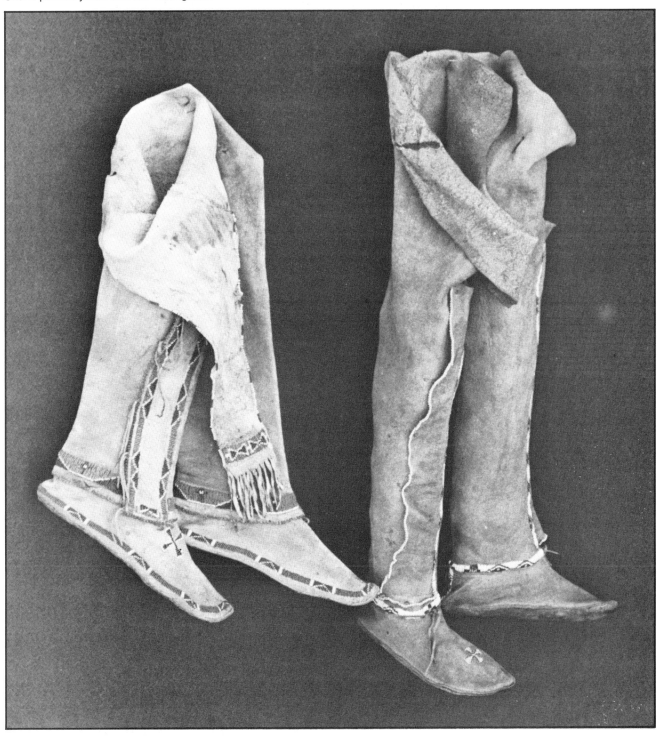

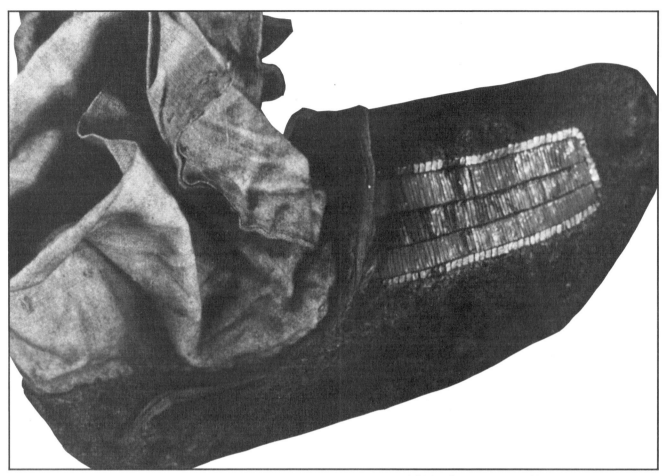

A Plains Cree moccasin with a quilled tongue-shaped design from American Museum of Natural History. Also pictured on page IV of the color section.

Fur trade era Northern moccasins were of the one-piece, side-fold, soft-sole type. The seam was sewn beginning at the base of the big toe and extending around the outer side of the moccasin to the heel. Their decoration often reflected the basic structure of the moccasin. A lane of quill or pony beadwork extended around the outer edge to cover the side seam but very often not on the inner edge where there was no seam. Catlin and Bodmer both illustrated this style of footwear (Hail 101).

Common decoration on such moccasins was a center stripe or tongue-shape in quills or pony beads such as Bodmer painted on a Teton Sioux woman in 1833 (Thomas and Ronnefeldt 47, 214). A keyhole design, pictured in Figure 32, was also used; Bodmer illustrated this on a Piegan Blackfeet woman in blue and white pony beads (Thomas and Ronnefeldt 214). Northern and southern Cheyenne women also used a keyhole design executed in quillwork in the North and cornhusks in the South. This was a sacred woman's pattern, while moccasins with horizontal quilled stripes among the Cheyenne were for men (Coleman).

Hard soles of buffalo rawhide were added to the one-piece, soft-sole moccasin of the North in the early- to mid-18th century. This rawhide sole was simply sewn to the

bottom of the one-piece moccasin. Later the moccasin was made in two separate pieces (Hail 101). Everday footwear was generally undecorated, but a woman's good pair had ornamentation in quill or beadwork. Remember that the fully-beaded, hard-sole moccasins so prevalent in museum collections are too late for the fur trade era.

On the southern plains, the two-piece, rawhide-sole moccasin was seen much earlier than up North. Berlandier collected such a pair from the Comanche sometime between 1828 and 1851. They are noted as being one of the earliest examples of the hard soled moccasin from the great plains (Berlandier 184). The high-top boot moccasin of the Cheyenne, Kiowa and Commanche has been discussed above and was noted by Abert among the Cheyenne in 1845 and by Berlandier among the Lipan Apache and Tonkawa in 1828. Arapahoe high-top moccasins sometimes had blue cloth uppers (Coleman).

Figure 32: Quilled "keyhole" moccasins of side-seam construction made by Cathy Smith. Also pictured on page VII of the color section.

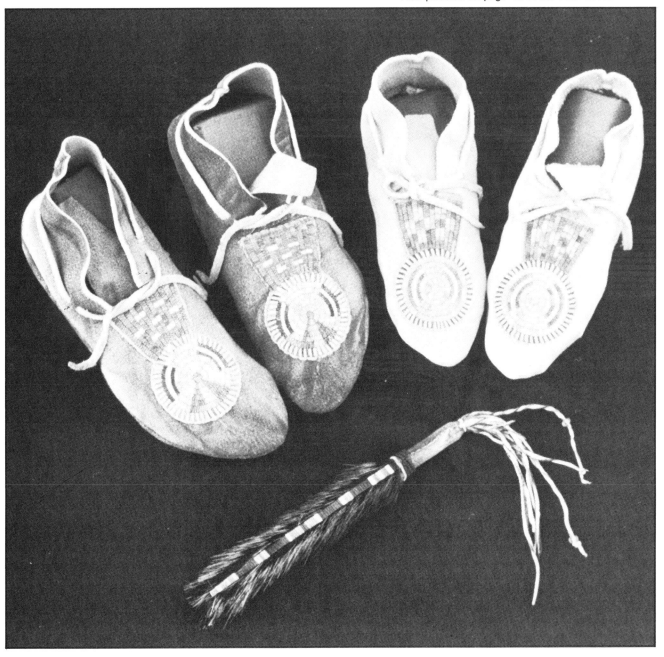

# ROBES

The buffalo robe or blanket was an indispensable part of a woman's costume. In his tabulation of clothing, Denig tells us that elk or buffalo cowskin robes were used in summer, but an everyday costume used a white blanket. In winter a buffalo robe, hair-on, was used. It was undecorated for everyday use and "much garnished with quills" for more costly dress (Denig, Assiniboin 588).

Women's robes were often painted in geometric designs; pictographic or figurative designs were men's. The "box and border" design, shown in Figure 33, was frequent among women. Bodmer painted a classic example of a Teton woman in such a robe in 1833 (Thomas and Ronnefeldt 47). This design was supposedly worn by a woman who had undergone the "Hunka," (adoption or tying a feather ceremony) one of the seven sacred rites of the Lakota Sioux (Schneider). Robes with quilled horizontal stripes originated with the Sacred Quillworkers societies of the Gros Ventre, Araphoe and Cheyenne (Coleman). Bodmer painted Assiniboin and Blackfeet warriors wearing robes such as these, while Lakota women and pubescent girls wore robes with red horizontal quilled lines, said to represent "the trail by which the woman travels" (Thomas and Ronnefeldt 135). Often the robes of unmarried women were decorated with a row of medallions or pendants made of short quilled strips, looped, with dewclaws attached to their ends (Powell 38).

Denig relates that in some parts of the North where buffalo robes were scarce, Cree women used a robe of rabbit skins. These were cut into strips, rolled up into a cord and connected by a bark chain and woven into a blanket "so firm as to be impervious to rain and to protect their persons from severe cold" (Denig, Five 129).

Kurz describes the robe and blanket as the vogue for women in 1850. They often belted their blankets, carrying their baby inside the blanket above the belt with their knife sheath hanging down in back. He further states that capotes were worn by Hidatsa, Crow, Assiniboin, Cree and Salteur men and children, but not by women! They wore robes with the head on the right, tail on the left and fastened with straps at the throat (Kurz 34).

Navajo Phase I Chief's blankets were in high demand on both the northern and southern plains. Abert notes attending a Cheyenne scalp dance at Bents Fort in 1845 where "nearly all [the women] were cloaked with Navajo blankets" (Abert 2).

The documented evidence, then, points to buffalo robes or blankets for a woman's cloak prior to 1850. Capotes worn by women seem to be one of the false impressions generated by the contemporary rendezvous experience. They have, as far as we have been able to ascertain, no basis in historical fact. If any reader has documentation to refute this, please point it out, as accuracy of interpretation is our prime concern.

Figure 33: Woman's "box & border" buffalo robe.

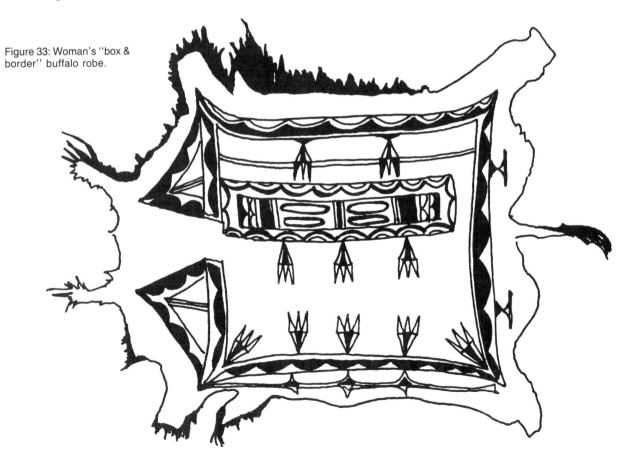

# BELTS AND
# ORNAMENTS

Early Cheyenne belts were made of painted parfleche (rawhide) tied together with buckskin thongs (Powell 43). Blackfeet belts were of the same, changing over to the tack belt on commercial leather at some time in the mid-19th century. How early this occured is again open to speculation (Conn, *Blackfeet* 124). Abert's painting of the southern Cheyenne woman in a belt studded with gilt buttons is the earliest reference to a tack belt that we have found (1845).

Figure 34 shows an upper Missouri belt of another style. It is made of soft, tanned buffalo hide in contrast to the wide, stiff belts described above. This belt is Oglala, but the style was also used by the Crow, Mandan and Hidatsa, Assiniboin and Cheyenne. Approximately 1½ inches in width, it is long enough to tie around the waist and hang down in front with quill-wrapped fringes about 4 inches in length as dangles. Sewn onto the belt is a square pouch, 2½ x 3 in-

Figure 35: A seed-beaded Comanche bag from the Berlandier Collection.

Figure 34: Oglala woman's belt from the American Museum of Natural History. This soft-tanned buffalo belt has a beaded and quilled pouch with a V-shaped flap. Also pictured on page IV of the color section.

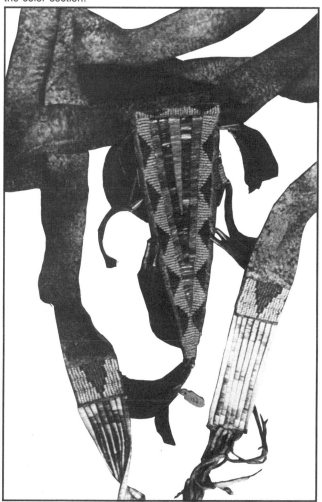

ches, with a V- or U-shaped flap approximately 8 inches long. This flap hangs from the belt, hiding the pouch behind, and is decorated with quill and beadwork. These units were made to hold a flint and steel.

In his paintings of upper Missouri women, Bodmer shows two belts, one of soft leather tied in a knot in front and a wide one pony-beaded in blue and white (Thomas and Ronnefeldt 69, 126). Another early belt in the American Museum of Natural History is fully quilled in a red background with a white undulating stripe through the center on fairly heavy buffalo hide.

Knife sheaths, strike-a-light bags, awl cases and sometimes whetstone cases were hung from the belt. It is not within the scope of this article to discuss these various accoutrements, save for one interesting example from the southern plains. Figure 35 is a drawing of a woman's pouch collected by Berlandier from the Comanche sometime prior to 1850. Made of red rubbed buckskin, it is 8 x 7.5 centimeters and is beaded in seed beads of red, yellow and blue with a few pink, green and white colored beads. This bag is proof that the type existed on the southern plains prior to 1850 and seed beads were available for its decoration (Berlandier 185). Figures 36 and 37 are examples of northern (Man-

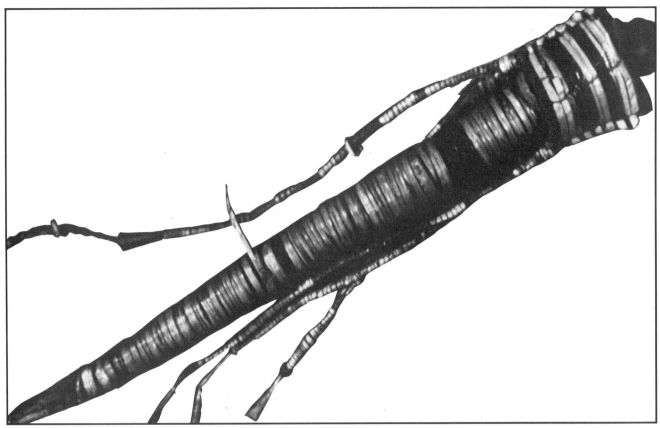

Figure 36: A Mandan/Hidatsa bird-quilled awl case from the American Museum of Natural History. Also pictured on page III of the color section.

dan) and southern (Apache) awl cases. As for ornaments, Denig relates:

*All Indians are excessively fond of display in ornaments . . . the value of their dresses depends entirely upon the nature and extent of these decorations. Small round beads of all colors are used in adorning every portion of their dress, as also agate for their ears, hair, neck and wrists, but these are by no means as valuable as several kinds of shells or as their ornamenting with colored porcupine quills. A shell, called by the traders "Ioquois," is sought after by them more eagerly than anything else of the kind. They are procured on the coast of the Pacific and find their way to our tribes across the mountains through the different nations by traffic with each other until the Crows and Blackfeet get them from some bands of Snake and Flathead Indians with whom they are at peace. These shells are about two inches long, pure white, about the size of a raven's feather at the larger end, curved, tapering and hollow so as to admit of being strung or worn in the ears of the women, worked on the breast and arms of their cotillions, also adorn the frontlets of young men, and are worth in this country $3 for every 10 shells. Frequently three or four hundred are seen on some of the young Crow and Blackfeet women's dresses. (Five 590-591)*

This is a great description of the first dentalium shell dress in the early 1850s.

Denig also described the blue or pearl abalone shell used as ear pendants. One shell was once worth $20 in trade but, by 1856, had depreciated to half that value due to the quantity

Figure 37: An Apache awl case from a private collection. Also pictured on page VII of the color section.

brought in by traders. Silver arm bands, hat bands, gorgets, brooches, ear wheels and ear bobs were common among the Sioux, while the upper nations preferred shells. Brass rings, wire bracelets, beads, hair pipe, hawk bells, thimbles and gold and silver lace were also traded (Denig 591).

# CONCLUSION

We have, so far, documented a wide selection of native dresses of the fur trade era from both the northern and southern plains. A correct outfit can range from a simple brain tanned hide wrapped around the waist or poncho with cloth skirt to an elaborate pony beaded, elk tooth, two-hide dress.

When planning your fur trade clothing, it is important to remember that you, as women, are involved in cross-cultural interpretation and that the culture you are interpreting is still alive and well. As such, it is very important to approach the project with sensitivity towards another culture, its taboos and restrictions, and to interpret with integrity. This means documenting every last detail. Research first-person journals of the time and study museum specimens. Don't mix time periods and tribal styles on the same outfit. A rendezvous at Bent's Fort would be the right place to sport a southern plains dress, while one in northern Montana would call for a two-hide dress. Quillwork in the old, natural colors and pony beads in two or three colors (basically white, black and blue) are correct. Limited use of seed beads might

also be acceptable on southern plains garments provided the color, size and pattern are right, but they would not be correct on a plateau or upper Missouri dress. Remember that southern plains beadwork was minimal, mainly one lane of lazy stitch border.

Good references for garments are Clark Wissler's *Costumes of the Plains Indians,* Susan Fecteau's *Primitive Indian Dress,* and *People of the First Man,* an account of Prince Maximilian's expedition up the Missouri River in 1833-34.

Before I close I would like to thank a few people for their help in the writing of this chapter. These include Benson Lanford for his assistance in letting me view his immense slide collection and for his pertinent comments, Dave Christianson for his persistant research of brain tanning methods and dress construction, the Field Museum of Natural History, the American Museum of Natural History, David Wright for his slides from the Ottawa Museum of Man, and Jerry Fahrenthold for contributing his section of this manuscript on two-hide dress construction.

## APPENDIX A: WORKS CITED

Abert, Lt. James W. *Through the Country of the Comanche Indians in the Fall of the Year 1845.* Ed. John Galvin. San Francisco: Howell, 1970.

Berlandier, Jean Louis. *The Indians of Texas from Prehistoric to Modern Times.* Ed. John Ewers. Washington: Smithsonian Institution Press, 1969.

Berthrong, Donald J. *The Southern Cheyennes.* Norman: University of Oklahoma Press, 1963.

Coleman, Winfield. "The Waltz of Traditions, The Swing of Fashion: Problems in Identifying Cheyenne Materials." Plains Indian Art Symposium. Cody, WY: 1987.

Conn, Richard. "Blackfeet Women's Clothing." *American Indian Tradition* (1961).

—. "Cheyenne Style Beadwork." *American Indian Hobbyist* (1961).

—. *Robes of White Shell and Sunrise.* Denver: Denver Art Museum, 1974.

Dorsey, George A. "The Mythology of the Wichita." Carnegie Institute of Washington, Public. No. 21, 1904.

Denig, Edwin T. *The Assiniboin.* Annual Report of the Bureau of American Ethnology (1928-29): 584-592.

—. *Five Indian Tribes of the Upper Missouri.* Ed. John Ewers. Norman: University of Oklahoma Press, 1961.

—. *Of the Crow Nation.* Annual Report of the Bureau of American Ethnology 151, 1953.

Ewers, John C. "Climate, Acculturation, and Costume: A History of Women's Clothing Among the Indians of the Southern Plains." *Plains Anthropologist* 25.87 (1980): 63-82.

—. *Indian Life on the Upper Missouri.* Norman: University of Oklahoma Press, 1968.

Fecteau, Susan. *Primitive Indian Dresses.* Cheyenne: Frontier Printing, 1979.

Feder, Norman. "George Catlin: Sometimes Accurate." *American Indian Art Magazine* (1980): 72-75.

—. "The Side Fold Dress." *American Indian Art Magazine* (1984): 48-55.

Gowans, Fred R. *Rocky Mountain Rendezvous.* Layton, UT: Peregrine Smith, 1985.

Gregg, Josiah. *Commerce of the Prairies.* Ed. Milo M. Quaife. New York: Citadel Press, 1968.

Grinnell, George Bird. *The Cheyenne Indians.* 2 vols. New Haven: Yale University Press, 1923.

Hail, Barbara A. *Hau, Kila!: The Plains Indian Collection of the Haffenreffer Museum.* Brown University, 1980.

Harmon, Daniel W. *A Journal of Voyages & Travels in the Interior of North America.* New York: 1903.

Henry, Alexander and David Thompson. *The Manuscript Journals of Alexander Henry & David Thompson, 1799-1814.* Ed. Elliot Coues. 3 vols. New York: Harper, 1897.

Hungry Wolf, Adolf and Beverly Hungry Wolf. *Blackfoot Craftworker's Book.* Vol. 15. Skookumchuck: Good Medicine Books, 1983.

Isham, James. *James Isham's Observations on Hudson's Bay, 1743.* Ed. E.E. Rich. Toronto: Champlain Soc. Public. HBC, Ser.12, (1949): 109-110.

James, Edwin. *Account of an Expedition from Pittsburg to the Rocky Mountains Performed in the Years 1819 & 1820.* 2 vols. Philadelphia: H.C. Carey & I. Lea, 1823.

Kane, Paul. *Wanderings of an Artist among the Indians of North America from Canada to Vancouver's Island & Oregon Through the Hudson's Bay Company's Territory and Back Again.* Austin: University of Texas, 1971.

Kurz, Rudolph Frederich. *The Journal of Rudolph Frederich Kurz, 1846-1852.* Ed. J.N.B. Hewitt. Lincoln: University of Nebraska Press, 1970.

Lessard, Rosemary. "A Short Historical Survey of Lakota Women's Clothing." *Plains Indian Design Symbology and Decoration.* Ed. Gene Ball and George Horsecapture. Cody, WY: Buffalo Bill Historical Center, 1980.

Lyford, Carrie A. *Quill and Beadwork of the Western Sioux.* Boulder, CO: Johnson Publishing, 1982.

Thomas, Davis and Karin Ronnefeldt, eds. *People of the First Man: The Firsthand Account of Prince Maximilian's Expedition up the Missouri River, 1833-34.* New York: Promontory Press, 1982.

Newcomb, W.W. Jr. *The Indians of Texas from Prehistoric to Modern Times.* Austin: University of Texas Press, 1961.

Powell, Peter. "Beauty For New Life." *The Native American Heritage.* By Evan Maurer. Lincoln: University of Nebraska Press, 1977.

Quimby, George I. *Indians of the Frontier: Paintings by George Catlin.* Chicago: Chicago Natural History Museum, 1954.

Razka, Paul. "Identification: Ask the People." Plains Indian Symposium. Cody, WY: 1987.

Schneider, Mary Jane. *"Symbolism in the Border and Box Design."* 6th Annual Native American Art Studies Association Conference. Denver: 1987.

Smith, Cathy. "Quillworking." *The Book of Buckskinning III.* Ed. William H. Scurlock. Texarkana, TX: Rebel Publishing Co., 1985. 53-80.

—. "Silent Partners, Women in the Fur Trade, 1670-1987." *The Opposition Newsletter, A Company of Fur Trade Historians.* 87.3 (1987).

Tabeau, Pierre Antoine. *Tabeau's Narrative of Loisel's Expedition to the Upper Missouri.* Ed. Annie Abel. Norman: University of Oklahoma Press, 1939.

Wallace, Ernest and E. Adamson Hoebel. *The Comanches: Lords of the South Plains.* Norman: University of Oklahoma Press, 1952.

Wissler, Clark. *"Costumes of the Plains Indians Together with Structural Basis to the Decoration of Costumes Among the Plains Indians"* *Anthropological Papers of the American Museum of Natural History* 17.2 (1915).

# APPENDIX B: SUMMER AND WINTER DRESS

## WOMEN'S SUMMER DRESS

| | |
|---|---|
| Dressed cowskin cotillion.............. | 1 robe |
| Leggings of same..................... | ½ robe |
| Dressed cow or elkskin robe........... | 1 robe |
| Moccasins........................... | 0 robe |
| | 2½ robes @ $3 = $7.50 |

| COLORED BLANKET................ | 4 robes |
|---|---|
| Bleu or scarlet cloth dress............ | 3 robes |
| Garnishing of beads on same........... | 5 robes |
| Scarlet cloth leggings with beadwork..... | 2 robes |
| White deerskin moccasins with beadwork.. | 1 robe |
| Heavy bead earrings & necklaces........ | 4 robes |
| Brass wire wristbands and rings.......... | 1 robe |
| | 20 robes @ $3 = $60.00 |

| CROW WOMEN'S SUMMER DRESSES | |
|---|---|
| Fine white dressed elkskin robe......... | 1 robe |
| Fine white bighorn skin cotillion w/300 elk teeth.............................. | 25 robes |
| Neck collar of brass wire.............. | 1 robe |
| Fine antelope sking leggings w/porcupine quillwork........................... | 3 robes |
| Brass wire wristbands and rings......... | 1 robe |
| California shell ear ornaments.......... | 3 robes |
| Very heavy bead necklaces............. | 3 robes |
| Moccasins covered with beads.......... | 2 robes |
| | 39 robes @ $3 = $117.00 |

| SIOUX SUMMER DRESSES | |
|---|---|
| Fine white elkskin robe, painted........ | 1 robe |
| Fine white dressed antelope skin cotillion, heavily ornamented w/beads or shells on breast & arm... | 30 robes |
| Leggings of same ornamented with beads.. | 3 robes |
| Bead or wire necklace................. | 2 robes |
| Garnished moccasins & brass breat plate.. | 1 robe |
| Ear bones........................... | 3 robes |
| | 40 robes @ $3 = $120.00 |

| COMMON SIOUX, ASSINIBOIN OR CROW SUMMER DRESS | |
|---|---|
| White blanket....................... | 3 robes |
| Blue cloth cotillion or green cloth........ | 2 robes |
| Scarlet cloth leggings................. | 1 robe |
| | 6 robes @ $3 = $18.00 |

## WINTER DRESS

| | |
|---|---|
| Buffalo Robe........................ | 1 robe |
| Dressed cowskin cotillion.............. | 1 robe |
| Dressed cowskin leggings and shoes...... | 1 robe |
| | 3 robes @ $3 = $9.00 |

## WINTER DRESS: CROW

| | |
|---|---|
| Buffalo robe much garnished with quills... | 4 robes |
| Bighorn cotillion trimmed w/scarlet cloth & quills............................... | 3 robes |
| Leggings of elkskin, fringed & quilled.... | 2 robes |
| Wrist, ear and neck ornaments, say...... | 3 robes |
| | 12 robes @ $3 = $36.00 |
| | (Denig, 587) |

# Old-Time Music & Instruments

## by Eric A. Bye

ERIC BYE LIVES IN Cambridgeport, Vermont, with his buckskinning family: wife Barbara and children Olaf and Caroline. After earning a bachelor's and a master's degree in foreign languages, Eric was an educator for ten years. He presently works in the financial services field. His interest in black powder shooting began at the age of fourteen, and he has been a banjo player for a dozen or more years. He also has a passing acquaintance with the guitar, dulcimer and mandolin. He specializes in old tunes, and primitive rendezvous are the setting in which he most frequently performs. According to Bye, "The campfire creates such a friendly, relaxed atmosphere that rendezvous is the easiest place to loosen up and feel comfortable about playing and singing for others."

Bye has been a Vermont field representative for the National Muzzle Loading Rifle Association since 1983. Through the years he has had a number of articles published in *Muzzle Blasts*. Other interests include bicycling, cross-country skiing, smallbore rifle shooting and muzzleloader gunsmithing. When he's not pickin' and grinnin' by the campfire, he's most likely to be found at the rifle range.

ONE of the most rewarding facets of rendezvous life is live music around the campfires. Some of the music we hear at rendezvous is appropriate to the period we portray — roughly 1750 to 1850 — but some of it postdates that era. If bluegrass and sixties folk tunes don't jar the historical sensibilities as much as a set of Naugahyde buckskins would, gaining acceptance merely because they fall within the realm of ''folk'' or ''country'' music, it's only because we are less educated about true old-time music than we are about other aspects of rendezvous. We need to research our music and instruments with the same care we devote to our camp gear, firearms and clothing. Permit me to illustrate my point with a couple of examples.

Here's the scene: Around a campfire at a primitive rendezvous, buckskin- and calico-clad pioneer types are seated on stumps and on the ground. Tipis in the background reflect the campfire light. A camper lifts a brand from the fire to light his clay pipe while others pass a small stone jug. A bearded compatriot wrapped in a blanket coat approaches the fire, greets the others and settles into the circle. He reaches into a hardshell case, produces his Gibson Mastertone banjo and regales the company with a flashy rendition of ''Foggy Mountain Breakdown.'' The music and good spirits (both kinds) flow freely into the night.

What's wrong with that scene? Nothing, you say? Examine, then, this next scenario, which is not so different from the preceding one. Scene: the rifle range at the same rendezvous. The hour of the smoothbore match has arrived, and a score of contestants await the range officer's command to post their targets. Guns in evidence include fusils de chasse, Brown Besses, Charlesvilles, northwest trade guns and others. A late arrival unties the end of his blanket case and slips out his gun, a 12-gauge Remington Wingmaster. The other contestants justifiably raise a ruckus that can be heard

back at the main camp.

On the one hand, I've described a fairly commonplace scene and, on the other, an implausible one. Yet both scenes share this feature: the implements in question (the bluegrass banjo and the breechloading shotgun) are contemporaries of one another. The former is commonly accepted at rendezvous — surely not through intentional disregard for authenticity, but because many folks are not familiar with what real old-time music and instruments are really like.

I feel that live tunes of practically any kind are far more enjoyable than the slick and flawlessly staged music that most denizens of the 20th century are accustomed to hearing by means of the electronic media. I want to state for the record that I *like* bluegrass, ragtime, blues and lots of other types of 20th century music. My purpose in focusing on old-time music is not to foster dissatisfaction where none may currently exist. It's only that sometimes the rendezvous music I have heard has not enriched the voyage into the past as much as it could have — not because of the performer's skill or the quality of the setting, of course, but because, perhaps unwittingly, many folks are introducing modern music into an environment where we take great pains to eliminate intrusions of the present era. If we are to be the faithful preservers of bygone customs and ways that we aspire to be, our expertise and values should also extend to the music that we enjoy in camp.

I gave a couple of hypothetical examples above to illustrate how certain modern trappings like the bluegrass banjo are readily accepted in camp, yet others are not. Permit me to give one more example which is not hypothetical. At one major event, I saw a dog soldier call attention to a camper's non-period fishing gear. That same evening the very dog soldier I had observed earlier appeared at a campfire with a modern bluegrass-style mandolin on which he played 20th century music. In my opinion bluegrass, swing, jazz, country and western, blues, and contemporary folk music and some instruments commonly used in their performance are as out of place as fiberglas fishing rods and pump shotguns. I don't mean to suggest that the folks who have the talent to treat us to live music should be ostracized for a rendition of ''Rocky Top'' or ''The Tennessee Stud,'' but the fact remains that people in the era we portray never heard or played a note of bluegrass, which did not develop until the 1940s. Now, the music from which bluegrass and other modern idioms sprang is rich and beautiful, and all musicians who attend rendezvous could benefit from some extra research to broaden their repertory. That would keep our live entertainment as authentic, or nearly so, as the rest of our experience in camp.

I hope that you have concluded correctly from the foregoing that it is not my intent to set up rigid guidelines by which instruments and musical styles might be banned from rendezvous. I believe we would all be much the poorer for that! Rather, my hope is to encourage in a positive sense a taste for the music and the instruments that might reasonably have found their way into camp life of the first half of the 19th century. Our best efforts in this vein will always contain a generous measure of conjecture, and since there is no one among us who was there, none can be presumed to be the ultimate authority on what is appropriate. My goal is to facilitate the adoption of instruments and playing styles appropriate to your chosen time period. If you want to fine-tune your choice of instruments and music, this chapter

should help. You'll soon see, for example, that if you portray the Western fur trade era, you can justify using a concertina but not if your preference is the French and Indian War period, since that instrument was first introduced in 1829 (Heatwole 5).

Before examining specific instruments or styles of playing, let's consider briefly what was happening on the music scene in the period of about 1750 to 1850. This background will help situate old-time music historically and give you a clearer idea of how it fits in with what we try to do at rendezvous. After all, as you studied history in school and researched Lewis and Clark and the fur trade, I'll bet you found mighty few references to the types of music and instruments that people enjoyed.

Starting in the 18th century, there arose in the New World a cultivated and ''genteel tradition'' in music, influenced heavily by European composers and performers, some of whom toured and performed extensively in this country. This vein of music was practiced in the cities. It was akin to what we might now term ''classical,'' and it included serious church music. Opposed to this orientation was the

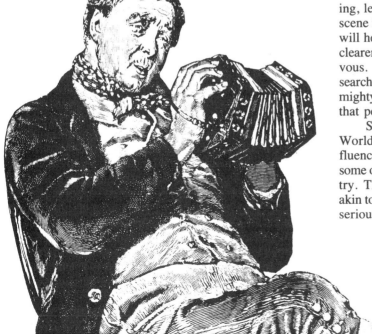

D. CHYWOOD 89

popular music, generally held in low esteem by proponents of the genteel. Popular music consisted of work songs, shantey tunes, chanteys, spirituals and minstrel tunes. It belonged to the country folk and used instruments alien to the genteel tradition. For example, the fiddle and banjo, now highly regarded, were once considered the devil's instruments. That popular conception was reflected in some figures of speech of the times. People were wont to remark such things as, "Yep, we cotch a mess o' fish, all right, but the skeeters was thicker 'n fiddlers in Hell."

Some performers seemed to have combined successfully the appeal of the popular and the esteem of the genteel. A number of families toured extensively performing vocal music which espoused the current causes of temperance, women's suffrage, patriotism and abolition. The Singing Hutchinsons of Milford, Vermont, were among the most successful. Others included the Cheneys, also of Vermont, and such troupes as Father Kemp's Old Folks, the Harmoneons, the Moravians and the Orpheans (Howard 173). Some of

their tunes, which they generally composed themselves, can still be found in music history books and anthologies. I believe that their music would prove interesting if resurrected for the purposes of rendezvous, but this is about as far as I would penetrate the genteel tradition. I say that with a view toward remaining faithful to the character of the people who attended the original rendezvous, for . . .

*What the frontiersman wanted in his song were words and melody suited for a plain, common, democratic people. He had no use for sentimentality or sensationalism, and only contempt for snobbish descriptions of fashions and talk of city vice. At the same time he swept away the formal academic style of eastern songs. To his popular music he brought a gust of fresh wind and a spirit that was proud and free. "To the West" or "Shoot the Buffalo" had a lusty energy and manly vigor that would have been out of place in the stuffy atmosphere of an eastern parlor. (Ewen 42)*

Most of the music that would have appealed to the westward travelers and rendezvousers of the early 1800s was surely in the popular vein, and I suspect that by and large suits us just fine, too.

Dance music in the Eastern salons was naturally of the genteel kind. In the country, though, contra and other popular dances used the services of a fiddler and a caller. Sometimes the fiddler was joined by other instruments, such as a banjo. There was also some music for ritual dance as well as

social. For example, Morris dancing. Instruments used on these occasions included tin whistles, concertinas, drums, tambourines and bells.

There was plenty of music that did not exist for the entertainment of an audience and was not performed by trained musicians. Work songs prevailed on the plantations, at sea, in the trade canoes and in the lumber camps. Religious and ceremonial songs abounded at camp meetings and among the Native Americans. All of these merit at least a cursory examination.

The tribal music of the Indians would have been mostly unknown and alien to the whites living in the settlements, but westward travelers and trappers and traders surely had some exposure to it. We know that Indians were frequently at rendezvous and in and around the Western forts. I personally feel that the pulse of the tom-tom and Indian song and dance add immeasurably to the rendezvous atmosphere, but it does take something special for a white man to play successfully that type of music. Since Indian music is so closely tied to the natives' ceremonies and beliefs, it is understandable that its appropriation by whites, who may or may not be proficient in its performance and tuned into its spiritual significance, is a sensitive issue. I'll not pretend to be a knowledgeable source of information on this but pass on some general observations and a recommendation that those who wish to pursue Indian music further consult other resources and do their homework thoroughly.

North American Indians have a variety of instruments, most of which are percussive. These include the familiar drums (water drums, tom-tom, etc.) and rattles made of gourds, turtle shells, hooves and other materials. The main melodic instruments are flutes. The so-called love flute is blown at the end. It is about eighteen to twenty-four inches long, "pierced with six holes, and capable of playing a complete octave … . There are also small pipes, with three holes, that play up to five tones" (Chase 408).

Indian music is appropriate to modern rendezvous because it most likely figured into the original gatherings. Tony Warrior is shown adding his contribution to camp music.

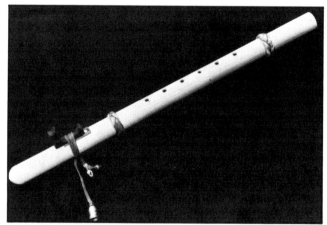

The so-called Indian love flute is blown from the end and different notes are made with the finger holes. This flute was made by Royal Forge in Bozeman, Montana.

It has been observed that of the three principal facets of musical structure — harmony, melody and rhythm — the last is the most important in Indian tribal music. Interestingly, the rhythmic independence of the drum beat and the singing voice is characteristic of tribal music. Our culture expects singing to "keep time" with the rhythmic beat, but in Native American music, that is often not the case. It can further be said that since the concept of harmony is alien to the Indian mind, songs are sung solo or in unison (Chase 406-408). There is much in Indian vocal music that is difficult for whites to grasp or quantify, as the following quotation from ethnologist Alice Fletcher (1900) shows:

*The continual slurring of the voice from one tone to another produces upon us the impression of out-of-tune singing. Then, the custom of singing out of doors, to the accompaniment of the drum, and against the various noises of the camp, and the ever-restless wind, tending to strain the voice and robbing it of sweetness, increased the difficulty of distinguishing the music concealed within the noise, — a difficulty still further aggravated by the habit of pulsating the voice, creating a rhythm within the rhythm of the song.* (Chase 408)

One might argue that the choice of words in that description shows how culture-bound the observer was. But the factual observations seem accurate in light of the Native American music I have heard and detract nothing from its appeal.

I will point to but one more facet of Indian music which may be of interest to us: the avoidance of clearly enunciated words, which are deemed to interfere with the melody. Indians feel that "we talk a great deal as we sing" (Chase 413). Lyrics to Indian songs seem scant to us, and the words that are present are frequently taken apart or modified to make them fit the melody and rhythm better (Chase 413). Given the fact that Indian music may have figured at the original rendezvous, I feel that it is appropriate to our latter-day gatherings. In the absence of Native American performers, some of us whites may successfully attempt to perform tribal music, but it is a difficult medium to master, and we would be well advised to do lots of research and practice diligently.

Around 1800, religious camp meetings became very popular throughout the country. Descriptions of the early meetings make them sound, in scope and activity at least, like our rendezvous, though of course the purpose was very different. Hundreds or thousands of people would gather and camp and, under the direction of circuit-riding ministers, would sing, dance and pray with great fervor. Previously sedate and staid hymns were taken up and enlivened; people "filled out partially remembered texts with much repetition, refrains, and choruses, and thus made them over into a rather roistering type of song . . . [which] went under the various names — spiritual songs, camp meeting songs, revival songs, and chorus songs" (Howard 607). Such camp meetings were all-denominational, and blacks apparently participated as well as whites. At these events it was inevitable that tunes of black and whites influence once another.

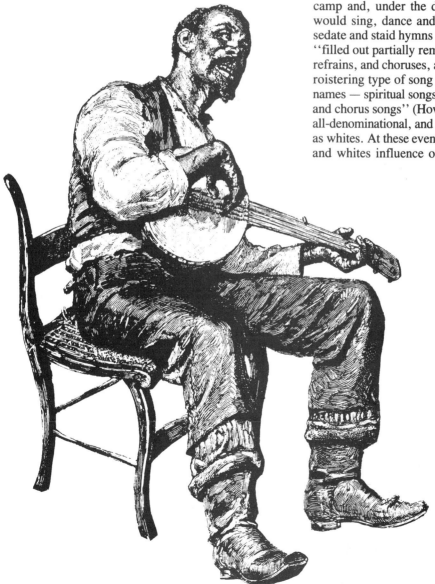

As everyone knows, black vocal music has contributed immeasurably to American music. In the early 19th century, it consisted of work songs or plantation songs and religious songs, the well-known spirituals. Whites were late in coming to an appreciation of this black music, and it was not until after the Civil War that it received much recognition (Chase 239). Yet as early as the 1820s its singular nature captured the attention of a few whites. Most of us are familiar with at least a few spirituals (for example, ''Michael, Row the Boat Ashore,'' ''Nobody Knows the Trouble I See''), so perhaps a few general conclusions will suffice. The spirituals were sung with great individuality, freedom, complication and variety. Originally, they were sung with a chorus and response pattern or a leader and chorus.

*The melody sung or chanted by a single voice, the chorus, joining in with the refrain . . . . Spirituals were used as working songs, e.g., for rowing and for field tasks, as well as at religious meetings. Some of the melodies resembled familiar European tunes, while others were ''extraordinarily wild and unaccountable'' . . . . The singing of the Negroes was characterized by peculiar vocal effects, difficult if not impossible to indicate by regular notation.* (Chase 250-251)

This type of music, like most others, will be more accessible if you can listen to some of it, rather than trying to learn it by reading notes on a printed page. Starting in the 1840s, some of this black music was appropriated by whites and made popular throughout the country, but more on that shortly.

Other fertile sources of work songs were the lumber camps and the seagoing vessels. Both places offered little by way of recreation, and a ''favorite form of entertainment for lumberjacks was to listen to minstrels sing songs and tell tall stories after the evening meal'' (Ewen 39). Shanteyboys sang about the lumbermen's work at day's end. In contrast, chanteys (sailor songs) were work songs performed during the execution of particular tasks (Ewen 40). Chanteys fell into four basic groups:

*Songs for tasks requiring short, heavy pulls were called ''short drags.'' They had abrupt rhythms, crisp accents, clipped phrases — as in ''Haul Away Joe'' or ''Haul on the Bowline.'' Songs for more sustained and heavier tasks, such as hoisting sails or casting anchors, were called ''halliards.'' A halliard like the famous ''Blow, Boys, Blow'' had a more even rhythm than the short drag, a more monotonous meter, a more flowing melody and more sustained choruses. For still more monotonous jobs there were ''capstans,'' long sustained melodies with slow march-like rhythms like ''Santy Anno.'' Finally, there were the ''Foc'sle songs.''* (Ewen 40)

This last category of song was performed in the living quarters after the day's work was done and in that sense was more akin to the songs of the shanteyboy. It may be worth a passing mention that in the early 1800s there was no chanteying on British ships, for that was not considered dignified enough for ships in his majesty's service. Instead, a fiddler was employed to relieve monotony and provide cadence for some tasks. Eventually, the demands of labor eliminated the music as the fiddler was pressed into helping with the physical work (Huntington 6). Songs of the lumber camps and seagoing vessels can be found in some of the resources listed at the end of this chapter. They are a great

source of tunes appropriate to rendezvous.

No discussion of work songs would be complete without reference to the songs of the voyageurs. We know that many French Canadians were engaged in the fur trade throughout the Western part of our country. Singing was part of their culture, and within each party there was often one voyageur of particularly robust singing voice who was paid extra to sing cadence. French paddling songs are an enormous repertory. In fact, ''it is difficult to exaggerate the richness of the voyageurs' legacy of songs . . . . In 1955 the Archives of Forklore at the University of Laval in Quebec had more than 13,000 texts of French Canadian songs. The collection testifies to the tenacity of folk memory, for nineteen out of twenty [songs] had originally been brought across the seas from France in the 17th Century'' (Blegan 3). The melodies of the French Canadian songs I know are very beautiful, and the antiquity of the texts is often very evident. Occasionally, you'll find English translations, but if you've had even a little high school language training, you can do a very creditable job with these songs, especially if you have a recorded version to emulate. It seems that words we might have trouble pronouncing in conversation are easier when sung. Many rendezvous which are blessed with a body of water include

canoe events, and paddling songs can contribute a lot of color as they ring out over the water. The songs sound fine around the campfires at night, too.

Earlier, I mentioned that while black music went largely unappreciated by whites until after the Civil War, some white entertainers had begun to exploit its richness as early as the 1820s. Its adaptation to entertainment ''came to be known as the 'Ethiopian Business' or 'Negro minstrelsy,' or simply 'American minstrelsy.' It brought to the whole of America, and to much of the rest of the world, a new type of humor and a new note of pathos that could have come only from the background of American plantation life'' (Chase

257-258). In the early 1840s, four friends joined forces to produce a more highly evolved and skilled minstrel show than had their predecessors during the previous dozen or so years. They consisted of Dan Emmett (fiddle), Billy Whitlock (banjo), Frank Brower (''bones'' or ''clackers'') and Dick Pelham (tambourine). They exerted a lasting influence on American music and theater, and their leader, Dan Emmett, won great reknown as the composer of ''Dixie'' (Chase 259). Some familiar tunes from this genre are ''Turkey in the Straw,'' ''Boatmen's Dance'' and ''Old Dan Tucker,'' the last two by Dan Emmett.

With the development of minstrelsy, we arrive at approximately the end of the time period we embrace at rendezvous. Much great music was yet to come, for instance ''Old Folks at Home,'' ''My Old Kentucky Home,'' ''Oh! Susanna!,'' ''Camptown Races'' and dozens of others by Stephen Foster and ''Grandfather's Clock,'' ''Marching through Georgia,'' and ''Kingdom Coming'' by Henry Clay Work. While in the strictest sense the appearance of these tunes and countless others of their period would be an anachronism, I can scarely imagine anyone standing on formality to the point that these songs would be objectionable. The foregoing history is offered in the spirit of acquainting the reader with the rich and exciting music scene in America up to about 1850. It should help us choose our repertory for rendezvous or gain a better appreciation of tunes we already know.

To the foregoing historical information, I might add one footnote. Old-time music has survived in certain geographical locations, where it can still be heard today much as it was played generations ago. With a few notable exceptions, old-time music survives in the country, rather than the city. I believe there's a great deal of truth in this observation:

*Civilization — and especially its age of machinery — does not provide fertile soil for folk songs. With our modern standardization of living, and such mediums as the talking pictures setting artificial standards even in the remotest places, the most rural countryman may soon acquire the manners and speech of the city dweller. Then he will sing the latest jazz hits instead of his own songs.*

*Folk songs are generally common to people whom civilization has touched the least . . . . Isolation from other people, hand labor, and lack of printed literature are factors that nourish and perpetuate folk music. A certain naivete is essential to the true people's song; sophistication is its deadliest enemy. True folk music is found among the Negroes, the mountaineers in the southeast Appalachians, the cowboys, the lumberjacks and shanty boys, the New England farm districts, among the wandering tribe of hoboes, with sailors and longshoremen, and often in the jails.* (Howard 633-634)

These are sources of great tunes for rendezvous, for the tunes we find among the mountain people of southern Appalachia, for example, have changed little since the 18th century. In many cases, then, our task is not so much to resurrect a discarded or forgotten music but to collect old tunes that are still current. But as we develop a repertory of old-time tunes, we don't have to restrict ourselves to music that originated *before* 1850. There are many old-time tunes of more modern origin, so this is not merely *old music*. Some of us may even compose tunes today which fit the mold.

Among the literature I have studied on the original

rendezvous, there is little specific mention of the music the old-timers heard in camp. But armed with our cursory knowledge of the music scene in early America, we can nonetheless consider what kinds of instruments and music we can call on to enrich our rendezvous life.

I will stick my neck out and voice the opinion that the instruments best adapted to rendezvous — for reasons of history, portability and suitablility to old-time music — are the fiddle, the dulcimer, the guitar, the mandolin, the voice and the banjo. There are plenty of other instruments that should be perfectly welcome in a strict rendezvous. Comments on these, plus a few of more questionable antiquity, appear at the end of this chapter.

The fiddle may be the king of the old-time instruments because of its universal presence and the vast number of tunes that exist for it. The fiddle is small and light, so it's not likely to be left behind by a traveler. Practically any fiddle can sound good when applied to old-time tunes. The physical differences between fiddles and violins are minor, consisting chiefly of details in setup. A fiddle may use the same strings as a classical violin, but steel strings are often used to provide more volume. The bridge of a fiddle is usually less rounded than that of a violin, for fiddlers frequently play double stops (noting on two adjacent strings at once). Some fiddlers may dispense with the chin rest, at least if they hold the instrument low, against their chest.

The fiddle has not changed in form or construction since the rendezvous days, and any instrument you're likely to find will be suitable provided that it's solid. Fiddles made in the Appalachian highlands may show a lot of variety in size, design and construction. I'm fortunate enough to have found a pair of them at a barn sale, and they are a delight. Despite their crude appearance, they play very nicely and have perfectly good tone. If you love to work with your hands, you might fashion a fine fiddle for yourself. *Foxfire 4* has a chapter devoted to this, and while the fiddle is clearly not a "bolt-together" instrument like the banjo, it should be a feasible project with the aid of such a good resource.

Fiddles are distinguished most clearly from classical violins by the way in which they are played. There are many styles of fiddle playing which are fine for rendezvous. Most styles vary according to region or ethnic type. French Canadian, New England, Appalachian, Irish and Cajun are some examples of playing styles. Your best bet is to get a couple of the records listed in the appendices to this chapter and listen to several styles. First, decide what you'd like to play, then find an appropriate instruction manual or teacher. A fiddler is in many ways a privileged musician: everyone else tunes to him and plays in his keys, he has perhaps more music to choose from than other musicians, and everybody loves his music.

Crooked Neck saws out an old tune on an antique, hand-whittled fiddle.

Stiff wire and a large woodscrew secure the hand-whittled tail piece to this Appalachian fiddle.

Above: The Appalachian dulcimer is a very popular rendezvous instrument and certainly dates back far enough. Right: A detailed view of the dulcimer shows the appropriate non-geared tuners at the top.

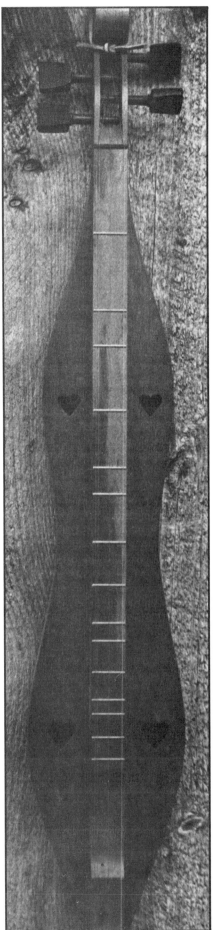

When folks remark that the dulcimer is the only true American instrument, they are probably referring to the Appalachian dulcimer. It has three or four strings in its usual forms. In either case, two are drones, and most of the noting is done on the melody string(s). The earliest known depiction of a dulcimer is a detail on a 12th century ivory book cover made in Byzantium (Sadie 5:701). Obviously, the dulcimer is old enough to qualify for our rendezvous! The American form, which is played on the lap, developed in the late 18th century in the Appalachians (Sadie 1:506). I have encountered references to strumming with the shaft of a goose or turkey feather and noting with a chicken bone (well degreased!) but haven't yet tried that technique. Nowadays, dulcimer players often strum with a guitar pick and note with their finger tips or a small piece of wooden dowel. The Appalachian dulcimer is not difficult to make or play, and there's an abundance of music on record and in instruction books that feature this instrument. It is well-suited to playing and singing since it doesn't drown out the voice. On the other hand, it's hard to hear when played with a loud banjo and fiddle. If you like the idea of a simple instrument that's as American as any, the Appalachian dulcimer may be the choice.

The other type of dulcimer we're likely to encounter is the hammered dulcimer. It bears scant resemblance to its distant cousin of the Southern highlands. Its many strings are not fretted and strummed but struck adroitly with small hammers made of wood, cane or metal. The sound of the hammered dulcimer is sweet and ethereal, and it's a real treat to hear.

The Publication for Black Powder Shooters

MUZZLELOADER

May/June, 1980                                                           $1.50

The guitar scarcely needs any introduction. It is universally accepted in the twelve- and six-string varieties at rendezvous. This instrument is the old stand-by in most countrified styles of music, and it has existed pretty much in its present configuration since the 18th century. An open sound hole (as opposed to one partially closed by a carved rosette) dates from the late 1700s, as do a flat back, metal frets, saddle pins to anchor the strings and machine tuning heads (Sadie 7:835). Originally gut strings were used, but even strict rendezvous folks don't seem to quarrel with steel or nylon strings. Ovation makes a line of guitars that feature a molded fiberglas back and a traditional wooden top and neck. They have a fine sound but look incongruous at rendezvous. I can't help but think, though, that they are suited to the rigors of playing outdoors in a falling dew, next to a campfire or in cold temperatures. Their synthetic back must resist some of

that punishment better than traditional wood. When I was in Friendship for the national shoots in 1983, my favorite traditional, wooden guitar came unglued in the week of 105° daytime temperatures and has never been the same. So, who's better off? The player with the traditional instrument that can't be used, or the one with the modern guitar which will play well under most conditions? I hope the choice is not

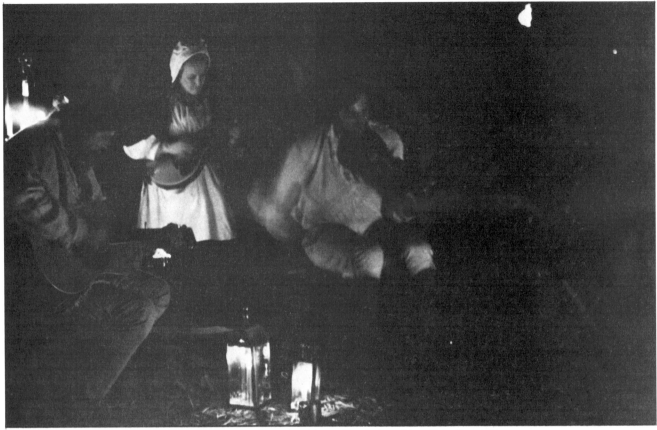

Rendezvous music often takes place after dark and long into the night.

often reduced to such absolutes! In the final analysis, whether or not guitars like the Ovation gain acceptance at rendezvous may be decided not by what is documented as historically correct but by what is *functional*. Playing around a campfire on a damp or cold night, when you've sidled up close to the heat to keep the fingers flexible, is a good deal more stressful for the instrument than playing in your living room! How important is music to *you*? How much are you willing to compromise to be sure that a musician will be able to play at the evening campfire?

If you are a staunch traditionalist and would like to build or find a guitar similar to what was played prior to 1850, a classical guitar with gut or nylon strings could be appropriate. Large-bodied dreadnought guitars are a later development, and a smaller guitar like the fine old Martin 0018 would be well-suited to rendezvous. If you like the idea of a primitive instrument, examine the cover of the May/June 1980 issue of *MUZZLELOADER* magazine. It depicts traditional musician Jimmy Driftwood with his dandy old-time guitar. I believe that this photo contains a clue to one fact of life in using a bona fide antique instrument: Jimmy has his instrument capoed up seven frets as he sings. Perhaps he finds, as do many of us who use antique instruments, that it's not desirable to keep an old instrument tuned up to pitch unless it's in exceptional condition.

Now for just a few peripheral notes about guitars. The references I have found to early playing styles indicate finger picking rather than strumming or flat picking. But I can't think of any style of playing an accoustic guitar, short of

bottle-neck slide, which would for historical reasons be out of place at rendezvous. Capos are a fact of life for guitar and banjo players, and their contributions at rendezvous will be undisputed. Metal finger picks are usually associated with modern bluegrass and other styles, but since there is nothing anachronistic about the material from which they are made, they will probably be accepted at rendezvous. I have begun experimenting with substitutes for the plastic flat picks we commonly use. Some materials such as sheet brass or German silver are out because of the wear and tear they'd produce on strings and wooden tops. Other materials like wood, ivory from old piano keys, tortoise shell and cowhorn may have some promise. This is for the true diehard, though, and the usual plastic pick will probably be lost with the molded Ovation guitar back in the shadows of the campfire.

50

The mandolin boasts an ancient lineage and is a fine instrument for rendezvous campfires. At the time of the original rendezvous, it had a gourd-shaped back. The flat-back mandolin developed later, well after the rendezvous days. If you ever play a round-back mandolin, you'll see why the flat-back was developed. The former is difficult to hold. The mandolin, despite its almost universal acceptance in old-time music nowadays, was late in making its way into Appalachia. The same is true of the guitar, by the way. These instruments weren't widely accepted until around the start of the 20th century (Irwin 83). The bowl-shaped madolins sound fine, and I still see some at flea markets and yard sales for reasonable prices. Condition is the crucial issue. Many I've seen are missing non-functional inlays, but far worse are the ones that have bowed necks or unglued seams. Most music played on a mandolin up to the mid 1800s would have been classical. In a popular vein, the mandolin may have been played with the fingernails or chorded and strummed more than it is today. Old Canadian or New England fiddle tunes and jigs and reels from the British Isles will also sound great on the mandolin. My earlier comments on pick materials will apply here, too. The more I learn about mandolins and their music, the better I like them. A round-back mandolin (or a non-bluegrass style flat-back) would be a fine addition to

Three fine Appalachian old-time instruments: A banjo made by Frank Proffitt Jr.; a small fiddle signed "No. 5, 1885 Made by Charlie Forrest, Walker, VA."; a larger fiddle, acquired at the same time, appears to be made by the same hand.

your rendezvous equipment.

It would be a mistake to overlook the voice as a great instrument for rendezvous. Even if you feel that your manual dexterity isn't up to playing an instrument, you may discover that you have a voice! The beauty of old-time music is that you don't need a trained voice. Old-time music is music of and by the common folk, and if you search out some of the records in the discography that follows this chapter, you'll find a number of performers in the old field recordings whose singing voices are less than sweet and melodious. The qualities which make them succeed as credible musicians are their sincerity and confidence and our tolerant attitude as listeners. Many drinking songs, insult songs (which are an old category of song unto themselves) and farm songs were sung a capella anyway, and an instrument might even seem

These mandolins look similar from the front, but the side view shows us that one is flat and the other round. The flat-backed mandolin is easier to hold and play.

51

to get in the way. If you don't feel comfortable singing solo, get folks to join you on choruses.

If there's an instrument as American as the Appalachian dulcimer, it's the five-string banjo. "The history of the banjo in America tells something of the history of the nation. The banjo takes place in our folkways, in our humor, and in the tragedies of our past. The banjo belongs to all of us: to blacks, to whites, to the first immigrants, and by adoption, to many of the latest" (Webb 1). Its origins are traceable to the "banza, banjer, bangoe, bangie, banshaw" referred to by early observers, including Thomas Jefferson (Webb 2). Initially, it had four gut strings and a back made from a gourd. By the early decades of the 19th century, it had evolved into a form readily recognizable to us. Joel Walker Sweeney (1813-1860) is popularly credited with having discarded the four-string gourd banjo for one of his own inventions: "He cut an old cheese box in half, covered it with skin, and strung it with five strings, thus inventing the modern banjo. He is credited with doing this as early as 1830; by 1840 his reputa-

tion was secure'' (Chase 262). Sweeney became a celebrated minstrel performer and traveled extensively. His original left-handed banjo is in the Natural History Museum of Los Angeles County. Sweeney's reputation as inventor of the five-string notwithstanding, there is no proof that he was responsible for the addition of the thumb string. Indeed, there is proof that the five-string banjo existed before Sweeney's birth. "A watercolour entitled The Old Plantation (painted between 1777 and about 1800 in South Carolina) . . . shows a group of slaves dancing to the music of a banjo. The instrument . . . is interesting in that it provides the first known illustration of the characteristic short thumb string'' (Sadie 2:120). Sweeney may not get credit for inventing the five-string banjo, but he surely deserves our thanks for populariz-

One of the most popular old-time banjos is the early Fairbanks Whyte Ladie #2. Being made after the start of the 20th century, it is less appropriate for the rendezvous than a fretless.

This beautiful, fretless, 5-string banjo by Henry Stichter, c. 1848, is a least twice the size we're used to.

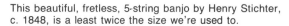

The old-time banjo on the right has a Waverly Fiberskin (plastic!) head - a very convincing counterfeit. It has an ebony tail piece tied on with gut, as well as the one on the lower left. The strings of the Appalachian banjo (upper left) are simply anchored to nails driven into the rim.

ing it and making it a permanent part of the American music scene.

Initially, banjos were fretless and strung with gut strings. Raised metal frets weren't advocated until about 1860, and they did not become common until around 1880 (Sadie 2:118). Strictly speaking, then, the most appropriate banjos for rendezvous are open-back (no resonator), fretless, fitted with a natural skin head and strung with gut (or failing that — gulp! — nylon) strings. The tuners should be straight-through violin-type pegs and the bridge a simple two- or three-footed affair (no bone inserts or fancy compensated bridges). The tail piece is a plain triangular or bell-shaped piece of hardwood tied to the external anchor of the dowel stick with the same strong gut used to tie on violin tail pieces. The accompanying photographs show some of these details. Appalachian fretless banjos have changed little for many generations, and they are equally appropriate. They are very simply constructed, and if you can build a rifle from a kit, you'll find such a banjo very easy to make. For good resources on building traditional banjos, consult *Foxfire 3* and ''A Simple Banjo'' by Richard Starr in *Fine Woodworking* magazine. Both contain enough information and illustrations to help you build a good instrument from scratch. The appendices to this chapter include addresses that will be useful if you need parts to build a new banjo or restore an old one.

The preceding paragraph describes a bona fide old-time fretless banjo, which should be the instrument of preference for experienced players who are concerned with authenticity.

Fretless banjos have a distinctive, plunky sound which I find irresistible. Granted, playing such a banjo is more difficult, the sound is not as brilliant as the more modern banjo you may be used to, it's tricky to tune up or capo up to play with a fiddle or mandolin, it's hard to play barre and other cords, and it takes practice to play above the seventh fret or so. But, I'd say that your flintlock poor boy doesn't shoot as straight or as fast as your modern deer rifle, either, but you make the choice based on what's historically correct and what feels right. I'll add another observation: If you already play banjo and hesitate to attempt a fretless, I'd say that the change is akin to learning to shoot a flintlock smoothbore with no sights when you've been used to firing a caplock rifle. The transition can be demanding, but you may be rewarded in proportion.

But let's again be pragmatic. If you're not an experienced banjo player, you'll find a fretless one difficult to manage. Gut strings are expensive and hard to find, nylon strings are available but also expensive and both types are rather quiet. With a natural skin head, you will experience

The anchor on the rim of this antique, fretless banjo is tied to an ebony tail piece. Gut or nylon strings are tied to the tail piece.

A fine, wood-top banjo by Fred LaBarre of Bristol, Vermont.

changes in volume and brightness of tone with variations in humidity. You can learn to live with these or become adept at tensioning the head under various conditions. At a recent rendezvous, I brought just one banjo, my favorite skin-head fretless, and the falling dew at night softened the head. The feet of the bridge sank into the head and the strings kept popping off the bridge. I was essentially *hors de combat* for the rest of the evening. From now on I'll bring a second banjo along with a Fiberskin head just in case. This is a modern plastic head which is impervious to moisture, but instead of being frosted or clear like most banjo heads you've seen, it is grained like a natural hide. It really looks like a skin head! It seems that the Fiberskin would be the answer to setting up a banjo to play under rigorous conditions, but the last I knew, it was available in only one size, eleven inch. If I had an old banjo with a usable natural skin head, I probably wouldn't change it at all.

I've mentioned earlier that bluegrass three-finger picking is a style of playing which was introduced about a hundred years too late for strict historical accuracy at rendezvous. The styles that *are* appropriate include classical, clawhammer (also referred to as drop-thumb, frailing, rapping and undoubtedly a few other descriptive terms) and two-finger picking. It's beyond the scope of this chapter to treat these styles in detail, so the best way to get a sense of these styles, if you don't have access to a good teacher, is to arm yourself with a passel of records and instruction books from the appendices of this chapter. I taught myself to play banjo that way, and there is some satisfaction in going it on your own. But I'd be leagues ahead of where I am now if I'd had the benefit of learning from a good teacher.

As you learn to play, you'll also learn to be a better listener. In regard to written music, I've always taken to heart the comment of the old-timer who, when asked if he could read music, replied, "Not enough to hurt my playin'." The point is that there's a difference between playing notes, what you read on the page, and playing *music,* the sound that your heart and fingers produce together. It was probably the same crusty old-timer who declared about his banjo, "Hell, they ain't no notes to it; ye jest *play* the damn thing!"

Making music in cold weather is tough on hands and instruments.
Capes and capotes can warm hands between tunes.

Much of the music you'll find for the instruments I've discussed so far is written in tablature rather than true musical notation. Tablature is easy to learn, as it is a visual representation of the strings on the instrument and where they are to be stopped. It will help immeasurably to learn tablature for your instrument. If you dig into some old sheet music for good antique tunes, they will surely be in musical notation. I don't read music, so I have to depend on my wife to play an unfamiliar tune for me on the violin until I can translate it into banjo. Virtually every good source book of tunes I've seen for banjo, mandolin, guitar and dulcimer has an introduction that covers adequately how to read tablature and chord notations and play the music in the book. A lot of records will help you add music to your repertory, for

they have word sheets and tablature which accompany them or which can be ordered separately.

If you'd like to get started playing old-time music but need an appropriate instrument, you might find one at a flea market, antique shop, yard sale, music store or through a classified ad. If you buy from a music store, you might not find a bargain, but you probably will be served by a knowledgeable person who can help you start on the right foot. My most delightful finds have been at flea markets and used furniture shops, where I have landed some jim-dandy instruments, including most of the fiddles and banjos I photographed for this chapter.

In shopping for a used stringed instrument, you need to verify that the neck is absolutely straight. Otherwise, it will not note accurately, and it will be difficult to play. You can lay a straight edge along the frets (or the bare fingerboard in the case of a fretless banjo) and see if there is contact all the way. If not, the neck may be unusable. If you find a banjo with a warped neck but a good pot, you might consider having a new neck installed, at least if the price

is right. In the absence of a straight edge, you can sight along the fingerboard by holding the instrument close to your eye, like sighting a rifle. If the skin head of a banjo is torn, if frets are worn or if brackets, tailpiece, inlays and bridge are gone, that's all relatively minor as long as that damage is reflected in the purchase price. If you like to restore old guns to their former beauty and utility, you'll find much enjoyment in fixing up old instruments, too.

One final word about playing your cherished instruments at rendezvous: they may require unaccustomed care when played and stored outdoors. Remember the earlier example of the guitar held close to the campfire for the comfort of its player? The back of that instrument might be cold and its top and strings wet from dew, which is a pretty stressful environment for a delicate instrument. Wood and strings should be wiped dry before returning the instrument to its case for the night. You may have to replace the strings on a rendezvous instrument more frequently and apply guitar or fiddle polish more regularly. Watch out for your big hand-forged iron belt buckles, or they'll make the back of your instrument look like a bear-clawed tree. Keep the instrument in a good case at night, under cover, preferably off the ground

and in a place where a sleepy camper exiting the tent at nature's call won't fall over it. You may even find it desirable to keep your best instrument at home and take a spare to rendezvous.

Experiment and discover what you can add to the evening music sessions. As a contributor to life around the campfire, relax and enjoy the chance to share a tune with kindred spirits who know how to have a good time, folks who know that the campfire is not Carnegie Hall and who will love you for trying. If you are not inclined, despite my pleas, to take up an instrument, at least be a good listener! Music around the campfire should be participatory, so join in on the choruses! And remember that many of the musicians at rendezvous have never met before. When they get together to play, they may be simply jamming, so don't expect every tune to be concert ready!

Music that's a century and a half old shortens the distance that separates Jim Bridger, Dan Emmett and Jim Crow from us. Unlike other relics, the music doesn't rust, rot or wear out, so it can be as fresh for us as it was for them. As we escape into a different era, old tunes make the illusion more complete. Music may be the best entertainment

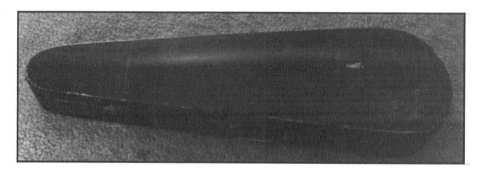

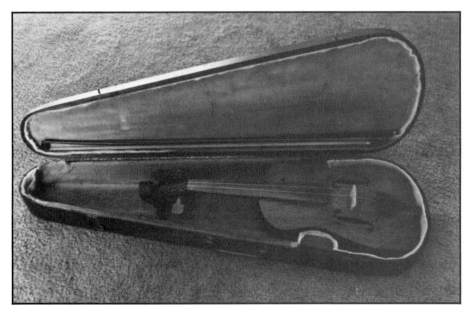

Wooden fiddle cases from the 19th century, like the one pictured, still turn up inexpensively at flea markets. Modern, hard-shell cases look out of place at rendezvous.

Music is always an important ingredient in the great life at rendezvous.

camp life offers, as Stephen Foster suggests:

> *The Time is never dreary*
> *If a fellow never moans;*
> *The ladies never weary*
> *With the rattlin' of the bones.*
> *So come again, Susannah,*
> *By the gaslight of the moon;*
> *We'll thump the old piano*
> *When the banjo's out of tune.*
> *Ring, ring the banjo,*
> *I love that good old song!*

Ring the banjar, and long live the old music! The camping gear, the guns, the clothing and other trappings of the period we portray are links to the material world of our forebears. The music we can preserve is a spiritual connection, for it reflects their tastes and values, their aspirations and their preoccupations. If you can truly appreciate the old-time music, you are a step closer to entering the skins of the people we admire from past generations.

# APPENDICES

## APPENDIX A: OTHER INSTRUMENTS

**ACCORDION:** The piano accordion and button accordion (also called melodeon) are traceable to the organ-accordion of Busson (1859) and farther back in other forms (Sadie 1:40). The button accordion, with its more archaic appearance, would probably fit in better at rendezvous than the piano accordion. The latter, from my experience, seems to be overendowed with snazzy chrome-plated fittings and mother-of-toilet-seat plastic.

**AUTO-HARP:** This chord zither was invented in the last quarter of the 19th century. The first American patent was granted in 1881 to C.F. Zimmerman, who began commercial production of these instruments in 1885 (Sadie 1:741-742). Technically, the auto-harp is a late comer for rendezvous, but since it is suited to traditional music, its tardy appearance may be overlooked by most people.

**BAGPIPES:** In their various forms (Irish, Scottish, English, French, etc.), the pipes date back to about the 13th century (Sadie 2:20). I've met a couple of people who are not fond of the pipes, but I've always loved them. For volume they can't be matched, and I find the music stirring and altogether appropriate for rendezvous.

**BANJO VARIANTS:** Variations of the banjo such as the banjeaurine, bass banjo, tenor banjo, plectrum banjo, piccolo banjo, guitar banjo and others are mostly contributions of the Victorian era and therefore out of place at a rendezvous. Equally to the point, most are suited to a music which had not evolved by mid-century.

**BODHRAN** (pronounced ''boron''): This Celtic drum is clearly of ancient origin. It is held in one hand by the rossed dowel sticks which keep it round and flailed upon with a double-ended drumstick held in the other hand. It sounds great with tunes from the British Isles.

**BONES:** This simple percussive instrument may boast the greatest antiquity of all. Bones are shown on Egyptian vases dating from 3000 B.C.

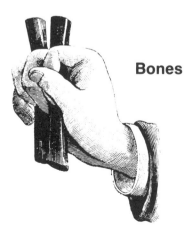

**Bones**

A Celtic bodhran and an 18th century military snare drum from Cooperman Fife and Drum Co.

(Barber 7). They are always amusing to listen to and watch, for the "virtuoso player does not merely play; he dances the bones" (Barber 8). Bones can be made of wood or, as in olden times, rib bones. American players often use a pair of bones in each hand. Spoons serve a similar percussive function.

**CONCERTINA:** As indicated earlier Oliver Wheatstone patented this instrument in 1829. There are two types that we're likely to encounter: Anglo, and English. The former plays a different note on squeeze and draw; the latter plays the same note. Either type is fine for playing, and I don't believe that one is easier to learn than the other. Buying a concertina can be tricky. The bellows must be in good shape. Original instruments may not be pitched properly to play with other instruments. Concertinas with wooden ends and ivory buttons may be generally less desirable than ones with metal ends and buttons. In the former case, the reeds are probably of brass, and they may not have withstood the ravages of time as well as steel reeds. If a concertina needs reeds and bellows, the repair bill can be substantial. The concertina sounds great with sea chanteys.

**HARMONICA:** The patent for the harmonica dates from 1821 and is ascribed to Christian Friedrich Ludwig Buschmann (Sadie 8:164). Oliver Wheatstone developed a type of harmonica, the symphonium, in 1829. It was an intermediate step in the development of the concertina. Today, there are two types of harmonica: the diatonic, and chromatic.

**JEW'S HARP:** References to this instrument date to the 16th century. Jew's harps and harmonicas have been part of the old-time music scene in the Appalachians since the arrival of the first settlers in the 1700s, and remnants of both instruments "have been found in the ruins of the earliest military forts in this area" (Sadie 9:645).

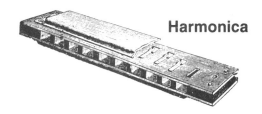

**Harmonica**

This hexagon concertina with ivory buttons and carrying case was made for the Crystal Palace Exposition of 1851. Oliver Wheatstone patented the concertina in 1829, the same year as Pierre's Hole Rendezvous.

The jaw harp is easily learned and can be packed anywhere.

The banjo-mandolin is technically a latecomer. However, it might serve well where a traditional mandolin cannot be heard above the other instruments.

**MANDOLIN OFFSHOOTS:** Instruments such as the bouzouki and the banjo-mandolin may lend themselves to rendezvous music. Strictly speaking, the banjo-mandolin was invented too late (Victorian era) for rendezvous, but mandolin players who play in an outdoor setting with other musicians may find that it gives more volume than a traditional Neapolitan (round-back) or flat-back mandolin.

**MISCELLANEOUS INSTRUMENTS:** These might include such things as the ocarina or sweet potato, though it dates from about 1860 (Sadie 13:487); the washtub base; the washboard; the limberjack, which is as much a percussion instrument as it is a toy when it is danced skillfully on its paddle; the carpenter's saw, struck or bowed to produce notes; and the jug. Military music and its instruments are also no stranger to rendezvous, where fife and drum corps sometimes march and perform.

**PENNY WHISTLE OR TIN WHISTLE:** This instrument is great in instrumental tunes from the British Isles. Generations is the brand of penny whistle found most commonly in music stores. The whistles are made in numerous keys, D being the usual choice. If you want to avoid the glaring plastic mouthpieces of the Generations whistles, get a tin whistle from the

Cooperman Fife and Drum Company listed in the appendix of resources. Theirs is made only of metal and wood.

---

# APPENDIX B: DISCOGRAPHY

Some of the records listed here may no longer be in production. A library with a good record section may be able to provide some records that music shops can't. The following records are almost entirely old-time music of the type that would be appropriate to rendezvous. These records will impress upon you the nature of true old-time music, as opposed to bluegrass or 60's folk music, more effectively than any written treatise. They will also help you learn specific tunes as you take written tablature

and try to transform it into music. Tablature tells you only which notes to play, and you'll benefit from having a recorded version of your new tune to discover how it should *sound*.

In the following list, I have not included a separate category for guitar and mandolin only because these instruments figure prominently on a number of the records. Some records are classified only as general, because numerous instruments and voice are featured on them and any other classification would be inaccurate or incomplete.

Finally, I have for the most part restricted the discography to American

music. There is an abundance of great music from other countries which is appropriate to rendezvous. Some traditional performers from the British Isles I can recommend are The Battlefield Band, The Boys of the Lough, Do'A, Jean Redpath and Ian Robb.

**AUTOHARP:**
*Traditional Music Played on the Autoharp.* Folkways FA 2365.

**BANJO:**
Burke, Kevin. *Plain Singing and Fancy Picking.* Kicking Mule 207.
Bursen, Howard. *Cider in the Kitchen.* Folk Legacy, FSI-74.
*Burt Porter and Tom Azarian.* Fretless 102.
*Clawhammer Banjo.* County 701.
*Clawhammer Banjo.* Vol. III. County 757.
*Folk Banjo Styles.* Elektra EKL 7217.
*Frank Proffitt.* Folk Legacy FSA-1.
George, Frank. *Traditional Music for Banjo, Fiddle, and Bagpipes.* Kanawha 307.
Levy, Bertram. *That Old Gut Feeling.* Flying Fish 27271.
*Melodic Clawhammer Banjo.* Kicking Mule 209.
*More Clawhammer Banjo Songs and Tunes from the Mountains.* County 717.
*Ola Belle Reed.* Rounder 0021.
Porter, Burt. *Living Just the Same.* Fretless 126.
*Roscoe Holcomb and Wade Ward.* Folkways FA-2363.
Rosenbaum, Art. *Art of the Mountain Banjo.* Kicking Mule 203.
—. *Five String Banjo.* Kicking Mule 108.
*Southern Clawhammer Banjo.* Kicking Mule 213.
*The Old-Time Banjo in America.* Kicking Mule 204.
*Uncle Dave Macon at Home.* Tennessee Folklore Society DU-TFS-101.
*Uncle Dave Macon: Early Recordings.* County 521.

**CONCERTINA:**
*Father Charlie: Traditional Irish Songs and Tunes.* Green Linnet SIF 1021.
*Irish Traditional Concertina Styles.* Topic/Free Reed 12TFRS506.

**DULCIMER:**
Cronshaw, Andrew, et al. *Times and Traditions for Dulcimer.* Trailer LER 2094.
*Edna Ritchie, Viper Kentucky.* Folk Legacy FSA-3.
Kretzner, Leo and Jay Leibovitz. *Pigtown Fling Dulcimer Sessions.* Green Linnet SIF 1019.
—. *Dulcimer Fair. Traditional Songs on the Mountain Dulcimer from Simple to Advanced.* Michigan Archives. MA002.
Mitchell, Howard W. *The Mountain Dulcimer.* Folk Legacy FSI-1.
Roth, Kevin. *The Mountain Dulcimer Instrumental Album.* Folkways FS 3570.
—. *Kevin Roth Sings and Plays Dulcimer.* Folkways FA 2367.
—. *The Other Side of the Mountain.* Folkways FTS 31045.
Schilling Jean. *Old Traditions. Traditional Southern Appalachian Mountain Music Played on Dulcimer.* Traditional Records JS5117.

**FIDDLE:**
Beaudoin, Louis. *Louis Beaudoin.* Philo 2000.
Carignan, Jean. *French Canadian Fiddle Songs.* Legacy LEG 120.
Courville, Sady and Denis McGee. *La Vieille Musique Acadienne.* Swallow LP 6030.
*La Famille Beaudoin.* Philo 2022.
*New England Traditional Fiddling 1926-1925.* JEMF-105.
*Old-Time Fiddler's Repertory.* R.P. Christeson, ed. University of Missouri Press. ISBN 0-8262-0199-7.

**HAMMERED DULCIMER:**
Caravan, Guy. *Green Rocky Road.* June Appal 021.
Ecker, Douglas, et al. *More Path Rent.* Eckerworks 001.
Spence, Bill. *The Hammered Dulcimer.* Front Hall FHR01.

**STRING BAND:**
Cranberry Lake. *Old Time and Jug Band Music.* Swallowtail Records ST-8.
*Debbie McClatchy with the Red Clay Ramblers.* Innisfree/Green Linnet SF1003.
Deseret String Band. *Land of Milk and Honey.* Ohkedokee Records.
Highwoods String Band. *Fire on the Mountain.* Rounder Records 0023.
*Kenny Hall and the Sweets Mill String Band.* Vols. 1 and 2. Bay 103 and TPH 727.
*Putnam String County Band.* Rounder Records 3003.
*The Hollow Rock String Band.* Rounder Records 0024.
*The Old Reliable String Band.* Folkways FA 2475.
*The Old Scratch Band.* California Condor Records CCLP-1.
*The Red Clay Ramblers with Fiddlin' Al McCanless.* Folkways FTS 31039.

**VOCAL:**
*Five Days Singing.* Vol. 1. Folk Legacy FSI-41.
*Blow, Ye Winds in the Morning.* Traditional sea songs, dances and chanteys. Revels Records, RS1084.

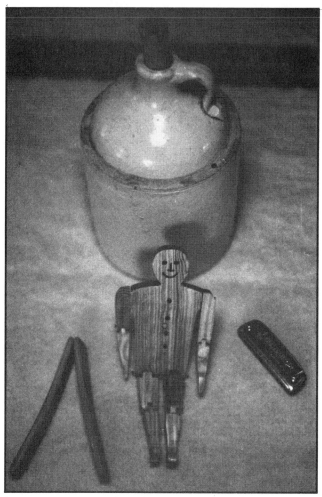

A pre-1850 music session can take place with the jug, bones, harmonica and Limber-Jack. The jug changes tone as it empties.

MacArthur, Margaret. *The Old Songs.* Philo 1001.
—. *An Almanac of New England Farm Songs.* Green Linnet SIF 1039.
—. *Folksongs of Vermont.* Folkways FH5314.
—. *On the Mountains High.* Living Folk LFR 100.
—. *Make the Wildwood Ring.* Front Hall FHR 027.
McCutcheon, John. *How Can I Keep from Singing?* June Appal 003.
Morton, Craig. *Them Liverpool Judies.* Philo 1002.
Ritchie, Jean. *Traditional Ballads in the Southern Mountains (Child Ballads)* Folkways FA 2301 and 2302.
Roberts, John and Tony Barrand. *Mellow with Ale . . . From the Horn.* Front Hall FHR 04.
—. *Across the Western Ocean.* Swallowtail ST-4.
Seeger, Peggy. *The Best of Peggy Seeger.* Prestige FL 14016.
X Seamen's Institute. *Heart of Oak.* Folkways FTS 32419.

**GENERAL:** You'll find plenty of good examples of all the major instruments and voice on these recordings.
*Allan Block and Ralph Lee Smith.* Meadowlands Records. MS-1.
*Beech Mountain, N.C. Traditional Music.* Vol. 2. Folk Legacy FSA-23.
*Brandywine Mountain Music Convention.* Vol. 1. Heritage VI.
*The Child Ballads 2.* Topic 12T161,
*Folk Festival of the Smokies.* Vol. 1, FFS 528; Vol. 2, FFS 529.
*Goin' Down the Valley.* Vocal and Instrumental Styles in Folk Music from the South. New World NW 236.
*Grand Musick.* Fife and Drums. Old North Bridge Records ONB1775.
Hutton, Bruce. *Old-Time Music; It's all Around.* Folkways FA 2402.
*I'm Old, But I'm Awfully Tough.* Traditional Music of the Ozark Region. Missouri Friends of the Folk Arts 1001.

*Instrumental Music of the Southern Appalachians.* Tradition Records TLP 1007.

Kirkpatrick, John and Sue Harris. *Shred and Patches.* Topic 12TS355.

Lomax, Alan, ed. *Folk Music of the United States, Anglo-American Ballads.* Library of Congress Music Div. AAFSL1.

MacArthur Family. *Make the Wild Woods Ring.* Front Hall Records. FHR-027.

McClatchy, Debbie. *Lady Luck.* Innisfree/Green Linnet SF1017.

*Oh My Little Darling.* Folk Song Types. New World Records NWR 245.

McCurdy, Ed. *A Treasury of American Folk Song.* Elektra EKL-205.

*Mountain Music of Kentucky.* Folkways FA 2317.

*Music from the Hills of Caldwell County.* Physical Records 12-001.

Nagler, Eric and Martha Nagler. *A Right and Proper Dwelling.* Swallow Records BS1002.

Ritchie, Jean. *British Traditional Ballads in the Southern Mountains.* Folkways 2302.

Ritchie, Jean, Paul Clayton and Richard Chase. *American Folk Tales and Songs.* Tradition Records TLP 1011.

Smith, Henry, ed. *Anthology of American Folk Music. Vol. I: Ballads.* Folkways FA 2951.

*The Sounds of History.* Vols. II, III and IV. Life History of the U.S. Records.

Tannen, Holly and Pete Cooper. *Frosty Morning.* Plant Life Records.

*That's My Rabbit, My Dog Caught It.* New World Records. NWR 26.

Tuft, Harry. *Across the Blue Mountains.* Folk Legacy FSI-63.

Robichaud, Jerry. *Maritime Dance Party.* Fretless.

To bolster your repertory, take in some old-time music festivals. This one featured Leroy Troy, banjo virtuoso in the Uncle Dave Macon tradition.

PHOTO COURTESY OF JOHN RICE IRWIN MUSEUM OF APPALACHIA

## APPENDIX C: RESOURCES

Alpine Dulcimers, Box 566M85, Boulder, CO 80306. Dulcimer kits (and muzzleloading rifle accoutrements) by and for buckskinners.

*Banjo Newsletter,* P.O. Box 364, Greensboro, MD 21639. Monthly magazine; $18.50 for 12 issues.

Cooperman Fife and Drum Co., Essex Industrial Park, Main Street, P.O. Box 276, Centerbrook, CT 06409. Sources for *authentic* fifes, drums, tin whistles, wooden games and amusements from the past.

Dulcimer Dave McNew, 2313 Kingsman, Virginia Beach, VA 23456. A devoted buckskinner who builds the nicest dulcimers I've seen, all on a custom basis.

Kicking Mule Records, Box 3233, Berkeley, CA 84703. Many fine records of old-time music; also books containing tablatures and words to music on the records.

Mandolin Brothers, 629 Forest Avenue, Staten Island, NY 10310. Vintage instruments; catalog available.

Museum of Appalachia, P.O. Box 359, Norris, TN 37828. The museum has an outstanding collection of old and primitive instruments. Also, every October, the museum is host to a homecoming event which features old-time music, crafts and activities of every description. The museum is a must-see any time you are in this part of the country.

Music Emporium, Inc., 2018 Massachusetts Avenue, Cambridge, MA 02140. One of the most complete selections of old-time musical instruments you're likely to find.

Stewart-MacDonald, 21 North Shafer Street, Box 900A, Athens, OH 45701. Copious source of banjo parts, supplies, kits. Catalog available.

## APPENDIX D: ADDITIONAL READING

Investigate these sources as well as those listed in the bibliography.

Burke, John. *Old Time Fiddle Tunes for Banjo.* New York: Amsco, 1968.

Carlin, Bob, ed. *Southern Clawhammer Banjo.* New York: Kicking Mule, 1978. (Accompanies Kicking Mule record of same title, KM 213.)

Carlin, Richard. "Dating Wheatsone Concertinas." *Mugwumps* 7.1 (June 1981): 16-18.

Erbsen, Wayne. *Back Pocket Old-Time Song Book.* New York: Pembroke Music, 1981.

Hunter, Ilene and Marilyn Judson. *Simple Folk Instruments to Make and Play.* New York: Simon and Schuster, 1977.

Jumper, Tim. *The Banjo Player's Songbook.* New York: Oak, 1984. This is my favorite resource book of old banjo tunes.

Krassen, Miles. *Clawhammer Banjo.* New York: Oak, 1974. An excellent book, with sound sheet, for beginning players.

—. *Appalachian Fiddle.* New York: Oak, 1973. Another good book; it contains fiddle versions of many tunes in *Clawhammer Banjo.*

Lee, Lorraine. *The Magic Dulcimer.* Cambridge, MA: Yellow Moon Press, 1983.

Levy, Lester. *A Century of Humorous Songs in America: 1805-1905.* Norman: University of Oklahoma Press, 1971.

Magee, Rogers. *Let's Play the Dulcimer.* Aiken, SC: The Dulcimer, 1972.

McQuillen, Bob. *Bob's Note Book: Jigs, Reels, and Other Tunes.* Dublin, NH: Bob McQuillen, 1978.

*Melodic Clawhammer Banjo.* New York: Kicking Mule, 1977. (Accompanies Kicking Mule record of same name, KM 209.)

*Mugwumps Special Reference Issue.* Vol. 3 No. 4. Silver Spring, MD: Mugwumps Instrument Herald, 1974. Information on dating old instruments by serial number.

*One Thousand Fiddle Tunes.* Chicago: M.M. Cole, n.d.

**Ocarina**

Perlman, Ken. *Melodic Clawhammer Banjo.* New York: Oak, 1979.
Rosenbaum, Art. *Old-Time Mountain Banjo.* New York: Oak, 1968.
Sandberg, Larry. *The Original Banjo Case Chord Book.* New York: Acorn Music Press, 1978.
—. *Complete Banjo Repair.* New York: Oak, 1979.
Seeger, Pete. *How to Play the 5-String Banjo.* Beacon, NY: Pete Seeger, 1962.

Starr, Richard. "A Simple Banjo." *Fine Woodworking* 53 (July/Aug. 1985) 38-40.
Taussig, Harry. *Teach Yourself Guitar.* New York: Oak, 1971.
Waring, Dennis. *Making Folk Instruments in Wood.* New York: Sterling, 1982.
Wigginton, Elliot, ed. "Banjos and Dulcimers." *Foxfire 3.* New York: Anchor, 1975. 121-207.
—. "Fiddle Making." *Foxfire 4.* New York: Anchor, 1977. 106-126.

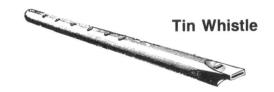

**Tin Whistle**

# APPENDIX E: WORKS CITED

Barber, Sue. "How to Make and Play the Bones." *How to Play Nearly Everything.* Ed. Dallas Cline. New York: Oak, 1977. 7-17.
Blegan, Theodore. *The Voyageurs and their Songs.* St. Paul: Minnesota Historical Society, 1966.
Chase, Gilbert. *American Music From the Pilgrims to the Present.* New York: McGraw-Hill, 1955.
Ewen, David. *Panorama of American Popular Music.* Englewood Cliffs, NJ: Prentice-Hall, 1957.
Heatwole, Oliver. "The Invention of the Concertina." *Mugwumps* 6.5 (1979): 5-8.

Howard, John T. *Our American Music.* New York: Thomas Crowell Co., 1939.
Huntington, Gale, ed. *Fiddle Tunes 1801-1802.* Vineyard Haven, MA: Hines Point Publishers, 1977.
Irwin, John Rice. *Musical Instruments of the Southern Appalachian Mountains.* Exton, PA: Schiffer, 1983.
Sadie, Stanley, ed. *The New Grove Dictionary of Music and Musicians.* 20 volumes. London: MacMillan, 1980.
Webb, Robert Lloyd. *Ring the Banjar!* Cambridge: M.I.T. Museum, 1984.

# Trade Goods for
# Rendezvous

## by Charles E. Hanson, Jr.

CHARLES HANSON KNEW what a working cowboy's life was all about by the time he was ten years old on a Nebraska ranch. He trapped, hunted and camped in his spare time and made his own moccasins, fringed shirt and muzzleloading shotgun when he was sixteen.

Then followed an active life as an engineer, writer, historican and, for the last eighteen years, director of the Museum of the Fur Trade. He has written three books: *The Northwest Gun, The Plains Rifle,* and *The Hawkin Rifle: Its Place in History;* plus 130 articles for historical, archaeological and collector journals. He has also edited *The Museum of the Fur Trade Quarterly* for the past twenty-four years.

Hanson has been active over the last twenty years as a museum consultant and research specialist. He holds a ''Graybeard'' membership in the American Mountain Men, a lifetime ''Gold Card'' from the Maryland Arms Collectors Association and life membership in the National Muzzleloading Rifle Association, the Bordeaux Creek Fur Trade and Muzzleloading Association, the Wyoming State Muzzle Loading Association and the Buckhorn Skinners of Colorado. In addition to all this, he has been a long-time member of the Ohio Gun Collectors Association, the National Rifle Association and the American Society of Arms Collectors.

After a long career as an administrative assistant for public service organizations, Hanson's wife, Marie, is his co-worker and research assistant. His three sons are Charles III, professional gunsmith and author of two frontier gun sketchbooks; William, long-time Alaska resident, engineer, big game hunter and match shooter; and James, director of the Nebraska State Historical Society and author of ten popular books on Indians and all phases of buckskinning.

THE North American fur trade didn't start after
1800 in the Western mountains. It started in the
16th century along our Eastern Seaboard. It was
called "the fur trade" because it wasn't trapping; it was buying furs from native hunters and trappers using European
goods for currency. Our original thirteen colonies were
established with capital derived from this trade. Traders
traveling up the St. Lawrence established Canada, and
English ships going into Hudson's Bay brought the first goods
to trade with the Indians for the furs of the Far North.

Before the Revolution English traders were packing
goods across the Appalachians to trade with the Indians of
the Ohio Valley and the Deep South. At the same time,
French traders were established all around the Great Lakes
and most of the Mississippi Valley. By 1800, the French
trading families of St. Louis were taking trading goods to
the Osages and to tribes on the Missouri like the Kanza, Oto
and Omaha, while the Nor'westers were beginning to buy
beaver skins from the Blackfeet, Mandan and other upper
Missouri River Indians.

It was only after the Louisiana Purchase that a flood
of American backwoodsmen began to hunt the beaver
themselves in the new virgin territory that was suddenly
opened to them. Most of them could hunt, shoot and trap,
so it was much easier for them to produce beaver pelts
themselves instead of buying them from the plains Indians
who had very little trapping experience. This was the birth
of the mountain man era, and the rendezvous was created
to serve the mountain men in lieu of the time-honored Indian trading post. Consequently, the mountain men and their
rendezvous were really atypical portions of the whole
300-year fur trade story. In addition, many of the trade goods
at rendezvous were not what one would find at the typical
Indian trading post.

In the first place, trade goods for the rendezvous went
over tough routes to impossible places while goods for the
Indian trade were moved along rivers or other established
"highways" suitable for boats or wagons. Trading posts
were always at favorite Indian camping locations with ready

access to travelers, while rendezvous were held at locations close to mountain trapping operations and were specifically selected for the availability of forage and water for thousands of horses and mules.

Secondly, the customers at the rendezvous were different from the ordinary tribe of Indians. The principal customers were white men working at a specific job, anxious to outfit themselves for another long year in the mountains. The only real time they had to make things for themselves was when the weather was bitterly cold and heavy snow covered everything.

For this reason a rendezvous supply train carried halters, halter chains, horseshoes, horseshoe nails, saddles, trap chains, razors, shaving soap, even pencils and paper. Trade goods were always part of the cargo, however, because hundreds of Indians congregated around most rendezvous sites and a small amount of trading resulted. But a more important reason was that trade goods were the currency of the country. Indians had no use for money, and trade goods were needed to buy horses, robes or provisions from them. There are many recorded instances of an emergency purchase of a horse from various tribes by brigade leaders. Sir William Drummond Stewart noted that the people in Independence recommended that he take cases of English powder plus some coarser powder for trading (96).

The bulk of the money involved in putting a supply

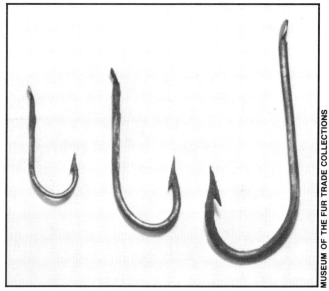

Three sizes of trade fish hooks from the first half of the 19th century. The top ends are flattened instead of having a hole like modern hooks.

Indian-made items like this buckskin jacket and quilled possibles bag were a part of the fur trade, but trappers depended on trade goods brought to the rendezvous for their livelihood. Shown here are a Standish beaver trap, a Hawken rifle and an old pack saddle. This photo is also reproduced on page III of the color section.

*THE SUMMER RENDEZVOUS.*

caravan together went for horses, horse gear, traps, tools, supplies, rum and "white man" items like razors, soap and spurs. Some items — awls, flints, firesteels, combs and cloth — could be used by both Indians and whites. The third category of goods was strictly for Indian trade: ribbons, rings, beads, jewelry, vermilion, shells, and fancy cloth.

Lists are dull things, but a few are necessary to identify the things that really came to a rendezvous. Ashley's accounts for his 1825 rendezvous are a classic source.[1] Following are the obvious "trapper items":

| | |
|---|---|
| Pack cloths | Rum |
| Horseshoes | Soap |
| Girths | Pepper |
| Bridles | Salt |
| Axes | Pipes |
| Trap springs | Fish hooks |
| Pans | Gun locks |
| Tin cups | Flannel |
| Pistol | Russia sheeting |
| Pen knives | Large chisels |
| Kegs of tobacco | Assorted files |
| Gunpowder | Razors |
| Bar lead | Spurs |
| Bags of coffee | Lead pencils |
| Bags of sugar | Men's shoes |
| Flour | Hats |

These items could be used by everybody:

| | |
|---|---|
| Awls | Northwest guns |
| Flints | Combs |
| Fire steels | Mirrors |
| Kettles | |

The third category was obviously intended for Indian trade:

| | |
|---|---|
| Ribbon | Women's shoes |
| Beads | Sewing silk |
| Rings | Tomahawks |
| Sleigh bells | Blue and scarlet cloth |
| Earrings | Verdigris (green paint) |
| Vermilion | Indian trinkets |
| Shells | Cochineal |

Of course this last category included many items bought by trappers as presents for Indian wives or girl friends.

Experience and the desire to be very specific are reflected in the price list which Ashley gave to Smith, Jackson and Sublette in 1826 (Morgan 150-152). Here are some new notations from that list:

| | |
|---|---|
| Butcher knives | Washing soap |
| Horseshoes and nails | Shaving soap |
| Shot | Thread |
| Traps | Buttons |
| Best James River tobacco | Binding |
| Tin pans | Blankets |
| Dried fruit | Squaw axes |
| Allspice | All kinds of cloth |
| Raisins | |

---

[1]Morgan 107, 112-113, 118-129.

Another primary source for early rendezvous supplies is the Harrison Rogers Daybook containing a memorandum of merchandise taken by Jedediah Smith on his South West Expedition in 1826 and the accounts with the men who participated (Brooks 205-213). It should be borne in mind that these men had just been outfitted at the rendezvous. Issues to the men included:

- Six wiping sticks (for rifles) at $1.50.
- One and a half pounds of hard soap, five cakes of shaving soap at 50¢ each and two other sales of unspecified soap totaling $3.00..
- Fifteen butcher knives at $1.50 and one at $1.00. Two are identified as "Wilkinson" knives and one as "Wilson."
- Nine and one-half pints of rum at $3.00, all of it sold in increments of one pint, half-pint or gill (one-fourth pint) on August 15 and 16, 1826, when they were repairing their guns at "Blacksmith Fork."
- Thirty-three and one-fourth pounds of "tobacco" at $1.50 plus 6½ pounds of "chewing tobacco" at $1.50 which were sold December 6, 1826, at San Gabriel Mission. Most of the tobacco was sold in one-pound or half-pound increments. It is not known whether the chewing tobacco was plug, but it may have been. Plug was generally popular with mountain men.
- Six cups of coffee at $2.00, one cup of tea, four cups of sugar.
- Seven "mokason awls" at 25¢.
- Five handkerchiefs, apparently all black silk.
- One and one-half pounds of powder and 1¾ pounds of lead.
- Miscellaneous items, including two "Beaver chissel & spear," one surcingle, 1½ yards red stroud, one looking glass, one 2½-point blanket, one 3-point blanket, two skeins of silk, two dirk knives, two tin pans, two pairs of moccasins at 33¢ and 40¢, a $5.00 charge for shoeing a horse.

While at San Gabriel, the men bought six dozen finger rings for $2.00 a dozen plus a few beads, probably for romantic presents.

In addition the brigade made some small presents to Indians encountered on the trip which included red ribbon, red stroud, some razors, powder and balls, rings, mirrors, combs, buttons, awls, hawk bells and a few knives including two with green bone handles and one with a brass handle (probably a cartouche knife).

Surviving accounts made at rendezvous are the surest way to tell what was sold there. The other available records are the lists of items charged in St. Louis to a rendezvous brigade going to the mountains. In this case it is occasionally difficult to determine exactly which provisions, guns, clothing and horse equipment were to be used by the men,

Playing cards are not always listed in rendezvous accounts but someone had to bring them. Nathaniel Wyeth did and he took 54 decks to the new Fort Hall he built after the rendezvous. They were probably like these cards made by Thomas Crehore (1801-1846) of Dorchester, who was one of the most prominent early card makers in Massachusetts, Wyeth's home state.

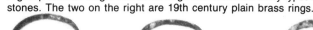

A group of trade rings. The three rings on the left are early types set with glass stones. The two on the right are 19th century plain brass rings.

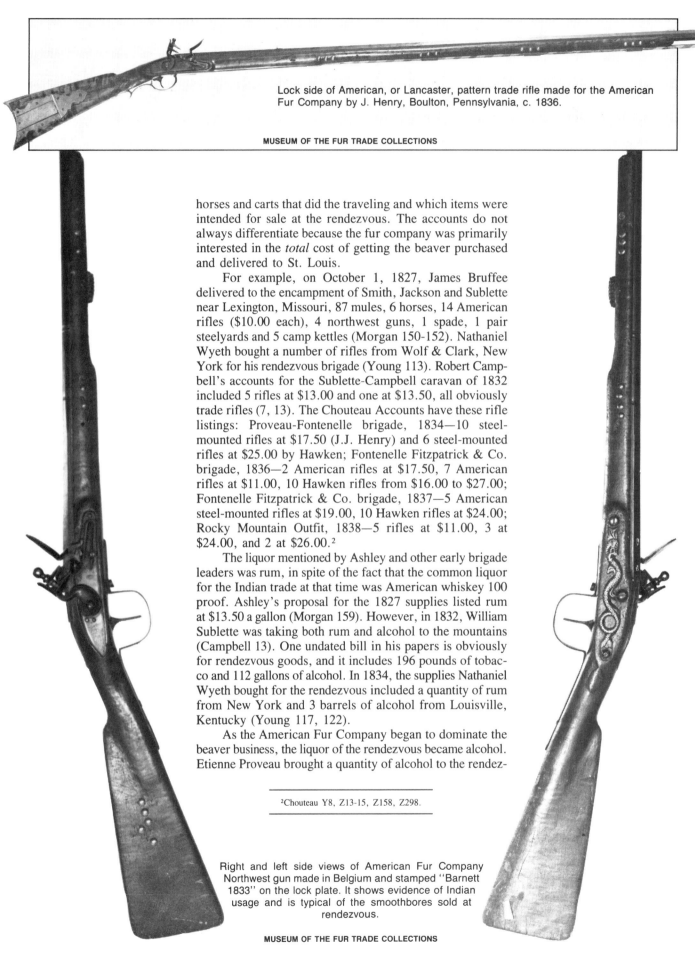

Lock side of American, or Lancaster, pattern trade rifle made for the American Fur Company by J. Henry, Boulton, Pennsylvania, c. 1836.

horses and carts that did the traveling and which items were intended for sale at the rendezvous. The accounts do not always differentiate because the fur company was primarily interested in the *total* cost of getting the beaver purchased and delivered to St. Louis.

For example, on October 1, 1827, James Bruffee delivered to the encampment of Smith, Jackson and Sublette near Lexington, Missouri, 87 mules, 6 horses, 14 American rifles ($10.00 each), 4 northwest guns, 1 spade, 1 pair steelyards and 5 camp kettles (Morgan 150-152). Nathaniel Wyeth bought a number of rifles from Wolf & Clark, New York for his rendezvous brigade (Young 113). Robert Campbell's accounts for the Sublette-Campbell caravan of 1832 included 5 rifles at $13.00 and one at $13.50, all obviously trade rifles (7, 13). The Chouteau Accounts have these rifle listings: Proveau-Fontenelle brigade, 1834—10 steel-mounted rifles at $17.50 (J.J. Henry) and 6 steel-mounted rifles at $25.00 by Hawken; Fontenelle Fitzpatrick & Co. brigade, 1836—2 American rifles at $17.50, 7 American rifles at $11.00, 10 Hawken rifles from $16.00 to $27.00; Fontenelle Fitzpatrick & Co. brigade, 1837—5 American steel-mounted rifles at $19.00, 10 Hawken rifles at $24.00; Rocky Mountain Outfit, 1838—5 rifles at $11.00, 3 at $24.00, and 2 at $26.00.[2]

The liquor mentioned by Ashley and other early brigade leaders was rum, in spite of the fact that the common liquor for the Indian trade at that time was American whiskey 100 proof. Ashley's proposal for the 1827 supplies listed rum at $13.50 a gallon (Morgan 159). However, in 1832, William Sublette was taking both rum and alcohol to the mountains (Campbell 13). One undated bill in his papers is obviously for rendezvous goods, and it includes 196 pounds of tobacco and 112 gallons of alcohol. In 1834, the supplies Nathaniel Wyeth bought for the rendezvous included a quantity of rum from New York and 3 barrels of alcohol from Louisville, Kentucky (Young 117, 122).

As the American Fur Company began to dominate the beaver business, the liquor of the rendezvous became alcohol. Etienne Proveau brought a quantity of alcohol to the rendez-

---

[2]Chouteau Y8, Z13-15, Z158, Z298.

---

Right and left side views of American Fur Company Northwest gun made in Belgium and stamped "Barnett 1833" on the lock plate. It shows evidence of Indian usage and is typical of the smoothbores sold at rendezvous.

Early 19th century mold for making six one-pound lead bars, with two of the finished bars. Usually the rendezvous brigade was furnished with bar lead, but a mold like this was shipped from St. Louis for the use of the Rocky Mountain Outfit for 1838.

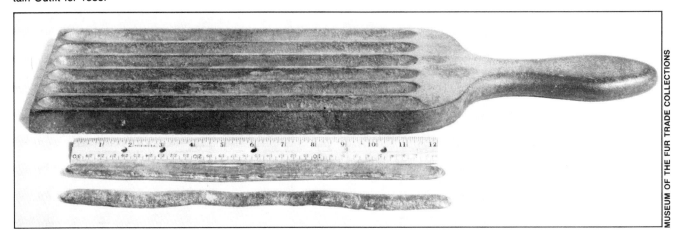

Typical wooden powder keg, c. 1830, with split hickory bands.

vous of 1834 for Lucien Fontenelle, and other shipments to rendezvous by Fontenelle Fitzpatrick & Co. are 540 gallons in 1836 and 321 gallons in 1837.[3] Much of it was put up in 10-gallon iron-bound kegs. John Townsend noted in 1834, "The principal liquor in use here is alcohol diluted with water. It is sold to the men here at *three dollars* the pint!" (83).

The very complete Chouteau invoices for rendezvous in the 1830s give us a good idea of the supplies available to the trapper customers in that period.[4] Alcohol was always available. It often came in 10-gallon kegs, but it never came in heavy, breakable containers like jugs or bottles. The usual drinking container was a tin cup. If a quantity of liquor was carried about the camp, the trappers used a small kettle just as the Indians did. Any use of an old-fashioned pottery jug at a rendezvous was *extremely* rare.

Dupont gunpowder came in 50-pound kegs. Small bar lead was always available, shipped in boxes of about 250 pounds. Two-thirds of the tobacco was in plugs, generally of one-pound size. Most of the rest of the tobacco was in small twists, but there was usually a box of fine Cavendish tobacco for the more discerning smokers. Three thousand pounds of plug tobacco were sent in 1838.

There were always plenty of bags of green coffee and a few 6-pound boxes of Young Hyson tea. The average rendezvous sold about three-quarters of a ton of brown Havana sugar. In those days white sugar was an expensive luxury.

Men who had just put in a year eating mostly meat, and

[3]Chouteau Y9, Z16, Z159.
[4]Chouteau Y6-9, Z10-16, Z156-159, Z294-299, Z304.

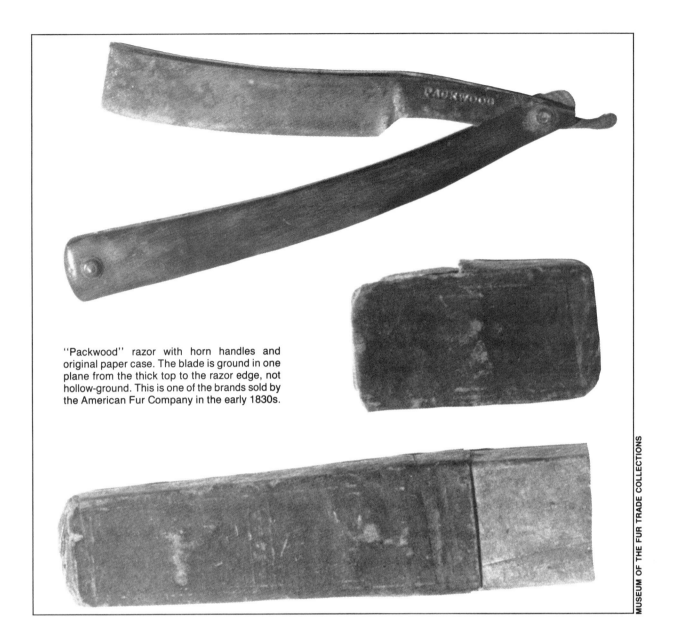

"Packwood" razor with horn handles and original paper case. The blade is ground in one plane from the thick top to the razor edge, not hollow-ground. This is one of the brands sold by the American Fur Company in the early 1830s.

sometimes not enough of that, welcomed a few exotic groceries even at the inflated prices. As an example the outfit for the 1837 rendezvous included lots of black pepper, 4 boxes of raisins, one barrel each of dried apples and dried peaches, two barrels of flour and 150 pounds of rice. Chocolate as a beverage was there, too. An undated bill in the Sublette Papers includes all kinds of rendezvous items sold to an outfit, and one item is "20 lbs. sweet chocolate." At the 1839 rendezvous, Dr. Wislizenus noted that cocoa beans sold for $2.00 a pint cup (87). The bread was "hard tack." The 1838 outfit included 8 barrels of "Navy Bread" and one barrel of "Pilot Bread."

The idea of ready-made clothing for trappers has been buried in a welter of fringed buckskin for 150 years. However, it really existed. In 1833, Charles Larpenteur described the trappers' "little outfits" as consisting of "blankets, scarlet shirts, tobacco and some few trinkets to trade with the Snake Indians" (Coues 34). In 1837, Osborne Russell wrote of trappers consoling themselves "with a blanket, a cotton shirt or a few pints of coffee and sugar to sweeten it" (63). Campbell's outfit in 1832 included flan-

nel shirts, check shirts and wool socks. A Sublette bill to the Rocky Mountain Fur Company Sept. 9, 1833, included "46 flannel shirts." Another undated bill in the Sublette Papers has "Louis Vasquez" noted on the back. It includes 1½ dozen red flannel shirts, 15 calico shirts and 18 pairs of pantaloons. The 1836 outfit had 236 red flannel shirts, 157 calico shirts, 129 checked ones, 51 in plaid, 12 plain and 7 in pink!

Trousers were not quite as popular, but there were 105 pairs of satinet "pantaloons" and 25 pairs made of duck in 1837. Satinet was a cheap trouser fabric with cotton warp and wool filling and woven so that it had a close, smooth wool surface. Corduroy trousers were not in much demand, but 22 pairs were sent in 1836 (these would have been made of old-style wide-wale corduroy).

The 1837 supplies also included 71 tailor-made blanket capotes in blue and green and six dozen pairs of wool socks. In addition, if you had a local seamstress you could buy any

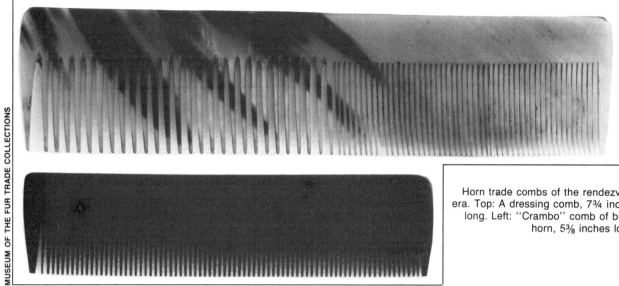

Horn trade combs of the rendezvous era. Top: A dressing comb, 7¾ inches long. Left: "Crambo" comb of black horn, 5⅜ inches long.

Above: 19th century English package of twelve round pencils, 6¹⁵⁄₁₆ inches long. Below: Two 19th century English manufactured quill pens with the original cardboard box.

Two types of rendezvous tobacco: a one-pound bright plug, 13½ inches long; and a small tobacco twist in eight-to-the-pound size, 5¾ inches long.

kind of trade cloth, stroud, flannel or calico, plus thread and buttons.

For some reason green blanket coats seem to have been popular. When John Townsend and Thomas Nuttall arrived in St. Louis in 1834, Nathaniel Wyeth took them to a store to be outfitted for the trip to the rendezvous. He selected several pairs of leather pantaloons, ''enormous overcoats, made of green blankets'' and white wool hats with round crowns and five-inch brims (Townsend 11).

Cheap wool hats were available at the rendezvous. In 1837, there were 2 dozen black ones and 15 white ones. In 1838, there were 2 dozen wool caps, apparently voyageurs' style. Handkerchiefs were offered in quantity. Black silk ones seemed most popular, but there were also bandannas and red or blue printed cotton handkerchiefs. Blankets were the ordinary point blankets, most of them 3-point size in white, green, red or blue, with a few smaller ones in white. A few ''Spanish blankets'' from the Rio Grande found their way to rendezvous also. Sublette's account with the Rocky Mountain Fur Company in 1833 included ''1 Spanish blanket.''

Personal equipment available to the trappers included single-edge ''crambo'' combs, larger ''dressing combs,'' Indian awls, gun worms, fire steels, fish hooks (of which hundreds were sold every year), pocket knives, tailor scissors, light common axes and lots of half axes. The last were the workhorse axes for the trappers. The common trade axe or ''squaw axe'' was completely unsuitable. The half axe was of better material, easier to sharpen and adapted for driving stakes.

Other personal accessories were usually available, including pocket compasses, files, razors in paper cases, quill

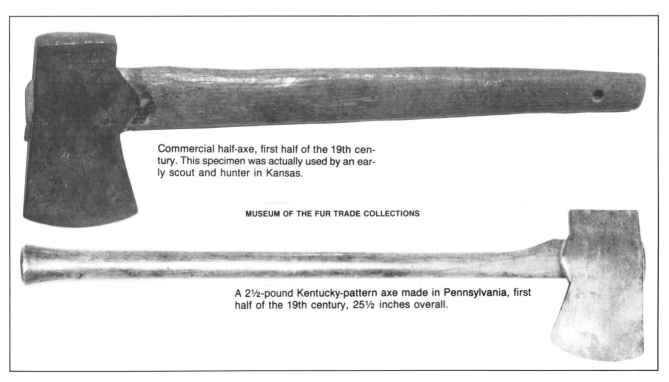

Commercial half-axe, first half of the 19th century. This specimen was actually used by an early scout and hunter in Kansas.

MUSEUM OF THE FUR TRADE COLLECTIONS

A 2½-pound Kentucky-pattern axe made in Pennsylvania, first half of the 19th century, 25½ inches overall.

A good example of a sheet-iron kettle from the first half of the 19th century. This specimen is 8 inches high and 8¼ inches in diameter.

pens, blank books, foolscap paper, ink powder, lead pencils and powder horns. Occasionally an outfit included chisels, gimlets, hand vises, iron-bound wood canteens, spades, saws or drawknives. One of the Ashley bills from Siter Price & Co. for rendezvous supplies in 1832 lists 5 "spy-glasses" with achromatic objectives and sunshades (Sublette). The reader is referred to various definitive articles previously published in the *Museum of the Fur Trade Quarterly* concerning ink, pens and pencils, powder horns, combs, fish hooks, axes, lead, tea, tobacco, scalpers, butcher knives and cartouche knives.

At the top of the hardware list stood beaver traps and replacement trap springs. Tin cups were always available, along with tin pans and tin or sheet iron kettles. We found no specific references to cast iron, brass or copper kettles. They were probably too heavy. Each outfit brought heavy cords and quantities of manila rope.

Surprisingly enough, the most numerous knives brought for sale were the cheap "scalpers" with blades set in a saw cut made in a solid wood handle. This might be true because

scalpers were in constant demand by the Indians and were therefore good trade items. The 1837 outfit had 84 dozen warranted scalpers, 17 dozen Wilson butcher knives, 16 dozen cartouche knives and 6 dozen knives with green bone handles. According to several observers, the butcher knife was the mountain man's favorite. Most of the identified butcher knives on the invoices were Wilson, a few were Wilkinson. An undated Sublette bill for rendezvous goods includes one dozen Wilson knives. Nowhere, so far, have we found an identified trade order for Russell "Green River" knives before 1843, Ruxton notwithstanding. The cartouche knife was, of course, the common kitchen knife or "case knife" of the period.

Horse gear was certainly important. The "Spanish saddle" was ubiquitous, and the name referred to its *tree pattern* and *not* the place of origin. Most of them were made somewhere from St. Louis to Pittsburgh. The common pack saddle was the "sawbuck" pattern. Some were made in St. Louis, but there were also references to the men making them in the field. Bridles were manufactured and sold complete.

A group of cartouche knives. Left to right: wood-handled knife marked with Maltese cross; "brass inlaid" knife with cast brass design pressed into horn handles; wood-handled knife by Hiram Cutler, found along Niobrara River; large bone-handled knife by Wm. Greaves & Son, maker to the American Fur Company, 7-inch blade.

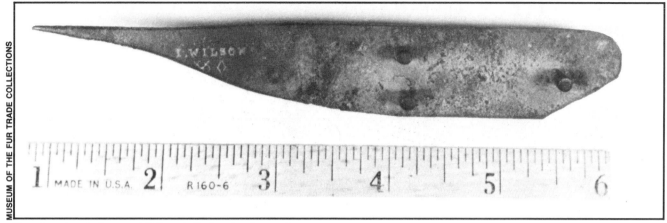

Remains of an Indian-used Wilson knife bearing the marking used by John Wilson during the rendezvous period. Knives with this type of marking are extremely rare today.

The 1836 outfit had 7½ dozen snaffle bridles and 9 dozen curb bridles. In 1837, there were 60 snaffle bridles. The designations, of course, refer to the types of bit used. Generally, the snaffle bit was most common. Halter chains with hooks were always part of an outfit, along with sets of front hobbles and a few sets of side hobbles.

Repair supplies for sale included a gross or so of wide roller buckles, horseshoes, muleshoes, horseshoe nails, shoeing hammers, some sides of heavy leather, replacement stirrup leathers in large quantities and 100 to 200 leather "surcingles." This is an old term for a girth, but even in those days saddle girths were generally of something at least somewhat yielding and absorbent. The surcingles may have been used to go over the saddle and hold padding in the seat as was customary in the army, or they may have been used for packing.

Another item we haven't been able to identify were "leather powder bags," which usually cost about $3.00. Some were sent every year. While we have no documentation, it seems plausible that powder bag was a bookkeeper's abbreviation for "powder horn bag" or what we refer to now as a hunting bag. A number of bags with early Western association have been shop-made of heavy leather for hard service. Old hunting bags made of beaver skin may be as romantic as a Frederick Remington trapper's beard, but it is doubtful that any "plew" would be wasted on such a mundane piece of equipment. There is certainly good authority for the reluctance of most trappers to use a beaver skin for a cap, preferring instead to use badger or kit fox at 50 cents instead of four dollars.

A third item a bit out of the ordinary was goggles. On the Teton Fork in 1832, Robert Campbell sold 12 pairs of goggles to O'Fallon and Vandeburgh at $4.00 each (64). The 1836 Rocky Mountain outfit included "1¾ dozen Green Goggles" for a total of $11.13. Another half-dozen pairs were sent in 1837 (Chouteau Z13, 156-159). These goggles protected the eyes from dust, sand or snow glare. Trade orders through the years were very specific in differentiating "goggles" from the "green spectacles" frequently sold to the Indians, which were simple metal-framed spectacles with

A pair of 19th century "goggles" showing colored lenses and wire gauze frames with the original cheap japanned metal case.

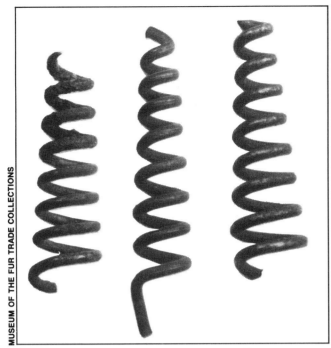

Three typical wire gun worms for Northwest guns. These were screwed on the plain end of the rod.

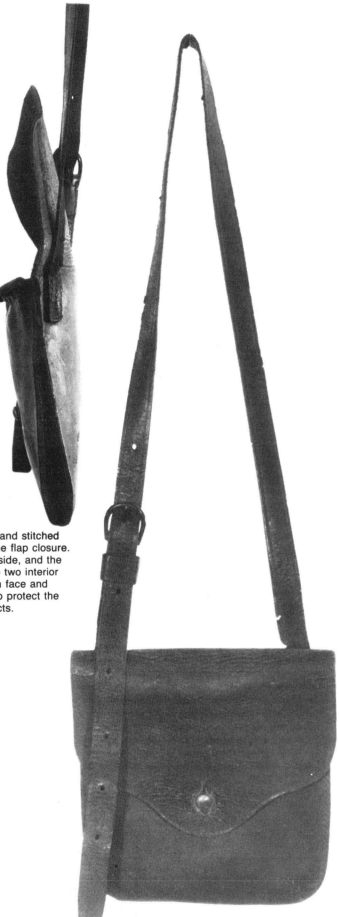

green glass lenses (sunglasses). The goggles had small oval lenses set in truncated cones of wire gauze so each eye was completely protected. The Hudson's Bay Company was trading goggles in quantities by the 1860s, and they were still popular with American travelers in the 1880s. We have been unable to find a pair as early as 1836, but ones used by Arctic explorers in 1845 fit the description of the pair

Two views of a shop-made hunting bag. It was hand stitched and had a regular, military-style brass stud for the flap closure. The side view shows the short gussets on each side, and the bottom of the bag is folded (no seam). There are two interior compartments. The top inner edges of the pouch face and divider have had narrow bindings of sheepskin to protect the user's hand and help prevent spilling small objects.

shown in the accompanying illustration. Having a pair in your possibles sack would have provided good insurance against snow blindness.

The ''moccasin spur'' is a new term that has appeared in buckskinner circles, but I've never encountered it in the literature. The standard spur sold at the rendezvous (as well as at trading posts and country stores) came fastened on a large display card to sell. They were light, plain and had small rowels. Most of them were tin-plated to avoid rust. There was no reason why a mountain man couldn't adopt the Spanish spur if he wished, and a few of them did, but they didn't buy them at a rendezvous unless some Santa Fe trader was there.

A few final observations can be made of weapons. Each annual outfit included a few dozen northwest guns with corresponding flints. Sometimes a few pistols were brought out; the 1836 outfit had 4 pairs of pistols with iron barrels. Thousands of rifle flints were brought each year, but we have

78

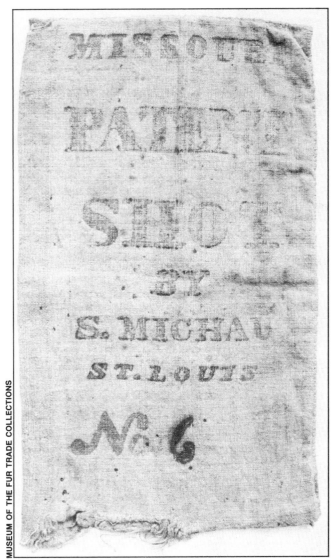

The shot which went to the early rendezvous could very well have been in bags like this one. St. Amand Michau began operations in 1823 at New Hartford, near St. Louis, and advertised his shot in the *Missouri Gazette* that year. He died in 1845. This is a 25-pound linen bag for No. 6 shot.

only observed percussion caps a few times. Sublette's account with the Rocky Mountain Fur Company September 9, 1833, included three boxes of percussion caps. Ten boxes (1,000 caps) were sent in the 1836 outfit and 10 more boxes in 1838. Replacement rifle locks were also a standard rendezvous commodity. Nearly every outfit included a few bags of shot.

The last, but a very important, category of rendezvous goods was the list of Indian trade goods. Aside from northwest guns, cloth, awls, knives and blankets, there were usually hawk bells, pound (pony) beads in red, white and black, brass tacks, brass wire, shawls, squaw axes, vermilion, hawk bells, ribbon, earrings and worsted binding.

Vermilion was the main pigment sold to the Indians, but small amounts of cochineal and verdigris were also sold. Vermilion was primarily a product of China, made from mercury ore in powder form and of a brilliant flame color. It was a very important trade item for 200 years. Vermilion could be rubbed into buckskin, and mixed with water or grease, it was used for face or body paint. For painting robes or wooden objects, it was mixed with prickly pear juice or mucilage made by boiling a beaver tail.

Small amounts of cochineal appear in several rendezvous accounts. Even Peter Ogden listed one-half ounce of it in his accounts for the Snake River Expedition of 1827. Cochineal was a soft, velvety crimson powder made from tiny insects which feed on cactus. It was an important product of Mexico and was used as a dye for woolens, for artists' pigments and as rouge for facial adornment.

Another important trade pigment for painting faces and objects was verdigris, a green powder which formed on copper plates exposed to vinegar or the refuse of grapes used for winemaking. It was used from ancient times until about 1850, when "chrome green" took its place. Trading outfits usually included about three times as much vermilion as verdigris.

A great many mountain men used small wedge tents. Many of them came from St. Louis, but others may have been made in the field since linen "Russia sheeting" was usually available. It is interesting to note that the Sublette-

Roll of percussion caps containing ten boxes (1,000 caps).

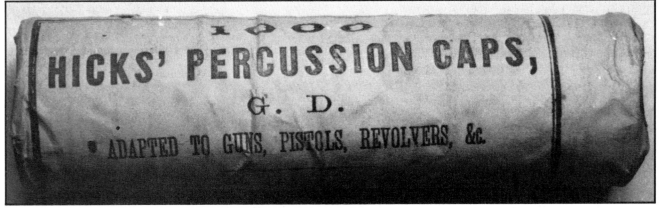

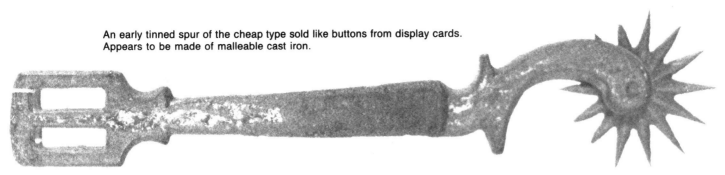

An early tinned spur of the cheap type sold like buttons from display cards. Appears to be made of malleable cast iron.

MUSEUM OF THE FUR TRADE COLLECTIONS

Campbell caravan in 1832 had tents with jointed poles. The bill from Robert Campbell includes charges paid for jointing the poles and making slides for the joints (70).

A study of the various annual outfits shows that many stock items like saddlery, cloth, blankets, coffee, sugar, tea, flour, powder and trade goods ran consistently year after year. Others varied in amount considerably from year to year, and some items might be sent one year and not the next. This could be because of particular requests received one year at a rendezvous and filled on the next trip, different judgements by various leaders who made up the outfits or the fact that Sante Fe merchants or other competitors started bringing some things of better quality or cheaper prices.

The existing records thus give a fair idea of the goods taken to the usual trappers' rendezvous of the 1830s. The information they supply may help solve some of the many questions of authenticity which seem to arise at every modern rendezvous. The modern events, of course, commemorate the original gatherings which ended nearly a century and a half ago. Times are different and so are the basic situations. but the old-time spirit lives on in the dedicated buckskinners of today. Anything the historian can do to make future rendezvous more realistic and enjoyable is certainly worth the effort.

MUSEUM OF THE FUR TRADE COLLECTIONS

The American Fur Company regularly purchased flints in "papers of 500." This is one of the only known surviving examples of these packages.

## APPENDIX A: WORKS CITED

Brooks, George R., ed. *The Southwest Expedition of Jedediah S. Smith.* Glendale, CA: Clark, 1977.

Campbell, Robert. Sale Log of Robert Campbell. 1832. Robert Campbell Family Collection of Historical Papers. St. Louis Mercantile Library, St. Louis, Missouri.

Chouteau Accounts. Missouri Historical Society, St. Louis, Missouri.

Coues, Elliott, ed. *Forty Years a Fur Trader on the Upper Missouri.* Vol. 1. New York: Harper, 1898.

Morgan, Dale L., ed. *The West of William Ashley.* Denver, CO: Old West Publishing, 1964.

Russell, Osborne. *Journal of a Trapper.* Boise, ID: Syms-York, 1921.

Stewart, William Drummond. *Edward Warren.* London: G. Walker, 1854.

Sublette, William. Sublette Papers. Missouri Historical Society, St. Louis, Missouri.

Townsend, John Kirk. *Narrative of a Journey Across the Rocky Mountains to the Columbia River.* Lincoln, NE: Nebraska University Press, 1978.

Wislizenus, F.A. *A Journey to the Rocky Mountains in the Year 1839.* Glorietta, NM: Rio Grande, 1969.

Young, F.G., ed. *Sources of the History of Oregon.* Vol. 1. Eugene, OR: Oregon University Press, 1899.

# Tipi Know-How

## by Bill Walter

WILLIAM T. WALTER, born November 1, 1927, in Lansing, Michigan, attended the Art Institute of Pittsburg, Pennsylvania, after his discharge from the Navy. He has worked in sales, as an industrial technician and craftsman and as a silversmith and goldsmith. Bill started building shelters part-time in 1968.

Bill was introduced to black powder by Ken Stuck and is a member of the Sauk Trail Longrifles. In 1979, Bill and his wife, Lila, went to the National Muzzle Loading Rifle Association's fall shoot and made the decision to build shelters full-time. That winter Four Seasons Lodges was born.

Since 1980, Bill and Lila have been full-time builders of tentage for historical reenactors and black powder shooters. Four Seasons Lodges initially offered only tipis and lean-tos but now offers over 60 sizes and styles spanning 2000 years. Bill and Lila recently changed the business' name to Four Seasons Tentmasters to reflect this expanded time span.

AS I sat at my dining room table looking out the window, I saw snow blowing angrily around my yard. My mind began to drift back in time, thinking particularly about the brave people who had survived the long, bitterly cold prairie winters without the convenience of today's technology. These thoughts led me to reflect upon my first experiences with a tipi, the experiences that set the course I was to follow for the next twenty years.

I remember well my first encounter with a tipi. I was walking up a hill, and as I reached the top, I saw a tipi sitting against the backdrop of a clear blue sky. Smoke swirled from the top of its smoke hole. This impressive sight drew me closer. As I approached the door, some friends who were expecting me invited me in. I was greeted by about twenty men sitting around a fire with a pot of stew cooking in the center. The men were in their shirt sleeves, warm and comfortable in a smoke-free environment. I remember being amazed at the time-proven comfort of this dwelling. ''This is for me!'' I thought. The outside temperature that day was −20 degrees and a very strong wind was blowing. This scene took place in February, 1968.

A short time later at a rendezvous I attended, I encountered an entirely different tipi. This lodge was decorated with quill rosettes and painted with pictures of shields, feathers and animals. Streamers flew from the tops of the poles. I stared at the beauty of this lodge, but had the feeling it was very different from the one I had seen earlier in the year, and the difference was definitely not the decoration. After studying the scene for a while longer, I noticed what made it so vastly different. This tipi was clouded with thick, dense smoke. Smoke hovered over the smoke hole like a heavy curtain. Smoke was pouring out the door and from under the bottom of the cover, which appeared to be twelve to

fourteen inches off the ground. Smoke even hung around the people as they entered and exited the lodge. It was not a pleasant sight or a comfortable situation for its occupants. The day was about 50 degrees and only a light breeze was blowing. It was April of the same year.

As I continued thinking about these two entirely different experiences, I began to wonder what the tipi was really about. I had observed firsthand that it is not necessary to put up with smoky discomfort in order to enjoy tipi life. Yet I was discouraged by the miserable smoky scene I had also witnessed. The concern I felt was strong because I had already begun the construction of my first lodge. I was not really interested in spending my time in a miserable, smoke-filled environment, so I began to seriously study the details that made these two lodges so very different.

It was during the construction of my own lodge that I launched my long learning experience, which, by the way, has never ended. I have spent much time traveling from rendezvous to rendezvous studying the nature and function of the tipi as it is being used today. I also read all of the information on tipi life that was available at that time. Unfortunately, most of that information dealt only with the styles and sizes of various lodges. I felt that the most important information, the understanding of the lodge itself, was omitted. Therefore, many of my questions were left unanswered, and I was forced to continue the search on my own. I found the answers to my questions through experiencing and experimenting with the tipi itself. Like it or not, the tipi must be approached as a scientific principal in action. Unless its function and construction are understood, the tipi cannot be made to work to one's advantage.

I will share with you, based on my twenty years of experiences and observation, this comprehensive and even somewhat controversial information on the use and management of this glorious dwelling. Be informed that I am not here to address style, size or even trivial tipi facts. I will thoroughly address attention to every other detail of the tipi. It is this detail that is the key difference between the two previously mentioned lodges. Also keep in mind that only one setup is ever needed for your lodge. Comfort in all seasons depends on the proper management of a well-constructed lodge and attention to its detail. This functional construction will provide the dweller smoke-free heat in cold weather and a natural cooling system for hot weather comfort. I will attempt to dispel some of the negative rumors surrounding tipi life and reinforce the vesatility of this dwelling. Therefore this article will cover in logical sequence the necessary steps that, if followed, will allow a tipi to be used to its maximum potential.

Though not for everyone, tipis lend an air of beauty to a rendezvous camp. On a cool night when fires are built inside of them, the lodges glow like Chinese lanterns.

# PREPARATION

The primary step in insuring a successful tipi experience is the proper preparation of the various components needed. Those to be discussed are the poles, cover, stakes, lace pins and ropes. Preparation time spent on these details *before* the first setup will be greatly rewarded with a positive experience.

Poles not only contribute to the beauty of the lodge, but they must fit the cover. Therefore, pole preparation is extremely important. It has been my experience that the poles should project a minimum of 6 feet above the tie point for aesthetic reasons. Note in Figure 1 that lodge ''A'' has a more graceful and pleasing look than does lodge ''B.''

A good rule of thumb to use in determing adequate pole length is to add 6 feet to the diameter of the lodge. For example, an 18-foot lodge should have poles no shorter than 24 feet long to achieve the appearance as seen in Figure 1A. The poles contribute as much to the grace and beauty of the lodge as does the cover.

Another critical aspect in ensuring a proper setup of poles is the determination of the poles' diameter at the base of the tripod. It is also important that they be as small as possible yet still maintain the stability of the lodge. Bear in mind that the diameter of the pole at the base will determine the diameter of the pole at its tie point and the tie point diameter is as important as the base diameter. I recommend that the diameter of each of the poles at the tie point be about the same size. The diameter of a pole at its base should be from 3 to 5 inches depending upon the size of the lodge. The poles of a smaller lodge, 15 to 18 feet in diameter, should have a base diameter of 3 to 3½ inches. A larger lodge, 21 to 24 feet in diameter, will have poles that measure 4 to 5 inches at the base. The base diameter and tie point diameter will be determined to a large degree by the type of tree used. See Figure 2.

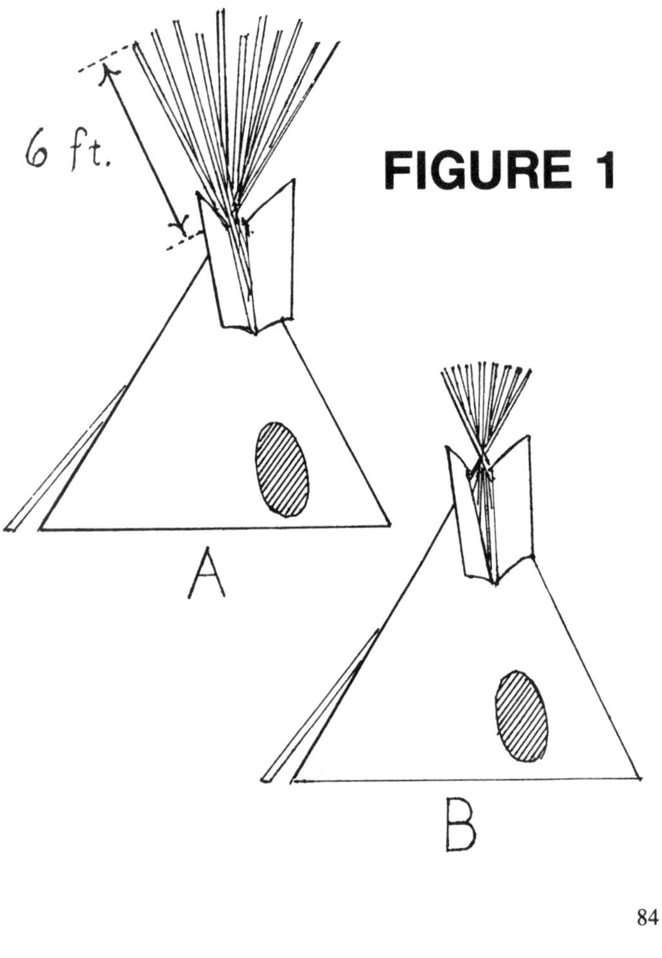

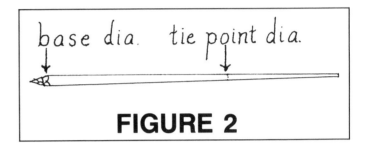

**FIGURE 2**

At this time you can measure the tie points of the tripod poles and the lift pole, along with the length of the smoke flap poles. You will take measurements from the lodge cover. It is vital to fit the poles to the cover, not the cover to the poles. This set of measurements has been a source of controversy among many tipi advocates. The present controversy centers on the false idea that the tipi cover must be off the ground and that a separate winter and summer setup is necessary. I will attempt to dismiss this idea by demonstrating with one set of measurements how the tipi cover can be varied to adapt to all types of weather. This involves raising and lowering the cover at the ground as the situation necessitates without removing the stakes. I discuss this further under ''Tipi Management.''

**FIGURE 1**

6 ft.

A

B

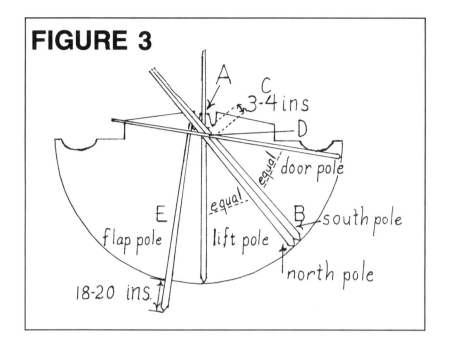

# FIGURE 3

To determine the correct tie point measurements for most lodges, unroll the tipi cover on the ground. Take care to eliminate as many wrinkles as possible. Place the lift pole on the cover with the base of the pole centered at the bottom edge of the canvas and laying across the tongue of the cover where the ties are located. Make a permanent mark on the pole at the tip of the tongue, as shown in Figure 3 detail A. It is recommended that the stoutest or longest pole be used as the lift pole, since this pole does not add to the bulk of the pole gathering. I will discuss this further on in the chapter.

Next, choose three poles to be used for your tripod. The tripod poles consist of the north, south and door poles. These should be the stoutest of the remaining poles. Lay your north and south poles together on the canvas halfway between the lift pole and the edge of the door as shown in Figure 3. Mark these poles three to four inches below where the tongue is sewn to the cover. This measurement is accurate for most manufactured lodges on the market today. This critical measurement must also be adjusted for poles that have a diameter that is too large or too small in the tie point area. A larger diameter pole will need to be marked at a lower point, and a smaller diameter pole will need a higher adjustment. The reason for this adjustment is that the diameter of all the poles at their proper places determines the critical diameter of the smoke hole opening.

The third pole of the tripod is the door pole. Lay the door pole on the canvas alongside the door opening. Mark this pole at the point that it crosses the north and south pole. Record these measurements on the tongue of your tipi or where they will always be with your lodge. This will save much time and trouble in the event of a broken pole, when a new one must be marked. If there is a significant difference in the measurement of the north, south and door poles, the tipi will be of the classic, leaned back style as in Figure 4. If the measurements of these poles are close to the same, the tipi will take on a conical shape.

For your smoke flap poles, pick out the two slightest poles. It is important that the tips of these poles be no smaller

As you examine the pole arrangement on a standing tipi, the poles on the far left and right are the south and north tripod poles. The pole on the right side of the cover tongue in the "V" is the door pole. Notice the symmetry of well-laid poles.

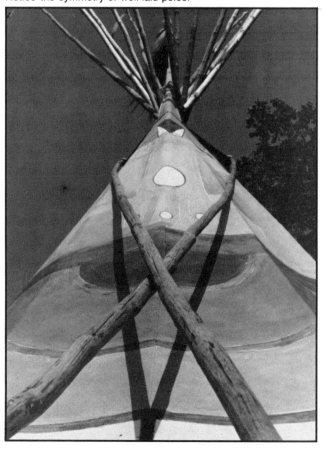

than broom-handle size. It might be necessary to trim the tip to this size. The thicker size of the tip of the flap pole will help to minimize breakage and prevent the bowing of these poles. Lay one smoke flap pole on the canvas according to the diagram in Figure 3. Make sure the tip is inserted into the flap pocket. Approximately two feet of pole should extend below the bottom edge of the canvas. Cut the pole accordingly and use it as a guide to cut the other flap pole. Shortening the flap poles will help keep the poles close to the tipi cover at ground level yet will allow the flaps to be pushed upwards rather than outwards, an important factor in tipi management. I recommend that you sharpen the broom-handle end of the flap pole into a spoon shape as shown in Figure 5. Shaping the poles this way will eliminate some trouble in the bothersome task of inserting the flap poles into the pockets.

Finally, make sure all of the poles are smooth and clean. Smooth, clean poles will help eliminate drips of rainwater caused by rough surfaces. Sharpen the north, south, door and lift poles approximately ten to twelve inches from the bottom, as in Figure 6. Sharpen the flap poles approximately five to six inches from the bottom. Sharpening the poles helps keep them from slipping during the erection of the tripod. This is especially helpful if the lodge is to be set up by one person. With sharp, light poles, I can set up a 21-foot lodge by myself. A sharpened lift pole provides leverage for raising the stout pole which is made heavier by the added weight of the cover.

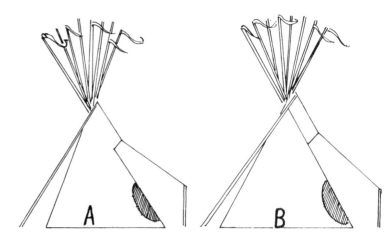

## FIGURE 4

more strongly in the ground. The rest of the bark may be left on the stake for decorative purposes. Rope notches on your stakes are not necessary.

Lace pin preparation is quite simple. The size of the lace pin hole will determine the diameter of the lace pins. The type of wood used in the construction of the lace pin is not important. They can be made of maple, willow, oak, choke cherry or even doweling. The crucial factor in lace pin construction is uniform diameter. The lace pins should fit snugly into the holes. If all of the lace pins are not uniform in size, the lace pin holes will become stretched to various sizes. This may cause the smaller-sized pins to slip on subsequent insertions. The decoration of lace pins by using beads, feathers, bones and other items can create a very attractive appearance. The bark may also be left on for decorative purposes.

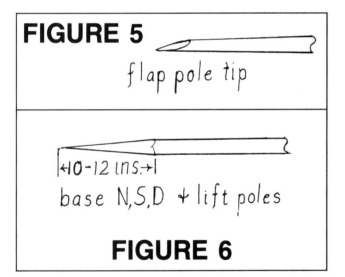

**FIGURE 5**

flap pole tip

|←10-12 ins.→|

base N,S,D + lift poles

## FIGURE 6

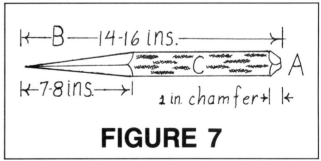

## FIGURE 7

Another important aspect of preparation is making a good, sturdy set of stakes. Tipi stakes need to be made of high-density, close-grained wood, which is not pithy or knotty. The best types of wood for this purpose are oak, ash, maple and choke cherry saplings. Once you have chosen the wood, cut the stakes to a length of 14 to 16 inches. Ensure that the diameter of these stakes is 1'' to 1½.'' After cutting the stakes, they need to be sharpened. First, chamfer about one inch at the top of the stake. See Figure 7. This procedure will help keep the stake from flattening and splitting where it is pounded. After chamfering the stake, sharpen it 7'' to 8'' from the bottom. I recommend a square cut rather than a round cut because a square cut seems to hold the point

The final step in lodge preparation is the ropes. It is not necessary to cut the ropes before the first setup, but it is important that an adequate supply of the proper types of rope be available. All rope should be untreated, oil-free Manila or sisal. Use a good quality rope that is either braided or twisted. Oil-free rope is important because it will not leave unsightly stains on the canvas. Tripod ropes should be ⅜'' in diameter, but all other ropes need only be ¼.''

In order to ensure an adequate supply of rope, use the following guidelines. You determine the amount of rope needed for the tripod by taking a measurement from the door pole. Measure the door pole from the base to the tie point and add 12 feet. To determine liner rope length, measure the overall length of the top of the liner and add 8 feet. Smoke flap ropes can be measured right from the cover. Measure from the bottom of the smoke flap to the bottom of the door and add ten feet. Remember, two smoke flap ropes are needed.

## SETUP

Now that all the preliminary preparations are complete, setup at the site should be quite simple. When selecting a site, it is important that the area be reasonably flat and free of overhead obstructions. Avoid low spots and observe the surrounding terrain in order to determine the water runoff pattern in case of rain.

Once you have chosen the site, decide in which direction the door will face. There is no question that having the door face east is very romantic, but it is not always practical. For good tipi management, it is necessary that the door be in the direction opposite local prevailing winds. These winds may vary seasonally. Sometimes you will have no choice of direction because of rendezvous traffic patterns. In that case it is important to keep your door toward the traffic flow.

You should take the following steps when laying out the tripod poles. Lay the north and south poles side by side with the north pole lying to the left of the south pole when you are standing at the base of the poles. The base of the poles should be 45° to the left of the proposed door location, as in Figure 8. Figure 8 also illustrates how the door pole should be placed on top of the north and south poles, crossing at the previously marked tie points. This procedure must be absolute. There can be no variations because this establishes the three crotch areas. The formation of these areas determines where the rest of the poles must fit. When the tripod is up and the poles are in place you will observe that the bulk of remaining poles are in the smoke hole and the cover itself wraps around only four poles, poles 9, 10, 11 and lift. Any variation will change the size of the hole at the tie point. The object is to have as small a hole as possi-

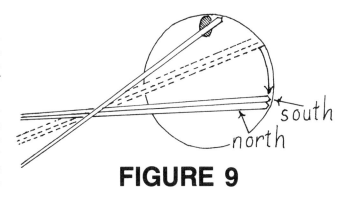

## FIGURE 9

ble at the tie point when the smoke flaps are completely closed.

Now that we have established the importance of a correct setup, you can erect the tripod. To do this take the tripod rope and tie the tripod poles together as they lie on the ground. There is no type of knot that *must* be used, although many people use the clove hitch. The important fact is that the knot not slip. After tying a secure knot, make sure to wrap the rope around the tie point no less than four or five times and finish with a square knot. The next step is to swing the north and south poles away from the door pole until the rope begins to creak. This creaking indicates that the knot is adequately tight. Refer to Figure 9.

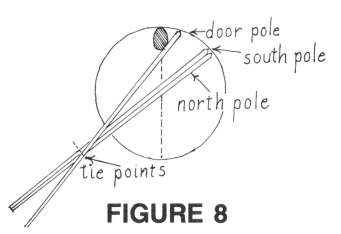

## FIGURE 8

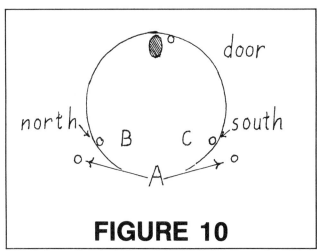

## FIGURE 10

At this point you can raise the tripod off the ground. You accomplish this by lifting the tripod at the tie point to approximately shoulder height. Force the sharpened poles into the ground for leverage. Walk up the north and south poles using a hand-under-hand method (similar to that of walking up an extension ladder) until the poles are just less than vertical. During this process the door pole does not need to be attended, since it goes along for the ride. When the poles are almost vertical, be careful that the poles do not go beyond center. It is very easy to loose control at this time and cause the entire tripod to fall.

The north pole is now the farthest pole to the right. Walk this pole clockwise, leaving the south pole in its place, until the tripod is stable and self-supporting. Refer to Figure 10. For extra support walk the north and south poles back another three to four feet. This is extremely important because the front crotch of the tripod must support the weight of eight poles, and failure to do this has been the cause of hundreds of broken poles. The tripod plays an integral part in the pole sequence numbering pattern. I do not agree that the spread

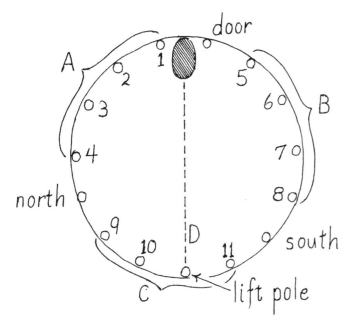

# FIGURE 11

distance of the tripod can be pre-measured. The tripod poles will later be rearranged in the uniform spacing of all the poles, so no further moving of the poles is necessary at this time.

Now that the tripod is secure, you can place the rest of the poles in the respective crotches formed by the tripod. Follow the numbered procedure in Figure 11 to accomplish this placement. Make sure that you place poles 9, 10 and 11 in the crotch to the left of the door pole. This will also help to minimize the size of the smoke hole opening. Notice also in Figure 11 that pole 1 becomes the other side of the door, and the lift pole will eventually be opposite the door opening with seven poles on each side.

At this point all of the poles should be in their respective crotches and ready to be secured. To secure the poles,

take the whip end of the tripod rope and walk it around the outside perimeter of the lodge in a clockwise direction. The rope will wrap around the outside of the tie point. Be sure to pull the rope snugly as it is wrapped. After the rope has been wrapped around the poles four times, tie off the remaining rope to either the north or south pole. ***Do not move the poles outward to their fullest position at this time!*** Move the poles only enough to evenly space them. Remember, the poles must fit the cover. The final spreading of the poles will take place *after* the cover is laced. Do not be concerned about measurements because the poles were marked according to the measurement of the lodge before setup. No change can take place.

It is now time to put the cover on the poles. To do this place the lift pole on the ground with its butt end between poles 10 and 11. See Figure 11. It is imperative that the cover be rolled narrowly enough to lay on top of the lift pole. This is necessary so that you can hoist the cover as it lies on the lift pole, instead of it hanging like a flag. Many lift poles have been broken because of the strain of a flapping cover on a windy day. The time to roll the cover, if it is not already rolled, is when the cover is on the ground to measure the poles. Roll each side of the cover toward the center, keeping the roll as narrow as possible. Then, starting at the base, roll the entire cover into a ball ending at the tongue.

Lay the rolled up cover on top of the lift pole so that

the tongue of the cover matches with the tie point mark on the lift pole. Tie the tongue securely to the lift pole. Again, the type of knot is not important, however, the cover must be tied securely to prevent it from slipping down the lift pole once it is hoisted into the air. Unroll the cover down the lift pole and gather the cover and the lift pole together. Push the sharp end of the lift pole into the ground and raise it into its proper position. The position of the lift pole is into the same crotch as poles 9, 10 and 11, which is to the *left* of the door pole.

The canvas can now be unrolled toward the front of the tipi, and the advantage of the pole location will become evident. Unroll the cover one side at a time. On a windy day, it is advisable to unroll the side that the wind is blowing *against* first. The wind will help hold this side down. I also recommend that the side be held in place by driving a stake at the door opening.

Once both sides are unrolled, secure the cover of the lodge with a few reachable lace pins. This will stop the cover from blowing around while the rest of the lace pins and whatever is being used to reach the high lace pins are gathered and set up.

An important observation must be made at this time. Make sure that the bottom of the "V" formed by the tongue and the right flap of the cover is close to the door pole as in Figure 12. This will be a verification of a correct tie point on the lift pole. If the door pole is not close to the "V" of the canvas, it will be necessary to readjust the tie point mark. If the chance arises, observe other tipis, noting that when you see a small smoke hole opening, the door pole is close to the "V" of the cover.

Now that all of the lace pins are in place, it is time to adjust the poles. Make the adjustments from the inside of the lodge, starting with the lift pole. The lift pole must be centered behind the door opening. Refer back to Figure 11. Once the lift pole is in place, start at one side of the door pole pushing each pole outward. Continue this process for each pole around the canvas. It may take several times around to gain the correct adjustment. At no time should the canvas

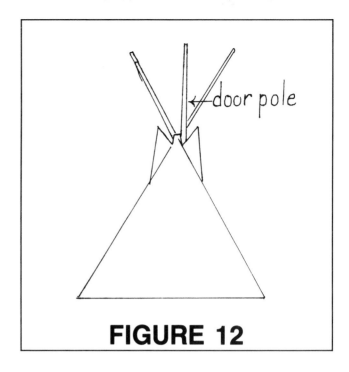

## FIGURE 12

be more than 2'' to 3'' off the ground. After you drive the stakes in, the cover will touch the ground. If the canvas is higher than 2'' or 3'' at any point, move the poles inward to reach the optimum cover height. You should make the final adjustment of the poles after the cover is staked down and stretched. This will give a wrinkle-free, smooth lodge. Setting the poles out those few extra inches trying to gain more diameter will result in total discomfort in adverse weather conditions.

I recommend, from experience, staking the tipi down in the following way. Starting in the back of the tipi, alternating from side to side, pound in the stakes working toward the front. This procedure eliminates the twisting of the canvas and aids in removing the wrinkles from the cover. When pounding in the stakes, use something with a large flat striking surface. This will keep the stakes from flaring out and splitting (Figure 13).

I would like to mention that there is a great deal of variation in the way the peg loops are attached to the cover. Some of the variations do not lend themselves to my multi-purpose concept. It is my experience that peg loops should be located nine to ten inches above the edge of the canvas and spaced between the poles. This will minimize the number of stakes needed and will aid in the placement of the poles. This arrangement of peg loops is the only way a multi-purpose setup can be accomplished. It will also alleviate the necessity of removing stakes after they have been driven into the ground. If stakes are to maintain maximum holding power in the ground they should not be disturbed. If the peg loops of your lodge are not in the recommended position, you can make this modification very easily. Figure 14 illustrates the procedure.

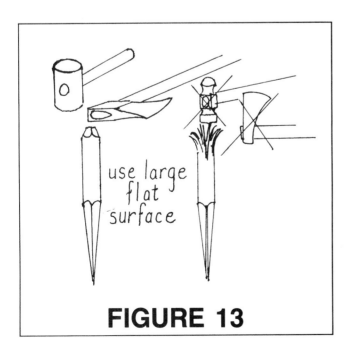

use large flat surface

## FIGURE 13

A smoke-free living environment is especially important when cold-weather camping dictates having a fire inside the lodge almost constantly.

By inserting the stake into the peg loop and twisting it tightly as in Figure 15, a rope notch on the stake is unnecessary. Be sure to twist the rope tightly to avoid slippage. It is necessary to have the rope on the stake as close to the ground as possible, and this cannot be done with a notched stake. A notched stake creates too much leverage in the ground, causing the stakes to loosen. Variations in the hardness of the ground will also determine how far the stake can be driven into the ground. By using a stake without a rope notch and the twisted rope technique, a stake can be adapted to all types of ground conditions. I also advise driving the stake into the ground straight up and down to further minimize leverage.

It is finally time to give the poles their final adjustment, making sure that the cover touches the ground. The cover touching the ground is key to the multi-purpose setup. I will discuss this in further detail later in the chapter.

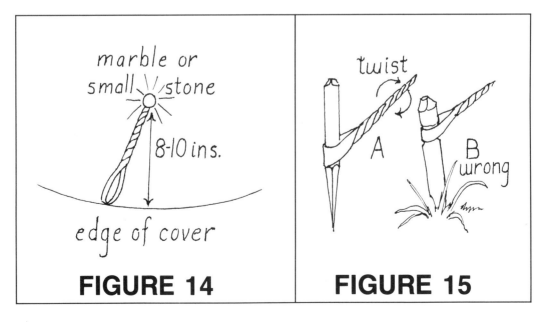

**FIGURE 14**     **FIGURE 15**

The primary purpose of a liner, as illustrated in Figure 16, is to create a dead air space that protects the occupants from the elements at ground level. After the lodge is in place and all of the final adjustments have been made, the liner can be set up. Once again, there are many variations in the design of liners and in the interpretations of its purpose. But, the use of a liner along with the correct setup of the cover is the main difference between a cone-shaped tent and a tipi.

A dead air space will give the tipi dweller an airtight, draft-free living environment. The only time you will need overhead ventilation is during warm weather or in rare ideal situations void of problems. *The function of the liner can be cancelled out by an uncontrollable cover that does not touch the ground.*

Some liners have their ties placed in random patterns. The most workable type of liner is made in one piece with the ties attached at the bottom matching the tipi peg loops. This type of liner eliminates the use of two sets of stakes because the peg loops and the liner ties can share the same set of stakes. The top loops of the liner should line up with the bottom loops whenever possible. These loops should be between the poles, which helps in pulling up the liner with a liner rope.

I do not agree that the liner rope needs to be wrapped around each of the poles, requiring bothersome rain sticks to stop dripping from the ropes. If the rope is not wrapped, it cannot cause dripping. The liner rope need only be run behind the poles. The poles and cover are enough to hold the liner rope in place.

It is much easier to work with two liner ropes. Therefore, cut the liner rope into two equal pieces. Start at the lift pole and work toward the door with one rope. Start the second rope at the lift pole also and work toward the door in the opposite direction. Tie off each rope to the opposite door pole. The ropes should be the same height as the liner.

Allowing for approximately 12 inches of liner flap turn-in, attach the bottom of the liner to the bottom of the lift pole. Then tie the top of the liner to the lift pole. Run the liner from the lift pole to the door on each side, attaching the liner to the rope along the way. Pull the liner up tightly at the door one side at a time. Secure the liner at the door by whatever method the builder has suggested.

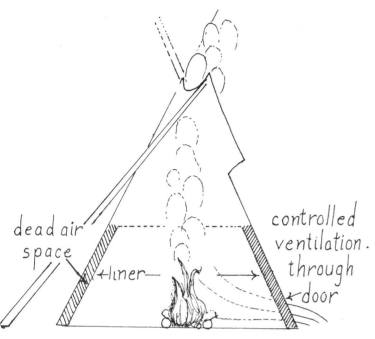

**FIGURE 16**

With the bottom of the tipi cover set tightly to the ground, the owner can manage the lodge for comfort in almost any weather.

# TIPI MANAGEMENT

The actual managing of the tipi began with all of the preparation and setup. It is a result of the attention paid to detail. Without this attention to detail, tipi management cannot be effective. Thus, managability is dependent upon: an efficient, effective setup; the ability to set up the lodge the same way every time, which was accomplished by marking the tie points; and the realization that attention to detail is the key to a successful setup. Once this efficient setup is completed, you can turn your attention to other important details.

Managability of the fire is the next most important detail in achieving a comfortable camp. I suggest that the fire be placed as far forward as possible while still allowing easy access to the door, as illustrated in Figure 17. It is also important that the location of the fire be such that the smoke will immediately begin to exit from the bottom of the smoke hole. This allows a larger living area, since the space in front of the door is usually used for storage.

A tipi fire has three functions, which are, in the order of their importance: heating the lodge, cooking, and socialization. In order to effectively accomplish these purposes, it is necessary to keep the fire on the ground, out of a hole whenever possible. Heat radiates outward, and a fire in a hole heats the sides of the hole, not the lodge or the people. See Figure 18. The tipi is not heated by retaining heat but by heat constantly radiating from the fire.

It is difficult to draft a fire that has heat barriers, so it is necessary to keep the fire area clear of clutter. Do not hang cook gear in the fire area unless they are actively being used in cooking. These utensils will act as heat barriers that block the radiating heat, keeping it from warming the lodge. Also, trunks and large pieces of furnishings need to be moved to the perimeter of the lodge since they are also heat barriers. People themselves are enough of a heat barrier, causing cold spots behind them, without the added cold spots caused by unnecessary clutter.

Hot coals give the maximum amount of heat with the minimum amount of smoke. Hot coals are a much better heat source than a blazing flame. They are also better for cooking

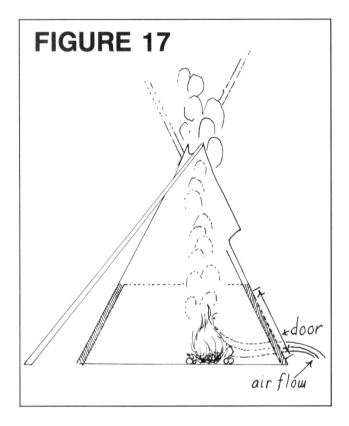

**FIGURE 17**

door
air flow

The typical, off-the-ground setup will work in favorable weather but will become unmanageable when conditions take a turn for the worse.

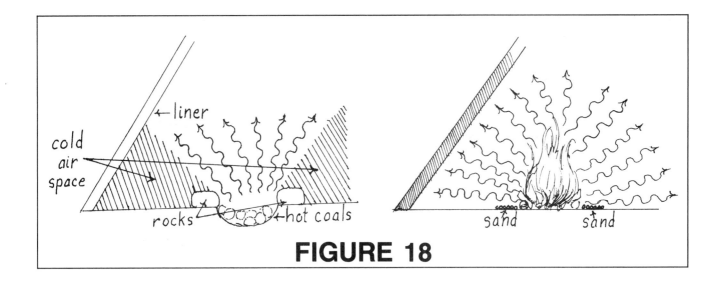

**FIGURE 18**

and provide for a less smoky social environment. In order to achieve hot coals, it is necessary, whenever possible, to use small pieces of wood that will burn easily. If the wood has bark on it, make sure it is placed on the fire *bark up.* Wood placed bark up will eliminate excess smoke and will catch fire more quickly.

There are three pieces of equipment necessary to achieve a fire consisting of mainly hot coals. They are a buck saw, a hand axe or knife large enough to split small pieces of wood, and a fire ring. Use the buck saw to cut the larger pieces of wood down to smaller lengths which can be more readily split. Splitting these shorter pieces will be much easier and can even be done in the lodge with the hand axe or knife. The purpose of the fire ring is for leaning the burning wood against. This will keep one end in the fire and the other end up off the fire to prevent smoking. A piece of wood laid flat on the fire has a tendency to burn in the center and smoke on the ends.

Even a well-built fire will be the source of some smoke. This is where adequate ventilation for the fire and the removal of smoke comes to play. However, this type of ventilation does not come from a cover that is off the ground!

Smoke is removed from the tipi by a rising column of hot air exiting the lodge through the smoke hole. It is also removed by the wind blowing across properly adjusted smoke flaps, creating a suction similar to that of a window vent on an automobile. Thus, you create a venturi effect. It is also important that this column of hot air be as undisturbed as possible. Any breeze created by a cover off the ground or by any other source disturbs this column, causing the smoke to hang heavy at liner height. A natural balance of air intake and exit is created when the cover and liner are in correct positions. A cover off the ground will disturb this balance by forcing more air into the tipi than can be exited. The result is *smoke!* The principle is similar to that of a wood stove. Rolling the door flap up or down is the primary control measure in adjusting the air volume created by the wind blowing across the flaps.

I will now discuss the operation of the smoke flaps in relation to the working unit of the lodge. If you disregard even one of the factors I have discussed previously, the entire system can be cancelled out. Therefore, all of the details are crucial if the system is to work. If you overlook even one detail, there can be no effective use of the flaps.

For the smoke flaps to be used to their maximum potential, three components of the lodge are important. These components are pole streamers, flap poles and the flap rope pole. See Figure 19. The streamers, as well as being decorative, tell the wind direction. The smoke flap poles keep the flaps wrinkle-free with a good straight edge. You accomplish this by pushing the smoke flap poles up, not out. I referred to this when I discussed cutting and shaping the smoke flap poles. The smoke flap poles also move the tops of the flaps. The tops of the flaps need to be moved in accordance with the wind direction, which you determine by observing the streamers. The flaps should point the direction in which the streamers are blowing. The smoke flap rope pole must also be moved as the smoke flaps are moved. This allows for the movement of the entire flap with the wind, not just the top half, which eliminates the snow fence effect. See Figure 20.

Moving the entire flap with the wind is also important on warm days. The flap so moved will help to create the maximum movement of air in the lodge. This cooling system is the natural updraft formed as the warm air rises and is replaced by cooler air.

The reason it is important to be able to close the entire smoke flap becomes evident in the rain. The closed flap will help to keep it from raining into the lodge. Take care to close the flap completely. This means one flap overlapping the other. The reason for this is to avoid the formation of a trough which will cause a steady stream of rain to pour into the lodge.

The importance of the cover being on the ground now comes into play. It gives choices, alternatives and absolute control of ventilation when needed. As a result of the setup

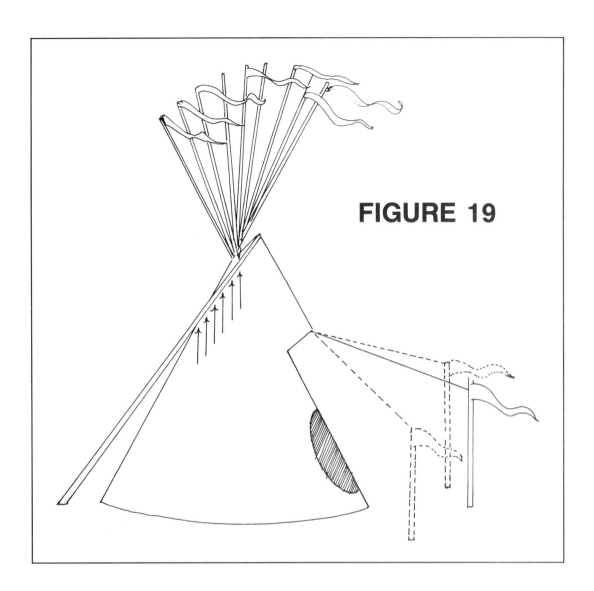

**FIGURE 19**

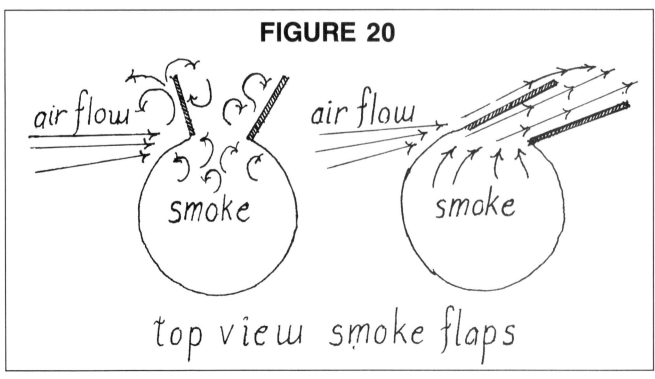

**FIGURE 20**

air flow

smoke

air flow

smoke

top view smoke flaps

Streamers tied to the ends of the poles aren't just for decoration. They are also used to judge wind direction so you can adjust the smoke flaps accordingly.

The smoke flaps can be adjusted to meet a variety of weather changes. Left: With the wind from the left, the smoke flaps are adjusted to the right. Middle: The flaps here are adjusted for rain only. Right: When high winds and rain are expected, closing up the flaps tight will protect the lodge.

procedures explained earlier, the cover is now multi-purpose and functional. The cover works in combination with the liner and the wind direction to give comfortable living in all seasons. This functional cover is especially useful in very hot or very cold weather. There may be those rare situations in the absence of wind where it might be helpful to roll up a portion of the cover to help eliminate excess smoke. An example of this might be the necessity of cooking in the lodge on a hot, windless, rainy day or just on a hot, windless day to escape the heat.

On those hot, sunny days, the rising hot air created by the canvas can be utilized. The ability to roll up the cover in order to circulate the air is determined by the location of the peg loops. If the peg loops are in the correct position, you can roll up the cover without removing the stakes.

Roll up the cover and liner on the shady side of the tipi. As the hot air rises and exits out the smoke hole, cool air will be drawn in on the shaded side of the tipi, as shown in Figure 21. Remember, the position of the shade will change with the movement of the sun, so it may be necessary to change the roll of the cover and liner. There may be times that randomly rolling the cover is all that is necessary to achieve the movement of air. If there happens to be a breeze on a warm day, move the smoke flaps with the wind. This will help to draw in more air at ground level.

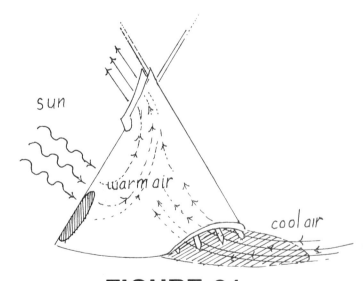

**FIGURE 21**

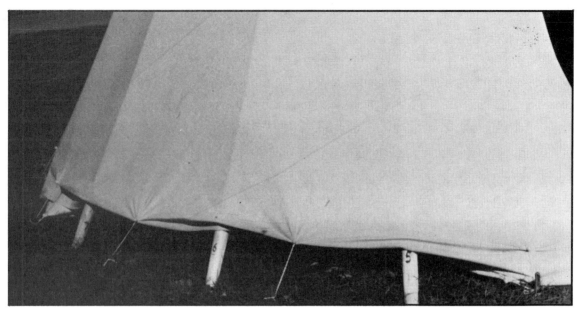

When it's hot you can increase the air circulation by rolling up the cover and the liner.

The challenge really comes on a cold day. The object is to keep the cold air from rolling up over the liner and down the backs of the occupants as in Figure 22, which happens if the cover is off the ground. A cover and liner tight to the ground eliminates the hot face, cold back syndrome so frequently faced by many tipi dwellers.

Unfortunately, it is not possible to have ideal situations at all times. Therefore, it is during times of adverse conditions that everything needs to be working to its optimum potential. It is these times that tipi management becomes a critical necessity.

Now that setup and management have been properly taken care of, I will address some of the extra items that add a touch of romance to tipi dwelling. I discuss these last because these extras mean nothing to managing the lodge.

A beautiful addition to a lodge is creating a bonnet effect with the poles as in Figure 23. A bonnet is very easy to make but it is important to cut and mark each pole so they will be put in the same place at each setup. To achieve a bonnet, lay the poles on the ground, cut them and mark them as shown in Figure 24. If the tipi style is of the classic lean-back shape and all of the poles are the same length, a natural bonnet will occur with no work at all. If the poles are not the same length or the lodge has a conical shape, laying them out as in Figure 24 will be necessary to achieve this look.

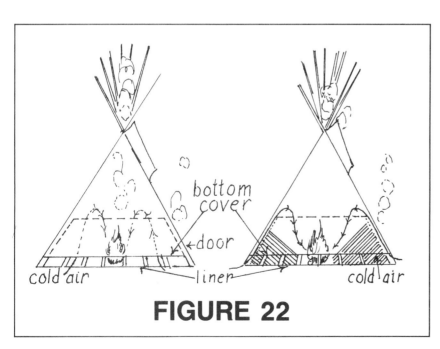

**FIGURE 22**

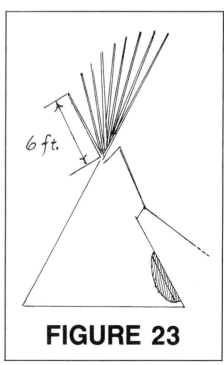

**FIGURE 23**

A large tipi like this 24-footer is impressive and will shelter a lot of peole. The bonnet effect of the poles is evident on this setup.

Another functional yet decorative feature of the lodge is liner staves. Liner staves are an extra set of short poles. These poles sandwich the liner between themselves and the lodge poles, eliminating the need for liner ropes. These staves can also be decorated attractively for a special touch.

Painting the lodge and liner is another attractive means of decoration. Use acrylic paint only, *no latex.* Keep the canvas wet and the nap of the fabric brushed up in the area you are painting. Always finish an entire area before stopping, because overlapping on dry areas will cause color demarcation. Some types of fabric do not lend themselves to this procedure. Waxy finished or blended fabrics fall into this

Here's another view of the bonnet effect of the poles as seen on Bill Walter's lodge.

You can decorate your tipi by painting (actually staining) it like Bill Wallace's lodge shown here in 1983. Ask for a scrap of canvas from your tipi's maker to practice on.

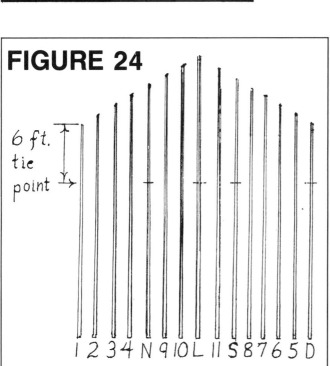

# FIGURE 24

6 ft. tie point

1 2 3 4 N 9 10 L 11 S 8 7 6 5 D

category.

Speaking technically, the fabric is actually being stained, not painted. Because of this fact, it is advisable to use only one teaspoon of color per ½ gallon of water. This can be varied slightly to achieve the density of color desired. I recommend practicing with the color before trying to paint the actual lodge. Practice painting can be done on a scrap piece of fabric or on the transport or storage bag.

I will now discuss the ozan. The ozan is a modern adaptation to solve the problem of the cold back, hot front created from covers being off the ground. The purpose of the ozan is to create a ceiling of sorts to trap warm air and to prevent water drippage from the smoke hole overhead. Water dripping on bedding is a problem usually associated with smaller lodges. Because of their smaller diameter the smoke hole is usually over the bedding.

The use of an ozan is a point of personal preference. I feel that an ozan is not needed for larger lodges. It is an accessory that does not lend itself to the managing of the tipi as mentioned in this article.

---

# CONCLUSION

---

As a final note, I would like to give a few precautions on take-down. Basically, you reverse the setup process when the lodge is taken down. First, I recommend that you relax the cover slightly. This is done by moving the poles inward just a bit. This takes the strain off of the lace pins and lace pin holes. Next, in order to eliminate pole breakage after the cover is off, move out the north and south poles to give extra stabilization to the tripod. Last, move poles 4 and 8 slightly forward to stabilize them. These two poles are the most frequently broken during take-down, and a little extra time can save costly damage.

I wrote this article using firsthand experience. Over the last 20 years, I have observed and experienced many struggles with the setup and management of the tipi. I have also learned many hard and costly lessons. The lessons I learned were the result of a lack of firsthand knowledge and over-simplified instructions. I hope my article will save many of you the long and painful learning experiences I have encountered.

# Engraving & Carving

## by G. L. Jones

BORN AND RAISED IN THE WEST, G.L. Jones was influenced by pioneer history and cowboy folklore. His first introduction to the mountain man era came when he responded to an ad for muzzleloaders while in high school. Little did he know that the ad would have such an impact on his future. After owning and shooting his muzzleloader for a while, Glen's interest in the past increased and his muzzleloading became more than a mild involvement. His hobby soon became a part-time gun building occupation and then, since 1979, a full-time profession.

G.L. Jones has a wife, Annette, and two children, Shanna and Seth. Glen and Annette live near Williamsburg, Virginia. Glen has an associate degree in commercial art and worked for Sears as a commercial artist for five years before becoming a full-time gunmaker. He is an originator and member of the Western Long Riflemen Association, a pre-1800 national organization. Says Jones, ''I have always had a great love for history and consider myself lucky to be one of the few individuals that are able to combine their zeal for the past with what they do for a living. I remember back when I saw my first Davy Crockett movie. There was an excitement that arose inside of me because I realized that there was a more romantic time to have lived in. Now I enjoy reliving that era, both as a hobby and a profession.''

101

The art of engraving and embellishing implements of war and personal effects dates back thousands of years. Evidence of early engravings has been found in the tombs and graves of ancient Egyptian pharoahs and aristocrats. Swords, shields, knives and other personal effects were engraved either to depict important events and personal triumphs or just for decoration. As man progressed engraving became more of an art form and was used to embellish and set apart items of endearment or establish social class. Early Roman military leaders wore breast plates that were heavily embellished as opposed to the common soldier. As time went on, the ways of engraving and embellishing became more sophisticated and developed into a high art form. This art is performed well by many of our present-day engravers, McKenzie and Churchill to name a couple.

The embellishing on a rifle is what distinguishes it from another with the same components. Engraving gives the gun character and personality, so to speak. At many rendezvous I have had people bring me rifles to be engraved that they have made for themselves. I've spent many hours engraving other people's rifles, and there is always a sense of pride on their faces when they read their name after the phrase, ''This Rifle Made by . . .'' But often they will comment, ''I can build a pretty fair rifle, but I just can't seem to engrave.''

There are always a few comments I receive when I am engraving at a gun show or rendezvous. ''Wow, there is a dying art!'' or, ''I just got the tools, and I'm learning to engrave, too'' are some examples. Many folks will say, ''How can you do that? I can't even draw a straight line.'' My reply is, ''Neither can I, that's why I use a ruler.'' Like anything else, you can learn to engrave. I am going to outline some basic steps that you can use to start engraving and upon which you can build your skills. Remember that as a beginner, you should not get discouraged by comparing your work with others, especially that of more accomplished engravers. I've had the opportunity to talk to, observe and receive pointers from several highly skilled engravers and they, too, had humble beginnings. Henry Frank, maker and engraver, told me that he would like to gather all the pieces he engraved when he first started and bury them somewhere. I have often had the same thought.

The three keys to successful engraving are: layout (knowing what you are going to engrave and planning ahead); using the correct tools; and execution or making the right cut.

## THE LAYOUT

This is the area for which most beginners fail to prepare properly. There are many types and styles of engraving, the most common being the single line pattern or border, often referred to as the open background style. This is one of the easiest patterns to execute and a good one for the beginner to start with. This type of engraving gives you a minimal amount of coverage yet is attractive to look at and dresses up most pieces. You can add some additional lines and cuts

**FIGURE 1**

to this and make it almost three-dimensional with a little bit of shading, as shown in the three steps in Figure 1.

At this point you should try to become familiar with the many different styles of other engravers. Looking through books, magazines and other publications, you can copy and simplify their designs and eventually develop your own style of engraving. It is beneficial to me to look at and handle other engraving to study the various types of cuts used to produce the pattern.

One big mistake beginners make is trying to go too quickly. They make a few cuts on a sheet of brass, do a few rough layouts and then believe they are ready to begin engraving their rifle. On several occasions I've seen someone attempt to engrave a gun worth $300 or $400 and wind up with a piece that is worth less than the original cost of the components. More time should be spent in practice.

Important tools for the layout are a pad of paper and a pencil. Taking ideas from other engravers, copy and lay out designs on the paper. Remember that if you can't draw it, you can't engrave it. If you can draw it on paper and you develop your skills of engraving, you will be able to recreate anything you sketch out. Almost all of the engraving you see is made up of S- and C-scrolls and straight and curved lines. As you are sketching, do not look at the tip of your pencil. Try to visualize the whole design and what it will look like when you are done. It is important that you practice drawing the scrolls on paper, paying close attention to the overall shape and size. After you have the feel of drawing a simple S- or C-scroll, try laying out various shapes and filling them with simple scroll work as in Figure 2. You should never have flat spots or eratic bends as shown in the "incorrect" example in Figure 3. Whether you are right- or left-handed, you will notice it is more comfortable to make a scroll in one direction than another. Practice drawing the scrolls in both directions, for as you start making cuts you will need to be able to go in both directions. There are few

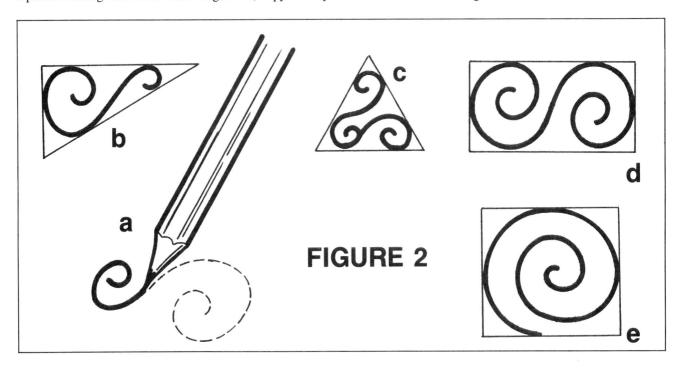

**FIGURE 2**

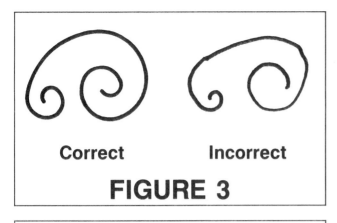

**Correct**         **Incorrect**

# FIGURE 3

# FIGURE 4

**S-Scroll**       **C-Scroll**

**Arc**      **Straight**      **Beauty**

**S-Scroll**

**Arc**

**Combination**    **Beauty**    **C-Scroll**
**Straight & Arc**

designs that you cannot accomplish by using the basic S- and C- scrolls, the beauty curve, arc and straight line. Figure 4 shows an example of scroll work using all of the above-mentioned cuts.

I cannot emphasize enough how important it is to plan ahead and carefully lay out your design before you engrave. Otherwise, you will wind up with a haphazard design as seen in the scroll in Figure 5. As you practice you will be able to elaborate and build upon simple scrolls. Figure 6 is an example of this. Your imagaination is the limit. I often spend more time deciding what I am going to do and laying it out than in the actual engraving, with the exception of relief engraving and inlay.

At this point I am going to explain different types of engraving and scroll work you might put on your rifle, pistol, or other item. A common mistake is putting a type of scroll work on a piece that would not have been done in a certain time period. For example, you would not put Nimsche scroll on a Kentucky longrifle. The best way to avoid such errors is to find examples of the type of rifle you would like to engrave in books and magazines and study the engraving that is upon them carefully. Some excellent sources are *Rifles of Colonial America,* volumes I and II, by George Shumway and *Kentucky Rifles and Pistols, 1750 to 1850* by Golden Age Arms Company and James R. Johnston. These books give close, detail shots of patchboxes and side plates and give you excellent examples of the type and style of engraving that Verner, Armstrong and others were doing during their time period. When I am engraving, I constantly refer to books and original pieces to ensure that I am using the proper engraving style on that particular piece.

# FIGURE 5

**FIGURE 6**

## USE THE CORRECT TOOLS

When I first wanted to engrave my rifles, there was no one near to give me information on hand engraving. I just ordered a few chisels from Dixie Gun Works that I thought were appropriate and went to work teaching myself to engrave. As the expression goes, ''Having lost all sense of direction, we have been able to double our speed.'' I was using palm chisels to chase with, a claw hammer for a chasing hammer, poor mechanics and improperly sharpened chisel tips. As you can imagine, the end result was not a pretty picture.

After using and misusing various engraving tools, I found that I prefer those produced by the NgraveR Company. After meeting one of their field representatives and having him demonstrate some of their tools and the correct way to use them, my engraving took a giant step forward. The NgraveR Company offers a variety of cutting and chisel tips, beginning with a number 1, along with numbers 2, 3

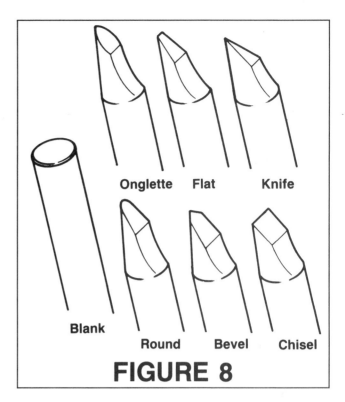

**FIGURE 8**

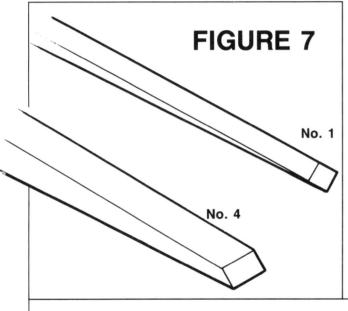

**FIGURE 7**

No. 1

No. 4

and 4, which are broader and squarer chisels as shown in Figure 7. One of my favorites is the blank chisel which you can grind into any particular chisel you like.

There are several companies that produce a wide selection of chisels such as the onglette, flat, knife, round, square and bevel. These are pictured in Figure 8. These chisels are offered in a variety of sizes in each type, usually with the finer point chisel having a smaller number and the larger number representing the bigger tip. Figure 9 shows the sizes using the onglette chisel as an example. Also available are a number of multi-lined chisels that allow you to cut a series of lines, from very fine to coarse, at the same time.

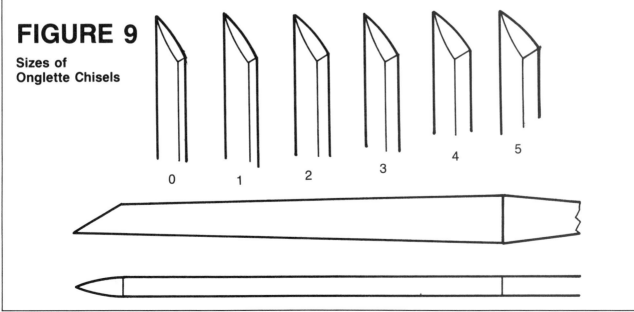

**FIGURE 9**

**Sizes of Onglette Chisels**

0    1    2    3    4    5

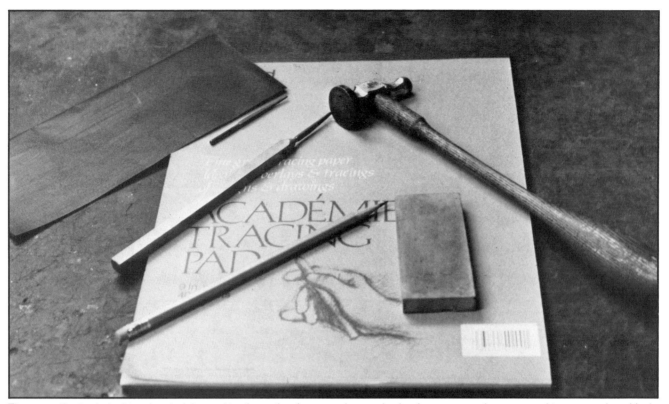

These are the basic tools and materials used by the author for engraving: a chasing hammer, numbers one and two engraving chisels (with handle), a fine whet stone for sharpening, a sharpened pencil, and some tracing and carbon paper.

On more than one occasion, I have been advised by accomplished engravers to stay away from multi-lined chisels. They feel it is best to make each cut separately to prevent the engraving from looking too mechanical. You will be able to accomplish about 90% of what I am going to outline here with the numbers 1 and 2 NgraveR chisels or similar chisel tips.

The tools you will need to make the first cut are: a chasing hammer, numbers 1 and 2 NGraver chisels (along with a handle), a fine stone for sharpening, some tracing and carbon paper, and a sharpened pencil. Starting with your number 1 chisel, you should have an approximate 45-degree angle on the tip. This will sometimes vary depending upon the type of metal that you are engraving. As you experiment with different types of metal, you will be able to decide upon the various angles that suit you for the type of engraving that you wish to do. Keeping the tip sharp is much more important than being off a few degrees on the angle of your chisel tip. NgraveR offers a small sharpening guide that you can clamp the chisel in as you sharpen it against the stone to get the correct bevels. I have one of these, but I prefer to use a grinding wheel with a very fine stone on it. One thing you must keep in mind when using a power grinding wheel is not to over heat the tip of your chisel as this removes the temper and ruins the chisel. Figure 10 shows chisel tips sharpened correctly and incorrectly. Remember that a sharp, clean edge will make a nice, clean cut, eliminating most burrs.

If you decide to use the blank chisel, Figure 11 shows a good example of grinding a blank to a number 1 square tip. Notice that the top half has been ground down. A smaller area sharpens quicker and easier than a larger surface. This is something you might want to do to other chisels that have

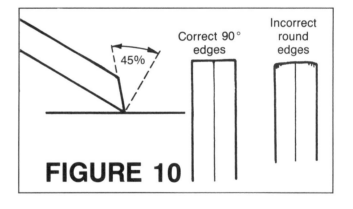

45%

Correct 90° edges

Incorrect round edges

**FIGURE 10**

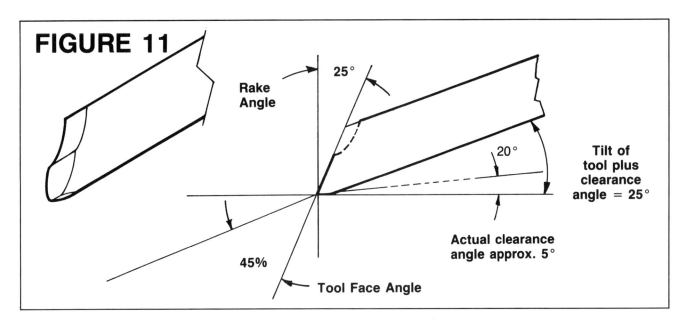

**FIGURE 11**

Rake Angle

25°

Tilt of tool plus clearance angle = 25°

20°

Actual clearance angle approx. 5°

45%

Tool Face Angle

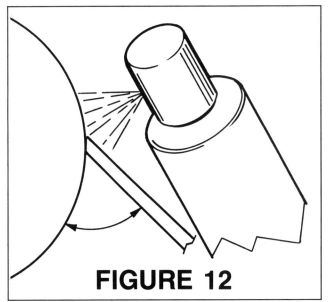

**FIGURE 12**

a very broad engraving surface. An excellent book that covers different sharpening techniques and the use of many types of chisels is *The Art of Engraving* by James B. Meek. This book goes into more depth than space here allows.

Figure 12 demonstrates a method of sharpening your chisel tips using a small, four-inch, fine stone grinding wheel. To prevent over heating your tip, you should wrap a small, wet paper towel close to the tip as you sharpen it and squeeze the water out of it to keep the temperature down. You could also have a cup of water to cool the tip down as you sharpen it. A rule of thumb is to have the tool in the water as much as it is on the wheel. I like using a small, fine mist squirt bottle, and as I touch the tip to the stone, I squirt it with the fine mist. However, if you are not careful, you still might over-heat the chisel tip and ruin the temper.

One essential item not mentioned before is a vise. If it is to be used primarily for engraving the rifles you build, I would suggest a large 5-inch vise that swivels. Mount it

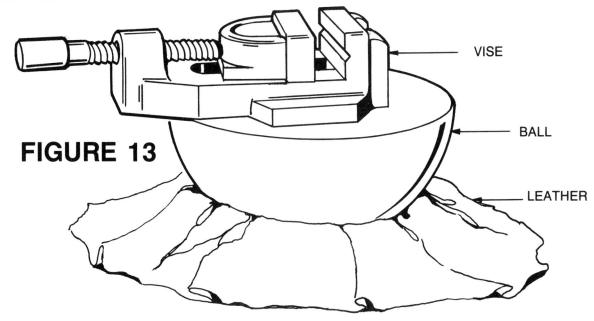

VISE

BALL

LEATHER

**FIGURE 13**

close to the end of a bench, allowing you to work around the gun as you engrave. For small items on a rifle, such as a trigger guard and side plate, I find it easier to remove them from the gun. You can mount these on a wooden block and clamp the block into the vise. The engraving on other items, such as patch boxes and butt plates, is sometimes better executed if they remain on the rifle. If you plan to do a lot of engraving, you might want to invest in an engraver's ball. These can be found in the $200.00 and up price range. If an engraver's ball is a little more than you wish to invest in, you can take an old bowling ball, cut it in half and mount a machine vise on top of it. Place the ball on a raised ring so the bottom of the ball is elevated slightly. Place a piece of leather between the ball and ring to help stabilize the ball while you are engraving. For a moderate investment, you have a fairly nice engraver's ball. An example of an engraver's ball made from an old bowling ball is seen in Figure 13.

Now that you have acquired all the proper tools and are ready to engrave, I would like to stress the importance of wearing safety glasses (prescription glasses are also appropriate) to protect your eyes from the small chips that might fly as you engrave. Do not allow anyone else watching you to put their face close to your working area without having their eyes protected also.

### EXECUTION

Now, let's start engraving. My favorite material to engrave is brass. Machine shops are ideal sources for obtaining shim brass, an inexpensive brass that is good to practice on. Taking a piece of this brass, secure it in your vise. Take a number 1 or 2 chisel, onglette or whatever manufactured chisel you have decided to use and put the point down where you have decided to start cutting. The angle of the engraver should be low at this point. However, if the angle of the chisel is too low, it will come out of the metal, and if it is too steep, it will bury itself into the metal, halting the progress of your chisel. A little experimentation at this point will give you a good feel for the chisel tip you are using. Just a warning: sometimes when people see that they can make a straight, smooth line, they jump right into fancy scroll work, initials or flowers. This results in bad habits. You are trying to learn too many things at one time. You wind up with ragged edges, burrs, poor coordination between the hands and chisel and poorly cut and executed designs.

To start practicing, trace out a few lines about ⅛-inch apart. Then cut the straight lines where you have traced. After you have made a half dozen or so cuts doing this, go back and try to cut a line between each of the previous lines, as in Figure 14. The purpose of this process is to learn to make a nice even cut, letting each cut end with the chisel coming up out of the cut, leaving no burrs. Remember not to watch the point of the chisel so much as where you are guiding the chisel as you chase it along and remember to tap the chasing hammer only slightly to ensure steady, even movement. This is the same rule as not watching the tip of the pencil as you draw out designs.

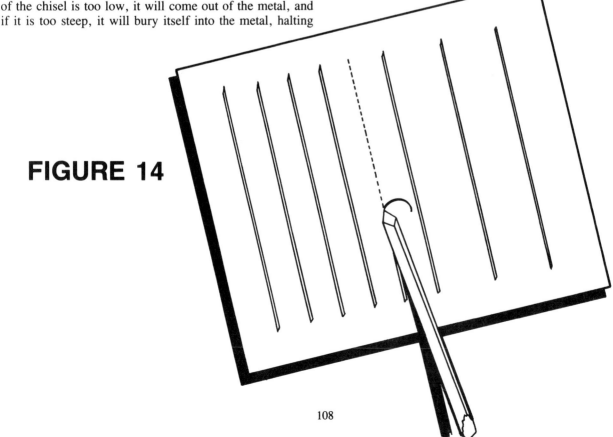

## FIGURE 14

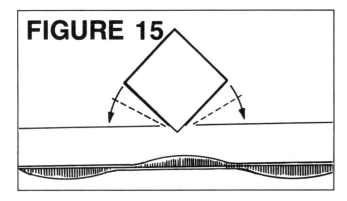

**FIGURE 15**

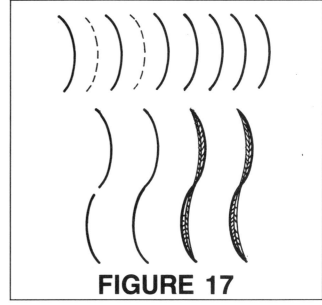

**FIGURE 17**

The next step, after you feel you have accomplished a nice, even, straight cut with even depth, is to rotate the chisel on its axis so that it cuts a wider strip. Look closely at Figure 15, which shows the rotation of the chisel tip and the results. Rotating the chisel back and forth on its axis and producing a wider cut gives a shading effect, which is useful when doing floral designs. Remember that moving the angle of the chisel up and down will determine the depth of the cut. By practicing all this repeatedly, you will develop good hand-eye control with the chisel and hammer.

After you have mastered the above cuts, get another sheet of brass and make a series of curved cuts. First, sketch out a series of curved lines where you are going to engrave. See Figure 16. Repeat the same process as with the straight lines. Go back and try to cut another set of curved lines between those. After practicing this, ending each cut with no burrs and even depth, mark out on another sheet of metal a series of arc cuts. Make one cut from one direction and a second cut from the opposite direction and try to make the points of the two cuts meet. You can also rotate the axis of the chisel to make a wider cut, then bring it back as you end the arc as in Figure 17. Practice, repetition and discipline is boring, but it is worth the end result. This will separate the accomplished engravers from the home shop hackers.

From the series of arcs and curves that you have been practicing, you should be able to start atempting letters and vines. We are going to try to make what has been referred to as a beauty curve, shown in Figure 18. This is accomplish-

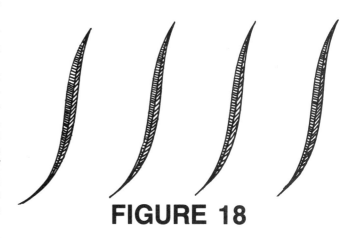

**FIGURE 18**

ed by making a slight "S" cut with your chisel, rotating it on its axis to the point where you reach the middle of the curve (the maximum roll of the chisel), then bringing it up slowly as you continue and finish the cut. A series of arc cuts, made with a rotating chisel, is shown in Figure 19. Notice the life and feeling accomplished by rotating the chisel on its axis as opposed to the sterile, bland look of those where the chisel was held straight up without rotation.

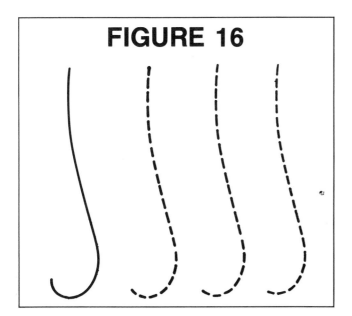

**FIGURE 16**

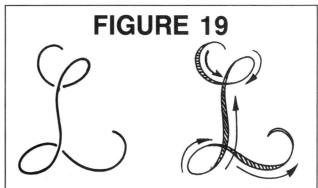

**FIGURE 19**

## FIGURE 20

At this point go back to all those drawings you did at the beginning with a pencil and start practicing those same curves and lines with chisels. Try at first to do it by making a simple cut without rotating the chisels. When you feel confident executing all of them without any burrs, go back and duplicate all of the cuts by rotating the chisel tip. A few examples are shown in Figure 20. The first set was made without rotating the chisel tip, but the chisel tip was rotated in the second set.

It is a good idea to repeat the exercises that we have outlined previously with a number 2 flat chisel. Place the corner of your number 2 chisel down and use it as if it was the point of your number 1 chisel. By placing the corner of the number 2 chisel down and rotating it on its axis, you are able to make a wider cut than with your number 1. This is shown in Figure 21. If you have been following along step by step and have not taken any shortcuts, you should have a real good feel for your chisels and how they work and a slight feel for a variety of points, such as the number 2 on up. Again, I stress the most important thing at this point is repetition and discipline. To become a quality engraver, like an accomplished pianist, you must practice. Anyone can beat out ''chopsticks'' and anyone can hack out a ragged line. Without a lot of practice, repetition and discipline you will not be able to accomplish the smooth flowing lines that are essential to quality engraving.

This is a good time to talk about borders. Borders are to engraving what frosting is to cake. Usually, engraving never looks quite finished without some type of border

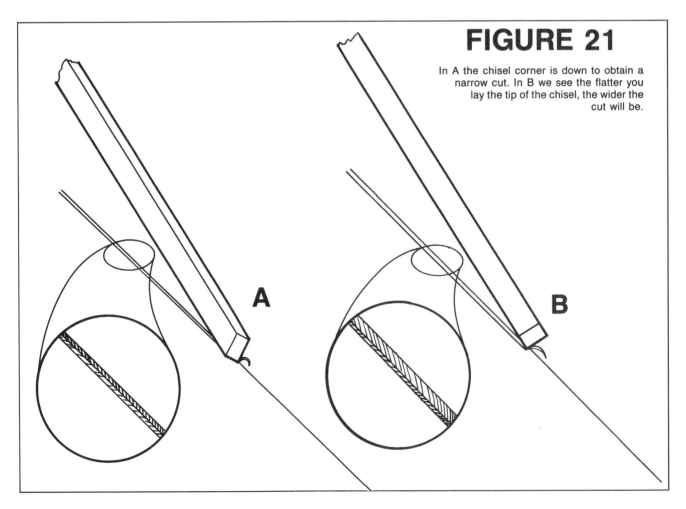

## FIGURE 21

In A the chisel corner is down to obtain a narrow cut. In B we see the flatter you lay the tip of the chisel, the wider the cut will be.

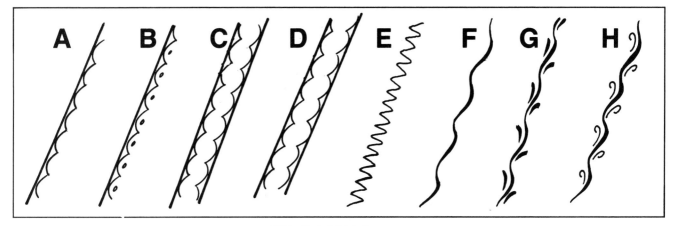

# FIGURE 22

around the edge. This can be very plain, like a single line, or a border of a variety of cuts. Generally speaking, the more elaborate the engraving design, the simpler the border should be so as not to detract from the main theme. On the other hand, an elaborate border may be called for where there is no central engraving pattern or perhaps only a monogram. Shown in Figure 22 is a variety of borders that I will discuss. Figure 22A shows what I refer to as a sawtooth border. This is made by rocking the tool uniformally on its axis as you

cut the line. I like to first scribe a line along the border where you wish to make the cut. Then mark off uniform increments ¼₆'' to ⅛'' apart along the cut line. Go back with your chisel and make a series of cuts inside your first cut, and as you come to each of the hash marks, rock or rotate the chisel to its extreme edge at that point and then bring it up. Figure 23 shows the steps to take in making this cut. This border takes a little bit of practice but is extremely simple once you master it. Figure 22B shows the same type border, only be-

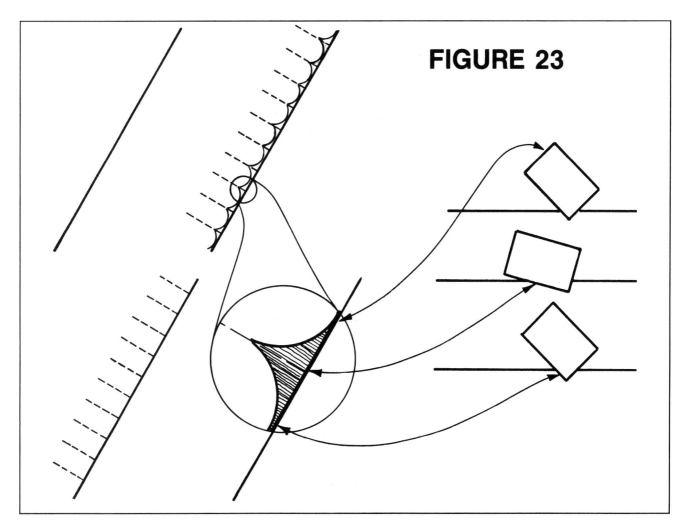

# FIGURE 23

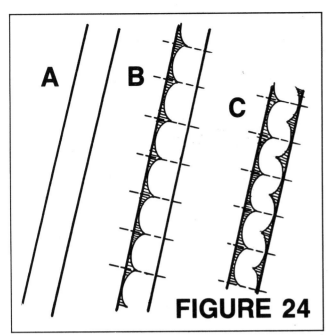

**FIGURE 24**

Scribe two lines in A. Mark off spaces and cut the first line as in B. Repeat the same cut on the opposite line in between the previous cuts, as shown in C.

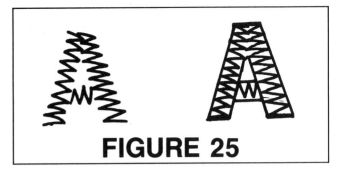

**FIGURE 25**

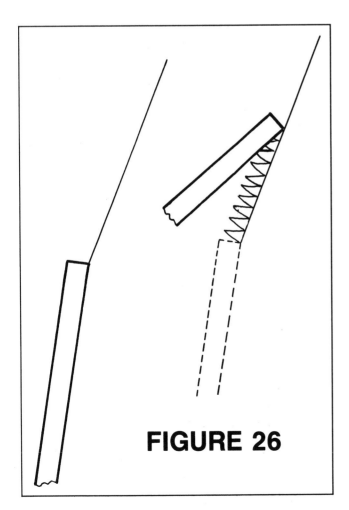

**FIGURE 26**

tween the points you hit it with a seed, a number 2 or number 1 dot. This border with the seeds or dots was extremely popular in a lot of European, especially English, engravings. The border in Figure 22C is a rope-like or zigzag border. This is done by repetitious, short plunge cuts, like what I have outlined in Figure 22A and B, but you mirror the image on the other side. This is done with repetitious, short plunges first with one corner of the chisel. After you have done the one side of the line, go back and scribe a parallel line to that and repeat the same process. The chisel is held at about a 30-degree angle to the work and its flat tip is cantered to about a 45-degree angle to the surface. Figure 24 outlines the steps to accomplish this border.

Figure 22D is done the same way, but instead of spacing your cuts between each other when you cut the opposite side, you make your cuts at the same places. Instead of a zigzag line, you end up with a bean or sausage-type design.

The next border, the Poor Man's Zigzag shown in Figure 22E, is probably the most popular border. This border is often used to fill in spaces. You can also make block letters using this same type of engraving. When you engrave the letters using the walking type of engraving, you can either leave the edges raw or you can outline them as shown in Figure 25. Figure 26 illustrates the best way I have found to execute this particular border. Begin by laying out a line. Lay your chisel down with one corner on your scribed or penciled line, then lift one edge of the chisel up and rotate it slightly forward. Lay the chisel down flat again. Pick up the opposite corner, rotate it forward slightly and set it down. Rock it back and forth, rotating the corners as if walking the chisel up the line. The further you rotate the chisel, the more narrow the pattern will be and the less the angle of the zigzag. Likewise, the shorter you rotate it, the wider the pattern will be and the steeper the angle. With a little bit of practice, this particular border can be utilized almost everywhere and executed very well. It is probably one of the simplest borders used.

Figure 22F is nothing more than a wavy line and a cut that you have practiced in learning how to use your chisel. This line can be accented, as in Figure 22G, by making simple flare cuts on either side. These are simply executed by rotating the chisel on its axis as you bring the chisel off its cut so you leave no burrs. Figure 22H is also the same wavy line, but a short C-type scroll is used to accent the line. It is good to scribe a line for this border, as for many of the

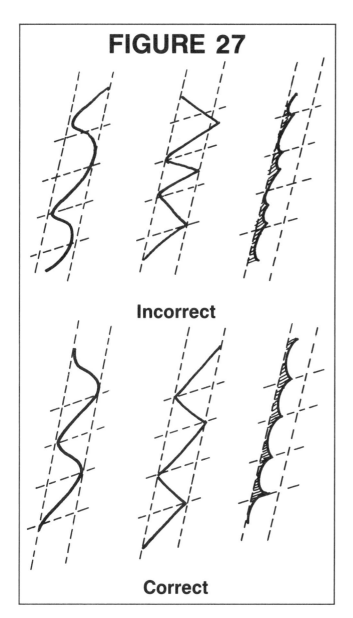

## FIGURE 27

Incorrect

Correct

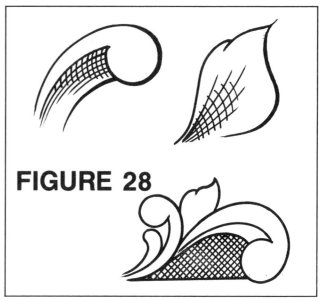

## FIGURE 28

borders, and engrave to it. This prevents any veering and inconsistency with the edge that you are cutting to. I scribe two lines to keep the wavy linen consistent as far as width and also mark off increments to keep all the waves equal. Figure 27 shows examples of correct and incorrect borders.

There are a multitude of borders you can execute by using these cuts and improvising other cuts. I could almost write a full chapter on engraving borders alone. This, however, will give you a good basis to work with. With a little experience making these cuts and looking at the metal, you should be able to see how the chisel was handled in order to make other borders.

At this point we will talk about crosshatching, which was very popular in the primitive-type engravings to indicate background and shading in the engraving patterns. Many of the Colonial gunsmiths used the crosshatching method of engraving, such as Albright, Fordney and Armstrong. Figure 28 shows several examples of how crosshatching can be used with simple line engraving. Here you do not rotate the chisel

## FIGURE 29

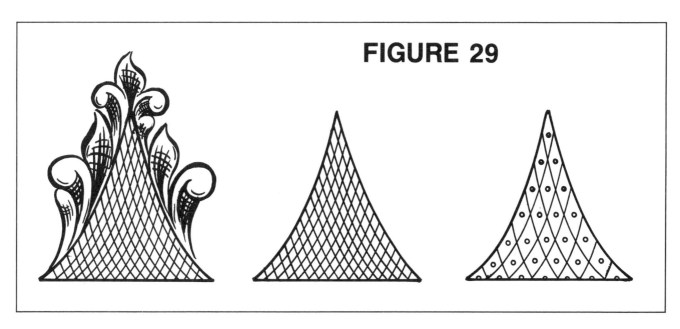

tip but make a plain, basic cut and then emphasize the cuts or the background using the crosshatch. The crosshatching can be used in a variety of ways to show depth in your stems and flowers and add a little depth to your engraving. You can also block off large areas. One is sort of a pyramid type, which was very popular on patchboxes and is shown in Figure 29. This can be done with fine crosshatching, or you can expand it and dimple it with a number 1, 2 or 3 seed punch.

There are always right and wrong ways to do things. Crosshatching is no exception. Crosshatching should flow with the engraving and not be a straight, sterile-looking checkerboard. Shown in Figure 30 are examples of correct and incorrect ways you might crosshatch or accent your engraving with crosshatching.

I have outlined quite a bit on the various types of cuts you can make: scroll, crosshatch, and borders. We will use all of the aforementioned engraving methods and lay out a design for a patchbox, trigger guard and side plate that you can apply to a rifle. The most popular rifle design seems to be the Lancaster style. Please note that all of the engraving shown here (Figure 31) on the hardware is not from the same rifle but from a variety of rifles made around the same time period (within a five- to ten-year time span). The same theme

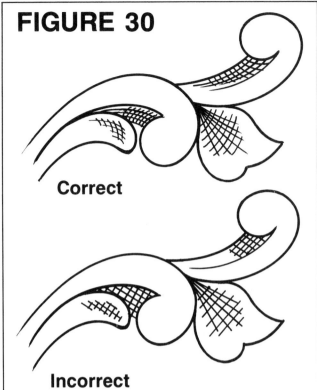

# FIGURE 30

**Correct**

**Incorrect**

# FIGURE 31

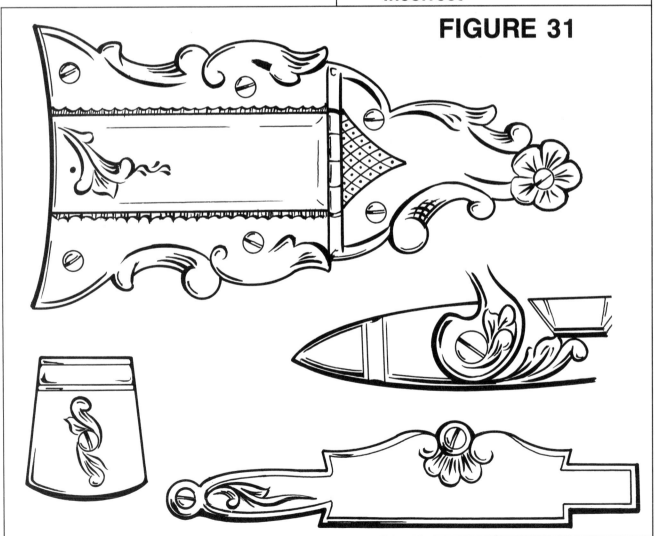

114

holds throughout the hardware we have engraved. I am using a line drawing here as we have throughout this part of the chapter to help emphasize details that might be washed out in a black and white print.

We briefly touched upon laying out your patterns before you engrave. I cannot emphasize this point enough. Now that you have some engraving skills and have spent a fair amount of time practicing various scrolls and borders, we will put some of that to use. Pick out a design or pattern that you wish to duplicate. This could be in a book, or you may have an existing piece of engraving that you'd like to copy. You will want to make a tracing of the object you are about to engrave and then sketch out the pattern on paper. This will act as a rough blueprint where you can work out many of the kinks before you put it on the metal. Remember that it is easier to erase the error on paper than to remove the engraving from the metal.

Throughout this article I have emphasized engraving upon guns, but everything that we have covered up to this point is also applicable to other objects, such as knives, gorgettes, buckles and tinder boxes. It would be a good idea to practice the pattern you have chosen on a piece of shim brass or steel. You should practice on a scrap of the same material that you are going to engrave the pattern on so you can get a feel for the metal. Different metals react differently to the chisels.

Before you can transfer the pattern, you must first prepare the metal to receive the layout. This can be done by applying a thin film of layout compound to your practice plate or the object you are going to be engraving on. Layout compound is a fast-drying fluid which is applied to the metal surface. When it is dry you can write on it with a pencil, pen or carbon. It makes drawing upon the surface a lot easier. The Ngraver Company has a nice compound that you can use, and Chinese White is another. I often take an item that is going to be cleaned up, browned or polished and scuff up the surface with 600 grit. This works quite well, too.

After you have prepared the surface of your patchbox, barrel, knife, or other item, there are two methods that you can use to transfer the pattern you are going to engrave. (One good thing about laying your entire pattern out on paper first is that you can save it for future references.) One is to simply lay the pattern next to the piece that is to be engraved and visually duplicate the design with pen or pencil. The second is to place the piece of tracing paper with your design over the item and secure it on one side with a piece of tape. Slip a piece of carbon paper under it and secure the other end, then trace over your pattern with a sharp pencil or pen, producing a carbon transfer of your pattern. After this is accomplished, remove the tracing paper and carbon. I like to go back over the tracing with a fine pencil and clean up any distortion that may have occured while tracing the pattern, as in Figure 32.

If you want to engrave a mirror image, where the right side is the same as the left side, tracing paper is an ideal way to do this (Figure 33). Take the paper and fold it in half. Draw your pattern on the tracing paper. After you have done this, turn it over and trace your pattern back through the other

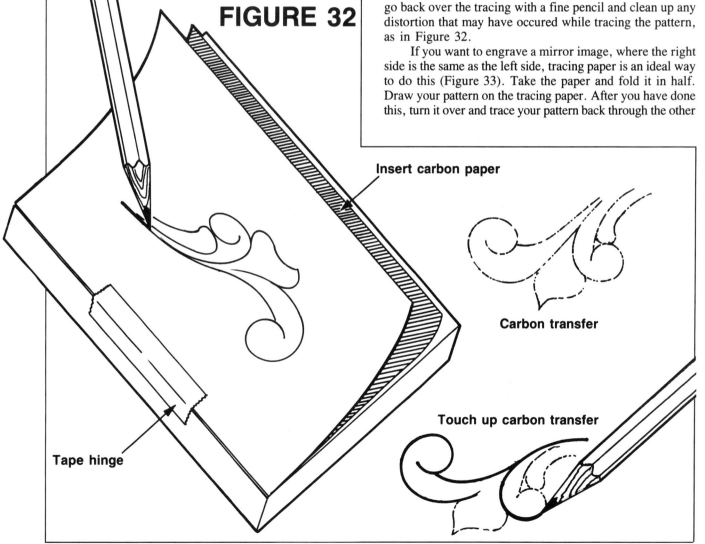

**FIGURE 32**

Insert carbon paper

Carbon transfer

Touch up carbon transfer

Tape hinge

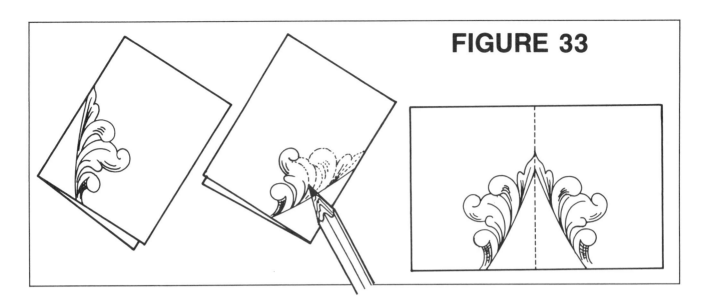

FIGURE 33

side. When you unfold it, you have a mirrored image. You can then take this and trace it on the object you are going to engrave. Keep in mind that when you engrave an item, most of your time will be spent in preparation. The actual execution may only take 20 or 30 minutes. You will find that this process will become easier with practice.

sophisticated than their execution of figures and animals. It was in the 19th century that the figures took on the more sophisticated look, close to what we have today. This is somewhat of a generalization and there are always exceptions to the rule. Figure 34 shows a typical hunting dog and hunter as engraved by an 18th century artisan. These sketches are based upon some Twigg engravings. Next to it in Figure 35 is a spaniel that is typical of 18th and 19th cen-

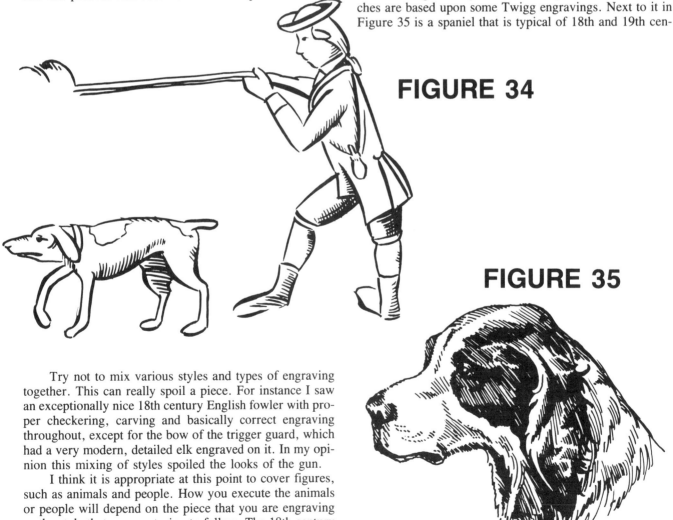

FIGURE 34

FIGURE 35

Try not to mix various styles and types of engraving together. This can really spoil a piece. For instance I saw an exceptionally nice 18th century English fowler with proper checkering, carving and basically correct engraving throughout, except for the bow of the trigger guard, which had a very modern, detailed elk engraved on it. In my opinion this mixing of styles spoiled the looks of the gun.

I think it is appropriate at this point to cover figures, such as animals and people. How you execute the animals or people will depend on the piece that you are engraving or the style that you are trying to follow. The 18th century engraving of scrolls and designs seemed much more

116

Engraving on trade silver and gorgets can range from rather sophisticated to primitive.

tury engraving. This sketch is based on an engraving by Churchill. Notice the great contrast between the two.

Primitive art is another interesting facet in engraving. This type of engraving is quite appropriate on items such as trade silver and gorgettes. The engraving on these items ranges from rather sophisticated to very primitive, almost childlike. It takes a fair amount of talent in order to execute them properly, so that they do not look forced. There is a big difference between a drawing made by a child and one by an adult trying to imitate a child. In Figure 36 are a few examples of the primitive-type engraving that you might find on trade silver. This is also very appropriate on items such as tinder boxes, necklaces and pewter.

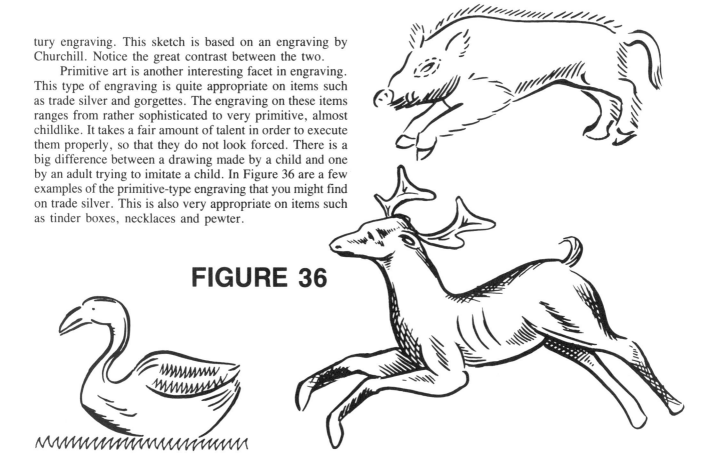

## FIGURE 36

## FIGURE 37

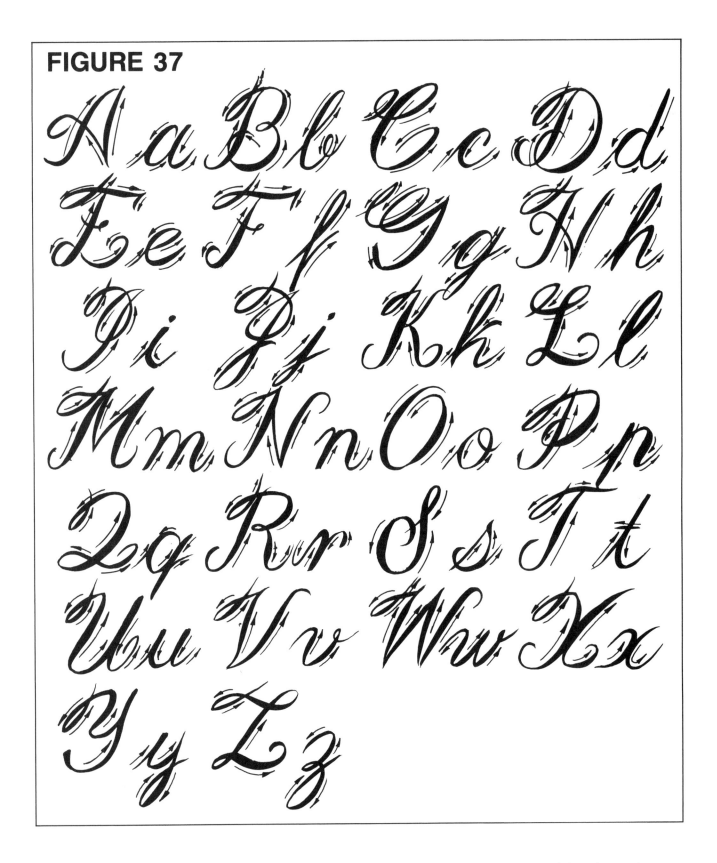

Last, but hardly least, is lettering. An entire book could be written on all the many types and styles. We are only going to discuss two very basic styles. One is script, probably one of the most popular because of its grace and beauty and for the way it compliments scroll work. The other is simple block lettering. The lettering is a somewhat stylized Caslon, an early 1700s type face which has thick and thin lines with serifs.

There is much you can do with lettering, script especially. You can elaborate the scrolls in it and decorate with the lettering as well as write. This is particularly true with monograms. However, before you write anything or make a monogram, it is important that you know how to correctly engrave the letters.

When you engrave letters, almost 90 percent of your

FIGURE 38

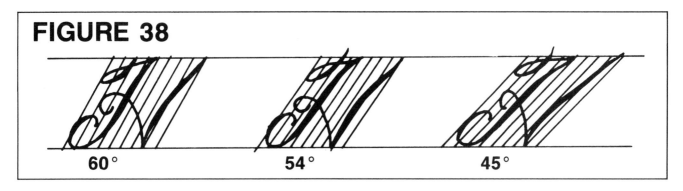

| | | |
|---|---|---|
| 60° | 54° | 45° |

engraving will be done on the upstroke. Almost every letter is a series of different cuts. What I mean is that you don't try to engrave the complete letter ''C'' or any other letter. It's a matter of executing a number of cuts properly and together they form a pleasing, flowing letter. I'm often complimented on my handwriting when I'm engraving, but when the truth is known, my writing is atrocious and at times barely legible. You should engrave lettering much the same as scrollwork. You should lay out what you are going to engrave. This will allow you to see how it will look and will

**FIGURE 40**

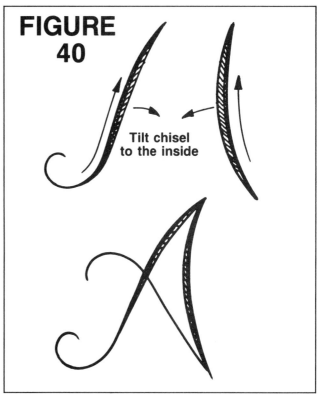

**Tilt chisel to the inside**

**FIGURE 39**

help prevent mistakes. At one time when I felt very comfortable with script, I engraved people's names on their barrels by just laying out the guidelines and not the letters. As I stated before, the letters are nothing more than a series of cuts. Once when I was concentrating more on the series of cuts I had to make than the letters, I spelled a gentleman's last name, ''Litttle.'' Needless to say, I no longer engrave letters without laying out the name correctly.

In Figure 37 I have outlined the script alphabet, both upper and lower case letters, with arrows indicating the direction your chisel should cut. Upon close examination of the letters, you can see that many are made of cuts we have previously covered. The beauty curve is one that is seen throughout most of the letters in script, particularly the upper case letters.

Script is done on an angle. The degree of the angle can vary with personal taste. I personally like a 60-degree angle. Figure 38 shows a variety of angles: 60, 54, and 45 degrees. In the book *The Art of Engraving* by James B. Meek, he suggests using a series of ovals when laying out the script to get a feel for spacing and design. In Figure 39 you can see

# FIGURE 41

study the engraving of the old masters as well as established modern engravers.

After the script (which we just barely covered), comes block lettering. The upper and lower case letters are made the same, with the exception that the lower case letters are smaller. You will find this in a lot of old and new engraving where they have used block lettering and the first letter is dominant and just a little larger. Figure 42 outlines the Caslon typeface that I like to use. The majority of the letters are straight cuts with very few curves. Almost all of the letters are accented with serifs, which are at the top or the bottom of the letter. The serif is simply executed with a quick, gouge-type cut, similar to the one we discussed earlier in the sawtooth border. One difference between laying out a phrase or a name using the block letters is that rather than using the oval-type layout illustrated in Figure 39, you mark off spaces for each letter. A standard rule is that for each letter such as ''A,'' ''B,'' ''C'' or ''D'' mark off one space. Characters like ''I'' and ''1'' take only a half space, and letters like ''W'' and ''M'' require a space and a half. This is illustrated in Figure 43. A small space separates each of the letters. This illustrates how you would lay out the word ''TIME,'' giving the letter ''I'' a half space and the ''M'' a space and a half. This method of dividing up the space for

how using the oval technique helped lay out the initials ''G.L.J.'' When cutting script letters, I like to keep the sharp edge to the outside and the more beveled cuts to the inside. Figure 40 shows that in making the first stroke of the letter ''A'' you tilt your chisel to the inside of the letter as you make the cut. The same is true when you make the second cut of the letter ''A.'' The chisel is tilted to the inside of the letter. This gives a sharp, clean definition to your lettering.

As a rule when you are engraving script lettering, there should be very little change or alteration in the characters with the possible exception of monograms. With monograms, as opposed to simply writing out one's initials, the letters entwine or lock together. This can be from very simple to extremely elaborate to the point where the letters are barely identifiable. Figure 41 shows a set of basic script initials, a set of more elaborate initials and a monogram. You will notice that in a proper monogram, the last initial is placed in the middle and is dominant, with the first initial to the left and the middle initial on the right. The area of monogramming and initialing is an area where you can display much of your personal style and technique. Remember, though, that script lettering has been around for centuries and is basically the same. You would do well to

## FIGURE 42

ABCDEF
GHIJKL
MNOPQ
RSTUV
WXYZ
123456
7890

**FIGURE 43**

the letters is useful when you are trying to center a name or phrase in a location. This rule will vary some depending on how broad you make some of the strokes and how large the serifs are. When you lay a series of letters out, also keep in mind that although each letter is given a specific space, it may need adjusting so that it will be visually pleasing to the eye. Figure 44 shows an example of letters that are laid out correctly according to the space rule, but because of the letter that is next to them, you need to do a little adjusting so that the lettering does not appear so mechanical. The lower example shows where adjustments have been made to make the letters look more balanced.

After you get a feel for spacing, lay out a line and go over the steps to engrave it. Figure 45 shows the steps I like to use when laying out the block lettering. In Figure 45 I have laid out the name I am going to engrave. This has both upper and lower case letters. Note that the upper case letters are just slightly larger than the lower case letters. I make all my primary straight and curved cuts, then my secondary cuts and finally add serifs to the letters. I like making all my serif cuts at the same time. This helps sharpen the lines and makes them more even.

Remember, this is how I engrave, and by going through the above steps, I achieve the best results for myself. When each letter is engraved separately in its entirety, I've found the results resemble the lower example in Figure 46, where the letters are not uniform in height and the line appears ragged.

One thing to keep in mind when using block lettering

**FIGURE 44**

## FIGURE 45

This figure shows the steps for engraving the letters. In A we see the letters laid out with pencil. In B the primary cuts are made with the No. 1 chisel. The secondary cuts are shown in C. Finally all the serifs are added in D.

is that the size of letters makes a difference in how you will execute them. In Figure 47 the letter ''E'' is executed two different ways depending on its size. The smaller letter ''E'' is one that you might engrave on the top flat of a barrel, a lock plate, or an inscription on a watch. The second illustrates the cuts for a larger block letter that you might use on a snuff

## FIGURE 46

KENTON

KENTON

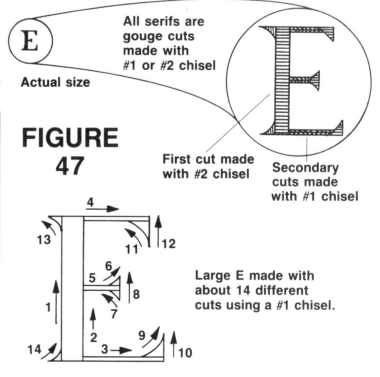

E
**Actual size**

**All serifs are gouge cuts made with #1 or #2 chisel**

## FIGURE 47

**First cut made with #2 chisel**

**Secondary cuts made with #1 chisel**

**Large E made with about 14 different cuts using a #1 chisel.**

## FIGURE 48

LOCK

*LOCK*

antique guns by Twigg and Quinn who were both English gunmakers.

In summary, remember that no matter how much you engrave you are going to make a mistake now and then. Everyone does. One thing that separates the masters from the amateurs is the masters' ability to disguise the errors they make.

I remember once while I was engraving at a rendezvous, a young lad about eight or nine years old watched me for hours. My first "groupie," I thought at the time. I thought I had impressed him. After a few hours of observation, his parents came to take him back to their camp, but he quickly objected. "No, I want to see him make a mistake." I went from a hero to a bum just like that.

I am often asked, "What do you do when you make a mistake?" My answer to that is, "I simply change my design." The key to this is to carefully lay out your pattern and pay close attention to what you are doing. You will find that the errors and mistakes will be fewer and smaller. I have

## FIGURE 49

*Twigg* LONDON

*TWIGG* LONDON

box, buckle, patch box or gorgette. On these large letters, the serifs are engraved using a number of line cuts rather than a quick gouge cut. You can also enhance these letters by shading or filling in the body with crosshatching or even walking engraving.

You can italicize this block lettering by engraving at an angle similar to script lettering. A 60-degree angle is again what I prefer. Figure 48 shows a word in plain block and one that is in italics. For example a maker might put his name in italics and the place the gun was made in plain block. You can also mix script and block in the same manner. Figure 49 shows two examples. These have been taken from various

yet to lay out a fair-sized design where I haven't had to alter a pattern to compensate for a small error. Should you make a mistake, do not panic but carefully go over the options to correct the mistake.

You have probably noticed that I have used numerous figures and examples as instruction in this chapter. You will find that in engraving "A picture is worth a thousand words," as the saying goes. Even after you get a feel for making the different cuts, you must still study examples of engraving. I strongly urge you to purchase the book *The Art of Engraving* by James E. Meek, which gives you more detail on the topics I have just briefly outlined for you.

**On the ride** into the 1988 Western Rendezvous, time is taken to water the horses at a mountain stream. Bob Schmidt and Tom Bryant's chapter beginning on page 229 explains how to build the pack saddles and panniers needed for extended horseback trips. Also see page VIII of the color section for more horseback travel scenes.

I

II

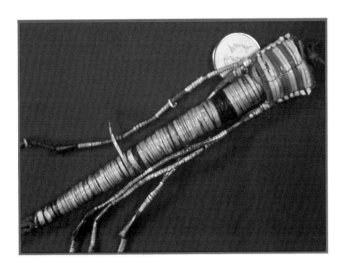

*Facing Page:* **A Cree** side-fold dress in the Ottawa National Museum of Man. Intricate bands of quill-wrapped fringe decorate the yoke, sleeve and bottom. *Clockwise from top left:* **A Mandan/Hidatsa** bird-quilled awl case from the American Museum of Natural History. **A Blackfoot** dress from the Ottawa National Museum of Man. The yoke was rubbed with yellow ochre. Note the triangular motif in the enter of the dress. **Mountain man** clothing and equipment used and traded at rendezvous: Indian-made buckskin jacket, Standish beaver trap, Hawken rifle, quilled possibles bag and pack saddle.

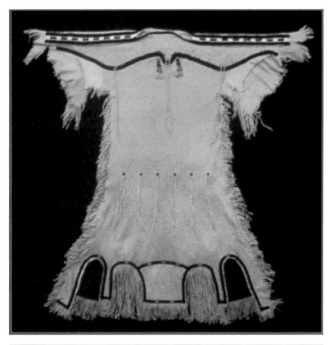

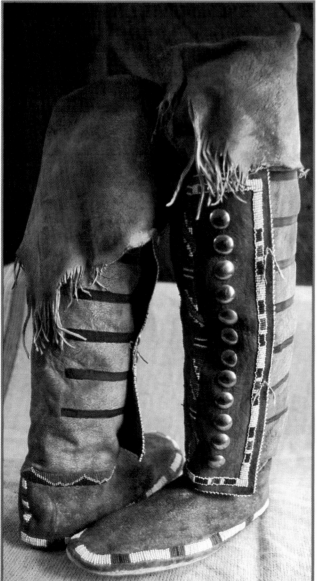

IV

*Facing Page - clockwise from lower left:* **Southern Plains** boots with blue coup stripes painted on a verdigris-rubbed background. The boots are trimmed with silver buttoms and one-lane-wide beadwork. Made by Cathy Smith. **An Upper Missouri** two-hide dress made by Cathy Smith. It has blue and white pony beadwork and deep crescent cutouts with wool plugs. **A Plains Cree** moccasin from the American Museum of Natural History. It has a quilled, tongue-shaped design on top of the foot. **An Oglala woman's** belt from the American Museum of Natural History. This soft-tanned buffalo belt is beaded and quilled at each end. The V-shaped, beaded and quilled pouch in the center is attached to the belt. *Above:* **An Upper Missouri** dress with quilled shoulder strips and deep crescent plugs on the bottom contour. Also shown are quilled ''keyhole'' moccasins and a quilled bag made by Cathy Smith.

VI

*Facing Page:* **A Southern Plains** poncho and skirt made and modelled by Cathy Smith. The decoration includes partial painting with yellow and red ochre, old peso buttons, tin cones and twisted fringe.

*Clockwise from top right:* **An Apache** awl case decorated with beadwork and tin cones from a private collection. **An Oglala** quilled legging from the American Museum of Natural History. **Two pairs** of quilled ''keyhole'' moccasins of side-seam constructon and a porcupine-tail hairbrush made by Cathy Smith. **Cheyenne** three-hide dress made by Cathy Smith. The yoke is rubbed with yellow ochre, the bottom with vermilion.

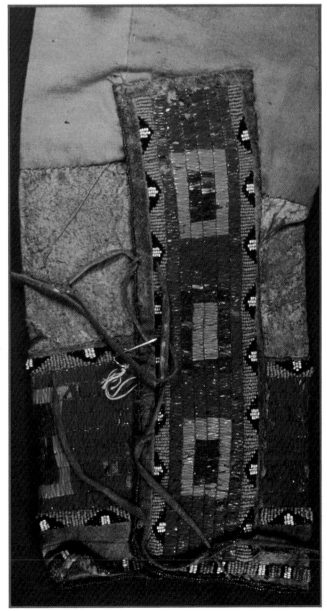

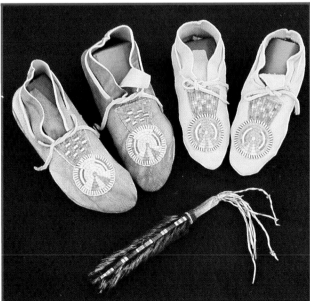

VIII

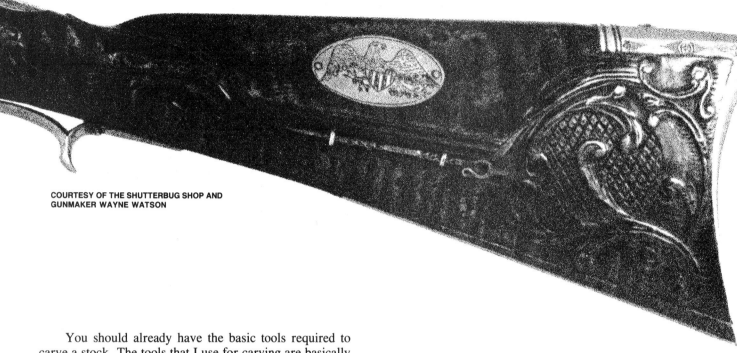

**COURTESY OF THE SHUTTERBUG SHOP AND
GUNMAKER WAYNE WATSON**

You should already have the basic tools required to carve a stock. The tools that I use for carving are basically the same ones that I use to build a rifle, except for a set of small vinyl palm chisels. I like using the small vinyl chisels, which may be purchased at any good art or office supply outlet. I find these chisels ideal for getting into small areas and executing fine detail in the carving. Figure 50 shows the tools. The palm chisels are in the upper left corner. Another set of tools that I find extremely useful is the rifle files that are in the upper right of the print. These I bought from Dixie Gun Works a number of years ago, and I understand that they still have them for sale.

When carving, the steps are basically the same as those discussed in engraving: lay out and design, use the correct tools, and execute the design.

### THE LAYOUT

It is essential to have a clean, geometrically sound, symmetrical rifle. When laying out a design on a rifle, I like to mark out grids on the breech tang, entry thimble and around the wrist, and unless the gun is symmetrically correct, this technique will not work. The layout will look uneven and not as clean or professional as you would like it to be. In Figure 51 you see both sides of a clean, symmetrical rifle that is ready for carving.

You are ready to lay out your design and carve after the gun is basically finished. You should have it all shaped and sanded down to a 120 finish. As you can see in the illustrations, if you were not going to carve the rifle, it would be complete following the final sanding and staining and browning.

Once again, go back to your books and study them before you attempt to do any carving. Get a good feel for

# FIGURE 50

**FIGURE 51**

the type and style of carving that is appropriate for your rifle. The rifle that I am going to use as an example is an Allentown-Bethlehem style. All of the designs that we will be laying out on this gun I have taken from originals and they are appropriate for this piece and time period. I prefer George Shumway's books for reference on carving and engraving because they show many more detailed pictures and give more dimensions than other books often do.

After you have chosen the carving that is appropriate for your rifle, it is time to start laying the design out on your rifle. What we will be doing on this rifle may be a little more elaborate than what you may wish to attempt, but the principles are the same with the relief and incised carving. Figure 52 shows a design behind the cheekpiece which I'll be carving into this rifle. It is very similar to a design that I have used on some of the Grand Rifles that Jack Garner and I produced. Figure 53 is a design that is much simpler than what I will demonstrate. This style of relief is one that I refer to as primitive, because it does not have the form or detail the other design has. But as stated before, if you choose a design as simple as this, the principles as far as layout and execution are the same.

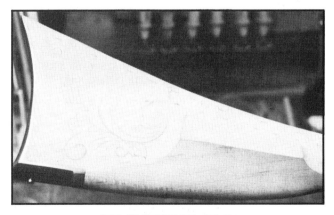

**FIGURE 52**

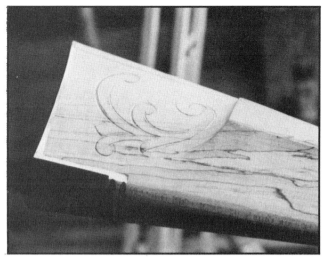

# FIGURE 53

As you will notice in Figure 52, I have also laid out a few hash marks along the belly of the butt and below the cheekpiece. These indicate the spots where I will lay out the molding in each of the areas. The molding that runs along the belly of the butt of this stock usually tapers as it runs from the butt to the wrist. Sometimes it is a straight line, but on most of the originals I've examined, the molding tapers toward the wrist. The molding that is underneath the cheekpiece should either run parallel to the belly molding or taper toward the belly molding as it runs toward the wrist. In Figure 54 you can see where I have connected the lines and finished the molding along the butt. Figure 55 is an example of correct and incorrect lines.

# FIGURE 54

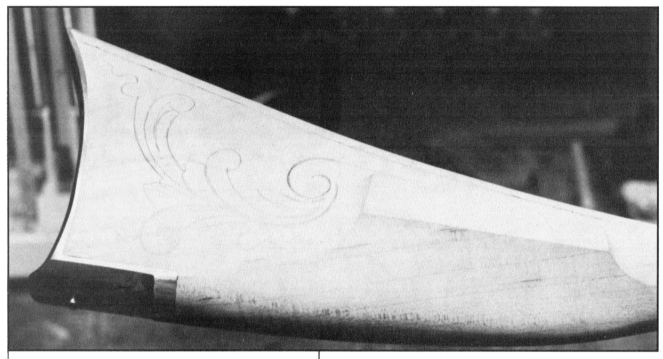

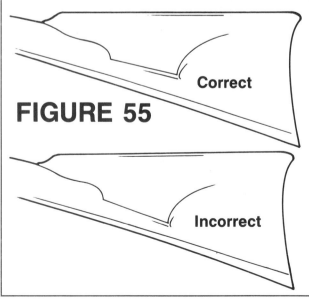

Correct

## FIGURE 55

Incorrect

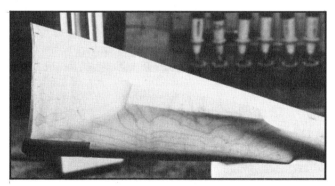

## FIGURE 56

One thing to keep in mind with a curved butt, such as in the Bethlehem school in a Verner-style rifle as an example, is that you will need to measure off more hash marks in order to get a smooth line for your molding. Figure 56 shows a Lancaster-style rifle with just a few hash marks on it. When you have a straight belly, such as in the Lancaster school, you may not need to make any more lines than just at the beginning near the wrist and at the end near the butt. Then lay a straight edge down on the two lines and connect them.

In Figure 57 you can see where I have finished the molding along the belly of the butt. I have also laid out a design to finish off the molding under the cheekpiece, which I brought up into the wrist and around the nose of the comb. Also notice in the illustration that I took a line off of one of the lock panels and ran it down the wrist towards the butt. From this line I have taken a series of measurements and marked out a small grid which we will use for laying out the beaver tail on the molding around the lock panels. Using a grid is one instance when it is very critical that your rifle be symmetrical. Otherwise, the designs will not turn out the same. I like to have the beaver tails flow into the wrist and not up toward the comb or into the belly. This makes the lines of the rifle nicer.

## FIGURE 58

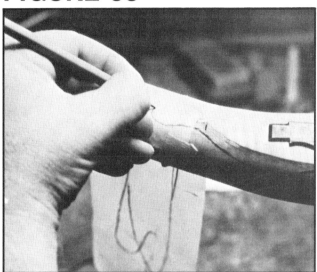

## FIGURE 57

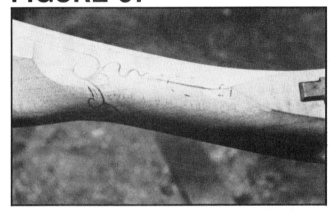

At this point we are going to use a little trick similar to one I described in the engraving portion of this chapter, where you take a piece of tracing paper and lay it over a design to transfer it to another portion of the rifle. In Figure 58 I have finished sketching out the molding on one side of the rifle and have laid a piece of tracing paper over it, se-

## FIGURE 59

## FIGURE 60

curing it with masking tape. After you have traced it, remove the tracing paper and go over the traced lines with a soft lead pencil, preferably an HB, but you should not use anything harder than a number 2. Darkening the lines should be done on a flat hard surface so you do not damage the tracing. The next step is to turn the rifle over, as seen in Figure 59, and lay out a grid on the opposite lock panel, using measurements identical to the other side. Then turn the tracing paper over so the tracing is face down. Lay the beaver tail traced from the opposite side of the rifle over the grid of the lock side and be sure your drawing is against the wood. Line it up with the grid that we have marked off from the other side of the rifle and secure it with masking tape. Take a hard, sharp pencil and trace over it. Remove the tracing paper, then go back over the beaver tail, darken it in and smooth out the lines.

Transferring the design by using tracing paper is a technique I have found to be very helpful when you are duplicating a design from one side of the rifle to the other, such as the breech tang, beaver tails and the molding near the entry thimble. However, the areas where you use this method should be relatively flat and without curves.

After I finish the beaver tails, I like to complete the molding along the belly on the lock side. In Figure 60 you will notice the belly has a series of hash marks across the bottom. I have taken the measurement from the other side where the molding exists. Just above the hash mark, make a mark identical in depth to the molding on the opposite side. After that it is just a matter of connecting the dots. Once again, I stress the fact that on a curved butt, you must make more hash marks to ensure smooth matching molding lines.

After the beaver tail and molding has been drawn on both sides of the rifle, I like to lay out the carving that will be on the lock side of the wrist. The reason for putting the beaver tail and the molding on is to see how much room I have to work with and what designs will look well in the limited area. Often the carving that is on the wrist, other than the beaver tails, is similar on both sides but not the same. This is because of the interference of the cheekpiece and the patchbox. Figure 61 shows a series of carvings taken from different original rifles which illustrates how the carving can be similar though not identical on both sides of the wrist and still compliment each other. I have copied, using the tracing paper method, the design on the cheekpiece side of the ri-

# FIGURE 61

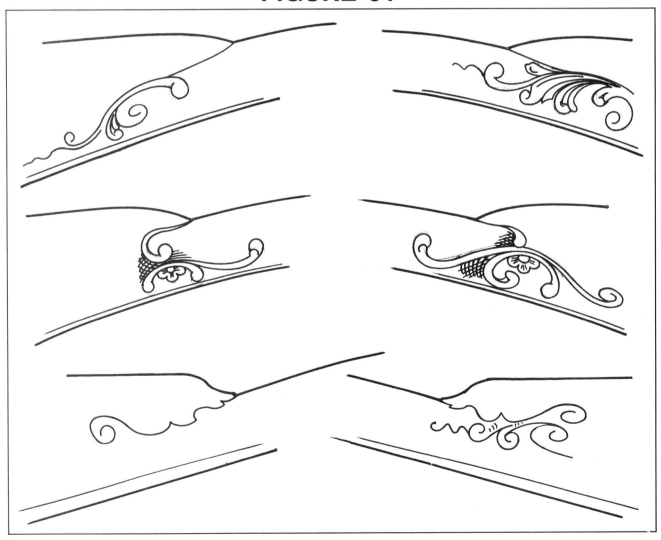

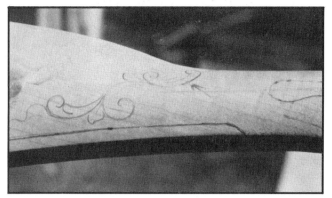

## FIGURE 62

## FIGURE 63

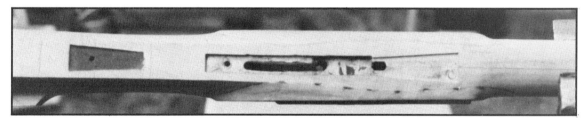

## FIGURE 64

of the shape of the panel I have used a lot of measurements, and it takes very little at this point to run a line between the hash marks. You would use the same method as we used for the beaver tail to complete the front of the lock molding.

The last area around the lock panels and breech is the breech tang. In Figure 65 I have laid out a design that has a floral pattern directly behind the tang. This area will be relieved, and the molding that goes around the lock panels that runs up into the pattern will become incised lines. This is an excellent place to use the transfer method with tracing paper. Figure 66 is an example of a different style where the tang is accented by elaborate incised carving. The molding and beaver tails around the lock panels are basically the same but fade into the incised carving. These are just

fle. In Figure 62 you will see the carving is now all laid out and an arrow points to a portion of the design. This arrow indicates that from this point up is a mirror image of the opposite side and from there down I have elaborated on the design.

From this point, I move back up the lock panel and finish laying out the design for my lock molding. If you have done the studying that I suggested, you will have found that there is a wide variety of lock moldings, depending on the school, and even within the various schools the moldings vary a great deal. In Figure 63 I have chosen what I consider a pleasing molding that has a slight flare at the rear and the front of the lock panel. After laying out the molding completely on one side, you may use a couple of methods in transferring the design to the opposite side of the rifle. In Figure 64 you see the bottom of the rifle with the measurements taken from one side and marked on the other. This is using the grid method. You will notice that because

## FIGURE 65

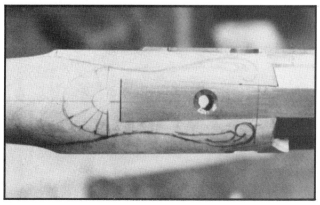

two examples of many styles or patterns that you can use around this area of the rifle.

The final area that we need to lay out on this rifle is the molding that runs along the ramrod channel and entry thimble. It is very important that you make sure your ramrod channel runs straight and true so that the molding along the ramrod channel will look correct. The molding should run parallel with the channel. As a rule I run a line that is anywhere from ¼'' to ⅜'', although it can even be wider

**FIGURE 67**

depending upon the school of the rifle. On this particular piece, the molding is just a little over ¼''. The principles of laying this out are essentially the same as laying out the molding on the butt of the stock. As the molding comes into the area of the entry thimble on this piece, it takes a very gradual slope upwards and flows into a C-scroll with a pigtail or vine in front of the rear wedge plate (Figure 67). The entry thimble area is an ideal area for using the tracing paper method to duplicate the C-scroll design on both sides.

We have now basically laid out all the patterns that we

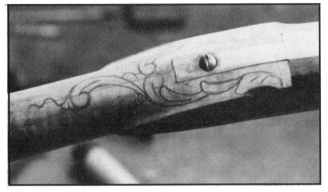

**FIGURE 66**

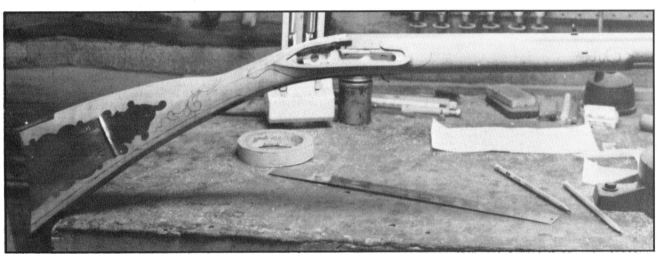

**FIGURE 68**

**FIGURE 69**

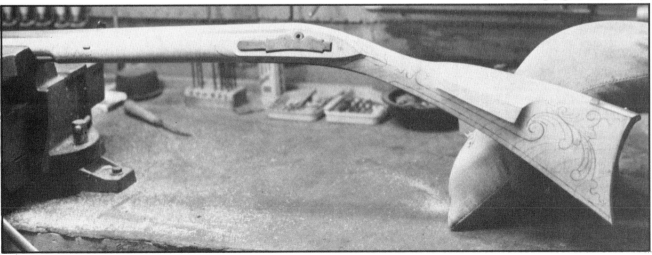

are going to carve into the stock. You can see both sides of the rifle in Figures 68 and 69. It would be good at this time to set the rifle aside and study what you have laid out to make sure you are happy and pleased with the design. It is much easier to erase a pencil line at this point and change your design than it is after you cut into the stock. I might suggest that before you cut into your rifle you pick up an inexpensive full or half stock to practice carving the designs that you've laid out on your rifle.

## EXECUTION

It is now time to execute the design. I usually start at the back of the rifle around the butt area and work my way up to the nose cap. The first step I take is to go through all my carving and cut an incised line that will accent the relieved carving. This incised carving will later be removed for the most part when you relieve your design. There is an important reason for doing this, although at first it might sound crazy to cut a lot of lines that will wind up as sawdust and chips on the floor. First, it gives you a feel for the wood that is in your stock. Each stock is different. Even two stocks that come from the same tree can vary. This is testing the waters, so to speak. Second, this gives you a chance to change your design if need be and to decide how you will approach the design in various spots of the rifle. Just as various metals react differently to a given chisel, so does

wood.

As mentioned I like to cut all my incised lines first and my lines for relief second. As a rule when I relieve I cut on the outside of the pencil line (Figure 70), otherwise your design may turn out smaller than you had originally laid out. In incised carving I straddle the pencil line with both sides of the veiner.

If you are making a good even cut when cutting the incised line around your pattern and the moldings, you should have the wood curl up in front of the chisel so that it resembles a small coil or the spring out of a ball point pen. This may not always be the case, especially when cutting across the grain, but it often indicates whether you are making a good even cut. If the stock is soft, the wood might have a tendency to tear when cutting across the grain no matter how sharp the chisel is. One trick I like to use is to moisten the surface of the stock slightly with a cotton ball as though you were going to whisker the stock. This helps to make a cleaner cut and prevents the wood from tearing or chipping. However, when you do this you quite often have to go back and repeat the cuts to clean them up and make them a uniform depth. You want to be rather sparing with the water. You apply it first, let it sit for a few seconds and then make your cuts. You shouldn't put too much water on, and if you do it correctly, it really doesn't add any moisture to the stock and is no worse than whiskering it.

In Figure 71 you will notice a series of little crosses around the design that I have laid out. These indicate the

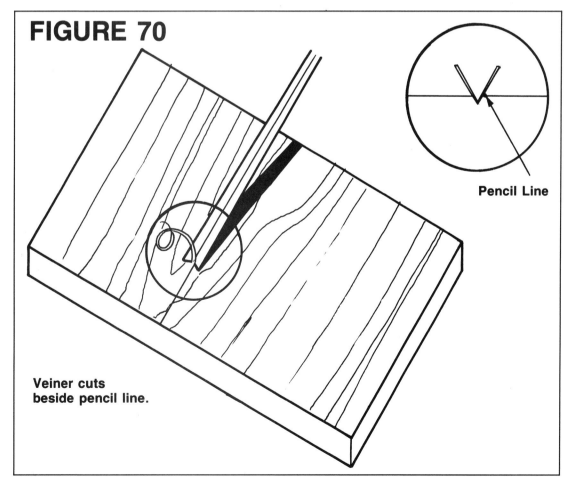

**FIGURE 70**

**Pencil Line**

**Veiner cuts beside pencil line.**

## FIGURE 71

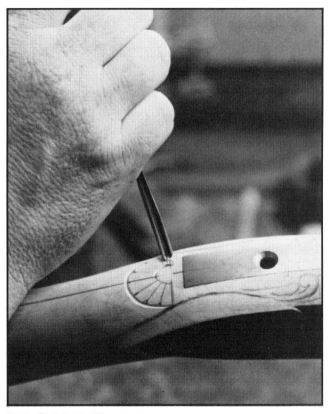

## FIGURE 72

places where I will relieve the wood from the pattern and where the relief carving will fade into an incised line as well. Use your large veiner to cut an incised line around the outside of your pattern behind the cheekpiece, being sure the inside blade of your chisel is next to the pencil line. One thing I want to mention here is that when you are cutting a design that has two incised lines that meet and form a right angle (Figure 72), it is important that you cut towards the corner and not away from it in order to achieve a sharp angle. Otherwise, you may produce a small dimple or flaw in your pattern (Figure 73).

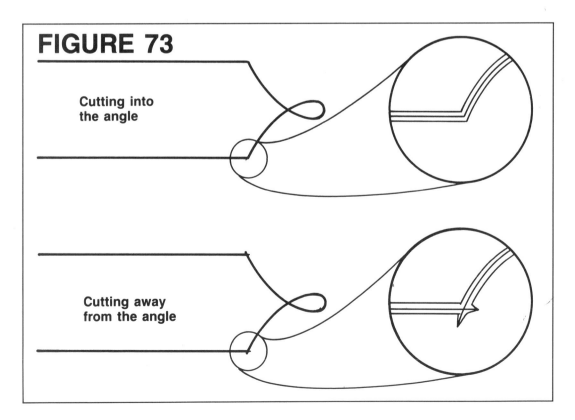

## FIGURE 73

Cutting into
the angle

Cutting away
from the angle

After you have made your cuts, you should still be able to see some of the pencil line. Repeat this process around the wrist, breech tang and lock moldings. However, cutting the lines for the moldings is one time that you would make the cut the same way even if the line is to be relieved or remain incised. Laying one side of the veiner against the pencil line will help to keep you from making a cut that is wavy. How you handle it after you have made the initial cut with the veiner will depend on whether it is to remain an incised line or become a relieved molding.

After you have gone all around the carving cutting an incised line, start relieving the wood around the pattern. Using a flat bent chisel, go around the places that we have marked off with Xs and make a small bevel cut around the outside of the design. When you are removing wood, it is very important to pay attention to the direction the grain flows in your stock. If you try to chisel against the grain or into it, you run a great risk of chipping or marring the wood and creating flaws that are hard to remove. Figure 74 illustrates the proper way to cut with the grain. Notice in the figure that the grain almost looks like arrows pointing the direction that you should cut. Ninety percent of the stocks that I have carved I have chiseled from the buttplate into the relieved carving behind the cheekpiece and carved from behind the cheekpiece down into the relief carving. Curly maple is notorious for chipping and flaking and having grain which switches back and forth on you. You might find it useful when cutting a bevel around your relief carving or

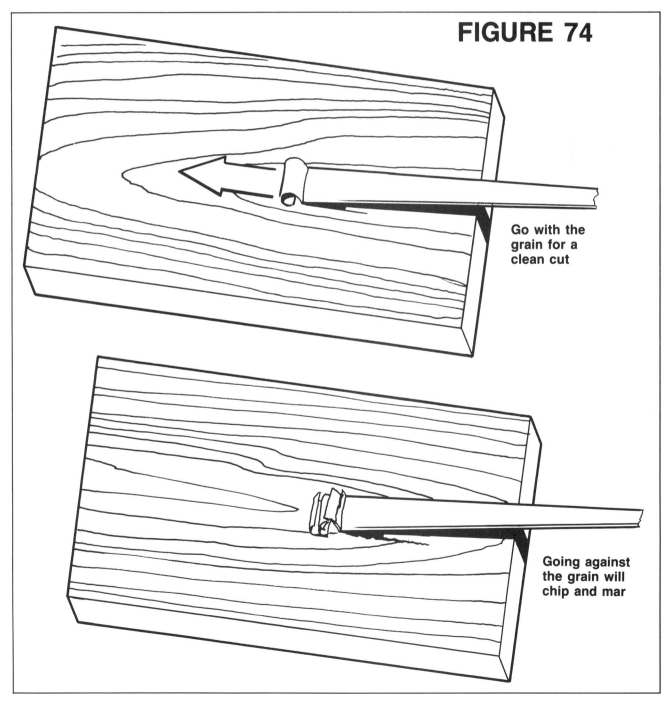

**FIGURE 74**

Go with the grain for a clean cut

Going against the grain will chip and mar

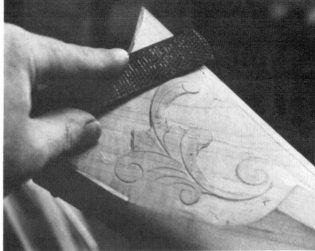

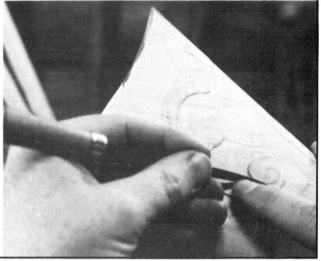

# FIGURE 75

A fine, flat riffle file (top left) is good for working the inside of the patterns. A large, rough combination file (top right) is good for removing a lot of wood fast. Use it on the easy-to-reach areas where great detail is not necessary. A tapered, V-shaped riffle (right) is excellent for tapering relief carving into incised carving.

when cutting across the grain to lightly moisten the wood as mentioned before. Then make a number of very light cuts, rather than trying to cut to the proper depth all at one time.

Figure 75 shows various rasps I use to remove the majority of the wood around the carving. I use anything from a rough bastard file to a number of fine riffle files, depending on whether I am blocking or fading the relief around the design. A crosscut section, Figure 76, illustrates the four steps in relieving a pattern around a stem: lay out the design, cut an incised line around the pattern, make a bevel cut around the incised carving, and remove the excess wood around the pattern using rasps. After you have blocked out and relieved your pattern, clean up the design with your sharp pointed chisel in areas you were unable to get to with your flat chisel and files.

In tight areas where the files can't reach, you can relieve the pattern with a sharp-pointed palm chisel.

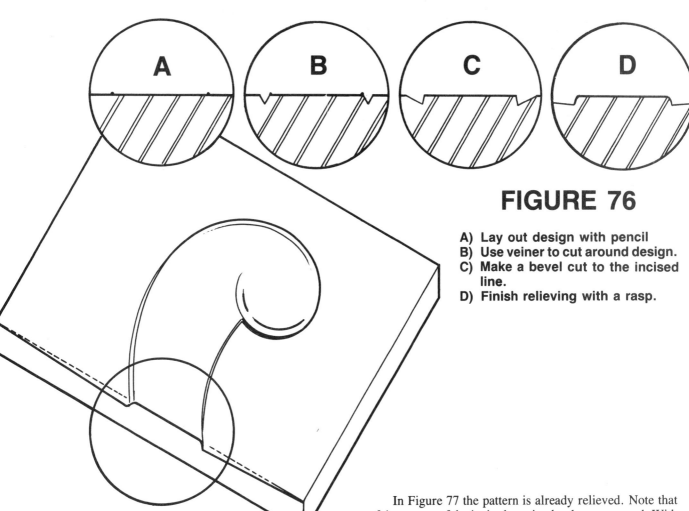

## FIGURE 76

A) Lay out design with pencil
B) Use veiner to cut around design.
C) Make a bevel cut to the incised line.
D) Finish relieving with a rasp.

# FIGURE 77

In Figure 77 the pattern is already relieved. Note that a fair amount of the incised carving has been removed. With a pencil, sketch the lines that were incised back onto the stock. This is as much detail as I put into the relief carving at this point.

After you have blocked out and relieved your basic design behind the cheekpiece, the next spot that I like to take care of is the molding. Up to this point, the molding has been left as an incised line. The next step is to straighten the line out, eliminating any slight waves that might have occurred. This can be done by running a three-cornered riffle file back and forth briskly, as shown in Figure 78. This makes your cut uniform in both depth and width. On a curved stock or butt like the one on which we are working, it is necessary

## FIGURE 78

**FIGURE 79**

to use a bent or riffle file. However, if you have a straight butt, such as a Lancaster style, you could use a long bastard or "V" type file. Figure 79 shows me straightening the incised line of a Lancaster. Note in this illustration that I do not use the full length of the file. Because of the short length of the incised line, it is wiser to use the front portion of the rasp. You would use the entire length of the rasp for the molding along the ramrod channel.

Whether the molding will remain an incised line or will be relieved is determined by the way you hold your rasps. For a relieved molding, using a half-round file, hold the flat surface of the file at a 90° angle to the wood. For an incised line, use only a 3-cornered file. Figure 80 is a cross section of both types of molding lines made with the files.

On this particular rifle, we will be relieving the molding

**FIGURE 80**

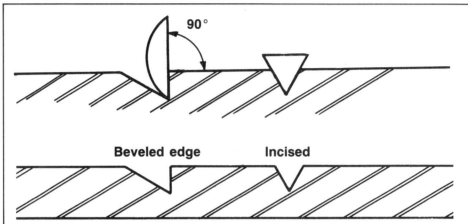

**FIGURE 81**

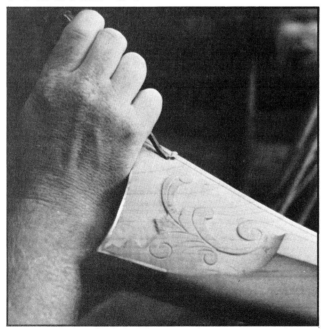

line. The next step is to finish with the flat bent chisel the bevel we started with the rasp (Figure 81). Note that on the patch box side you cut in the direction opposite from the direction on the cheekpiece side, as shown in Figure 82. This is because of the way the grain flows through the butt of the stock. Because of the taper from the butt plate to the wrist, it is uncommon in this area to cut in two different directions for your molding. But along the ramrod channel where you have a long, narrow piece of wood it is rather common. On occasion I have had to change the direction that I am cutting along the ramrod channel as many as three or four different times on one side. I will cover moldings in more detail later on

**FIGURE 82**

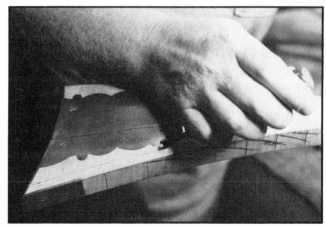

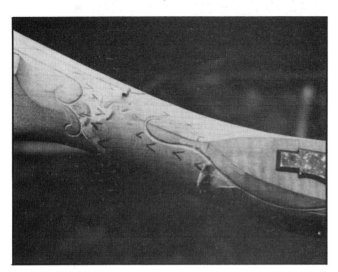

**FIGURE 83**

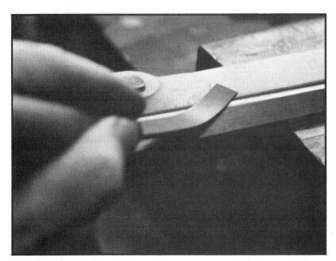

**FIGURE 84**

in the chapter. But for now finish off the bevel with a fine flat or riffle file.

Moving up into the wrist area, repeat basically the same process we followed behind the cheekpiece. The first step is to cut around your design with an incised line and then make the same beveled cuts outlined previously. In Figure 83 you see the wrist area where I have begun to make the beveled cuts into the moldings and design with the flat chisel. I have drawn a series of arrows showing you the direction that you should chase the chisel to make the initial bevel cuts. Notice how the direction changes because of the angle of the wood in various portions of the wrist. This is a difficult area to carve on a rifle, not only because of the way the grain grows but also because of the angle that you have cut the stock out of the wood. There are times that you will think you are cutting into the grain, but because of the dramatic slope, you are actually making more of a crossgrain cut, as at the top of the wrist. Once again, make shallow cuts to be sure you are cutting in the right direction. It may be a good idea to use your file rather than your chisels in some delicate areas. Figure 84 shows one area, the front of your lock molding, where this is advisable.

After you have made the beveled cuts around your lock moldings on both sides of the wrist, the next step is to remove the wood evenly from the wrist area using rasps. Your relieved carving should be raised slightly above and should not dish into the wrist area. Figure 85 shows the carving that comes down from the cheekpiece to the wrist and the beaver tail that is behind the lock mortice. The dotted line represents the original surface of the wrist. You don't have to remove a lot of wood here, but it helps define your carving.

On this rifle we are going to block out and relieve along the ramrod channel. This is done in the same manner as the molding on the butt of the rifle. It is not necessary to go into great detail or repeat what has already been explained, other than to mention that the molding should diminish and taper as it comes into the C-scroll and form an incised line.

Now that all the carving has been blocked out and relieved throughout the rifle, sand the entire stock down to

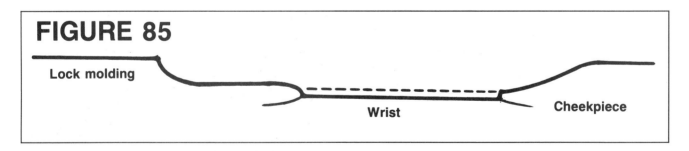

**FIGURE 85**

Lock molding

Wrist

Cheekpiece

a 220 finish. During this sanding you should eliminate all the scratches and flaws around the carving throughout the entire stock. By not putting any of the detail into the carving up to this point, we eliminate the danger of sanding out any of the fine relief carving. An ideal tool for sanding around the relief carving that you have blocked out and to get into the tight little corners is an emery board. These usually come with a 120 grit on one side and about a 220 grit on the other side. They may be cut into different shapes and bent in order to sand the small difficult areas and corners around the relief carving that otherwise are difficult to do with your fingers.

Now that the stock has been sanded down to a clean

## FIGURE 86

220 throughout, I go back and start to put the detail into the carving. I usually start with the molding along the butt and the ramrod channel and any decorative scallops that might be on the cheekpiece, which up to this point has remained a simple relieved molding. Figure 86 shows the belly of the rifle, where I have drawn two pencil lines. Within these two lines I am going to put a small scallop or dish, making a more decorative relieved molding. The same process that we use here you would also use along the ramrod channel. These molding lines are straight and not tapered. The first step is tó take a small round chisel and, making sure that you are going with the grain, cut a small round line within the pencil lines the length of the molding on the butt of the stock (Figure 87).

Next take a round riffle file and run it back and forth in the scallop that you just cut to even up the sides and the depth. This molding should be cut into the butt plate as well (Figure 88). These are almost the same steps you used to straighten up the incised line for the molding. Take a piece of sandpaper, wrap it around the end of a tapered dowel or pencil, depending on the size of the scallop you have made, and run it back and forth along the molding in the same manner as you did the file. Do not use your fingers because this

## FIGURE 87

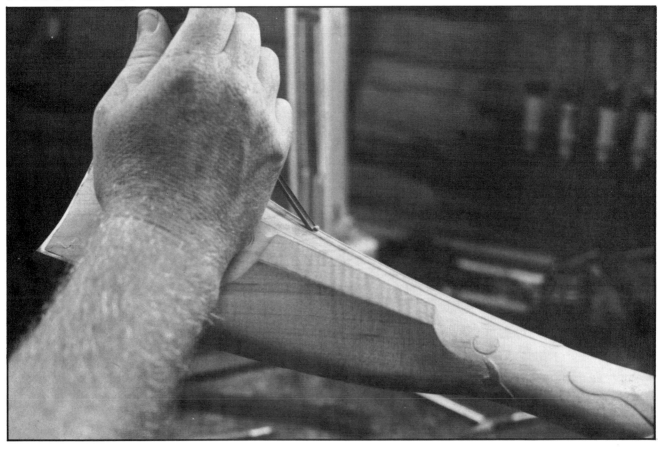

will give you an uneven line and ruin the sharp edges of the scallops. Start out with a 120 grit and then go down to a 360 grit.

Now that you have a feel for developing a straight molding, the next step is to create a tapered molding where one end is wider and heavier than the other end. On this particular rifle, we will be doing this on the cheekpiece. Sketch out a pattern, as in Figure 89, that your scallop will follow. In this picture you can see the pattern roll up and then dip down in a sort of S-shape. Draw the two outside lines first, then a third line that bisects the S-curve. After you have done that, take your veiner and cut along the top line. The cheekpiece will flow down into a large incised line, where the scallop will take over. Take a large half-round bastard file and run it back and forth, first to straighten the line out and then to begin rounding the top of the scallop on the cheekpiece. In Figure 90 the incised line has been made and I am in the process of straightening the incised line and developing the scallop. Now take a small round chisel and make a series of cuts on the bottom part of the scallop. These cuts should taper to a point at the front of the cheekpiece. Figure 91 shows the beginning of this, and Figure 92 shows a diagram of the various cuts that you make to achieve this.

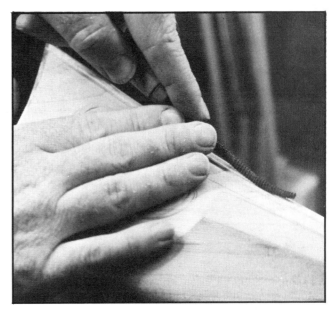

## FIGURE 88

## FIGURE 89

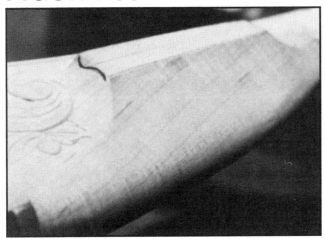

## FIGURE 90

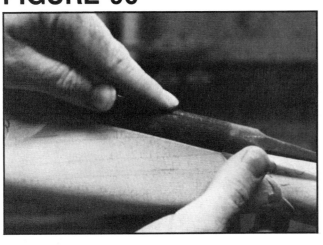

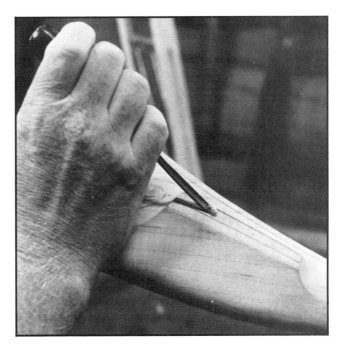

## FIGURE 91

# FIGURE 92

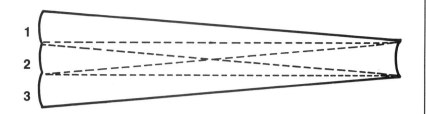

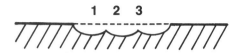

**The cuts made with the round chisel will overlap at the front of the cheekpiece.**

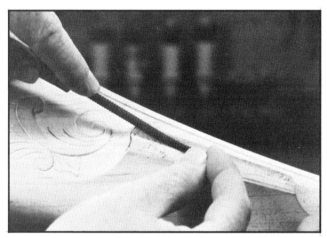

# FIGURE 93

In Figure 93 I am beginning to smooth out the concave part of the scallop. This is achieved with your riffle file. Lay the file down in the scallop at an angle, and as you rasp forward, you straighten the rasp out so that it runs parallel with the cheekpiece. Figure 94 shows the beginning and ending angle of the file. From this point it is just a matter of rolling and rounding the top portion of the scallop and dishing the bottom part to where it has an even S-type flow. After you have it roughly shaped and formed using the files, sand it

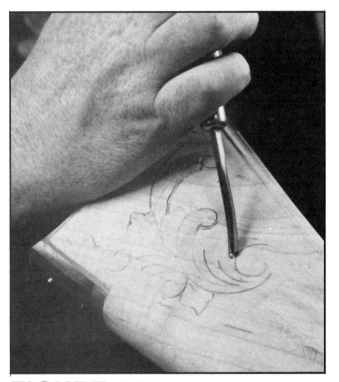

# FIGURE 95

down to a 360 finish.

We are ready to begin the detailed carving behind the cheekpiece. Figure 95 shows the completed cheekpiece with the scallop and the relief carving that we have blocked out.

# FIGURE 94

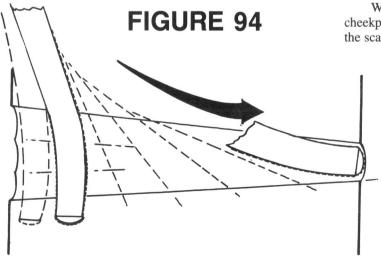

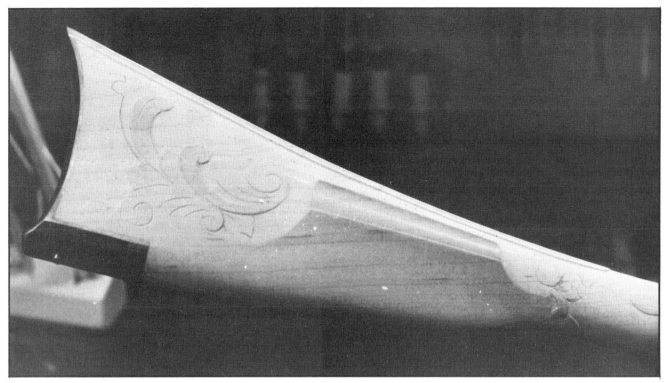

# FIGURE 96

I have drawn in all the incised lines that I had previously removed when I blocked out the relief carving. I have also gone back over the relief carving that was blocked out and have redrawn the edges of some of the scrolls that were damaged while relieving them. I am using the large veiner, laid on its side at a 90 degree angle, to clean up the edges of the pattern, making the scrolls round again where they might have been flattened. In Figure 96 you can see that

I have cleaned all the edges of our relief carving and have recut the incised lines.

Figure 97 shows that I have marked small Xs in the areas where I will tuck or bevel the existing pattern into or behind the other leaves or stems. This is done with a sharp pointed palm chisel. You should go very slowly, trying to take small cuts as I have stressed before, and make a very slight bevel so that it appears that the leaf flows from behind the other. I have crosshatched the parts of the leaves, illustrated in Figure 98, that will be dished. I did not draw

# FIGURE 97

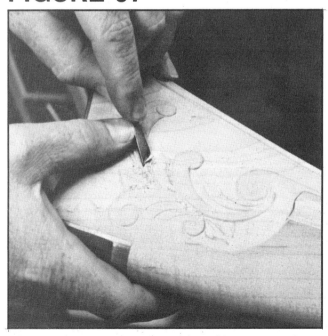

# FIGURE 98

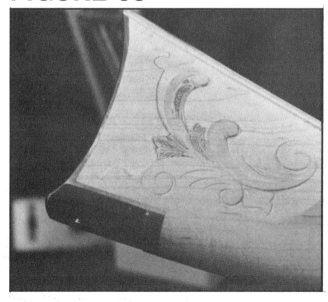

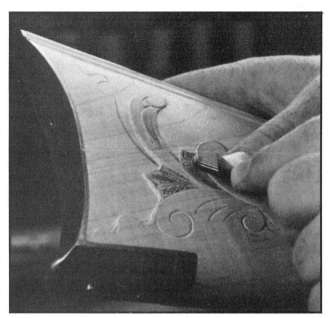

**FIGURE 99**

**FIGURE 100**

Through practice, you may come to prefer one chisel over another. After the concave sections of the leaves have been rounded out, smooth them with sandpaper. Most of the sculpting of your leaves and detailed carving is actually done with sandpaper as well as the small palm chisels. I use sandpaper folded over and pushed down using my thumbnail to get into the tight areas of the leaves as shown in Figure 101. I never trim my thumbnails; I let them grow to use them for wrapping sandpaper around to get into the tight spots. In Figure 102 I have wrapped sandpaper around a popsicle stick. You may use a small dowel or pencil tip, anything that will take the shape of the stem or the flower and sand the dish out smoothly. You also should round the edges of the stems

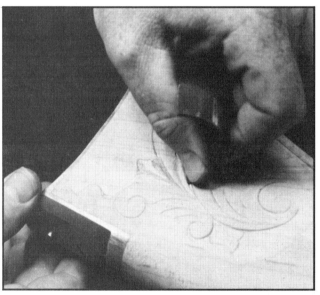

**FIGURE 101**

this crosshatching only for your benefit. When I'm carving, I draw on the stock where the carving will be dished and raised.

After you have determined which areas should be recessed, make a series of small cuts with a very small round palm chisel to dish out the areas. Usually the very small chisels work well if you rock them back and forth slightly as you make your cut. This is very similar to the cuts that we made in the cheekpiece, in which you used a smaller chisel than the area that you are carving out and made a series of small cuts that flow together into one (Figure 99).

In Figure 100 I am using a larger round palm chisel to cut the cove section around the flower at the end of the stem. Using a practice stock is really important to help you get a good feel for what these chisels can and cannot do.

**FIGURE 102**

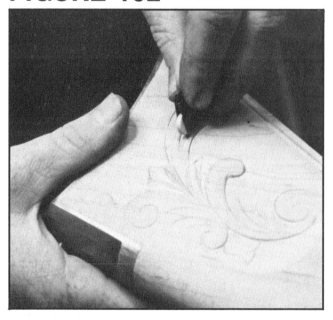

**FIGURE 103**

and flowers on the outside. I like to use a small veiner to go back and slightly undercut all of my leaves. This gives them great dimension and finer detail (Figure 103). Figure 104 shows me using the sharp-pointed palm chisel to cut a bevel on the edge of the stem leaf.

I have outlined here the tools that I used to achieve this look. Figure 105 is a blueprint of the carving with detailed

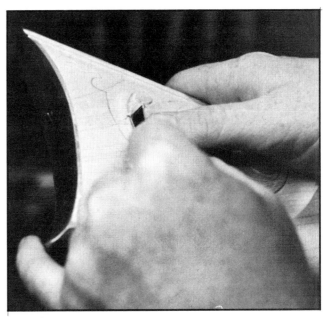

**FIGURE 104**

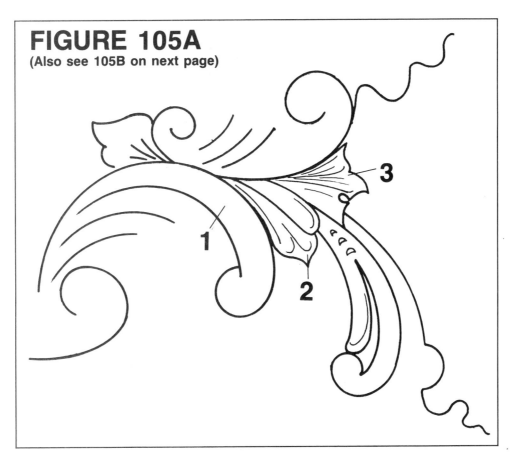

**FIGURE 105A**
(Also see 105B on next page)

1

2

3

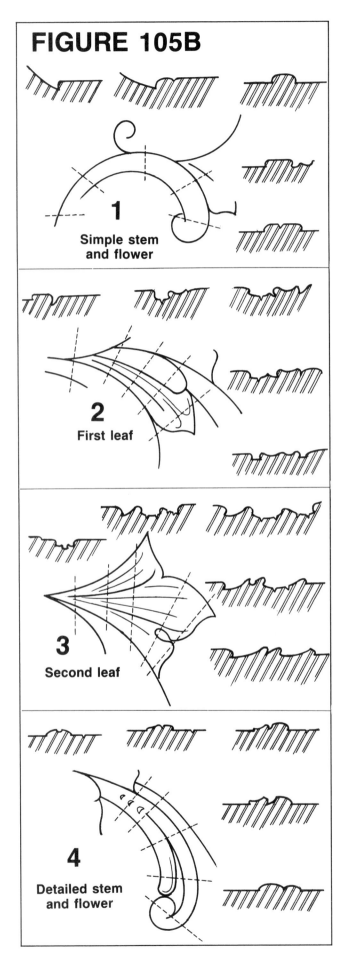

## FIGURE 105B

**1** Simple stem and flower

**2** First leaf

**3** Second leaf

**4** Detailed stem and flower

## FIGURE 106

crosscut sections of the various leaves and stems to better illustrate the cuts that I have described.

After you have completed the carving and sanded it down to a 360 finish, it is time to put in the finishing touches. In Figures 106 and 107, I am beginning to cut a series of dimples to accent the line behind the leaf and stem. The first

## FIGURE 107

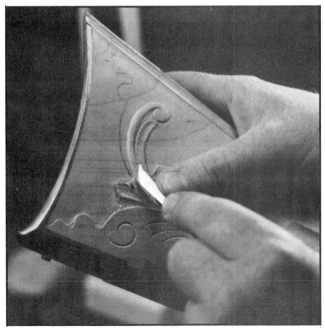

144

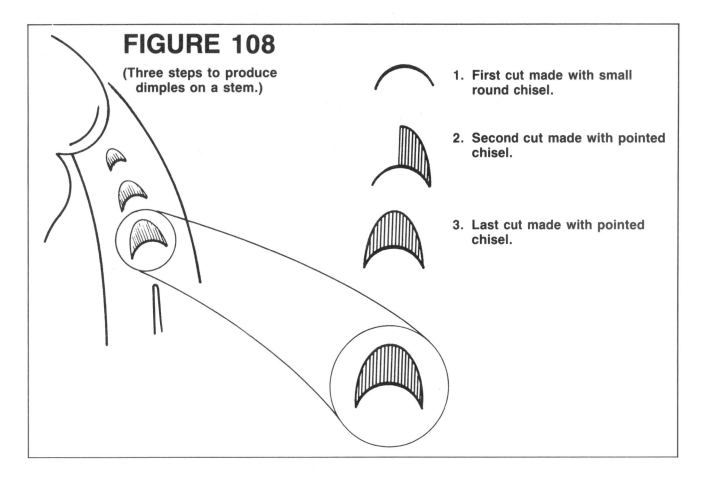

# FIGURE 108

(Three steps to produce dimples on a stem.)

1. **First cut made with small round chisel.**

2. **Second cut made with pointed chisel.**

3. **Last cut made with pointed chisel.**

cut is made with the medium curved palm chisel by pressing straight down so that the concave part faces the line where the stem and leaf come together. The first cut is accented with two bevel cuts into the back of it using the sharp pointed chisel (Figure 108). These dimples diminish in size when in a series (Figure 109). If you rotate your sharp chisel right, you can get a smooth, round cut that requires very little cleanup.

The other type of dimple is a sort of loop, which is on the full leaf. Make the first cut using the smallest round palm chisel, as seen in Figure 110. Then finish with two cuts, using

# FIGURE 109

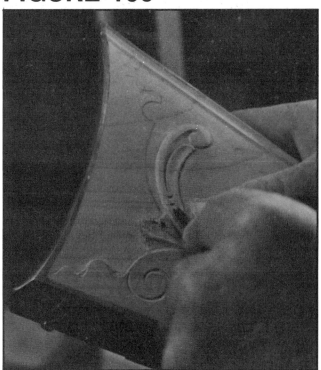

# FIGURE 110

the sharp pointed chisel, from each side of the half-round circle forming a point. Then it is just a matter of sticking in your half-round palm chisel again and popping out the teardrop (Figure 111). Figure 112 is the relief carving behind the cheekpiece completed and sanded to a 360 finish.

Moving into the wrist area, we'll go through the few steps necessary to complete the floral pattern that is behind the breech tang. We have spent a lot of time going over the detail in order to achieve what we did on the cheekpiece, and actually, you follow the same steps and use the same tools throughout the entire stock. So, it is not necessary to go into such detail in each of the remaining areas of the stock.

## FIGURE 111

## FIGURE 112

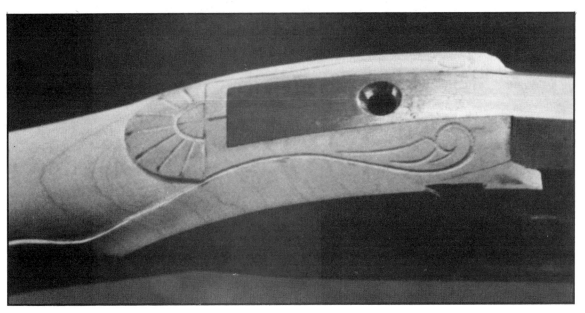

# FIGURE 113

Figure 113 shows the top of the breech tang. You can see that I have gone through all the carving cutting an incised line. Now go back between the petals with your sharp pointed palm chisel or small veiner and separate them with a very thin cut. Second, dish each one of the petals towards the center. Because of the way the grain flows through the wrist, you should push your palm chisel toward the butt whenever possible. You might find it necessary to rock the small chisel back and forth.

# FIGURE 114

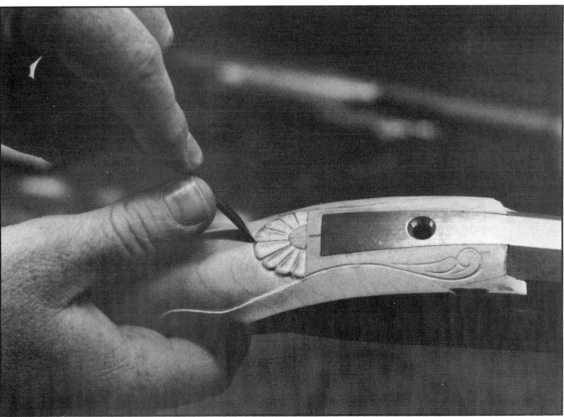

Notice in Figure 114 the petals have been dished, and I'm forming the outside of each one with the sharp pointed chisel. Next roll some 220-grit sandpaper around a pencil tip or a shaped popsicle stick to sand and clean up the petals. Cut a slight bevel around the outside of each one of the petals with your sharp chisel. After this is completed, smooth all the edges using 360 grit. Complete the petals by cutting veins into them using the pointed palm chisel or the fine veiner.

Figure 115 shows the pattern completed.

Using a combination of the large and small veiners, clean up the edges of the relieved border and accent incised lines around the wrist area on the lock side. Sand it all down to a 360 finish. Do the same around the lock mortices (Figure 116).

The last area, which really requires no more than cleaning up the edge with your large veiner and sanding, is

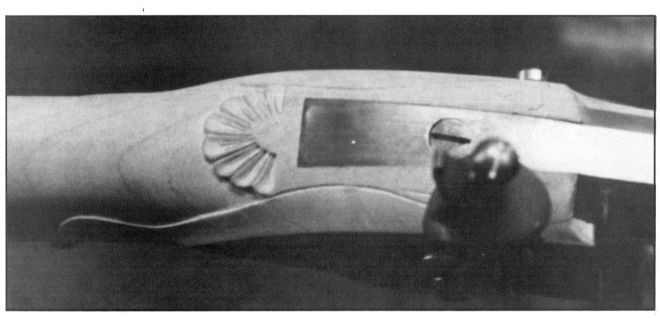

**FIGURE 115**

**FIGURE 116**

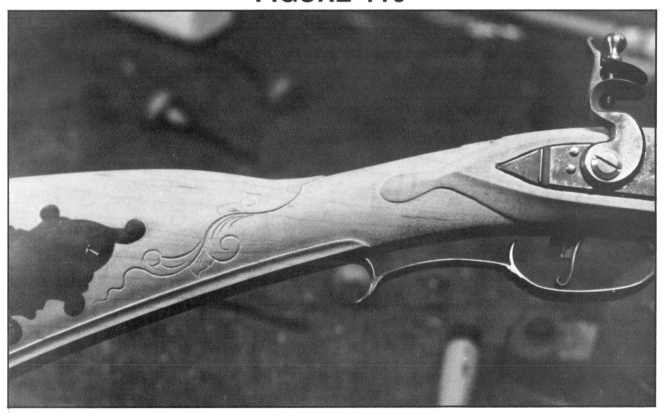

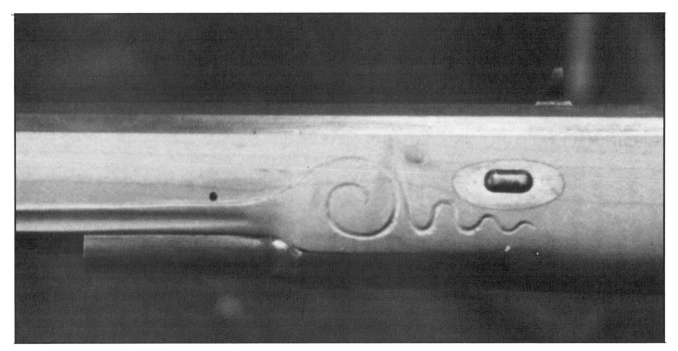

**FIGURE 117**

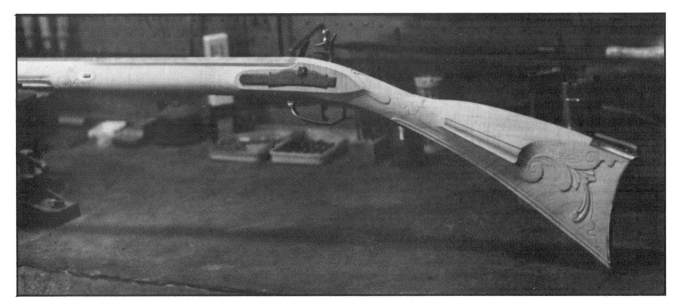

**FIGURE 118**

around the entry thimble. The dished molding fades out where it runs along the entry thimble and the relieved molding just fades into an incised C-scroll with a pigtail coming off of it, as shown in Figure 117. Clean up the edge of the molding and sand it down to a 360 finish.

Figure 118 shows the completed rifle. At this stage all that remains is to go over the entire rifle lightly with 000 steel wool and stain the wood. It is important to use a good stain. I try to use a stain which will not raise the grain when I finish a stock. This helps to preserve the detail in the carving. As a rule all that is required between coats is to rub the stock down with number 000 steel wool. If you cannot find a stain that you are pleased with, I have developed a

stain that I like to use and offer it through Colonial Arms.

I want to stress again that practice really makes the difference. What I have described and shown here is the end result of many years of practice. I use these exact tools and have carved literally hundreds of rifles. I know that I will continue to improve as long as I practice, and I feel that anyone who thinks they have arrived is either in the wrong place or has low standards. I want to encourage you to keep trying. Your first few tries may be discouraging but don't give up. Do your research, carefully lay it out, use the correct tool and then execute it properly. Then practice again.

## APPENDIX A: WORKS CONSULTED

Bleile, C. Roger. *American Engravers.* North Hollywood, Calif.: Beinfeld Publishing, 1980.

Fredrickson, N. Jaye. *The Covenant Chain.* Ottawa, Canada: National Museum of Man, 1980.

Johnston, James R., pub. *Kentucky Rifles and Pistols, 1750-1850.* Delaware, Ohio: Golden Age Arms, 1976.

Kirkland, Turner. *Dixie Gun Works, Inc.* Catalog. Union City, Tenn.: Dixie Gun Works, 1987.

Meek, James B. *The Art of Engraving.* Montezuma, Iowa: F. Brownell and Son, 1978.

Neal, W. Keith and D. H. L. Back. *Great British Gunmakers 1740 to 1790.* London: Sotheby, Parke, Burnett, 1975.

Phillips, Ray J. *How to Engrave...the NgraveR Way.* Oakdale, Conn.: Ray J. Phillips, 1986.

Scurlock, William H., ed. *The Book of Buckskinning IV.* Texarkana, Tex.: Rebel Publishing, 1987.

Shumway, George. *Rifles of Colonial America.* 2 vols. York, Penn.: George Shumway, 1980.

## APPENDIX B: SOURCES OF ENGRAVING TOOLS

The NgraveR Company
879 Raymond Hill Road
Oakdale, Connecticut 06370

Brownells, Incorporated
Rt. 1, Box 1
Montezuma, Iowa 50171

Hand Engravers Supply
4348 Newberry Court
Dayton, Ohio 45432

## APPENDIX C: SOURCES OF GUN STOCKS

Dixie Gun Works, Incorporated
Gunpowder Lane
Union City, Tennessee 38261

Tennessee Valley Manufacturing
P.O. Box 1125
Corinth, Mississippi 38834

# Historic Sites & Museums II

## by David & Susan Jennys

TO SAY THAT David and Susan Jennys have a passion for history is perhaps an understatement. The daughter of parents whose annual trek was "at least to the Rockies and back" (from northern Indiana), Susan grew up appreciating the beauty of America in its places of enduring splendor and the history of America as presented through museums, historic sites and special gatherings she has been privileged to frequent. Susan holds an associate and a bachelor's degree in education and is currently at work on a master's degree in cultural anthropology.

History has been a lifelong interest of David's, which has prompted his keen interest in books and in travel. He has had the opportunity to travel in Europe as well as within the United States. A direct outgrowth of his love of history is an avid interest in simulation strategy games. David has a bachelor's degree in social studies education and has taught world and United States history at the secondary level.

Together, David and Susan have been active on the rendezvous scene for many years. Proud members of the Brothers of the Wind of Indiana, they have an extensive affiliation with the NMLRA. They are active in their local historical society and are members of the Museum Association of the American Frontier. Susan and David have served as museum consultants and restorationists, as well as being guest speakers and demonstrators on plains Indian and Western fur trade life for many schools and civic organizations.

David and Susan firmly believe that the study of history should be active and "involvement oriented," not a stuffy list of facts and figures that means little to anyone. They carry this belief with gusto into their living history interests as well as into their travels, visiting many museums and historic sites on their frequent trips throughout the country.

IN light of the enjoyable chapter "Historic Sites and Museums" by Doc Carlson in the *Book of Buckskinning IV,* perhaps you are wondering, "Why another chapter on this subject?" The answer to this question is twofold. Hopefully, Doc's work stirred up the proverbial "coals" of interest in the museums and historic sites our country has to offer the student of history. This chapter is to be viewed as an expansion of the information offered by Doc Carlson, not a displacement. When the two chapters are viewed together, we hope you will be provided with a broader knowledge of the research facilities that are available to you.

Also included in this treatise is a special section devoted to the *use* of research facilities. All too often in our lives we are given a task to complete without being given the tools necessary to complete it. It is not enough to provide you with a lengthy list of museums and historic sites and a word of encouragement. You should also be familiar with the process of research if serious study or interest is expected.

Within the space of this second installment on museums and historic sites, it is our goal to help you, the reader, become familiar with the definition and purpose of museums, to address several common misconceptions about museums (which are spreading like wildfire in buckskinning circles), to discuss the responsible and full-fledged use of research facilities and to provide the reader with a supplemental expanded listing of major museums and historic sites throughout the United States.

Faced with the awesome task of contacting facilities, sorting information and making judgements on the appropriateness of these places for inclusion in a *Book of Buckskinning,* we would also like to offer our apology because this chapter is, necessarily, not comprehensive. Not only are there thousands of other fine facilities throughout our country that deserve listing, but even the facilities covered here are done so in a limited way due to the availability of space. Information about each of them has been condensed to several paragraphs, while available information could often

amount to volumes! We are indebted to the staff of each museum and historic site included in our listing for their gracious help and willingness to provide information about their facility.

## WHY GO TO MUSEUMS?

Since this chapter is the second in the five *Books of Buckskinning* specifically devoted to museums, historic sites and their usage, perhaps we can conclude that museum-going is on the rise in popularity among buckskinners and living history enthusiasts. However, from our personal experience with rendezvous goers, we have found that most of you reading this publication probably fall into one of two categories of enthusiasm about museum going: those of you who would go a good distance out of your way to *visit* a museum, and those of you who would go the equivalent distance out of your way to *avoid* a museum. No matter which category you find yourself in, the "avoiders" or the "visitors," we would like to propose that researching is of key importance to the sport of buckskinning. For the serious buckskinner or reenactor, museums should serve as the lifeblood of their interests. Museums and historic sites can be important tools in helping each of us grow and progress in our knowledge about the past.

If you are already a tried-and-true museum addict, we hope that the following considerations about museums and other research facilities will be a source of renewed enthusiasm for your ventures. If you are presently an avoider, we encourage you to take a careful, objective look at museums and what they have to offer you.

## WHAT IS A MUSEUM?

According to Webster's New World Dictionary, a museum is "a building or room used for exhibiting historical objects." Museums are not just large metroplex buildings made of granite and marble that take three days to walk through. Museums come in a variety of sizes and architectural styles, from large building complexes like the Smithsonian Institution in Washington, D.C., to small, one-room displays of historical objects in the basement of someone's home.

Museums also vary in the scope or material covered in their exhibits. A large-scale museum such as the Field Museum of Natural History in Chicago, Illinois, houses elaborate displays of cultural material from around the world, not just North America. Equally important to the researcher are the smaller, more specialized museums that focus their efforts toward one particular area of United States history like Ute Indian history or firearms of the American Revolution.

Finally, there are many different institutions that have the word "museum" incorporated into their names. Often living history enthusiasts overlook these facilities, thinking they are impertinent to their field of interest. These facilities include natural history, anthropological and art museums,

to mention a few. Names like this attached to a facility easily conjure up images in the potential visitor's mind of dinosaur bones, spear points or Michelangelo sculptures. Anyone who has ever frequented the Denver Museum of Art or the Lowie Museum of Anthropology can attest to the fact that natural history, anthropology and art museums are of equal importance to students of United States history as are the traditional museums of American history.

No matter what the museums' differences may be in size, structure, scope or name, they all share a common working goal: preservation of the past. Since our goal as living history personnel is also preservation of the past, perhaps it is safe to assume that we should desire to take full advantage of the historical knowledge and insight amassed at museums and historic sites. This knowledge can aid us in "fleshing out" our portrayals and furnishing our camps and persons in a truly historic manner. Individual museum's volumes of information contribute to the complete textbook on American history available to the student of history who travels widely and frequents museums and historic sites of all types.

Museums present their collections and findings in an organized and understandable manner that benefits the general public as well as the holder of a Ph.D. Museums are important endowments of knowledge that belong to us and to future generations. They have a function similar to the reference section of your local public library. This function is to arrange information for in-depth study while keeping the findings and materials on the premises. This assures that the articles will be protected and preserved for use and enjoyment by everyone in a nonexclusive manner.

Museums come in a variety of sizes and architectural styles and vary in the scope of material covered. The Native Center for the Living Arts in Niagara Falls is shaped like a turtle and offers many Native American cultural attractions.

PHOTO BY TIM JOHNSON

## FOUR COMMON MISCONCEPTIONS
## ABOUT MUSEUMS

Having misconceptions about something is a common trait of humanity. Misconceptions about museums seem to have found a foothold among buckskinners and reenactors. The following is an attempt to pin down and hopefully stop the perpetuation of these inaccurate ideas. We will discuss what we feel are the four worst misconceptions held among living history enthusiasts.

The most common misunderstanding concerning museums is that they are stuffy, tedious and present too much material, most of which is written in scientific jargon. If these thoughts have ever crossed your mind, take heart! You were simply suffering from a case of "museum panic." Chances are these thoughts have their root in an experience you had earlier in life. You know...the time you were taken to a major metropolitan museum and came face to face with its enormity when you were "generously" given a whole two hours to see it all. If you did not sit in the lobby or gift shop the whole time, you probably found yourself making a mad dash through the exhibit halls. Reading the captions on the displays was out of the question!

Does this sound familiar to you? Unfortunately we have all probably had a similar experience sometime in our lives. So how does someone overcome museum panic? Here is the key: Make sure you always go to a museum with a *goal*. Be sure to give yourself plenty of time to reach it. Scoutmasters and youth group leaders beware! Remember that when visiting a large museum, no *one* person can experience everything, especially in a short amount of time. If you or the group you are leading is interested in the Revolutionary War era, we suggest that after your arrival at the facilities, you proceed directly to the Revolutionary War displays. Be sure to take a pencil and notebook with you so you can write down your observations. As you tour through the collections, take the time necessary to read the captions or labels on the exhibits. Write down any questions or important comments that you might have about the subject matter presented. If you are a group leader, use these writings to spur a discussion at a follow-up meeting of your group. Your time will be well spent if you find that when the museum's closing time rolls around you are still in the same collections as when you first arrived at the facilities. So what if you do not have the opportunity to see the entire museum? Chances are good that the facilities will still be in operation should you decide to make a return trip!

Another common misconception about museums is that they have exorbitant admission prices. Generally speaking, this could not be further from the truth. How expensive are museums? We have found that admission prices for most museums or historic sites are considerably less of a dent in the wallet than admission to the commercial motion picture theatre. Museum entrance fees are often lower than the registration fees for local rendezvous!

A number of museums are free of charge on designated weekdays or holidays. Most research facilities have reduced rates for students, families, groups (if booked in advance), and senior citizens. Admission passes are available for historic sites administered by the National Park Service. These passes represent a significant savings on admission fees if several Park service sites are to be visited as the passes are good for an entire year at a time. Some museums and historic sites have no admission charge at all!

For the person truly interested in museum-going, the only major expense involved in visiting a museum or historic site is *time:* time to travel to the site, time to view it, and time to return home. As with any endeavor in traveling, careful planning and preparation are in order to insure that your time is well-spent. Responsible museum-going requires forethought.

A third misconception about museums centers on their *accessibility.* Many well-meaning folks have developed the belief that a person needs a Ph.D. to locate and enjoy museums. People who believe this have obviously alienated themselves from the notion that museums are *public* places, set aside for the cultural enrichment of everyone. Need proof? The next time you have the opportunity to visit a museum or historic site, take a moment to sit and watch the other people visiting there. The wide variety of folks who frequent museums may surprise you.

As for locating museums and historic sites, the road atlas is a great place to begin. Check the map notation key near the beginning of the atlas. Often significant historic sites and major museums will be represented on the maps by a small red square or other distinguishing symbol. Look over your anticipated route of travel and take careful notice of any of these symbols that fall in conjunction with your chosen highways. Plan your stops accordingly. If at all possible, write or phone ahead to the sites you anticipate visiting. Ask for information about the facility such as hours and days of operation, nearby accommodations, etc.

The American Association of Museums publishes a large listing of all the museums in its membership. A copy of this book might be found in your public library's reference section or at your local historical society. Look in the index under the desired subject heading (your interest). You will find a complete rundown on every museum in the AAM that has significant relevance to that subject.

Individual state tourism departments usually have a publication available that highlights the state's important museums and historic sites. Obtain this publication by writing or calling the state tourism department at the state's capital building. A local chamber of commerce can also provide you with addresses for these.

Publications such as the one before you are another source for locating museums. Perchance in your search you will find that there are museums and historic sites closer to home than you ever imagined.

Interpretive displays help bring meaning to the interesting things found in museums and historic sites. An actual demonstration, such as the spinning done here by Jan Dubbeld at Fort Dodge, helps show how the display pieces in the exhibits were a part of everyday life.

The fourth and final misconception about museums deals with the credibility of such places. Through communication with participants at rendezvous and reenactments, we have noticed a negative attitude about museums. This attitude manifests itself in around-the-campfire comments like, "Who needs museums anyway? If it's good enough for Friendship, it's good enough for me!"

Hopefully each of us as living history enthusiasts desire our facts to be solidly based on historical reality, not on heresay or foolishness. We believe this is especially true if we are in the habit of attending public-oriented events where we are expected to properly portray a certain time-period or culture. In other words, do we assume our articles of clothing or camp gear are authentic because they are "just like so-n-so's"? Or is our authenticity claim based on evidence like, "It's a replica of a documented museum piece"? Enough said.

Now that we have spent time considering what a museum is and looking at several misconceptions about museums, let us take a close look at how we as living history personnel can gain a better knowledge of the past by visiting museums and historic sites. The degree of our desire to carry out research determines the degree of our desire to visit or avoid museums or historic sites. For the avid buckskinner or reenactor, research provides the stuffing by which historical portrayals are "fleshed out" and the stitching by which those same portrayals are held together. Research is not a once in a lifetime activity but a lifelong passion for knowledge that brings with it a keen desire to dig for information about the past.

## UTILIZING RESEARCH FACILITIES

So how do we go about using these various research facilities? If anyone carries out a serious study in a given field of historical interest he will undoubtedly find himself confronted by unanswered questions and limited availability of materials. Everyone who researches comes up against these barriers. Research facilities exist to help us find answers to our questions about the past and provide us with subject material for our extended studies.

You can make use of research facilities in two ways: in person or long distance. If it is currently impossible for you to travel to visit a facility in person, you can still "visit" simply by picking up the telephone or a pen and paper. Phone calls and correspondence by mail are both important means to carry on personal research when it is impractical to do so in person. A simple procedure for long distance contact is first deciding which research facility would best meet your needs. Obviously, one would not expect to find lots of specific answers about Colonial history at a site devoted to the plains Indians. Next, write down the questions you have. Make sure they are not vague. Good questions should ask who, what, when, where, how, and why. Finally, contact the facility. Having questions already written down will aid you in writing your letter or in speaking with a curator. Keep in mind that it may take explaining who you are and what you want to several different people or having your letter shuffled from office to office before you are put into contact with the appropriate scholar. Sometimes this process can be a bit exasperating. Do not despair though! Research facilities exist

to serve. You will not be rudely hung up on, nor will your letter of serious inquiry be deposited in the proverbial "round file."

Having now discussed the long distance use of research facilities, let us turn our attentions to the actual visit. We would like to offer you the following tips that we have found helpful in our own research excursions. We encourage you to keep these ideas in mind as you anticipate *your* visit!

1. *Go with an open mind.* Remember that not everything we read or overhear at the local rendezvous or reenactment is necessarily in keeping with historical truth. For the serious living history buff, the popular excuse of "if they'da had it, they'da used it!" should cause all sorts of red warning lights to go off. In research we are persuing fact, not fiction. Sometimes in the pursuit of fact we must give up a preconceived idea of what is historic and be willing to change our thinking based on continued research. Keeping an open mind means letting the facts of history mold our personal thoughts about the way things were in our country's past, not vice versa.

2. *Write down specific questions to which you want specific answers.* Keep this list of questions handy as you visit the museum or historic site. As you find answers, check off the appropriate questions. If you run into trouble locating pertinent material that would provide answers to your questions, ask to speak to a curator or staff member. He will be happy to assist you. Contrary to a popular belief, curators DO NOT bite! Research facilities employ curators and staff who are respected scholars in their given fields of study. If you are given an "I don't know" reply to any of your inquiries, be grateful for the honesty behind such a statement. Make it a point to ask "Who might?" A referral is not a put-off. Look at it as your assurance that someone is not trying to play know-it-all. They are taking your inquiries seriously, which they are employed to do.

3. *What about picture-taking?* Remember that most research facilities have their own set of guidelines and restrictions on photography. It is no less than courtesy to ask if you may photograph permanent exhibits. To prevent confusion or mis-identification, be sure to write down a picture-by-picture description of the objects you photograph. This will help you correctly identify your photos when they return in a potential jumble from the developer.

4. *Become familiar with the use and purpose of archives.* Archives incorporate an organized storage and retrieval system through which items not on permanent display may be studied and preserved. Archives can be independent facilities not connected with a major museum, but most commonly they represent the major portion of a museum's collections. Often the archives of a particular

Permission for anyone to carry on research within archival holdings will be based on their satisfactory description of their purpose and specific area of study. Expect a credibility check to be done on you if you request permission to visit any archival facility. The museum will review your personal and professional references. You must have a definite reason for wanting to visit the archives. You must also be able to prove that you are a credible researcher. If you are asked to provide information about yourself when you request visitation permission, expect it to be thoroughly checked out. Though this sounds complicated and exclusive, keep in mind that it's just standard operating procedure.

5. *Many museums and historic sites offer seminars or workshops* on various history-related topics. Call or write ahead for information about the availability of such seminars and request registration materials if pre-registration is necessary. Also ask about any and all fees that might be charged in conjunction with the seminar and about materials (books, paper, pencils) you will need. Occasionally, college credit is available to people who successfully complete a seminar or workshop.

If a seminar is offered by a major museum or facility that is part of the National Park Service, you can be reasonably certain that the instructors will be highly qualified and the information presented and discussed will be well researched. The length and difficulty of these seminars will vary from place to place, so it is advisable to know what you are getting into when you sign up for one!

6. *Watch for special research facilities incorporated within a museum.* Included among these special facilities are libraries, microfilm files, photographic or pictorial archives, teacher resource centers (providing interesting classroom activities and information for teachers), working laboratories behind glass (where the public can watch archaeological work in progress), and video or audio archives. Museum policies differ in the visitation and usage of such special facilities.

Now that we have considered several aspects of museum-going, it's up to you to answer the question, "Why go to museums?" No matter what your answer might be, we hope this discussion has spurred you to seriously look at research facilities and to renew your excitement for visiting museums and historic places.

The following list of museums and historic sites will provide a "place file" for you to draw from as you travel and study. We also encourage you to keep your eyes and ears open as you travel, looking for billboards or highway signs that will point you to one of the many local historical sites or society museums that are available to the interested person. We have stumbled across a number of wonderful places in our travels that were not formally listed on the road map or in the tourist flyers. Visiting these places helps make for a more balanced view of our country's heritage, a heritage each of us as buckskinners and living history enthusiasts are interested in preserving for future generations.

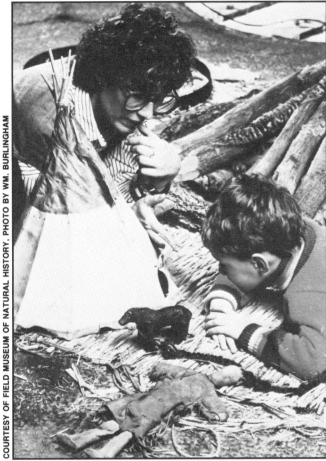

Exploring traditional Pawnee Indian culture becomes possible as visitors learn firsthand in the Pawnee Earth Lodge, the Field Museum of Natural History's full-sized replica of a typical Pawnee home, circa 1830. Visitors can examine actual clothing, tools, art, religious symbols and childrens' toys as shown here.

organization are housed in a separate building from the permanent galleries. A visit to archives of either type is done only on appointment basis. A museum curator or staff member will accompany the visitor and in certain instances he might be escorted by museum security personnel. As a rule of thumb, permission to take photographs within the archives of a facility is not implied along with permission to view items on hold there. Special permission must be secured for photography in the archives well in advance of an expected visit.

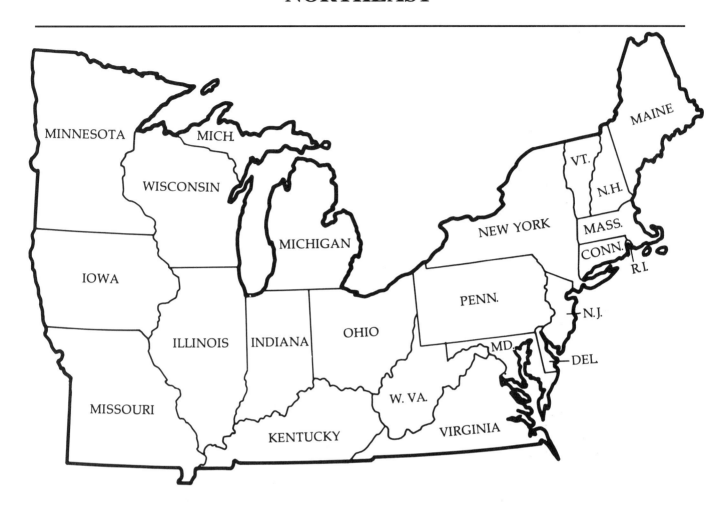

## CONNECTICUT:

### *Leffingwell Inn*
### *348 Washington Street*
### *Norwich, CT*

Built in 1675 by Stephen Backus, son of a Norwich founder, this historic inn began as a simple foursquare home. Even though extensive additions were made to the structure by later owners, the basic interior was never altered. Thomas Leffingwell bought the house in 1700 and converted it into an inn with an adjacent tavern room. An addition was built in 1715 as a result of the inn's booming business. Leffingwell's grandson Christopher later added an entire rear section as the inn became the town house of a leading Norwich family.

After having been restored, the inn is now open for visitors. It is completely furnished in late 17th and early 18th century style, complete with beds, tables, chairs and pottery. Also on display is a grandfather clock that was made to Christopher Leffingwell's exact specifications. It is housed in the George Washington Parlor, named for the famous general who actually entertained guests in that room during the Revolutionary War.

The Leffingwell Inn is open June through Labor Day. An admission fee is charged.

## ILLINOIS:

### *Field Museum of Natural History*
### *Roosevelt Road at Lake Shore Drive*
### *Chicago, IL 60605*

Ranked as one of the four great natural history museums in the world, the Field Museum in Chicago, Illinois, is truly an invaluable resource to students of anthropology, botany, geology and zoology. The Field Museum's collections are the third largest in the nation and encompass over 16 million artifacts and specimens. Included are the museum's own world-renowned collections of art and ethnographic artifacts from Asia, Africa, Oceania and the Americas.

The museum's exhibits and public programs deal with the world's cultures and physical environments. Over half of the museum's current displays are focused on anthropology. The Field Museum also serves as a vital research and teaching institution for the scientific community.

The exterior of Chicago's Field Museum is closely patterned after the Erechtheium, one of the Athenian Acropolis temples. Field Museum is located at the intersection of Lake Shore Drive and Roosevelt Road, just south of downtown Chicago.

Of particular importance to the student of Native American cultures is the Field Museum's outstanding collections of American Indian art and artifacts. Seven exhibit areas explore the Indian cultures of the Americas. Highlights of this exhibit include a full-scale replica of a traditional Pawnee Indian earth lodge, where visitors can sit inside on buffalo robes and listen to stories about Pawnee life, and the exhibit of Eskimo and northwest coast Indian cultures which

contains over 2,500 objects, including a totem pole "forest" and a model of an underground Eskimo dwelling.

The Webber Resource center for Native Cultures of the Americas is the first of its kind in America. Opened in September of 1987, the center brings together a tremendous range of people, material and audio/visual resources and places them in a comfortable, friendly center. Visitors may explore, ask questions, study, relax or just browse. The Resource Center is located on the first floor of the Field Museum.

A broad range of programs has been offered by the museum. Among these were "World Music," "Sizes," "Pawnee Life" and "Indian History of the Western Great Lakes." Programs include festivals, tours, workshops, performances, lectures and courses of study. A specialized museum library covers the fields of anthropology, archaeology, botany and many others. It is comprised of some 229,552 volumes in addition to the museum's rare book collection. The library is open to the public daily.

The Field Museum's staff takes great pride in the museum's statement of purpose, which is: "to preserve, increase and disseminate knowledge of natural history...to enhance in individuals the knowledge and delight in natural history." The museum itself is a treasure house of insight into the past.

Field Museum is open daily except for major holidays. A nominal fee for admission is charged, however, Thursdays are free. Teachers with I.D. and children under 6 are also admitted free.

## Ingram's Log Cabin Village
## Kinmundy, IL 62854

For an interesting and educational jaunt, the Log Cabin Village in Kinmundy, Illinois, gets a great rating. The village itself is made up of 17 authentic log buildings dating from 1818 to 1860. Thirteen of these are open to the public and are authentically furnished with rope beds, corner cupboards, chests, cradles and other historic items.

Many of the log buildings of the village were actual homes of early Illinois pioneers, while others were business buildings for an apothecary, an inn, a cobbler's shop or a grocery store. Each of the buildings has an important story to tell.

Several weekends in September and October are set aside for a demonstration and craft show. Over 100 craftsmen participate in this event. Crafts that have been demonstrated in the past include weaving, spinning, chair caning, pottery making, glass etching, copper punch work, broom making and woodworking.

A nominal admission fee is charged for the Pioneer Log Cabin Village. Hours for the village are seasonal and groups are advised to make prior arrangements.

# INDIANA:

## Eiteljorg Museum of the American Indian and Western Art
## 334 North Senate Avenue
## Indianapolis, IN 46204

This museum promises to be an important cultural/historical addition to the Midwest. It is presently under construction at White River State Park in Indianapolis, Indiana. The opening of the facility is scheduled for June of 1989. Upon completion the museum, which will be divided into three levels, will have approximately 23,000 square feet of exhibit gallery space, making it one of the largest museums

Artist's drawing of the Eiteljorg Museum of the American Indian and Western Art in Indianapolis. It's scheduled to open in June, 1989.

in the United States dedicated to American Indians and Western Art.

The collection of Native American art and artifacts offers representation from all regions of North America. The strength of the holdings is in the plains and Southwest. Highlights include pottery, basketry, northwest coast wood carvings and a rich representation of plains Indian beadwork and quillwork in the form of clothing and other accoutrements.

The American Western art consists of paintings, drawings, graphics and works of sculpture, ranging chronologically from the early 19th century to the present. It is one of the foremost collections of its kind and features painters of the widely acclaimed Taos art colony, the ''Taos Ten.'' The collection also includes works of 19th century painters who accompanied expeditions through the old West. Among these early artists are Alfred Jacob Miller, John Mix Stanley and Albert Bierstadt.

The museum will be easily accessible and admission will be charged.

# IOWA:

## Fort Dodge Museum and Historical Foundation
## P.O. Box 1798
## Fort Dodge, IA 50501

From its lowly beginnings as an Army outpost on the prairies of Iowa to its fully reconstructed palisades of today, Fort Dodge, Iowa boasts a unique and colorful history. The original name of the fort was Fort Clarke, however, the name was changed later in honor of Senator Henry Dodge, organizer of the United States Dragoons. Fort Dodge played an integral part in prairie history, housing infantry in the 1850s and protecting the farmers and settlers of the area from Indian attack.

''The past still lives at Fort Dodge,'' boasts its advertisements. Among the fort's special events are Frontier Days, Craftsman's Weekends, Buckskinner's Rendezvous and a 19th century Military Muster. During these events visitors can view and experience rodeos, historic encampments, historic foods and beverages, fashion shows and old-time muzzleloading rifle shoots. Also an integral part of the complex's facilities, ''Front Street'' at the fort museum depicts the early village of Fort Dodge. The fort museum features Native American artifacts, military history, pioneer settlement history, period furniture, clothing and accoutrements.

The Fort Dodge Museum is located close to Interstate 35 and is easily accessible. It is open from May to mid-October on a daily basis. Admission is charged. Tour groups are encouraged to make special arrangements in advance.

# KENTUCKY:

## Fort Boonesborough State Park
## 4375 Boonesboro Road
## Richmond, KY 40475

In 1775, Judge Richard Henderson of North Carolina obtained the land rights to a large portion of Kentucky. He sent Daniel Boone and a group of 30 axmen to clear the way to this little paradise. When Boone and his party reached the Kentucky River, they erected a fort for protection. Henderson, arriving several days later, was so pleased by what he found that he named the settlement ''Boonesborough.'' Boonesborough, Kentucky's second permanent settlement, was besieged by British troops and hostile Indians. Its compound of 26 cabins and four blockhouses provided safety and shelter for many pioneers working to carve a home out of the Kentucky wilderness.

Today, the visitor to Fort Boonesborough will see demonstrations of pioneer crafts by costumed interpreters. Several cabins are furnished as they would have been in Daniel Boone's day. During the month of October the Kentucky Corps of Longriflemen host an Interstate Invitational Tournament at Fort Boonesborough. This is a lively and fast-paced event which also includes a primitive camp and other activities.

Fort Boonesborough State Park proudly offers something for everyone. It has seasonal hours and an admission fee is charged.

# MAINE:

## Lumberman's Museum
## Rt 159
## Patton, MA 04765

In upper Maine there is a very unique place called the Lumberman's Museum. It was established to preserve a graphic record of the lumber industry as it existed in northern Maine in the 1800s. The collections and displays are housed in ten different buildings which exhibit the various aspects of lumbering. One building was made from logs salvaged from a building constructed about 1860. Other structures have been made in the old manner without the use of nails.

The displays house various equipment used by lumbermen in their trade, from utensils used by the cook to tools used in the cutting of the lumber. There are working models of saw mills and an extensive collection of tools used

Buckskinners Walt Dubbeld and David Parker demonstrate muzzleloading at Fort Dodge.

The Lumberman's Museum in Patten, Maine, houses 1,500 items dating from 1800 and ranging from loggers' scrimshaw carvings to huge log haulers.

by carpenters, millrights and coopers. Displays also include models, dioramas, photographs and paintings showing the life and times of the lumbermen. Other displays include a replica of a blacksmith's shop, a rack and pinion sawmill, a shingle machine and a replica of a lumber camp office.

The Lumberman's Museum truly preserves a unique but important part of our nation's history. The museum is located near Baxter State Park and is open on seasonal hours. A nominal admission fee is charged.

Located at the Lumberman's Museum are a blacksmith shop for a lumber camp of the 1890s (left) and a reproduction of a lumber camp for a small crew in 1820, built without a nail (right).

# MASSACHUSETTS:
## Peabody Museum of Archaeology and Ethnology
### Harvard University
### Cambridge, MA 02138

The Peabody Museum of Archaeology and Ethnology was founded at Harvard University in 1866 and is known for its devotion to scholarly research. Its collections total an impressive 2,000,000 artifacts with approximately half of the items originating in North America. The strongest collections are in the northwest coast, the Southwest and the plains cultures. The collections were accumulated by such notables as Captain Edward G. Fast, Roderic McKenzie and Lewis and Clark. Historic paintings and art work as well as photographic images are a prime resource for research at the Peabody.

A current renovation and expansion project is underway, one of the goals of this program being the opening of a large modern hall devoted to North American Indian art and artifacts. The creation of this new exhibit gallery is a long-awaited dream of the curatorial staff at the Peabody.

The scope of the collections at the Peabody Museum of Archaeology and Ethnology reflect the diversity of Native American culture. Anyone with an interest in Native American history will find this museum fascinating and helpful. The museum is easily accessible and the admission fee is modest.

A mid-eighteenth century ceremonial blanket from northern British Columbia, the Swift Blanket, collected by Benjamin Swift of Charlestown, Massachusetts.

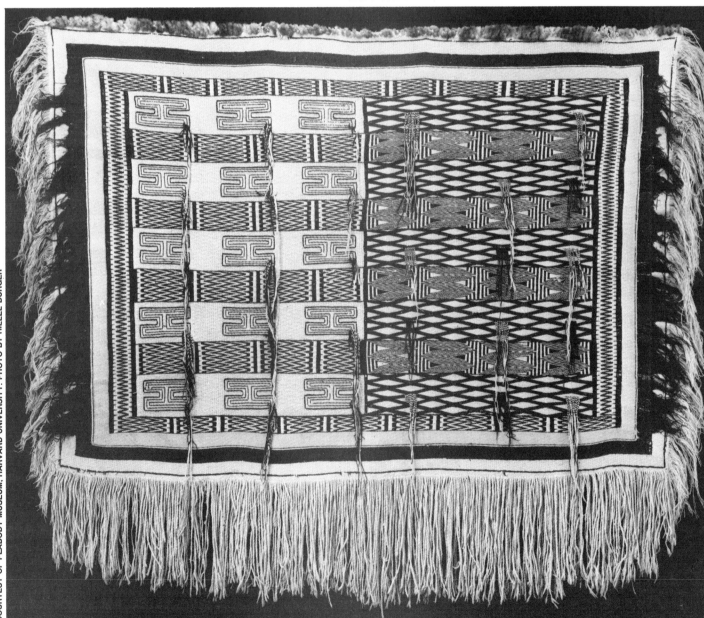

A sample of the pottery found in the Cranbrook Institute of Science in Bloomfield Hills, Michigan.

# MICHIGAN:

## Cranbrook Institute of Science
## 500 Lone Pine Road, Box 801
## Bloomfield Hills, MI 48013

Cranbrook Institute, founded in 1930 by Mr. and Mrs. George G. Booth, is one of the top-ranked natural history museums in the United States. The institute, committed to excellence in the scientific field, has as its stated purpose "...to actively encourage people to learn about nature, science and man through personal experience and the use of collection objects." Major collections housed at the facilities include minerology, zoology and anthropology. Among the anthropology collections is a sizeable holding of Great Lakes Indian clothing and accoutrements and a relatively new exhibit entitled "Gaweug: Native American Decorative Quill Work." This new exhibit features an unusual art form: boxes intricately designed with dyed porcupine quills. These are representative articles from the William M. Shurtleff collection.

A vital part of the Cranbrook Institute's outreach lies in its special programs and seminars. These cover a wide range of topics and interests. The Cranbrook Institute offers a little something for everyone of every age. An admission fee is charged.

## Historic Fort Wayne
## 6325 West Jefferson
## Detroit, MI 48209

In 1843, construction began on the third and last fort to stand on the Detroit River. The isthmus between Lakes Huron and St. Clair had long been recognized by colonizing Europeans as a strategic spot. The first to garrison the area were the French, who built Fort Pontchartrain in 1701 (renamed Fort Detroit in 1752). It was surrendered to the British in 1760 and then abandoned. In 1779, the British built Fort Lernoult and at the close of the American Revolution surrendered it to the Americans, whereby it was renamed Fort Shelby. Fort Shelby was allowed to fall into disrepair and in 1826 was demolished. When tensions mounted along the U.S.—Canadian border, the War Department made plans to build another fort. In 1849, it was named in honor of Gen. Anthony Wayne of Revolutionary War fame. For the next century, Fort Wayne served as a staging and training area for U.S. soldiers and equipment being shipped off to America's wars, from the Civil War to the Vietnam War. In 1971, the fort was taken over by the city historical department and extensive renovation work began.

Historic Fort Wayne features reenactors from the Civil

War era. However, a visitor on any given day will often see interpreters portraying personages from the area's other time periods. Historic Fort Wayne also hosts a number of reenactments of different time periods throughout the year. Inside the fort walls the visitor can view the fort's ramparts, powder magazine, casemate and connecting tunnels. Also for view is the blacksmith's shop, commanding officer's house and the soldier's barracks. The barracks have been turned into a museum depicting Detroit's military history. Outside of the fort are the parade grounds and an Indian mound dating 900 years.

In addition to the military history offered at Fort Wayne, one can take advantage of one of Michigan's most extensive museums on Great Lakes Indian cultures. The museum traces the history of Great Lakes Indians from the precontact period to the present day. Displays explain Indian life styles, religions and roles of tribal members. Other exhibits trace relations with the French explorers and missionaries, British soldiers and American settlers. The Great Lakes Indian museum is open to the public in the summer and is free upon admission to the fort.

Historic Fort Wayne is located in the city of Detroit and can be located by following the signs from Interstate 75. The fort is open seasonally. A nominal fee is charged.

# MINNESOTA:

## Pipestone National Monument
## Pipestone, MN 56164

Here on the vast Minnesota prairie lies a site of significant importance to Native Americans. For hundreds of years, Indians of many tribes journeyed to this area to quarry a blood red rock from which they fashioned their pipes. The name of this rock is Catlinite or more commonly, pipestone.

Although the site of the quarries is now a national monument and is administered by the National Park Service, Department of the Interior, active digging still takes place and may be viewed by the visitor. The Circle Trail, which begins at the visitor center, leads the visitor to the principal points of interest on the monument. The Spotted Pipe Quarry, the Nicollet Inscription, Inscription Rock, Inkpaduta Camp and various active and inactive quarries form the bulk of the sites to view at the national monument.

The pipestone quarries are rich in historical significance. All Indian tribes held the pipestone in considerable reverence and many legends surround its mythical origin. A general belief among Indian people is that the stone itself was formed from the flesh and blood of their ancestors, hence the deep red color. George Catlin, who spent eight years (1832-39) venturing among the Indians of the North American plains, described his visit to the quarries in words and sketches. The first U.S. Government expedition to visit the pipestone quarries was led by Joseph Nicollet, a French mathematician. Members of this expedition chiseled an inscription into the

Fort Wayne's annual Frontier Days chronicles Detroit's early settlers.

166

Living history interpretations are given daily from nine to five at Morristown National Historical Park.

stone, marking their passage.

Pipestone National Monument Visitor Center tells the geological and anthropological story of the pipestone quarries through dioramas, displays and an educational slide show. Visitors may purchase pipestone specimens from the Pipestone Indian Shrine Association in the park. Park hours vary by season. Admission is charged.

# NEW JERSEY:

## Monmouth Battlefield State Park
## R.D. #1, Box 258
## Freehold, NJ 07728

Monmouth Battlefield is an out of the way place located in central New Jersey between state road 33 & U.S. Route 9. The 1,520 acres that encompass most of the historic battle area are largely undeveloped, and the land has the same appearance it did in 1778. The battle was significant because it was the first battle in which the Continental Army applied skills they acquired from their training at Valley Forge.

The park features the Visitor Center where one can view a slide presentation about the battle and an electronic scale model map of the area depicting the troop movements. The Craig House is located on the battle site and has been restored to its 18th century appearance. Molly Pitcher Well is marked for the legendary woman who carried water for Washington's men and took her husband's place on a cannon crew.

The best features of Monmouth Battlefield State Park are the two living history events that take place on the grounds. A firelock and cannon shoot is held annually on the last weekend of April. The big event of the year is the Monmouth Battle reenactment held on the weekend that best falls on the date of the battle, June 28th. With these two events, Monmouth Battlefield State Park offers a splendid opportunity for the living history enthusiast.

The Ford Mansion at Morristown National Historical Park. This was Washington's headquarters in 1779 and 1780.

## Morristown National Historical Park
## P.O. Box 1136 R
## Morristown, NJ 07960

At Morristown National Historical Park, a visitor will find the story of an army struggling to survive. During two critical winters, the town sheltered the main encampment of the Continental Army. In 1777, George Washington brought the Continental Army to winter at Morristown after their exhausting victories at Trenton and Princeton. He had to overcome desertion and disease to rebuild an army that would be capable of fighting William Howe's redcoat veterans. When the Continental Army left Morristown in the spring, they did so greatly reinforced. In the two years following, many great events took place: a British surrender at Saratoga, Philadelphia's capture and subsequent abandonment, the hard winter at Valley Forge, and the failure at Savannah for a joint French-American siege.

In the winter of 1779-80, the military struggle was almost lost to starvation, nakedness and mutiny on the bleak hills of Jockey Hollow where the men lived in tents and began work on crude log cabins that were to serve as barracks. The winter was harder than anyone could imagine and was one of the Continental Army's severest trials. Under Washington's leadership, the army survived this time of discouragement and hardship.

Six integral sites are incorporated into the park area at Morristown: Washington's headquarters of 1779-80, the Jockey Hollow Encampment area of 1779-80, the Pennsylvania Line (bleak huts built as a "barracks"), the Grand Parade Grounds, St. Clair's Headquarters 1779-80, and the site of Fort Nonsense. Washington's Headquarters and the adjacent museum are open daily. Admission is charged. The Jockey Hollow Visitor Center and the Wick House (St. Clair's headquarters) are also open daily. Morristown is administered by the National Park Service, U.S. Department of the Interior.

One of the most valuable resources at Morristown National Historical Park is the research library. Housed in an addition to Washington's Headquarters Museum, it offers researchers a rich treasure of original books, manuscripts and other material on the Colonial and Revolutionary War periods of American history. Total holdings in the library consist of nearly 23,000 books and 44,000 manuscripts, including the Park Collection, the Lloyd W. Smith Collection, the Hessian Transcripts, the Ford Papers and the Diary of Sylvanus Seeley. Many of these books and manuscripts have been indexed and are available in transcript, photocopy or on microfilm to interested persons or organizations. The library is open Thursday through Saturday and other times by appointment.

# NEW YORK:

## The American Museum of Natural History
## Central Park West at 79th Street
## New York, NY 10024

The American Museum of Natural History is a museum of excellence and education. Within its walls are exhibits detailing human and animal life in various areas throughout the world. Some exhibits of particular interest to the living history enthusiast are the museum's extensive collections and displays of Native American art and culture. These exhibits highlight the native peoples of the northwest coast, the Eastern woodlands, the plains, the pacific and the Arctic. Typical displays include items such as clothing, tools, decorative art forms and hunting devices.

The American Museum of Natural History is open daily and hours vary by season. Admission is charged on a pay-what-you-wish system. Special traveling exhibits and displays as well as interesting seminars are offered throughout the year.

## Fort Ticonderoga
## Ticonderoga, NY 12883

Along the shores of Lake Champlain in the beautiful region of upstate New York is a historic site that brings the excitement of a restored fort alive for the visitor. Fort Ticonderoga is a splendid place to visit for those interested in the 18th century time period. During the fort's colorful history it witnessed the clash of four dynamic forces: the Mohawk Confederation, the British, the French, and the infant United States. All of these nationalities had a significant role in the history of Fort Ticonderoga.

A visitor to the Fort Ticonderoga Military Complex can take advantage of the four historic sites and the Military Museum. Fort Ticonderoga itself comprises of these sites: Mount Hope Battery between Lakes George and Champlain, Mount Defiance on the New York shoreline, Ticonderoga's sister fort and Mount Independence on the Vermont shore. Within the barracks of Fort Ticonderoga is the Military Museum which contains collections of paintings, etchings, maps, uniforms, powder horns, personal mementos and many other historic items. Another important collection on display at the museum is an excellent collection of swords, muskets and pistols. The museum's collections contain more articles used by Colonial and Revolutionary soldiers than anywhere else in the United States. A visitor can also enjoy the added realism of the historic site's living history interpretors. Regular drill and cannon firing demonstrations are

An aerial view of Fort Ticonderoga at the junction of Lake George and Lake Champlain.

The Frederic Remington Art Museum contains valuable art work both collected by and created by Remington, seen at left in front of a fireplace decorated with Western artificats.

given. Fort Ticonderoga is also the home of a fife and drum corp that performs regularly for the public.

The Fort Ticonderoga Military Complex is a definite must-visit site for the 18th century Colonial and military enthusiast. The fort is open between May 14 and October 16 and admission is charged.

## Frederic Remington Art Museum
## 303 Washington Street
## Ogdensburg, NY 13669

The Frederic Remington Art Museum is a treasure house of Western lore. In addition to Remington's art work, the museum houses much of his personal art collection and home furnishings. Remington's last studio has been faithfully recreated, which lends the visitor a unique glimpse into the life of this famed artist. The Remington Collection, the focal point of the art museum, contains 14 bronzes, 70 oils, 140 original water colors and several hundred pen and ink sketches by Frederic Remington.

Programs are held at the museum on a regular basis. Museum staff and volunteers provide special talks on Frederic Remington and the collection. Special programs and events are held throughout the year. Special exhibitions are held each year on a variety of themes and topics which appeal to the general public.

For the living history enthusiast interested in the Western fur trade, plains and Southwest Indian history, or

A 2½'' high basket decorated with feathers and shell beads from the Museum of the American Indian.

life on the great plains, this museum is an invaluable asset. Frederic Remington is recognized as the foremost artist of our old West. His work constitutes an extensive picturization of the Western wilderness days.

Museum hours vary by season. Admission is charged.

## *Museum of the American Indian*
## *Heye Foundation*
## *Broadway at 155th Street*
## *New York, NY 10032*

Perhaps housing one of the most important collections of Native American artifacts in the world, the museum of the American Indian can truly be considered a national treasure. The museum was organized by renowned anthropologist George G. Heye to collect, preserve, study and exhibit all aspects of the native peoples of North, Central and South America. The Museum of the American Indian's collections include over 1,000,000 artifacts that represent the world's largest assemblage of Native American materials. The facility's public galleries provide space for a permanent display area of over 10,000 artifacts. Special temporary exhibits on various aspects of Native American culture are presented frequently throughout the year.

Of particular interest to students of North American In-

dian cultures are the museum's outstanding collections of Southwest basketry, Eskimo tools and accoutrements, and painted hides and costumes of the plains Indians.

The Museum of the American Indian produces a biannual newsletter which gives a month-by-month update on special exhibits and programs going on at the museum's facilities. In the past these exhibits have ranged in topics from ''Silver Drum: Five Native Photographers'' to ''Gift of Double Woman: Quillwork of the Lakota.''

The Museum of the American Indian—Heye Foundation is closed on Mondays. Admission is charged.

The Native American Center for the Living Arts not only houses museum and art attractions but also features regular performances of native dance, drama and storytelling.

An 11'' diameter, red-on-white ware bowl from the Museum of the American Indian. The painted decoration represents an antelope.

## Native American Center for the Living Arts
## 25 Rainbow Mall
## Niagara Falls, NY 14303

According to the Iroquois people, the earth was created on the back of a giant turtle. The turtle appears many times throughout the art forms of many different Indian nations as a symbol of the earth and life itself. This recurring Native American theme is also an important part of downtown Niagara Falls' landscape . The Native American Center for the Living Arts is housed in a building shaped like a turtle. It is a unique and powerful structure which commands attention in an often busy tourist city.

From the Museum Orientation Hall of ''Voices From The Turtle Island'' to the National Indian Art Gallery and the Museum of Houdenosaunee (Iroquois, meaning ''People of the Longhouse'') Heritage, the Native American Center is a major cultural facility. Five years in the making, the Center serves the public by offering an outstanding museum collection, art attractions, theatrical productions and cultural/educational materials, all prepared by Native Americans. Represented in the museum collections are wampum belts, historic clothing and accoutrements, pottery, baskets and various other cultural materials.

Educational services offered by the Museum of Indian Heritage include guided tours, weekend classes, workshops, loan materials for teacher use in the classroom, and a speaker's bureau through which Indian speakers are available to lecture for schools and community organizations. An important part of the center's complex is a central performing arts amphitheater where drama, dance and storytelling occur on a regular basis.

The Native American Center for the Living Arts is a unique and valuable institution. Hours of operation vary by season. Admission is charged.

# OHIO:

## Fort Meigs
## P.O.Box 3
## Perrysburg, OH 43551

Fort Meigs relives the critical days of the northwest campaign of the War of 1812. The fort, located at the mouth of the Maumee River (near present-day Toledo, Ohio), played an important role in the land campaign of 1813. It successfully defended itself against two British sieges, helping to bolster the American morale of the time.

A visitor to Fort Meigs today will find the fort restored to its appearance during the first siege. The tour of the fort includes seven blockhouses. Each of these contains exhibits that help to show life as it was during the year 1813. Some of the blockhouses are set up in an ''as it was'' atmosphere, while other blockhouses have exhibits highlighting the history of the fort itself and the life of the typical soldier at Fort Meigs. Also to see at the fort are the Grand Battery, the visitors' center and the countryside abutting the fort grounds.

Special activities and historical seminars are presented throughout the year at Fort Meigs. Living history events are just one of these. Fort Meigs is located a few miles south of Toledo. Hours vary by season.

COURTESY OF FORT MEIGS

Living history events at Fort Meigs include reenactments of the British seiges during the War of 1812.

## Historic Fort Laurens
## c/o Ohio Historical Society
## Ohio Historical Center
## Columbus, OH 43211

Built in 1778 by troops of the 9/13th Virginia and the 8th Pennsylvania Regiments under the leadership of General Lachlan McIntosh, Fort Laurens became the winter hold out quarters of these militiamen caught in the wilderness amidst the hostile actions of Indians and British troops. McIntosh ordered that a fort be erected. He garrisoned it for the winter with 176 men and 5 women. When the four-sided palisade with corner bastions and blockhouse was complete, he and his troops left.

Over the ensuing winter, those who were left suffered at the hands of the elements and the whims of the Indians and British soldiers who frequented the area. In February of 1779, British forces under Captain Henry Bird surrounded the fort to begin what they felt would be a short wait to starve the garrison into surrendering. Colonel John Gibson, commander of the fort, realized that he had to act fast to counter the British strategy. He sent a barrel of flour out to the British and Indians to convince his enemy that the fort was well supplied. His trick worked!

Today Fort Laurens museum and the Tomb of the Unknown Patriot of the American Revolution stand as testimony of the ingenuity and fortitude of militiamen of the frontier. The museum exhibits artifacts unearthed from the fort site as well as uniforms, weapons and accoutrements of the American Revolution. Hours of operation at Fort Laurens are seasonal. Special programs and reenactments are an important part of the educational aspect of the site. A modest admission fee is charged.

## Piqua Historical Area
## 9845 North Hardin
## Piqua, OH 45356

The Piqua Historical Area is comprised of six significant parts. The John Johnston Farm has several buildings on view: the original farmhouse, springhouse and log barn; and a reconstructed cider house, fruit kiln and woodshed. The original structures date to the early 19th century and are furnished accordingly. The story of Mr. Johnston's life as a farmer and Ohio Indian agent (1812-1829) is told through graphic displays and a guided tour for visitors.

Located on a restored mile-long segment of the Miami-Erie Canal, which linked Cincinnati and Toledo and served the Piqua area from 1839 to 1913, is the historical area's canal boat landing. The dock is the departure point for the ''General Harrison,'' a mule-drawn replica of a mixed-cargo

canal boat of the 1840-50 era.

A modern building houses the Historic Indian Museum, a noted collection of artifacts and displays relating to the Indians of the post-contact period. Exhibits include information on Great Lakes/woodland Indians as well as items representing the culture of the plains Indians. The museum setup is geared to show the visitor how the introduction of white material culture led to the substitution of trade objects for native-made artifacts and the subsequent changes in traditional Indian design motifs.

Included in the Piqua Historical Area is the Johnston Cementary, a prehistoric Adena mound and the actual site of Fort Piqua, which was built in 1794 as a supply post for General Anthony Wayne's campaign against the Indians in northern Ohio. Hours of operation at the Piqua Historical Area are seasonal. Admission is charged.

The Piqua Historical Area includes a replica of a mule-drawn canal boat, the ''General Harrison,'' on a restored portion of the Miami-Erie Canal.

# PENNSYLVANIA:

## Fort Necessity National Battlefield
## Friendship Hill National Historic Site
## The National Pike
## R.D. 2, Box 528
## Farmington, PA 15437

To understand an era it is essential to understand its beginnings. War eras are not so cut and dried as to have only one beginning or cause, yet they do often have a spark that sets events in motion. Such is true of Fort Necessity National Battlefield. Under the administration of the National Park Service, Fort Necessity and the surrounding area offer a golden opportunity for those interested in gaining understanding of the French and Indian War time period. The park is open year round with varying hours, and a nominal fee is charged.

Jumonville Glen: Approximately six miles from the main park is the site of the skirmish between the Virginia militia under the command of young George Washington and the French forces under the command of Sieur de Jumonville. This little skirmish paved the way to what became known in America as the French and Indian War. A visitor to Jumonville Glen will find the site little changed from the time of the skirmish.

Fort Necessity: About a month after the clash at Jumonville Glen, the opening battle of the French and Indian War, the Battle of Great Meadows, was fought. After the Jumonville fight, Lt. Col. Washington decided to build a fortification and wait for supplies. Despite reinforcements, the Colonials were forced to capitulate after an eight-hour battle.

Afterward, the French destroyed the fort. A year later Gen. Edward Braddock led a large force to engage the French and built a road that cut through the forest past the remains of Fort Necessity. In the ensuing battle, Braddock was killed and his body was buried about one mile from the fort. Today, visitors can see the restored fort on its original site. There is a visitors' center on the park grounds and interpretive tours are conducted. The site of Braddock's grave is marked by a historic marker along U.S. 40.

Mount Washington Tavern: A half century after the French and Indian War, the National Road of the new nation was built near the Fort Necessity area. The National Road was in need of traveling accommodations for stagecoach riders. Roadside taverns were built to take care of this need, and a tavern was built on the site of the Battle of Great Meadows. The tavern, like others of its kind, went out of business with the advent of the railroad. In its time, however, it served a useful function in the growth of our country. The tavern was well-maintained for over a century and a half. The tavern today serves as a representative of a valuable segment of our country's early history, and it now serves as the park museum. Inside, the furnishings are symbolic of a tavern of its day and exhibits are displayed to tell the story of the National Road.

Friendship Hill: Located 20 miles away from the Fort Necessity National Battlefield is the Friendship Hill National Historic Site. The site, still under restoration, preserves the

Fort Necessity was reconstructed on its original site and is open for tours.

PHOTO BY CHARLES JOHNSON

PHOTO BY CHARLES JOHNSON

Mount Washington Tavern was originally built to offer traveling accommodations to stagecoach riders on the National Road. It is built on the site of the Battle of Great Meadows and houses the park museum.

country estate of Albert Gallatin. Gallatin, a Swiss immigrant, served this country in public and private and made significant contributions in the fields of finance, politics, diplomacy and scholarship. Visitors can tour the home and view the furnishings and architecture of an 18th century home. The site is open year-round on weekends and seven days a week between Memorial Day and Labor Day.

# WASHINGTON D.C.:

### National Firearms Museum
### The National Rifle Association of America
### 1600 Rhode Island Avenue
### Washington, DC 20036

Away from the Mall, the famous part of our nation's capital, is a museum that every rifle and historic weapon enthusiast should not miss. At the headquarters of the National Rifle Association is the accompanying National Firearms Museum. Overshadowed by the Smithsonian, the National Firearms Museum is perhaps one of D.C.'s better kept secrets. The museum is small (about two rooms in size), but it is distinct in its display. The grandson of Theodore Roosevelt recently donated his grandfather's pistol. He chose this museum over the Smithsonian because he felt that it would get lost there (the Smithsonian Institution has several fine firearms in its collection that aren't always displayed).

Contained in the museum are weapons ranging from a 14th century hand cannon to modern automatic rifles. The total number of exhibits on display is about 1,500. The National Firearms Museum displays examples of hand cannons, matchlocks, wheellocks, flintlocks, percussion fire, and many others. Some of the displays include personal firearms of Dwight Eisenhower and Theodore Roosevelt. Other displays include European pistols from the 1600s, Pennsylvania/Kentucky rifles and 19th century dueling pistols. There are 60 flintlocks on display of various ages and styles. A very interesting display is an illustrative piece on how the flintlock works.

A visit to the National Firearms Museum should prove to be a rewarding experience for the historic gun enthusiast (and for the modern gun enthusiast for that matter). Tours are available and the museum is well-marked to enable a visitor to tour at his own pace. The reference collection is available for personal study; one only needs to call ahead. Admission is free.

## National Museum of American History
## Smithsonian Institution
## Washington, DC 20560

The National Museum of American History is devoted to the study, display and care of artifacts that showcase the wide spectrum of American experiences. The museum offers many scholarly and public programs that aid in interpreting the American people. The collections are the focus for research, visitors' programs, publications and exhibitions. A large number of the museum's artifacts are on public display; most, however, are preserved in storage (archival) areas for scholarly reference and are carefully preserved and studied by museum staff members.

Topics of the public gallery include "After the Revolution: Life in America," "A Nation of Nations," and "Firearms and Ordnance." Items on exhibit include national treasures such as the original Star-Spangled Banner, scientific instruments, implements of everyday life from spinning wheels to musical instruments, clothing and textiles, Connestoga wagons, George Washington's field tent and an array of early American pottery and pewter.

In addition to its collections, the museum offers scholarly resource centers such as the Dibner Library of rare books relating to the history of science and technology and the Eisenhower Institute for Historical Research which focuses primarily on military history.

No admission fee is charged for the National Museum of American History. Visitors are urged to write in advance for information about special exhibits and programs current at the museum. For the student of American history, perhaps this could be called *the* museum!

## National Museum of Natural History
## National Museum of Man
## Smithsonian Institution
## Washington, DC 20560

The Smithsonian Institution brings our nation's cultural heritage to life. It is the largest complex of museums, art galleries and research facilities in the world. Visitors to the Smithsonian are often unaware of the wide array of research conducted behind the scenes by the curatorial and research staff at the institution. Seeking new knowledge is a tradition among Smithsonian researchers.

Among the Smithsonian's 14 museums and galleries is the National Museum of Natural History and Museum of Man. Included in the collections of this immense museum are anthropological artifacts that catalog cultures from all over the world. The Native American artifacts collection is one of the finest such assemblages in the world and represents a cross section of native cultures in North America. An Arapaho tipi which had been displayed at the Philadelphia Centennial Exposition of 1876 is on permanent display in the North American Indian Gallery, as are pottery and baskets of the Southwest peoples and ceremonial masks and accoutrements of northwest coast Indians. These displays are primarily located on the museum's first floor.

The National Museum of Natural History and Museum of Man offers seminars on various anthropologically and natural history-oriented subjects. A schedule of these seminars and programs is available by writing the Smithsonian Institution. Admission to this museum is free.

# WISCONSIN:

## Milwaukee Public Museum
## 800 West Wells Street
## Milwaukee, WI 53233

The Milwaukee Public Museum is considered to be one of the finest institutions of natural and human history in the world. Within its walls are exhibits on everything from the "Streets of Old Milwaukee," to Africa, Asia and the ethnic heritage of a European village. The living history enthusiast will take interest in the museum's fascinating galleries of "North American Indian Tribal Ways" and the back-in-time effect of the "Streets of Old Milwaukee."

The use of lifelike, life-sized dioramas originated in the Milaukee Public Museum. These dioramas have become the hallmark of the museum's quality and innovativeness. Atmospheric walk-through exhibits create a unique "you are there" experience for the visitor.

Special events abound throughout the year at the Milwaukee museum. These include notable programs and a variety of changing exhibits covering a wide variety of topics, such as the voyages of the first U.S. sailing expedition around the world and life in the Brazilian rain forest. The museum publishes a list of these special events. This listing is available to potential visitors by writing the museum.

# SOUTHEAST

## ALABAMA:

### Historic Fort Condé
### 150 South Royal Street
### Mobile, AL 36602

From the temporary wooden stockade built when the French founded Mobile in 1702 to the brick and mortar structure partially reconstructed today, Fort Condé has stood in the center of Mobile's activity. The fort was headquarters for the military rule of the coastal area by France, England and Spain. At one time it was the base for the entire French Louisiana Territory.

Reconstructed and furnished by the city of Mobile in a 1975-76 American Revolution Bicentennial contribution, Fort Condé now serves the city of Mobile as its visitor welcome center. Authentically uniformed French soldiers guide visitors through the fort and give demonstrations of cannon and rifle firings.

The history of Fort Condé is truly fascinating. For anyone insterested in the historic interplay of nations on our continent, Fort Condé will be an important part of piecing together information. No admission fee is charged for Fort Condé.

### Horseshoe Bend National Military Park
### Route 1, Box 103
### Daviston, AL 36256

For those interested in the War of 1812, Horseshoe Bend offers a unique historical experience. The battle that took place at the site of the bend in the Tallapoosa River brought about the end of the Creek Indian War (1813-14). The Creek Indian War was actually a war within the larger War of 1812. Horseshoe Bend National Military Park is administered by the National Park Service and a visitor can expect to find the same quality as in the rest of our nation's national parks.

A tour of the park starts at the visitor center. There one can view a slide program and see exhibits designed to help the visitor better understand the battle. The exhibits are on Creek culture, frontier life and the Creek Indian War of 1813-14. At the park flintlock and interpretive demonstrations are often given. To see the battlefield, one can follow a three-mile trail that loops through the area. It contains side trails and markers that help to make the tour both informative and interesting. Some of the highlights of the tour are: the overlook, where Gen. Andrew Jackson deployed his forces; the barricade, built by the Creeks at the narrowest point of

Storming the barricade at Horseshoe Bend, soldiers of the U.S. 39th Infantry followed by Tennessee militiamen pour over the log wall to attack the Creek Indians. The barricade was five to eight feet high. In the foreground the man with an arrow in his leg is Sam Houston, later of Texas fame.

the penninsula for defense; the Cherokee crossing, where Jackson's Indian allies crossed the river; and Tohopeka Village, where the Creek families stayed.

Horseshoe Bend National Military Park should prove to be a fun and interesting place to visit for young and old alike, and should appeal to those interested in either the War of 1812 or Southeast Indian culture. The park is located on Alabama 49 north of Dadeville and northeast of Alexander City. Camping is available near the park. The park is open to visitors year-round.

# FLORIDA:

### *Castillo de San Marcos National Monument*
### *Fort Matanzas National Monument*
### *1 Castillo Drive*
### *St. Augustine, FL 32084*

### *Fort Caroline National Memorial*
### *12713 Fort Caroline Road*
### *Jacksonville, FL 32225*

In 1565, the Spanish founded the settlement of St. Augustine in order to make good their claim to Florida and guard against French encroachment on that claim. That same year saw the capture of the French Fort Caroline and the end of the French threat in that area. St. Augustine lay in an excellent position. It was surrounded on three sides by water and was protected from the ocean by coastal islands. From the time of its founding St. Augustine was guarded by a number of wooden forts, all of which were destroyed in part by either fire, the humid climate or shoddy construction. In 1672, construction began on the stone fort or castle (castillo), which is now the oldest all-masonry fort in the continental U.S. The fort was called Castillo de San Marco. With the growth of the British threat, the Spanish constructed Fort Matanzas at the Matanzas Inlet to guard St. Augustine's back door. In 1763, Florida became a British possession and, in 1784, was returned to the Spanish. In 1821, Florida was ceded to the United States. Castillo de San Marcos was declared a national monument and later came under the administration of the National Park Service.

Castillo de San Marcos is now restored and a visitor can expect to see the fort as it appeared during the 18th century. Interpretors work at the fort to demonstrate and explain its rich history. Castillo de San Marcos is located in the old section of St. Augustine off of U.S. 1. Admission is charged and the fort is open year-round.

Fort Matanzas is located 14 miles south of St. Augustine. Visitors can get to the restored fort via Florida A1A, and a ferry boat service is available from Anastasia Island. A visitors' center is located on the island to further enhance one's visit. No admission is charged.

Thirty-eight miles north of St. Augustine is Fort Caroline National Memorial. A replica of the original fort has been constructed on the site, and a museum there depicts the French attempts at colonization in the area. Admission is charged.

# GEORGIA:

## Fort King George
## P.O. Box 711
## Darien, GA 31305

When George I became king of England he saw the need to protect the English interests in the Carolinas. The result was the colony called Georgia. Fort King George was built along the Altamaha River to protect the colony from possible invaders from Spanish-held Florida. Fort King George was garrisoned between 1721 and 1732 and was the southern outpost of the British Empire in North America. During this time the fort was manned by His Majesty's 41st Independent Company, commanded by Colonel John "Tuscarora Jack" Barnwell. After the fort was abandoned, a group of Scottish Highlanders came to the area and founded the town of Darien. For the next two centuries, the area saw the large-scale industry of sawmilling.

Today on the original site a replica of the fort has been built. Also, the remains of three sawmills can be seen from the fort. The museum on the site displays exhibits and a slide show that chronologically covers the Guale Indians, Spanish missions, the building and occupation of Fort King George, the settling of Darien and the 19th century sawmilling period.

The fort is administered by the Georgia Department of Natural Resources under the Division of Parks, Recreation and Historic Sites. Fort King George is open year-round and a small fee is charged.

Workers begin reconstruction on the 1721 British frontier fort, Fort King George, in Darien, Georgia.

COURTESY OF FORT KING GEORGE

# NORTH CAROLINA:
## *Cherokee Historical Association*
## *P. O. Box 398*
## *Cherokee, NC 28719*

Nestled in the beautiful Appalachian Mountains is the ancestral home of the Cherokee people. Today the hub of activity in this area centers on the town of Cherokee, North Carolina. It is here that past mingles with present to enable the visitor to experience the full historical spectrum of the Cherokee people. Cherokee offers a variety of things to see and do. Available to the cultural and historically oriented visitor is the Museum of the Cherokee Indian, the Cyclorama Wax Museum, the recreated Oconaluftee Indian Village, the renowned outdoor drama ''Unto These Hills'' and the Cherokee Heritage Museum and Gallery.

Both the Museum of the Cherokee Indian and the Cherokee Heritage Museum are dedicated to the preservation of the heritage of the Cherokee people through the presentation of art and artifacts of the past, education of the public about the Cherokee Nation and presentation of modern Cherokee art work. Both of these museums charge an admission fee, however, group discounts are available.

The Cyclorama Wax Museum portrays 300 years of Cherokee Indian history. Authentic scenes with life-size figures depict Cherokee history from the first recorded contact with white men to the tragic Cherokee removal (the ''Trail of Tears''). Oconaluftee Indian Village is a replica of a Cherokee Indian community of the 1750 period, created in live, authentic detail, with Cherokee guides to escort visitors through the village. Crafts going on at the village include pottery making, basket weaving, finger weaving and weapon making. Admission is charged for the cyclorama and the village. Hours are seasonal.

## *Old Salem*
## *Drawer F, Salem Station*
## *Winston-Salem, NC 27108*

Take a walk through streets of the past in Old Salem, a faithfully restored Moravian congregation town. Within Old Salem there are 91 historic buildings built between 1776 and 1860. Forty of these have been restored and 26 were reconstructed. Eight of the restored buildings and two of the reconstructed buildings are open as museums, interpreting life as it was in Old Salem through the 1850s. The entire complex covers two dozen city blocks.

It's craftsmen versus apprentices in a summer game of rounders on Salem Square as Single Sisters look on.

Visitors to Old Salem can see and experience the charm of the restored buildings; historic interpretors demonstrating early American trades such as smithing, pottery-making, baking, weaving and wood-working; and various educational programs at the extensive visitors' center and within the restored buildings. Old Salem is open year-round with special festivities occuring during holidays. Admission is charged.

## Museum of Early Southern Decorative Arts
## 924 South Main Street
## Winston-Salem, NC 27108

The Museum of Early Southern Decorative Arts is the only museum dedicated to exhibiting and researching regional decorative arts of the early South. The Museum of Early Southern Decorative Arts houses 19 period rooms and six galleries encompassing furniture, textiles, ceramics, silver and metalware made and used in Maryland, Virginia and the Carolinas through 1820.

Potential visitors to the Museum of Early Southern Decorative Arts are encouraged to obtain reservations, as visitation of the facilities is by guided tour. Tours are given seven days a week. Admission is charged.

Spinning on the walk behind the Miksch Tobacco Manufactory in Old Salem attracts visitors' questions.

One of the 19 period rooms at the Museum of Early Southern Decorative Arts is the Catawba Dining Room.

### Schiele Museum of Natural History
### 1500 Garrison Boulevard, P.O. Box 953
### Gastonia, NC 28053

The Schiele Museum is a facility truly dedicated to excellence in its many facets. Incorporated into the museum complex are the main exhibit building, a "Backcountry Farm Site," a reconstructed Catawba Indian Village, a planetarium, and various habitats presented within the large acreage of land surrounding the museum building.

The main building houses galleries detailing aspects of geology, paleontology, archaeology and others. Particular strengths of the collections lie in North Carolina archaeology and natural history. The newly finished "Hall of Earth and Man" reflects the history of the earth and man's involvement with it. The Backcountry Farm is not just a reconstructed home site but a reconstructed life style. Research and experimentation set the Schiele's program apart from most similar endeavors. The goal of the Museum Backcountry Lifeways Studies project is piecing together the details of everyday life in 18th century back settlements. Skilled and dedicated volunteers give life to this early Carolina farm site. They dress in detailed authentic period clothing and actively take part in crafts and skills from the past which include spinning, weaving, basket making, cabin construction, sheep shearing, blacksmithing, riving shingles and folk medicine. A 20-hour course in Colonial Lifeways Studies prepares the volunteer interpreters to assist with public programs.

The reconstructed Catawba Indian Village is an integral educational center for members of the Southeastern Native American Studies Program (S.N.A.S.P.). Participants in the Native Technologies Workshops offered by the S.N.A.S.P. "practice primitive" by recreating and using ancient technologies such as pottery making, weaving mats, working wood with fire and stone, and making and using an atlatl.

Workshops at the Schiele Museum of Natural History are offered on a pre-registration basis only. The Museum offers tours by reservation for organized groups, as well as having the facilities available to the self-guided wanderer. No admission fee is charged for the museum complex.

The Harvest Day feast at the Schiele Museum Backcountry Farm is attended by volunteers in authentic period clothing.

# SOUTH CAROLINA:

### Historic Camden
### Box 710
### Camden, SC 29020

Historic Camden, an affiliated unit of the National Park Service, is a site of great significance for the student of the Revolutionary War period of our country's history. Camden, the oldest existing inland town in South Carolina, evolved from instructions issued by King George II in 1730. By the mid-1770s, overriding Whig sentiment showed itself in the area in the selection of the town as a site for a powder magazine built in 1777. In the spring of 1780, when Charleston fell to the British, General Cornwallis established posts at several points, including Camden. Though the citizens had fortified their powder magazine with a moat and earth wall, it was no protection against the invading British. Cornwallis entered Camden on May 1, 1780, and set up his headquarters there. Three months after this an attempt to recapture the town by American troops under General Horatio Gates resulted in the disastrous Battle of Camden. Another subsequent battle between General Nathaniel Greene and Lord Rawton ensued in April of 1781, breaking the British hold on South Carolina.

The Museum of Appalachia is staffed by traditionally attired interpreters like (left to right) Searle Patton, Lucie Patton and Tom Patton.

Visitors to Historic Camden will see restored period homes, the battle sites, various exhibits concerning Colonial and Revolutionary War life, and sites where archaeological study is carrried out on a regular basis. Historic Camden is open to the public year-round but hours vary by season. A minimal admission fee is charged.

# TENNESSEE:

### *Museum of Appalachia*
### *Box 359*
### *Norris, TN 37828*

The Museum of Appalachia is truly a unique place. The museum is dedicated to the preservation and enhancement of southern Appalachian culture. The museum displays a host of interesting and unusual items and mountain relics which represent the culture of southern Appalachia. The founder of the museum, John Rice Irwin, felt that the best way to represent the culture was to display the everyday articles that the people made and used.

What makes the museum truly unique is that it was not developed to be a cold, formal, lifeless museum but rather to have a lived-in look. The operator's primary goal was authenticity. The Museum of Appalachia is actually an entire living mountain village fully staffed with traditional craftsmen and interpreters. A visitor can experience the sights and sounds of craftmaking such as shingle making, weaving and rifle making; of musicians such as fiddlers, dulcimer players and singers; of dancers such as buck dancers and cloggers; and much, much more.

A special annual event featured by the Museum of Appalachia every October is the Tennessee Fall Homecoming. The homecoming is a full-scale country extravaganza. Over 175 mountain activities and craft demonstrations are shared for all of the visitors and guests. Featured at the festival are numerous celebrities, musicians and writers. Every visitor can enjoy their company and talents and take part in all of the many activities. The Museum of Appalachia is located north of Knoxville off of U.S. 75. Admission is charged.

# SOUTHWEST

## ARIZONA:

### The Heard Museum of Anthropology
### Phoenix, AZ

Ranked among the top museums of anthropology in the country, the Heard Museum is a treasure house of artifacts from the past. The special focus of this museum is on Southwest history and cultures. Museum hours vary by season.

### Hubbell Trading Post National Historic Site
### P. O. Box 150
### Ganado, AZ 86505

Reservation trading posts were often the only direct point of contact between native and non-native Americans until well into the 20th century. Much of the change in native life styles came about through the agency of the reservation traders, and much of the early public awareness of native cultures resulted from such daily trade. The most notable of the traders with the Navajo was John Lorenzo Hubbell. Hubbell Trading Post, now a national historic site, is where he based an active trade with the Navajo people.

The post itself is a long, low stone wall structure. Within its walls are a wide variety of trade goods as well as an outstanding display of Navajo woven blankets and rugs, and silver Navajo jewelry. Hubbell Trading Post has changed very little since it was begun a century ago. It sill remains a strong bridge between native and white culture for the Navajo people.

Hubbell Trading Post is administered by the National Park Service, Department of the Interior. Admission is charged. Tour groups are encouraged to make arrangements in advance.

## CALIFORNIA:

### The Natural History Museum of Los
### Angeles County
### 900 Exposition Boulevard
### Los Angeles, CA 90007

The third largest natural history museum in the United States, the Natural History Museum of Los Angeles County offers a wide range of exhibits and educational experiences. The museum's collections include one of over 15 million

The interior of the Hubbell Trading Post in its early years.

specimens and artifacts from over 600 million years of the earth's history. The museum boasts the largest American and regional history halls in the Western United States. Highlights include a replica of a Colonial kitchen and a bell cast by Paul Revere & Son. One of the most prized items in the anthropological holdings of the museum is a grand selection of Navajo textiles from the William Randolph Hearst Collection. This includes nearly 200 rugs and blankets gathered by Hearst in the early 20th century.

Incorporated within the museum is the Seaver Center of Western History Research. This center is responsible for a large collection of photographs, manuscripts and maps that are an important resource for the public as well as history students and scholars. The museum's history collection of textiles, arms and culture of the Hispanic period of the American Southwest is extensive and would prove of interest to Southwest fur trade era enthusiasts.

Besides its fine exhibit galleries, the Natural History Museum of Los Angeles County offers a wide assortment of educational activities and programs. It also sponsors two annual events: the American Indian Festival, and the Folk Art Festival. A calendar of special exhibits can be obtained by writing the museum. Admission is charged.

This home model of the Florence sewing machine was based on a 1863 patent held by Leander W. Langdon. This sewing machine will be on display at the Natural Historical Museum of Los Angeles County in "Growth of the Nation," the new American history hall covering the 1815 to 1865 period.

### Robert H. Lowie Museum of Anthropology
### University of California
### 103 Kroeber Hall
### Berkeley, CA 94720

Founded in 1901, the Robert H. Lowie Museum of Anthropology is the largest museum of anthropology west of Chicago. The museum's primary function is to serve the instructional and research needs of the students at the University of California. It also provides resource material for faculty members, scholars and the general public. The museum is internationally recognized as a major research institution with collections of over 600,000 cataloged specimens comprising approximately 3.8 million items.

The Lowie Museum offers changing exhibitions in the exhibit hall and lobby to meet the varied interests and needs of university students and the public. Nearly 30,000 people a year visit the exhibit hall. The museum staff presents lectures on anthropological or other related subjects of interest.

The museum operates a gift shop where visitors can purchase books and objects pertaining to aspects of anthropology. A nominal admission fee is charged.

## COLORADO:

### The Denver Art Museum
### 100 West 14th Avenue Parkway
### Denver, CO 80204-2788

For the history student, a visit to the Denver Art Museum is a must. Notable exhibits of Americana include an entire gallery of textiles and costumes, a large gallery of art of the American West, Colonial period rooms painstakingly reproduced and the Boettcher Foundation Galleries which include an internationally acclaimed collection of American Indian art. Also within the museum complex are galleries for traveling exhibits, a restaurant and a museum shop offering a selection of quality art works and publications on a variety of topics. The museum is within easy walking distance of the Colorado State Capitol and the Natural History Museum. An admission fee is charged.

### The Leanin' Tree Museum of Western Art
### 6055 Longbow Drive
### Boulder, CO 80301

Recognized and acclaimed as one of the largest and finest collections of contemporary Western art in the nation, the Leanin' Tree Museum of Western Art houses over 140 original paintings by artists like Penni Anne Cross, Arnold

Just one of the over 600,000 catalog specimens in the Lowie Museum of Anthroplogy.

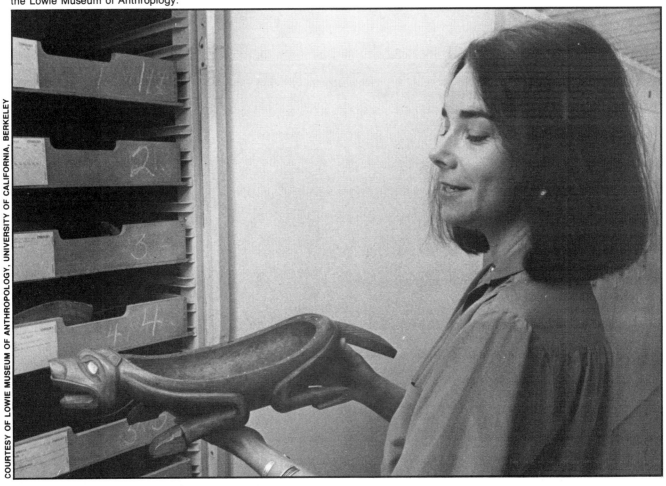

COURTESY OF LOWIE MUSEUM OF ANTHROPOLOGY, UNIVERSITY OF CALIFORNIA, BERKELEY

Friberg, Gerard Curtis Delano and Bill Hampton, and many outstanding bronze sculptures by Bill Moyers, Grant Speed, Joe Beeler and Harry Jackson, to name a few. These works of art are the collection of Mr. Ed Trumble, founder and chairman of Leanin' Tree. The collection was first put on display in 1974. Since it opened the museum has welcomed thousands of visitors from the United States and over 25 foreign countries.

The Leanin' Tree Museum of Western Art does not exhibit historical works of artists such as Russel or Remington. Instead, it focuses its attention on the works of contemporary and recently deceased artists. For the student of history, this is an important collection because it represents the enduring qualities of the old West. Anyone interested in the early history of our Western states will appreciate these collections. The museum is open Monday through Friday, closed on weekends and major holidays. No admission fee is charged.

### The Ute Indian Museum
### 17253 Chipeta Drive
### Montrose, CO 81402

The Ute Indian Museum in Montrose, Colorado, commemorates the life of the famous chief of the southern Ute Indian tribe, Ouray, and his wife, Chipeta. The museum, dedicated by the Colorado Historical Society in 1956, includes on its grounds Chipeta's grave, Ouray Springs and a historical marker honoring the 1776 Dominguez-Escalante Expedition. The museum's two galleries house the Colorado

A Tlingit rattle (early 19th century) made of unidentified hardwood, ivory and native paint. From the Native American Indian Collection of the Denver Art Museum.

The exterior of the Denver Art Museum in Colorado.

188

Part of the Thomas Gilcrease Museum's collection is this oil painting entitled "Fort Laramie" by Alfred Jacob Miller.

Historical Society's most complete exhibition of Ute Indian materials ranging from dance skins, beadwork and feather bonnets to leather garments, many of which are documented to have belonged to Ouray, Chipeta or other famous Ute Indians. The visitor to the Ute Museum is also introduced to Ute Indian religion through special dioramas and exhibits. Also incorporated in the facilities are galleries reserved for traveling exhibitions. Museum hours are seasonal. Admission is charged.

# OKLAHOMA:

## Thomas Gilcrease Museum Association
## 1400 Gilcrease Museum Road
## Tulsa, OK 74127

For a look at America's past through the eyes of the artists who witnessed history, this is one of the best places to go. Contained within the Thomas Gilcrease Institute of American History and Art is an internationally acclaimed collection of art, artifacts, rare books and documents that illustrate the development of the American West from pre-

Columbian times to the 19th century. The institute's American art collection contains works by artists such as Frederic Remington (1861-1909), Charles Russell (1864-1926), John J. Audubon (1785-1851), George Catlin (1796-1872), Thomas Moran (1837-1926) and many others.

Of particular interest to the buckskinner is the annual rendezvous held by the Gilcrease Museum. This event occurs near the first weekend of May and is highlighted not only by an early 1800s style encampment, but by the opening of the annual rendezvous exhibitions at the museum. These exhibitions feature art work by acclaimed Western artists. Special goings-on during the rendezvous include Indian dancing, clogging, a tipi raising, fiddlin' contest, muzzleloading demonstrations, Native American fashion shows, and various demonstrations by Indian and pioneer artists and craftsmen.

The Thomas Gilcrease Institute of American History and Art is open year-round. There is no admission charge. More information about the annual rendezvous and art exhibition may be obtained by writing the museum's public relations department.

An uncovered covered wagon on display at the Panhandle-Plains Historical Museum is part of its tribute to the pioneer sprit of Texas.

# TEXAS:

## Panhandle-Plains Historical Museum
## 2401 Fourth Avenue
## Canyon, TX 79016

The Panhandle-Plains Historical Museum is a tribute to the pioneer spirit in Texas history. Built in 1933, the building itself bears a State Antiquities Landmark designation for its unique architectural style. The Panhandle-Plains Museum is the largest museum in the Lone Star State.

If viewed systematically, the museum's exhibits chronicle the history of the southern plains from early Paleozoic times to the 1920s discovery and development of the panhandle oil and gas field. A hall of southern plains Indian cultures records the life of such tribes as the Apache, Kiowa, Arapaho and southern Cheyenne. Exhibits in this hall feature part of one of the finest collections of southern plains Indian artifacts in the Southwest. Everyday lives of cowboys and cattlemen are illustrated with guns, saddles, photographs and life-size dioramas in the exhibit "Texas Ranching: The First 300 Years."

Other integral parts of the Panhandle-Plains Museum include its galleries of art, historic fashions and natural history. A research facility, the museum's library-archive, contains many works dealing with history, archaeology and art. The research center is open to the public.

The museum is also host to many special events and exhibitions throughout the year. Events which have been presented in the past include the annual Museum Day, exhibits on Native American art and Southwest Native American jewelry. Admission is not charged. Museum hours are seasonal.

## Presidio La Bahia
## P.O. Box 57
## Goliad, TX 77963

In 1721, the Spanish built a fortification at an important crossroads. For most of its active history it was the scene of many battles. The Presidio was the most fought-over fort in Texas history. In fact, Presidio La Bahia is the only fortification on the North American continent to have participated in six separate national revolutions or wars for independence. The Presidio is the oldest fort in the United States west of the Mississippi River. It endured the longest siege in Texas military history. This was the site of the sad event known as the Goliad Massacre, which constituted the largest loss of life the Texans suffered during their revolution from Mexico. As a result of this, one of the largest graves in the U.S. is located just beyond the walls of the Presidio. La Bahia is also the site of the first offensive action taken by the Texans in the Texas Revolution.

More important to the visitor are facts like the following: La Bahia is the only fully restored Spanish presidio in existence in the United Stats. It is the only site in the entire state of Texas that appears as it did in 1836. The fort chapel is one of the oldest church structures in the country and is the only church structure from the Spanish Colonial period that has its original groin vaulted ceiling intact. Excavations in the area have revealed nine levels of civilization on the site.

Visitors to Presidio La Bahia will see an authentic Spanish fort manned by living history interpreters. A visitor will experience a unique display of part of Texas' turbulent history — which in a broader sense is also a part of the United States history. Living history events are held periodically throughout the year, and an admission fee is charged. Presidio La Bahia is located one mile south of Goliad on U.S. 183 and is open year-round.

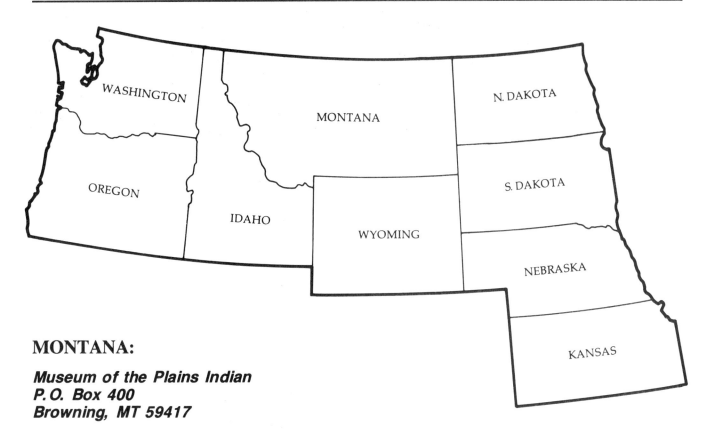

## MONTANA:

### Museum of the Plains Indian
### P.O. Box 400
### Browning, MT 59417

One of the finest museums dedicated to the study of Native Americans of the northern great plains, the Museum of the Plains Indian in Browning, Montana, offers its visitors a unique and in-depth look at the diversity of historic arts created by the Blackfeet, northern Cheyenne, Arapaho, Shoshone, Sioux, Flathead and Nez Perce people. A highlight of the historic exhibits is a display of the varied costumes of northern plains people in complete detail. Various other displays cover art forms related to the ceremonial and social aspects of different tribal cultures. Also incorporated into the museum's facilities is a multi-media presentation about the development of Indian culture on the northern plains called "Winds of Change," along with changing exhibit galleries which allow a further examination of various Native American arts and crafts of yesterday and today.

Many special events take place at the Museum of the Plains Indian throughout the year. These include demonstrations of Native American arts and crafts, events honoring Native Americans who have achieved fame in the performing arts, literature and art, and North American Indian Days. North American Indian Days is a major annual public event presented during the month of July in Browning, Montana. It is one of the largest gartherings of United States and Canadian tribes in the Northwest.

Tours can be arranged at the museum but are not necessary. The museum sends a special invitation to school groups to visit their facilities. The museum, founded in 1941, is administered by the Indian Arts and Crafts Board. Hours of operation are seasonal. There is no admission charge.

### Plains Indian Buffalo Culture Memorial
### Paul Dyck Foundation
### c/o Artists for Native America
### P.O. Box 158413
### Nashville, TN 37215

The year 1989 will see the opening of a brand new museum, the Plains Indian Buffalo Culture Memorial. The opening of this museum will take place in conjunction with the Montana State Centennial Celebration. So why another plains Indian museum? Paul Dyck, present owner of an extensive collection of plains Indian artifacts says that there are bits and pieces of the "buffalo culture" all over the world, but the Buffalo Culture Memorial will offer, for the first time, a representation of an entire culture in one place and in the appropriate educational setting.

The location of the museum will be on the Custer Battlefield National Monument which is situated in the heart of the Crow Indian Reservation, Montana. Many people visit the Custer Battlefield each year to see the site of the General's demise. After the opening of the Buffalo Culture Museum, visitors will also be able to see and better understand the culture of the Indians who fought the battle at "Greasy Grass" and the conflict of cultures which culminated in the battle.

The founders of the museum foundation have a goal to bridge cultures and promote understanding between peoples. With this in mind, the central museum structure will be con-

structed in the shape of a sun lodge with four wings to give the building the appearance of the morning star. The Paul Dyck Collection, valued at between 17 to 19 million dollars, is the most complete assemblage of plains Indian buffalo culture artifacts ever. The collection spans the era of 1700 to 1885. It contains 200 complete costumes, robes, blankets, horse gear, weapons, toys, pipes, religious materials, and three of the largest hide lodge covers in existence. In all there are nearly 20,000 items in the collection from which items for display in the museum will originate.

The opening of this museum promises to be an exciting opportunity for anyone interested in the plains Indian buffalo culture. It will definitely shatter myths and straighten misconceptions about the plains Indian peoples.

The Museum of the Plains Indian and Crafts Center exhibits historic and contemporary Indian arts, murals, dioramas and special exhibitions.

Two out of 200 "buffalo culture" costumes (circa 1830) displayed at the Plains Indian Buffalo Culture Memorial.

# NEBRASKA:

## Fort Hartsuff State Historical Park
## Route 1, Box 37
## Burwell, NE 68823

Fort Hartsuff came into being as a result of confrontations between the Indians (mostly Teton Sioux) and white settlers in the North Loup Valley of Nebraska in the early 1870s. After the War Between the States was ended, hundreds of homesteaders flooded into the area, eager to stake their claims to free government land. A fort on the Loup was needed to protect these settlers.

Construction on Fort Hartsuff began in the fall of 1874. The nine major buildings were constructed of concrete. These original buildings are still intact, now furnished in period style. Named for Major General George L. Hartsuff, the post served as a security station for Loup Valley settlers during its seven years as an active military installation.

As time went by, however, there became less need for this outpost. Orders for abandonment were issued by the Department of the Platte on April 13, 1881. Between 1881 and 1961, when Dr. Glen Auble presented the site to the state of Nebraska for preservation, Fort Hartsuff was farmed as private land.

Today, the fort is of special interest to the living history enthusiast because it is extemely well restored and furnished. The barracks are complete with 1872 composite beds. The post hospital and laundress quarters are also completely furnished. In addition, the blacksmith and carpenter shops have been reconstructed and are fully functional.

The fort is administered by the Nebraska Game and Parks Commission. More information can be obtained by writing the park in care of Superintendent Roye D. Lindsay.

Some officers brought their families to the plains during their tours of duty at Fort Hartsuff. Located near Elyria, the post is now a Nebraska state historical park.

## Harold Warp Pioneer Village Foundation
## Minden, NE 69595

Twelve miles south of Interstate Highway 80 near Kearney is a unique site for the person interested in the growth of the American West. At the Pioneer Village founded by Harold Warp, some 50,000 pieces of Americana are displayed in its 25 buildings. Many of the buildings are actual historic buildings that have been moved to their present locations. The displays are chronologically arranged so that the viewer can see the progression of the use of the items from the time of their invention to the time of their replacement. In this way the visitor can see the growth of the country from a wilderness outpost to a worldwide leader.

The historic buildings and displays are varied. A one-room schoolhouse is there, complete with its original furnishings. The St. Paul Lutheran Church of Minden was moved to the village with its original alter, pews, organ and baptismal font. Services are held every Sunday, June thru September. Moved from Franklin County, Nebraska, the Bloomington Limestone Land Office Building now stands in the village. The Elm Creek Fort was moved from Webster County, where it stood inside a stockage that protected five families during the Indian wars. Moved from the town of

Lowell is an old B & M Depot. A pony express station moved from Bridgeport, Nebraska, also stands in the village. Nearby is a reproduction of the Peoples' Store in Stamford, Nebraska, which is historically stocked to suit a pioneer's needs. Other displays (contained in modern buildings) include every aspect of a settler's life.

The Harold Warp Pioneer Village is located on U. S. 6 and is open year-round. Admission is $4.00 for adults and $2.00 for children ages 6-16. The admission fee is good for more than one visit. Also included in the self-supporting, non-profit complex is a 90-unit motel, campground and restaurant with reasonable rates.

## The Stuhr Museum of the Prairie Pioneer
## 3133 West Highway 34
## Grand Island, NE 68801

To catch a glimpse of pioneer life, particularly the era when the railroad had just linked East and West, motorists traveling through central Nebraska can pause at a crossroads in time on the southwest edge of Grand Island. The crossroads, called the Stuhr Museum of the Prairie Pioneer, is a 200-acre complex featuring two year-round exhibit buildings and a seasonal outdoor museum called Railroad Town, Nebraska.

The 40-acre town, patterned after those along the Union

STUHR MUSEUM

This sculptured grouping of a plains Indian family is the central exhibit in the Gus Fonner Memorial Rotunda, a separate building on the Stuhr Museum grounds which houses Indian and old west memorabilia of a noted collector.

Pacific in the 1860s, consists of 60 original shops, homes, barns and other structures that were moved to the site and restored and furnished to the period. From May to September, Railroad Town bustles with costumed interpreters living the parts of townsfolk and railroad men from the 1860s.

The Stuhr Museum's main building, designed by world renowned architect Edward Durell Stone, contains exhibits that detail the 1860 to 1910 period in Nebraska's history. These exhibits include clothing, furniture and other necessities of life for the Nebraska pioneer.

In the Gus Fonner Memorial Rotunda, an unusual building shaped like a wagon wheel, visitors can view the late civic leader's splendid collection of plains Indian and old West artifacts.

The Stuhr Museum complex is easily accessible. Its exhibits and reconstructions are of the highest caliber. For the student of the westward expansion period of United States history, this is a vital site for gaining knowledge and insight into life on the prairie. The Stuhr Museum is open year-round, however, Railroad Town is open only during the summer months. An admission fee is charged.

## OREGON:

### Portland Art Museum
### 1219 Southwest Park
### Portland, OR 97205

Founded in 1892, the Portland Art Museum is one of the oldest such establishments on the West Coast. More than 90 years of collecting art has earned the museum an international reputation for its outstanding holdings. Among the 35 centuries of world art represented at the Portland Art Museum is a wonderful collection of northwest coast Indian art. The Rasmussen Collection of Northwest Coast Art in-

corporates such cultural items as ceremonial masks and accoutrements, as well as a northwest coast Indian longhouse.

An admission fee is charged for the museum. Operating hours differ by day. The museum is closed on Mondays.

## SOUTH DAKOTA:

### Sioux Indian Museum and Crafts Center
### P.O. Box 1504
### Rapid City, SD 57701

Those interested in the lives of the Sioux Indians will not want to miss the Sioux Indian Museum and Crafts Center. Highlighted in the modern galleries are selected works from the museum's permanent collection of historic Sioux arts. These range from quilled pipe bags and beaded blanket strips to dolls and complete articles of clothing for both men and women. A special exhibition gallery is reserved for changing presentations that promote the creative talents of contemporary Native American artists and craftsmen. Special exhibits on Sioux culture are also an integral part of the museum's presentation. A special summer exhibition in 1988 was titled "Sioux Crafts — Adaptations" and featured outstanding works of adaptive art in quilling, beading, pottery making, quilting, painting and cross-stitch, to name a few. This exhibit focused on the adaptation of ancient patterns and creative forms to modern materials and mediums.

The Sioux Indian Museum was founded in 1939 through a joint cooperation of the federal and Rapid City governments. The museum program is administered by the Indian Arts and Crafts Board, an agency located in the U.S. Department of the Interior. The Arts and Crafts Board was developed to promote the growth of contemporary Native American arts in the United States. The museum is easily accessible in downtown Rapid City. There is no admission charge. Hours vary by season. The museum requests that potential photographers request permission to photograph the permanent exhibits well in advance of their visit. Photography in the craft shop, operated by the Tipi Shop, Incorporated, is prohibited.

## WYOMING:

### Buffalo Bill Historical Center
### P.O. Box 1000
### Cody, WY 82414

A visitor to the Buffalo Bill Historical Center will find an unparalleled collection of Western Americana. Contained within the four separate museums of the complex are: 13,500 artifacts and works of art, 14,000 printed volumes, and 25,000 photographic images.

*Buffalo Bill Museum:* This featured museum of the Buffalo Bill Historical Center is dedicated to displaying items pertaining to the life and times of the legendary William F. Cody. The exhibits showcase the various occupations he held in life, which included that of Pony Express rider, wild West showman, Indian wars scout, broadway actor and conser-

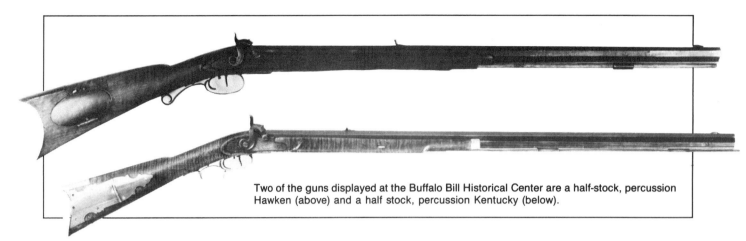

Two of the guns displayed at the Buffalo Bill Historical Center are a half-stock, percussion Hawken (above) and a half stock, percussion Kentucky (below).

vationalist. Also contained in this museum is the Boone and Crockett Club's National Collection of Heads and Horns.

*Plains Indian Museum:* Exhibited here is an exceptional display of art and artifacts representing selected tribes of the great plains. The culture of the Sioux, Cheyenne, Shoshone, Crow, Arapaho and Blackfeet is traced in addition to the changes and development of the Indians from past centuries to modern traditions and customs. Life patterns, religious practices and artistic expressions are represented in the Indian clothing, weapons, ceremonial items, beadwork and daily utensils on display

*Whitney Gallery of Western Art:* Paintings, sculptures, prints and drawings are exhibited here to give the viewer an invaluable image of America's Western heritage. Included in the collection are the works of Catlin, Bodmer, Miller, Moran, Bierstadt, Sharp, Russell, Remington, Koerner and Shreyvogel. The artwork in this world-renowned museum spans a century and a half, roughly from 1825 to the present day.

*Winchester Arms Museum:* This museum displays the expanded collection of noted firearms manufacturer Oliver F. Winchester. Today there are over 5,000 firearms and related weapons in the museum, 1,500 of which are displayed. The complete history of the development of firearms is diagramed and documented, including examples of matchlocks, flintlocks, percussion and repeating firearms, plus many examples of the unique. The displays represent technological differences, economic changes, historic associations, quality of ornamentation, and the variety of materials utilized in the production of firearms. The Winchester Arms Museum is a must for the firearm enthusiast!

## Colter Bay Indian Arts Museum
## Grand Teton National Park
## Moose, WY 83012

The Colter Bay Indian Arts Museum is located north of scenic Jackson Lake within the Grand Teton National Park. The museum displays represent items from most Native American cultural areas on the North American continent. Opportunities for extensive research are lacking, as the museum is small. Despite its small size, the Colter Bay Indian Arts Museum does provide the visitor with a cross section of Native American culture in its exhibits. Contained in the museum are examples of trade beads, pipes, sashes, shields, tools and utensils, moccasins, toys, baskets and clothings.

Since the museum is located in the Grand Teton National Park and is also near Yellowstone National Park, the visitor has numerous opportunities for recreation and education. The entire Jackson Hole region is also a wonderful place to learn about the Rocky Mountain fur trade. Admission is free to the Colter Bay Indian Arts Museum, but a visitor must pay the usual admission fee for entry into the national park.

## APPENDIX: SOURCEBOOKS AND AGENCIES

*Directory of Historical Societies and Agencies in the United States and Canada*
ISBN #0-9100-50-36-8
    American Association for State & Local History
    1400 Eighth Avenue South
    Nashville, TN 37205

*Official Museum Directory*
ISBN #0-87217-011-5
    American Association of Museums
    1055 Thomas Jefferson Street, N.W.
    Washington, D.C. 20007
    (202) 338-5300

National Register Publishing Company, Inc.
3004 Glenview Road
Wilmette, IL 60091
(312) 256-6067

*Off the Beaten Path*
ISBN #0-89577-253-1
    Reader's Digest Association, Inc.
    Pleasantville, NY 10570

# Games, Sports & Other Amusements

## by George D. Glenn

MUCH AS HE hates to admit it, George Glenn, seen at right contemplating his next lead in a game of whist, has been involved in muzzleloading, buckskinning and reenacting long enough to almost be considered an old-timer. His interest in old guns and all that goes with them was first kindled when his father gave him a Civil War Enfield musket at the age of 13 in 1951. He did not come from a gun- or shooting-oriented family (who knows what possessed his father), so shooting muzzleloaders had to wait until he turned 21 and could legally purchase a handgun in Illinois. He wasted no time in repairing to Gil Hibard's Gun Shop in Knoxville, Illinois, and laying out $90.00 borrowed from his college funds for an original 1851 Navy Colt, a Dixie bullet mold, a box of caps and a pound of FFF. He learned to shoot a rifle after he was married by building a flintlock from parts. He managed to make them fit together and actually work, much to his wife's bemusement. According to her it's been all downhill from there for the last quarter of a century.

Since then he founded the Turkey Foot Longrifles, which is celebrating its 20th anniversary this year and a muzzleloading business ahead of its time in devotion to authenticity in its offerings. George started writing for *MUZZLELOADER* in 1975 and has been a Special Features Editor since 1976. He thinks he may have been the first person in the country to offer a college-level course in muzzleloading. George took up buckskinning, then graduated to Revolutionary War reenacting and has committed other similar acts for which he will surely be called to account at the great Final Muster.

George Glenn is a member of the NRA and the NMLRA, is a charter member of the Iowa Black Powder Federation, and is the commander of the Sixth Virginia Regiment of Foot, Continental Line, in the North West Territory Alliance. This chapter marks his fifth appearance in the Book of Buckskinning Series.

ONE of the most significant aspects of a rendezvous or reenactment is recreating an authentic
and historic "slice of life" for the participant
as well as the spectator. This means that it is necessary to
recreate not only the physical environment—authentic
clothing, weapons, equipment, living quarters, etc.—but also
the life style of the period. The attraction of "living history"
for participants and spectators alike is the bringing to life
of what would otherwise be a sterile, untenanted museum
display.

I am aware that many rendezvous are for participants
only, with no outside spectators, but even in these cir-
cumstances, part of the pleasure of participation is in observing the authentic life of the camp unfolding around you,
of being, at one and the same time, participant and spectator.
The effect is not unlike that experienced by a musician in
the middle of an orchestra or by an actor in a play.

Many of the everyday camp activities that we as participants take for granted are fascinating to the observer, from
cooking over an open fire with authentic utensils to a shooting
match. But there is room for special events, too. We enjoy
shooting as well as watching a shooting match. Every card
or dice game attracts kibitzers. In other words the pleasure
of participants and observers can be enhanced and expanded
by providing more opportunities for relaxing with fun and
games, in this case authentic and appropriate fun and games.

So, this chapter will present a number of ideas and sug-
gestions for authentic games and amusements. The variety
will include examples from several historical periods as well
as several different kinds of games. The listing is not intended
to be exhaustive, and some may already be familiar to you.
We will look at games common during the Colonial/Revolu-
tionary War period, the fur trade and the Civil War, since
these are the most frequently reenacted periods. We will ex-

amine a variety of card games, dice games, board games and sporting contests from each period, recognizing that a game from one period may continue in popularity into another. Although I recognize that French and Spanish colonists and Native Americans had their own games and sports, I will concentrate primarily on those games introduced by the English colonists and further developed and played in the United States.

# CARD GAMES

## *Whist*

It is not known when whist was first invented, but it was already well-known as early as 1674. In that year Charles Cotton, giving the rules for a number of card games, declared that whist was "so commonly known in England in all parts thereof, that every child of eight years old hath a competent knowledge" (55). By 1742, whist was popular enough to stimulate Edmund Hoyle to publish his *Short Treatise on the Game of Whist.* Hoyle's book was the first scientific study of a card game, and it wasn't long before the phrase "according to Hoyle" was heard everywhere (Carson 58-59). Whist, sometimes also called "whisk" in the mid-18th century, became the favorite four-handed card game of the late 18th and early 19th centuries and, as everyone knows, was the ancestor of the modern game of bridge. The rules of play are relatively simple; the game's fascination and complexity comes from the fact that each player must remember the location of every card played and deduce the distribution and location of the remaining cards in the opposing players'

A candle-lit game of whist is a great way to relax after a hard day of reenacting.

hands.

Whist is played with a standard deck of 52 cards.[1] The game is played with partners, but unlike bridge there is no bidding and no exposed "dummy" hand on the table. As Cotton stated, the rules are simple. After shuffling the cards and presenting the pack to the player on his right to be cut, the dealer deals out all the cards, one at a time, beginning with the player on his left. The dealer turns up the last card; its suit determines the trump suit for that hand. The dealer restores the last card to his hand, and play begins by the player to the dealer's left playing a card from his hand to the center of the table. Each player in turn plays a card, following suit if possible, and the high card of the four played takes the trick, as the group of four cards is called. The player whose card was highest and thus took the trick (aces are high) then must lead (play a card from his hand) for the next trick. The dealer is partnered with the player opposite him, while the other two players also play as partners. Although either player of the partnership can take the trick if he plays the highest card of the four, the trick is won by the partnership.

As each trick is played, it is collected and placed face down in front of one of the players of each side. Usually the first to take a trick keeps the remaining tricks in front of him regardless of which of the team takes them. If a player cannot follow suit, he has the option of discarding a card from another suit or playing a card from the trump suit. If no other player plays a higher trump card, his will take the trick.

The first side to take six tricks has "made book" and every trick taken thereafter will count one point towards the score. The first side to accumulate seven points wins the game, the value of which is seven minus the losing side's accumulated score. For example, beginning the last deal of a game, one side has five points, the other side three. The former side wins three odd-tricks (three more than the six-trick book) and wins the game, but the score is $7 - 3 = 4$, not $8 - 3 = 5$, since the winning side can't score more than the game-winning seven points (Morehead and Mott-Smith 33). The best two out of three hands constitutes a winning "rubber."

Aside from the bidding and the use of the dummy, the strategy of play in whist is much like that of modern bridge. As the cards are revealed in play, the good whist player will keep track of them (suits and values) in his head and, by comparing them with the cards remaining in his hand, will have a pretty good idea of what remaining cards are distributed among the other three hands. Although he wrote over three hundred years ago, Cotton gives good advice on the play:

*Though you have but mean cards in your own hand, yet you may play them so suitable to those in your partners hand, that he may either trump them, or play the best of that suit on the board.*

*You ought to have a special eye to what cards are play'd out, that you may know by that means either what to play if you lead, or how to trump securely and advantageously. Reneging or renouncing, that is, not following suit when you have it in your hand, is very fowl play . . . . (55)*

To this I might add the rule that "when in doubt, lead trumps."

## Vingt-et-Un

Vingt-et-Un, otherwise known today as twenty-one or blackjack, is a very ancient game and was certainly being played in the eighteenth century. It remains a popular social and casino game today, and the rules are too well-known to need more than a brief restatement here.

The players can number from two to ten or twelve. The dealer is determined by having a dealer pro-tem deal the shuffled cards to the other players, one at a time, face up. The first person to be dealt an ace becomes the dealer/banker. The dealer reshuffles, and the cards are cut. The dealer then turns up a card, shows it to the other players and "burns" it by placing it face up at the bottom of the deck (a joker or blank cards may also be used). An ace may not be burned—the deck must be reshuffled and cut again.

Cards are dealt one at a time, beginning at the dealer's left. After placing his bet on the table in front of him, each player including the dealer receives one card face down. Next, each player receives one card face up. At this point any "naturals" are declared by the player announcing "twenty-one" or "vingt-et-un" (or, in a modern game, "blackjack"). A natural is any combination of two cards that totals 21 (a 10 and an ace or any face card and an ace). Ordinarily, aces can be played either high or low at the player's discretion. Naturals pay off at two to one; if both the dealer and another player have a natural, the dealer wins. A player getting a natural also gets the deal on the next hand. If more than one player gets a natural, the one closest to the dealer's left gets the deal.

If no player has a natural, the dealer, beginning on his left, again deals to each player in turn. A player may "stand" on the two cards he was originally dealt, or he may ask for another card by saying "hit me." The object is to be dealt as many as five cards (including the face down or "hole" card) without exceeding a count of 21. Face cards count 10, aces count 1 or 11 and all other cards are face value. If a player exceeds a count of 21, he is "busted" and loses that hand. His cards are gathered and placed face up at the bottom of the pack. A player may stand at any point before reaching 21.

After dealing to all the other players, the dealer then deals to himself. The dealer may stand or draw (in casino play the dealer must draw if his count is 16 or less, and he

---

[1]It should be noted that early cards, unlike today's, had no numbers in their corners. It wasn't until towards the end of the nineteenth century that numbers began being added to the corners of cards.

must stay if his count is 17 or more). If the dealer busts, he pays off the remaining players. If he stays he matches his hand with those of the remaining players, collecting from those who have a count less than his, paying those whose count beats him. Ties pay the dealer.

If, on the initial deal, a player is dealt a pair, he may choose to face the hole card, request two more down cards from the dealer and play the two hands at one time.

Basic strategy is to always stand on 17 or higher, particularly if you're playing casino rules where the dealer must draw on 16 or less. Hit on 12 or under; count any ace as 1 for any number up to 17. If several players before you have stayed, you may stay on a count as low as 12 or 13, since the dealer must try for a high number and may bust (Morehead and Mott-Smith 180-183; Scarne, *Cards* 142-151).

## Cribbage

Cribbage is another of those still-popular games that has existed almost without change since the 17th century. The game is supposed to have been invented by the great English poet Sir John Suckling (1609-1642) and was brought to America by the early Colonists (Morehead and Mott-Smith 156). It was originally a two-hand game (although three- and four-player variants are known today).

Cribbage is such a fast-scoring game that the cribbage board was devised to aid in scoring (see Figure 1). Each side of the board has two rows of thirty holes marked out in 5-hole segments plus two starter holes at the home end. Each player has two pegs for keeping track of the score. Once around and back home completes a game of 61 points (the modern game consists of twice around or 121 points). Each player begins pegging points on the outer row and returns on the inner row, using two pegs and advancing the rear peg past the front peg for each point scored. For example, a player would begin scoring a count of 2 by advancing his first peg from the starter position to the outer row, hole 2. If his next point is a 3, he advances peg #2 three holes past peg #1 and so on, leapfrogging pegs. The board thus always shows the current score and the last score played (Scarne, *Cards* 404).

The dealer begins by dealing five cards (six in the modern game) to each player, beginning with the non-dealer. Each player then selects two of his cards and puts them face down in a pile by the dealer—this forms the dealer's "crib," which he will score after play of the hand is completed. Every strategist from Cotton onward stresses that the strategy here is for the dealer to select two of his best cards and the non-

dealer two of his worst—say a 2 and a 9—for the crib.

Play begins by the dealer next turning up a "starter" card from the pack; this card is used in common by both players. Play commences by each player evaluating and scoring the cards in his hand, although "you must not see (your opponent's) cards nor he yours; if you think he plays foul by reckoning too much, you may count them after the hand is played" (Cotton 52). This is another departure from the modern game, where this "melding" is completed after the hand has been played (Scarne, *Cards* 407). The non-dealer scores his hand first, called "showing." Each player scores the three cards still in his hand plus the common starter card. Any combination of cards which counts up to fifteen (aces count 1, face cards count 10) is good for 2 points. Other combination that score are:

| A pair | 2 points |
|---|---|
| A pair-royal (3 of a kind) | 6 points |
| A double pair-royal (four of a kind) | 12 points |
| Run of three | 2 points |
| Run of four or more | 1 point for each card |
| Flush of three or more | 1 point for each card |

In addition, if you hold a jack in your hand that is of the same suit as the starter, it is called "knave noddy" ("his nobs" in modern lingo) and scores 1 point (Cotton 51-52). In the modern six-card game, there are other possible scoring combinations, such as double runs, which Cotton does not use (Scarne, *Cards* 407; Morehead and Mott-Smith 159).

Following the meld, play begins by the non-dealer selecting one of his cards and laying it on the table in front of him, announcing the value of the card as he does so. For instance, assume that the dealer holds a 9 and two 6s after laying off two cards to the crib, while the non-dealer holds a 4, 5 and 6. Also assume that a 6 was turned up as the starter. In the meld the dealer would have scored a total of 12 (a pair-royal—three 6s—for 6 points and three 15s for 2 points each). The non-dealer would have a total of 8 (a run of three in his hand for 2 points, a run of three counting the starter for 2, a count of fifteen in his hand for 2 and a count of fifteen with the starter for 2). Cotton suggests playing this hand as follows:

*He that dealt not plays first, suppose it a six, if you have a nine play it, that makes fifteen (announcing "fifteen—2" as you play), for which set up two, the next may play a four*

# FIGURE 1 The layout of a cribbage board, standard since the invention of the game.

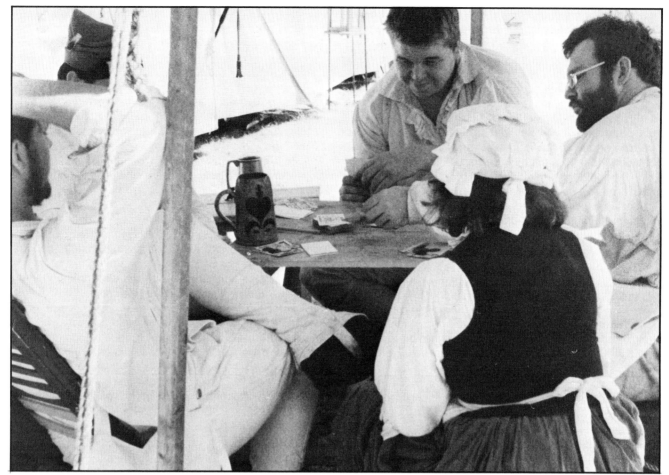

Only the British could have hard money on the table
in a fast game of loo between battles.

*which makes nineteen, you* [play] *a six, twenty-five, and he
a five that is thirty, you not being able to come in, having
a six in your hand, he* [scores] *one (for it is one and thirty
you aim at in playing the cards), because he is most, and
two for Sequences four, five, six, which were his four after
the fifteen, you five, and his six; and that doth not hinder
them from being Sequences, though the six was play'd between the four and the five; but if an Ace, Nine, King, Queen,
or the like, had been play'd between, they had been no Sequences, so the two for the Sequences, and the one for thirty
being most (as at one and thirty) makes him three . . . . (53)*

The object is to get as close to a count of 31 points as
possible. If you can't play a card and not carry the point total
over 31, you must say, "Go." If your opponent then cannot play under 31, he also calls "Go," and you peg 1 point.
If your opponent *can* play and keep the total under 31, he
pegs 1 point—and can peg 2 points if he can come to an exact 31 total. After a go, play resumes, counting again towards
a new 31-point goal. The final card played is considered a
go and scores 1 point for last and 2 points if it totals 31
(Scarne, *Cards* 406-407; Morehead and Mott-Smith 157).

"Lastly," says Cotton, "you [the dealer] look upon
your Crib; if [you] find no [point] in them, nor help from
the [starter], then [you are] bilkt . . . . Thus they play and deal

by turns till the game of sixty one be up" (53). There is one
other chance to score: "If you get the game [61 points] before
you adversary is forty five . . .you must then say, I have *lurkt*
you, and that is a double game for whatever you play'd with
six shilling, or a greater summ" (Cotton 53). Modern cribbage says you are "lurched" and lose a double game if you
haven't made it halfway around by the time your opponent
scores 61 (or 121).[2]

## Loo

Loo was a popular, high-stakes game in the 18th century and was also known as lanterloo. Cotton gives the rules
for a five-card game, but by the 18th century, a simplified
three-card game had evolved (Carson 66 ff). The game was
so popular that a special round table with compartments
around the edge to hold the counters was devised. The compartments were called "fish ponds," from the popular fish-
shaped counters, usually valued at sixpence each (Carson
67).[3]

The game is suitable for any number of players but

[2]For strategy and scoring tables for the modern game, see Scarne or
Morehead and Mott-Smith.

[3]See Neumann and Kravic, page 129 for a photo of Loo counters.

202

seems to work best with around five to seven. Play begins by cutting for the deal; high card deals. Cotton suggests that you can play with a deck from which the threes, fours, fives, sixes and sevens have been removed so that the players "may not be quickly Lood; but if they would have the Loos come fast about them then play with the whole pack" (69).

The players place their bets in the "pool" in the middle of the table. The dealer then deals three cards to each player and, if the complete pack is being used, three cards to an extra hand or "miss," sometimes called the "widow." He then turns up a card to determine a trump suit.

After the deal, the eldest (the player to the left of the dealer) has the option of leading a card, passing (and losing his ante) or turning in his hand and playing the miss. If he chooses the miss, he must play. If he passes, the next player in line may choose to play the miss, and so on. Once the miss has been taken, the remaining players must either pass or play.

The first player to play must lead his highest trump, if he has one, by placing it on the table in front of him. The players do not toss their cards into the center of the table but, as in cribbage, simply place their cards in front of them. The remaining players must follow suit if they can, and if a trump was not first led, they may trump if they can't follow suit. Aces count 11, face cards 10, etc. There is no ranking of suits. The winner of the first trick then leads for the second, and so on. A player who takes no tricks is *looed;* the players who are looed in a hand must make up the pool for the next hand. The winners of the three tricks divide the original pool up in the ratio of a third for each trick won. Carson describes a typical example of dividing up the pool:

*If five players originally contributed six counters each, the pool of thirty is divided thus: Player A passed; he receives nothing and contributes nothing to the next pool. Player B took one trick; he receives ten counters. Player C took two tricks; he receives twenty counters. Players D and E were looed; they receive nothing and each contributes fifteen counters to the next pool. If the game is unlimited, then D and E each contributes thirty counters, and the next pool is sixty. (280)*

If there are five players, two at least are bound to be looed. In the unlimited game, the pool gets very large very fast, since each player who is looed must contribute the entire amount of the last pool to the next pool. Carson quotes a report from the *Virginia Gazette* from 1768 that reports that a London lady lost a thousand guineas in an evening's play at loo (68). Carson also mentions that if only one player stands in (does not pass), then the dealer must play his hand (or the miss)—he cannot pass.

Some variants in the older five-card game are: (1) A player who holds a five-card flush loos the table, that is, wins the whole pool. If more than one player hold a flush, the eldest flush takes precedence. (2) The knave of clubs is wild and is called *pam.* Pam can take the ace of trumps.

Nor were the seventeenth and eighteenth centuries ages of innocence. Cotton warns, "if one of the gamesters have four of a suit and he want a fifth, he may...make an exchange out of his own pocket if he be skill'd in the cleanly art of conveiance, [but] it is not my business to teach you how to cheat..." (69-70)

## Fan-Tan

A game played in Colonial times, fan-tan is a simple card game suitable for children as well as adults. Since the entire pack of 52 cards is dealt out, it works better with more than two or three players, especially if the hands holding the cards are small ones. After the deal the players place their bets in the center of the table. It is best to use counters or chips and establish a common ante, say, one counter. Because some players will have fewer cards than the others, the players with fewer than the maximum number of cards must double the initial bet.

The eldest player begins play by leading a seven to the center of the table. If he has no seven, he must pay another counter to the pot. The next player then plays, either his seven or building in sequence next to the cards already played. The four 7s are kept in a pile, the 6s to the left of the 7s, the 8s to the right, and so on. Aces are low and go next to the twos; the kings are played on top of the queens. As with the sevens, any time a player cannot play a card from his hand (either building on a card already played or starting a new pile in sequence), he must put another counter in the pot. The player who first gets rid of all his cards wins the pot (Strobell 29).

## Poker

The card games so far mentioned all originated in or before the eighteenth century and were popular for a considerable time, some even up to the present day. They are thus suitable for almost any period. Other games came into being after the eighteenth century, however, and are more appropriate for the period of the fur trade, the Civil War or later. Of these card games, by far and away the most popular and enduring are the several variants of poker.

The origins of poker are lost in the mists of time, but some authorities trace it to an ancient Persian (Iranian) game called *as* from which we supposedly get our term "ace" (Scarne, *Cards* 231). At any rate a game that was recognizably poker, and which was called that, was being played on the Mississippi steamboats in the 1830s (Scarne, *Cards* 230). This early Poker game was played with twenty cards, the aces through the tens. Each player was dealt five cards, and the maximum number of players was obviously four. According to Scarne this was the game that was first included in *The American Hoyle* in the 1860s, although that work called the game "Bluff." By 1887, the game had been recognized again as poker.

Modern draw poker is probably as close to the original game as one needs to get. Draw poker is so well-known and widely played that it is unnecessary to elaborate the rules here. Refer to the standard sources, such as Scarne or Morehead and Mott-Smith.

## Faro

Family tradition has it that my wife's Grandpa Focht, a private in an Iowa regiment in the Civil War, came back from the war with enough money to buy a farm or two in southwestern Iowa. How did he do it? He was a faro dealer. Faro was an extremely popular gambling game from the seventeenth century through the nineteenth century and would be a wonderful game to reproduce at a reenactment except for the equipment needed to run the game. Aside from the table cloth with the layout of a suit of thirteen cards painted on it, the game requires a faro dealing box which will permit one card at a time to be dealt; a casekeeper, or counter, to keep track of the cards played; a rack of chips; a supply of markers to denote bets; and some betting coppers, traditionally the nineteenth-century large cent piece. An ambitious reenactor who could come up with authentic equipment could put on quite a display, redolent of old-time river boat gamblers, but it's all too much for most of us to manage.

## Spanish Monte

However, a faro family game that was popular in the pre-Civil War Southwest, Spanish monte, can be played without all the faro paraphernalia. The dealer, or banker, established by cutting the low card, shuffles the cards and presents them to the player on his right to be cut. He then deals four cards face up to the center of the table in the following manner: he takes the first two cards from the bottom of the deck and places them face up; he next takes two cards from the top of the deck and places them face up below the first two cards, forming a rectangle. The cards should be relatively close together. If any of the four cards are of the same rank—two sixes, for example—there is a "no play," and the cards are redealt.

Beginning at the dealer's left, each player now bets on any two of the four cards, betting that one of them will be matched by a card drawn from the deck before the other will. The player indicates this by placing his bet on the exposed cards in a way that the bet is mainly on one card, but just touching another. If the two cards so marked are a four and a six, the player is betting that a four will come up before a six.

After all the bets are down, the dealer turns the deck face up, exposing the bottom card. If it should happen to match one of the four cards either the dealer or a player (or players) wins. The dealer keeps taking cards off the pack, exposing each subsequent card, until all the bets on the cards are won or lost.

The dealer can establish any betting limit he chooses. The deal passes to the left after each hand played (Scarne, *Cards* 185-187).

# DICE GAMES

Hammering a die out of a .75 caliber musket ball.

Dice have probably been around longer than cards—dice of various types have been traced to prehistoric times. The typical six-sided cubical die of today is identical to dice that can be identified as being Egyptian and Roman. Dice made from flattened musket balls have been excavated from Revolutionary War campsites. In this country the Native Americans were great dice-game gamblers, using a variety of dice made from such things as bones, shells, fruit stones and pebbles.

## *Hazard*

Prior to the early years of the nineteenth century, the favorite dice game was hazard, which can be thought of as a forerunner of the modern preferred game of craps. Craps, or at least the ancestor of craps, was basicaly invented early in the 1800s by the black laborers on the waterfronts and steamboats from New Orleans up the Mississippi. Generally speaking, hazard is an authentic game up to the 1830s, while craps takes over after that time, even though craps didn't appear in the big casinos and gambling clubs until the 1890s (Scarne, *Dice* 1-19).[4]

---

[4]For the rules for craps see Morehead and Mott-Smith 236 ff; or Scarne, *Dice* 1 ff.

Although the game was called hazard in the 18th century, the scene would be familiar to every serviceman in every war since the Revolution.

The rules for hazard are spelled out by Cotton and didn't change much if at all from the seventeenth through the nineteenth centuries. Hazard, Cotton says, "is a proper name for this game; for it speedily makes a man or undoes him; in the twinkling of an eye either a man or a mouse" (82). The game is played with two dice, "but there may play at it as many as can stand round the largest round table" (82). The person throwing the dice is called the "caster" (in today's parlance, the "shooter"). If another player (the "fader" in craps) desires to bet against the caster, he places his stake on the table. "When he has done this, if the caster agrees to it, he knocks the [dice] box upon the table at the person's money with whom he intends to bet, or mentions at whose money he throws" (the second edition of the *American Hoyle*, quoted in Scarne, *Dice* 15).

The caster begins by throwing the *main,* or the "company's" (fader's) point. The main can only be a 5 through 9; if any other number is thrown, it doesn't count and the caster must try again. Once the main is established, the caster must throw to establish the *chance,* or his point. The chance can be any number from 4 through 10. If, when throwing for the chance, the caster matches the main, it is a *nick* and the caster wins. Other winning nicks occur if the main is a 6 or an 8 and the caster throws 12; or if the main is a 7 and the caster throws 11 (throws of 6, 7, 8 would also nick mains of 6, 7 or 8). Losing throws, *outs,* occur automatically if the caster throws "ames-ace" (1-1, or the modern snake-eyes) or deuce-ace (3). Ames-ace and deuce-ace were also called "crabs." If the main is 5, 7 or 9 and the caster throws

a 12 (modern box-cars), it is an out and he loses. If the main is 5, 6, 8 or 9 and the caster throws an 11, it is also an out.

If none of the above things happened—that is, if the caster threw neither a nick nor an out, then the number thrown becomes the caster's point and he continues throwing until he either matches his chance, in which case he wins, or matches the main, in which case he loses. There is some indication that there could be another round of betting before the caster tried to throw his chance. Players also placed side bets among themselves, betting whether the caster would nick, out or match his chance (Cotton 82-83; Scarne, *Dice* 15-17).

The gambling odds are complex, and although in Cotton's time it was recognized that 7 was the easiest number to throw, it took Hoyle to lay out the first mathematical odds tables (for a summary of Hoyle's odds, see Carson 290). Scarne points out that "because the odds against a 6 coming before a 5 are different from those of a 5 coming before a 7, or a 9 before a 10, etc., etc., the expert Hazard player

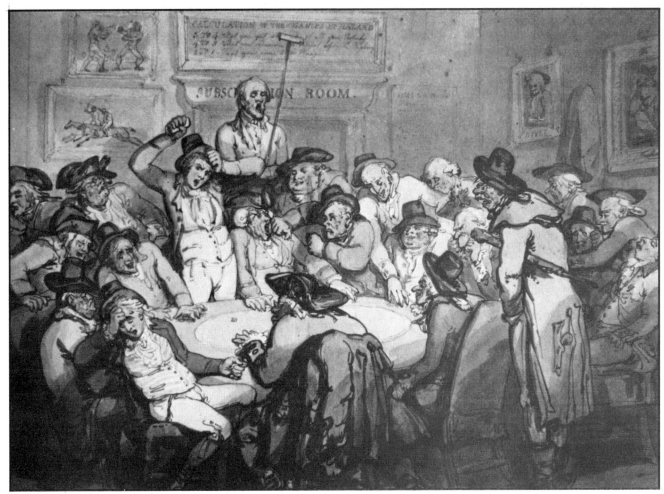

"The Hazard Room," by Rowlandson. Notice the portrait of Hoyle on the wall on the right and the odds table on the wall above the door.

had to have a remarkable memory and a very clear head'' (17). Cotton's summary of the game still can't be bettered:

*Certainly Hazzard [sic] is the most bewitching game that is plaid on the dice; for when a man begins to play he knows not when to leave off; and having once accustom'd himself to play at Hazzard he hardly ever after minds any thing else... To conclude, happy is he that having been much inclined to this time-spending-money-wasting game, hath took up in time, and resolved for the future never to be concerned with it more; but more happy is he that hath never heard the name thereof.* (84)

Sorry about that.

## Dominoes

Dominoes is a very old game that was popular in France in the seventeenth and eighteenth centuries but doesn't appear to have been popular in England until later in the eighteenth century or the beginning of the nineteenth. Carson notes that no reference to the game has been found in the records of Colonial Virginia (82). However, this doesn't mean that the game couldn't have been played elsewhere in the English or French colonies in the eighteenth century, and it was certainly popular from the beginning of the nineteenth century until the present day.

Dominoes probably evolved from dice, for each domino tile, or bone, has marked on it one of the twenty-one possible combinations that can be thrown with two dice. To make up the standard twenty-eight piece set, seven more bones are added with at least one blank on one side, plus one double blank.

The game is started by spreading all the bones out on the table face down. Each of the two players then draws seven bones from the *boneyard.* If three or four are playing, each draws five bones. Each player stands the dominoes he drew on edge facing him to form his hand. The player with the highest doublet (6-6, 5-5, etc.) begins play by laying it in

the center of the table. Play then rotates to the first player's left.

The second player then attempts to match one end of the first bone with one of his. Each player in turn continues to build off either open end. For example, if a 6-6 was first laid down, player #2 could match it with a 6-4. Player #3 could then play a 6-2 on the other end of the original 6-6 or a 4-3 off the end of player two's 6-4. There are always two open ends on which to play, even though other doublets are played crosswise.

If a player cannot play from his hand, he draws from the boneyard until he finds a bone he can play. The game ends when a player either gets rid of all the bones in his hand, or when no player can play. The player with the *lightest* hand (the hand with the lowest total number of spots) wins, and scores the total of the spots in the other hands. The usual game is to 50 or 100 total points.

## Sweat-Cloth

This three-dice game was originally known as "sweat-cloth" in England in the eighteenth century and as "sweat" when it came to America at the end of the century. It is known today as "chuck-a-luck" or "the bird cage," since the dice are enclosed in a spinning metal cage. The cage, although a part of the game, is not really necessary, since the banker can throw the three dice from a cup. The table is marked with a layout of the numbers 1, 2, 3, 4, 5 and 6, corresponding to each side of a die. The players place their bets on the numbered spaces, and if that number turns up on a die, the player wins even money. If the number appears on two dice, the bank pays 2 to 1, and the bank pays 3 to 1 if the number comes up on all three dice.

In this game it is a good idea to be the bank, since Scarne figures that the odds are 7½% in favor of the house (*Dice* 330-331).

Will he have to go to the boneyard after she makes her play? A tense moment in a game of dominoes.

# BOARD AND TABLE GAMES

## Chess, Draughts & Tables

There are a great number of board and table games that are appropriate and authentic for the period we are considering, including chess, checkers (draughts) and backgammon. These three in particular are ancient, their origins lost in the proverbial mists of time. All three are played today pretty much the way they were two or three hundred years ago. The only problem in playing an authentic game of chess is to find authentic chess pieces. The basic rules of play haven't altered for at least 350 years, as reference to Cotton will show (24-38).

The same can almost be said for checkers, or draughts (pronounced ''drafts'') as it was called then and is still so called in England. There were two versions known in the eighteenth century, the so-called French and Polish draughts. Confusingly enough, French draughts, played on a chess board of eight squares a side with sixteen men per player, was the game played in England and is the game we know today. Polish draughts, on the other hand, was played in France and by the French in America. The Polish board was ten squares on a side with twenty men a player, and in the play the men could capture backwards as well as forwards, and a king could move from one corner of the board to another if not opposed by two men close together (Strutt 415-416).

By far the oldest game extant seems to be the game of tables, or as we know it, backgammon. The rules as outlined in Morehead and Mott-Smith's *Hoyle's Rules of Games* are as authentic, as well as being complete and easy to understand, as any (224-232). As played in the seventeenth and eighteenth centuries, the game was called ''Irish'' and was the same as the modern game except there was no doubling (Cotton 74-75). The game Cotton called Back-gammon was the same game as is played today, with doubling (76).

## Goose

The Royall and Most Pleasant Game of the Goose was invented in Italy and was discovered there by the London printer John Wolfe. Wolfe published and copyrighted the

A father and his son enjoy a game of draughts on a warm summer's afternoon.

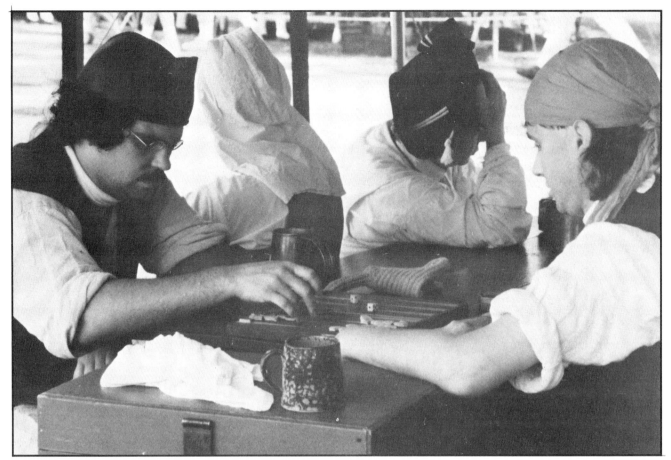

Members of a British regiment playing at tables, or backgammon.

An original goose board (Carson 91).

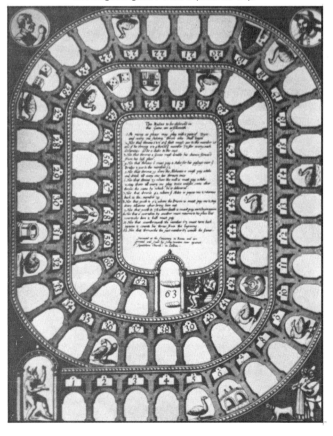

game in 1597, and it remained popular into the nineteeth century. The board contains a track of sixty-three numbered spaces, spiraling in towards the center. Most of the spaces are blank, but thirteen of them have a picture of a goose (on spaces 5, 9, 14, 18, 23, 27, 32, 36, 41, 45, 50, 54 and 59); two have a pair of dice (spaces 26, 53); while there is one each of a bridge (6), an alehouse (19), a well (31), a maze (42), a jail (52), and Death (58). The players cast a pair of dice and move tokens along the path the same number of spaces that show on the dice. The object of the game is to get your token to space 63 before the other players. To play the game, one really needs a reproduction of the original board, which contains the rules in its center:

*1. As many as please may play with a paire of Dyce and every one stakeing* [betting]. *Throw who shall begin.*

*2. Hee that throws 6 & 3 at the first must goe to the number 26 and if he throws 5 & 4 then to the number 53 for every such advantage add a stake to the rest* [double your bet].

*3. Hee that throws a Goose must double his chance forward from his last place* [move twice the number on the dice].

*4. Hee that throws 6* [the space with the bridge] *must pay a stake for his passage over the Bridge & goe to the number 12.*

*5. Hee that throws 19 where the Alehouse is must pay a stake and drink till every one has thrown once.* [That is, he must skip a turn].

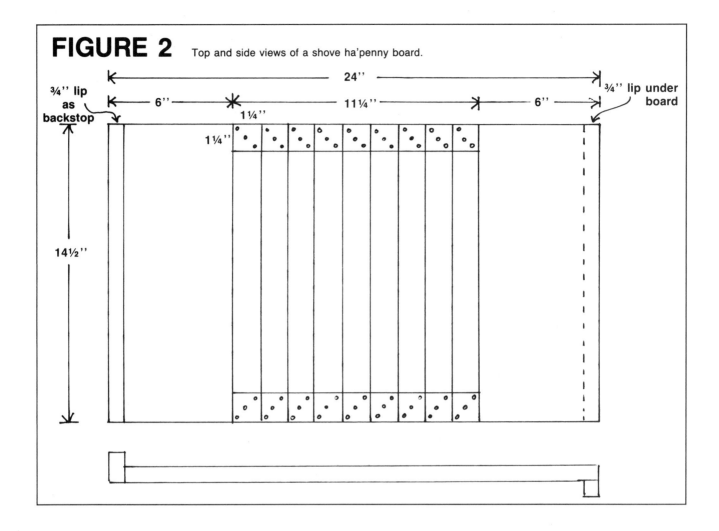

**FIGURE 2**  Top and side views of a shove ha'penny board.

---

6. *Hee that throws 31 where the well is must pay a stake & stay there till every one play twice unlesse some other throw the same by which he is delivered.*

7. *Hee that throws 42 where the Maze is payes one & returnes back to the number 29.*

8. *Hee that goeth to 52 where the Prison is must pay one & stay there till some other bring him out.*

9. *Hee that goeth to 58 where death is must pay one & begin again.*

10. *Hee that is overtaken by another must returne to his place that overtooke him & both must pay.*

11. *Hee that overthroweth the number 63 must turn back again & count his throw from the beginning* [e.g., if the counter is on 62 and the player throws a 3, he must move his counter forward one space to the finish, and then back two spaces to space 61 (Diagram 17)].

12. *Hee that throweth the just number 63 wineth the game. (Carson 293)*

### Shove Ha'penny

Shove ha' penny was played in England at least as early as the sixteenth century and continued to be popular as a tavern game well into the present. It requires a simple board constructed so that it has a lip which hooks over the end of a table and another lip on the opposite end which keeps the halfpennies (or other coins used as playing counters) from going off the board (see Figure 2). The board is 24'' long by 14½'' wide and is marked out into several zones. The middle 11¼'' of the board is divided into nine beds, each 1¼'' wide. Two lines marked 1¼'' from the sides limit the playing area and include three holes for each bed to hold pegs for keeping score. One player scores on the left side of the board and one player scores on the right.

Each player has five halfpennies (or other coins) to use as counters. The old English halfpenny was 1'' in diameter, so any smooth metal disc 1'' in diameter can be used (Diagram Group 180). The counters are placed one at a time over the front edge of the board and are struck with the palm of the hand to send them into the playing area. The ones that end up in one of the beds, without touching a line, score. The ones cutting a line are "dead" and won't score unless a subsequent counter knocks them clear of the line. The first player to score three times in each bed is the winner.

The players shoot each counter in turn. Those that go beyond the beds are immediately removed from the board, as are those that end up more than halfway into one of the marker squares at the sides of the boards. The ones less than halfway into a marker square remain on the board, but they can't score unless they're knocked back into a bed. After each player shoots his five counters, the ones laying in a bed are scored, and a corresponding peg is placed in a marker hole. The beds may be filled in any order, but once a player

211

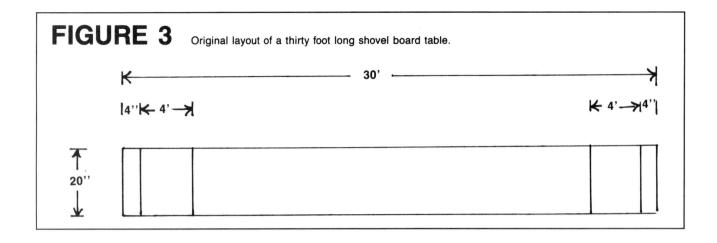

# FIGURE 3  Original layout of a thirty foot long shovel board table.

has landed three coins in a bed, any subsequent counter of his that lands in that bed is credited to his opponent if he still needs a score in that bed. The final point of the game must be scored by the winning player.

If a counter stops short of the first line, the player shoots it again, but if it reaches the first line, it must remain on the board. It may be knocked further on by a subsequent shot, but if that counter in turn remains short of the first line, it cannot be lifted and shot again. Striking one coin with another is obviously allowed. If one coin ends up on top of another, neither scores. The best playing strategy is to fill the farthest beds first (Bell 123-124).

## Shovel Board

Similar to shove ha'penny and the ancestor of today's shuffleboard, shovel board was originally played on the long, narrow sideboards that stood in the halls of most country mansions. It was later adopted to smaller tables and was a popular game in inns and taverns in Elizabethan England. The original boards were 30 feet long and 20 inches wide, with a line four inches from each end and another line 4 feet from each end (See Figure 3). The game can be played on smaller tables by adjusting the inner lines proportionally. Each player has four metal discs and players alternate in shoving their discs down the table. When two players play, they shoot from the same end, but when four play they are divided into two teams with partners at opposite ends of the board.

A disc hanging over the far end of the table (but not falling off) scores 3 points. One between the edge and the 4'' line is 2 points and between the 4'' and the 4' line, 1 point. Discs stopping short of the 4' line don't score unless they are knocked past the line by a subsequent shot by either player or team. Discs falling off the table don't score, and a disc halfway on a line scores as in (just like scoring a muzzleloading target). If, at the end of a round, there are no discs in the scoring areas, the one closest to the 4' line counts as in and scores 1 point. A game for two people is 11 points, while the partnership game is 21 points (Bell 130-131).

## Nine Men's Morris

This is an ancient "board" game that was played indoors and out. It supposedly was played much by shepherds on a board marked out on the ground but also was popular as an indoor game. The board consists of three squares, one within the other, with lines connecting the middles of the squares (see Figure 4). Each player has nine men, which can be anything as long as they can be distinguished from each other. Play begins by the players alternately placing a man on one of the intersections marked on the board. Strutt states that if, during this initial placing of the men, a player forms a row of three men, known as a "mill," he may remove one of the other player's men, as long as it is not part of a row of three men (417). This removal of an opponent's

# FIGURE 4  The layout for nine men's morris.

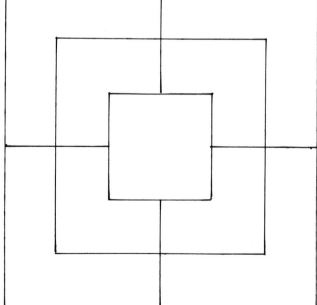

man is called "pounding." After each player's alternating nine moves to place men on the board, the players alternately move their remaining men from point to point, trying to create new mills or rows of three and thus pound the opponent. Moves are to unoccupied points and are one space at a time. As in the initial period of play, as soon as a player has three men in a row, he removes an opponent's man if it is not part of a row, unless no other man is available. The game is won when a player cannot move, either because all of his men have been captured or because they are blocked by his opponent's places.

Carson states that the skillful player will initially try to place his men on all three squares and to cover as many corners as possible. Early in the play, he should try to set up a "see-saw" movement that will allow him to open one row of three and close another in the same move. Carson warns that "if his opponent cannot break up the see-saw, he soon loses all his men" (298). Strutt speculates that the game gets it name from the morris dance-like patterns of the movement of the men.

## Fox and Geese

Fox and geese is similar to nine men's morris, except that the game is played on a cross-shaped board of twenty-squares (see Figure 5). There are seventeen "geese" and one "fox."[5] The fox is usually placed in the center of the board (but can be placed anywhere), and the geese are arranged as shown in Figure 5. The object of the game is for the geese to hem in the fox so that he cannot move. The fox can move in a straight line in any direction, but the geese can only move forwards or sideways. The geese cannot take the fox, but the fox can take a goose by jumping it, as in draughts (checkers), as long as the space on the other side of the goose is unoccupied. Again as in draughts, the fox must take a jump if there is no alternative move available. The game is over either when the fox is hemmed in and cannot move or when the fox has taken all the geese. According to Strutt the advantage is with the geese if they are played by a skillful player (418).

During the nineteenth century, two changes were made in the game to give the fox a better chance: twenty-two geese opposed two foxes, and diagonal lines were added for use by the foxes (Carson 299). An 18th century board with diagonal lines is illustrated in the *Collector's Illustrated Encyclopedia of The American Revolution* by Neumann and Kravic. With diagonal lines connecting the corners of the squares, the fox (or foxes) can move in any direction diagonally, while the geese are still restricted to forward movements, including the diagonals.

---

[5]A modern set of rules calls for only 15 geese and one fox (Diagram Group, 30).

## FIGURE 5

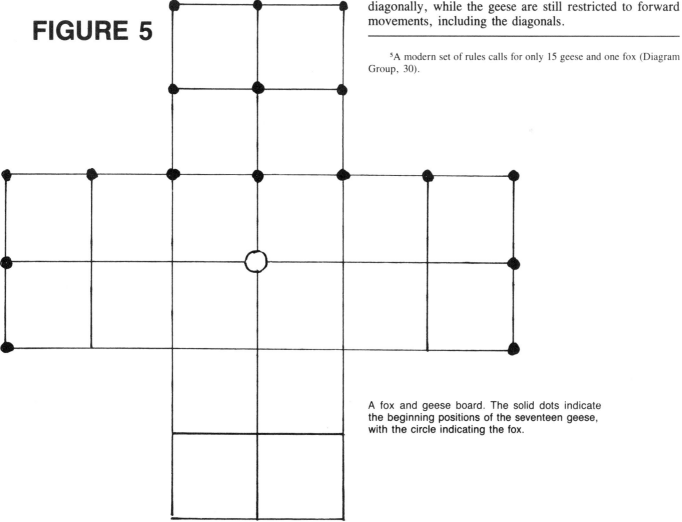

A fox and geese board. The solid dots indicate the beginning positions of the seventeen geese, with the circle indicating the fox.

# GAMES AND SPORTS

George Caleb Bingham's "Shooting for the Beef," 1850 (Twombly 30).

Many of the sports popular from the Colonial period through the Civil War are still popular and still played in one form or another today, and many are already common at rendezvous and reenactments. Shooting contests, for example, were very common and popular throughout the period, as were such contests as knife and tomahawk throwing. Hunting was universally popular, not only as a survival activity on the frontier but also as a sport in more settled areas. Horse racing was very popular but is not a sport that is usually found at a rendezvous or reenactment. Ball games of various types were common and provided the forerunners of our modern football and baseball. Bowling games were played, and golf was known, although it is doubtful that it was played in the Colonies. Wrestling, boxing, fencing and foot racing were common amusements.

Some very popular sports are no longer indulged in legally or openly, such as cock fights, rat pits, bear and bull baiting, and frontier rough-and-tumble fighting where one of the objectives was to gouge out the eyes of your opponent. But there are many other games and sports which are suitable not only as authentic recreations but as spectator sports for the public. We'll look at a few of these, beginning with some children's games and then moving on to games for adults as well as children.

## Marbles

While I don't see kids today playing marbles, it hasn't been that long since I was playing marbles for keeps in the schoolyard and in my neighborhood. Although the game may be dying out—how can it compete with Space Invaders?—the games we played in the late '40s and early '50s were exactly the same games that were played by kids in the 1740s and later mentioned by Mark Twain in *Tom Sawyer*. There were two basic games; one, called "Taw" by Strutt (491) and "Ringer" by Strobell (17), was played with the marbles enclosed in a circle drawn on the ground; the other, which Strutt calls "Hit and Span," "Boss Out" or "Boss and Span," is a "follow-the-leader" game. The only equipment needed for either game is a supply of marbles (round clay in the 18th century, glass today) and a larger marble used as a "shooter."

The simplest form of taw begins with drawing a circle

on the ground. Each player then puts an equal number of marbles in the center of the circle. Taking turns, each player "knuckles down" at a point on the perimeter of the circle, and by flipping his shooter out of his hand with his thumb, he attempts to knock the other marbles out of the ring. The player must have a knuckle of his shooting hand on the ground. The easiest shooting technique is to tuck the shooter in the crook of the forefinger and flip it out with the thumb, but a more advanced (and preferred) technique is to position the shooter between the thumbnail and the tip of the forefinger. The latter technique tends to put backspin on the shooter so that it will stop in place when it strikes another marble. The first shot is from outside the ring, and subsequent shots are from inside the ring as long as the player has knocked a marble out of the ring on his first shot. He keeps shooting as long as he knocks marbles out and as long as his shooter stays in the ring. As soon as he misses or goes outside the ring, his turn is over. In a friendly game, the player who knocks the most marbles out of the ring is the winner. In playing for keeps, each player keeps all the marbles knocked out of the ring.

A more formal version of the game is described by Strobell (17). This game, which she calls "Ringer," is played in a circle 10' in diameter with 13 marbles arranged 3'' apart in a cross as in the illustration (see Figure 6). Two lines, the "pitch" line and the "lag" line, are drawn as illustrated, and the players knuckle down at the pitch line and shoot towards the lag line to determine who will shoot first. The player who gets his marble closest to the lag line shoots first, the next closest shoots second, and so on. Like taw, the first player knuckles down anywhere on the circle and tries to shoot the interior marbles out of the circle. If the player shooting misses, he picks his shooter up no matter where it ends up, and on his next turn, he again begins from the outside of the circle. The winner is the player who knocks the most marbles out of the circle.

Hit and Span doesn't use a ring; it is a two-player game where the first player shoots his marble to any distance. Shooting from the same point, the second player then tries to hit the first player's marble. If he hits it or can touch both marbles with his hand span, he wins a point or the marble. If he doesn't come within a span of the first marble, the first player then shoots at *his* marble, and so on alternately. The hand span rule is Strutt's. When we played it as kids you had to hit your opponent's marble to win.

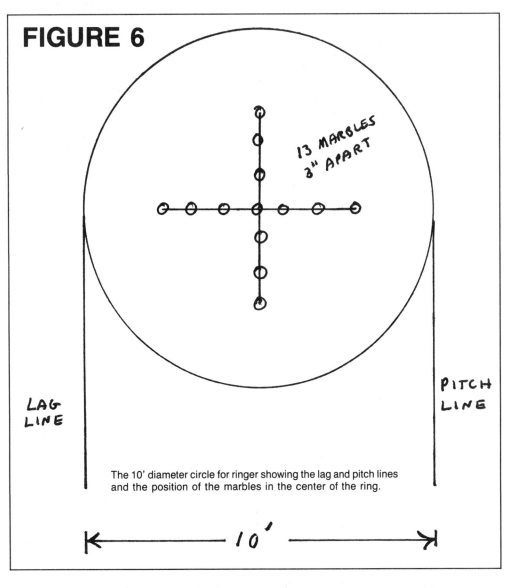

**FIGURE 6**

13 MARBLES 3'' APART

LAG LINE

PITCH LINE

The 10' diameter circle for ringer showing the lag and pitch lines and the position of the marbles in the center of the ring.

10'

215

Some historical sports are not legally or openly engaged in now. A good example is shown in Hogarth's "The Cockpit" (Carson 163).

## *Jacks*

Also known as jackstones, this game is a derivation of the ancient game of knucklebones, which was played with the knucklebones of sheep. We are all of us familiar with the metal jacks and small rubber ball with which the game is played today. A very modern-looking jack was excavated from Fortress Louisbourg, which indicates that 18th century soldiers, or perhaps their children, played the game (Neumann and Kravic 128).[6]

The game begins by casting five or six jacks or knucklebones on the ground. Originally, one of these was used as the "jack" which was thrown into the air. Later a small wooden ball was used which was ultimately replaced with a rubber ball which could be bounced. The object of the game is to throw the jack or the ball into the air and manipulate the remaining jacks on the ground in various ways before catching the ball. The simplest sequence is to throw the ball up and pick up a jack before the ball is caught. This is repeated until all the jacks on the ground have been gathered. Then the sequence begins again, only this time two jacks at a time are gathered up and so on, until at the last all of the jacks must be gathered up in one sweep of the hand before the ball is caught. If the player fails at any stage, drops the jack or the ball, or touches a jack not being picked up,

he loses his turn and the next player takes over. When play gets around to the first player, he can either take up where he left off or be made to start it all over again with "ones." The difficulty can be increased by having each player throw the ball, pick up the required number of jacks and clap his hands before catching the ball.

A second variant has been called "jumping the ditch." Four jacks are laid in a line. The ball or a fifth jack is tossed into the air, and before it is caught, the first and third jacks must be picked up. On the next throw the second and fourth jacks are picked up.

In "horses in the stall" or "pigs in the pen," the jacks are scattered on the ground and the left hand is placed on the ground with only the finger and thumb tips touching the ground. Each time the ball is tossed up, a jack must be placed in one of the openings formed by the spread fingers before catching the ball. Then, in the same way, the "horses" are removed from the "stalls."

Other long-lasting children's games include tag, kite flying, rolling a hoop, hide and seek, blindman's buff and ducks and drakes. I played the latter as a child and even taught it to my kids without knowing that it had a name. Ducks and drakes is simply the old entertainment of skipping a flat stone or shell across the water. The winner is the one who can coax the most skips from his stone.

---

[6]Along with other reproduction toys, Cooperman Fire & Drum Co., Centerbrook, CT 06409, makes a nice set of jacks with a small wooden ball.

## Mumblety-Peg

When I was a boy my Grandfather Smith, who was born in the 1870s, taught me this game of his childhood. Of course mumblety-peg is much older than that, apparently originating in England. Since the game requires an open or bare-blade knife, it should be played by older children or under adult supervision.

Mumblety-peg is simply a stick-the-knife-in-the-ground game. The challenge comes from the various ways the knife must be held or manipulated in the throws to stick it. Any number of variations is possible, and as with most of the games and sports described in this chapter, there is no "official," unalterable way to play, although certain moves seem to be pretty standard.

The game requires two or more players, each with his or her own pocket knife. The first player goes through a series of throws until he fails to stick his knife, at which point the second player starts through the same series. When he fails the first player takes up where he left off. The winner is the player who can get through the predetermined series first. The game gets its name from the penalty imposed on the loser: The winner drives a wooden peg into the ground as far as he can with three blows of his knife, and each loser must "mumble" it or pull it out with his teeth.

Some of the standard moves are:

1. The knife is held in the palm of the right hand with the point outward (pointing the way the fingers are pointing). Flick the knife so that it revolves towards the player and sticks in the ground.

2. Hold the knife the same way in the left hand except with the point towards the player. With a downward flick of the hand rotate the knife away from the player and stick it.

3. Repeat moves 1 and 2 but with the knife on the back of the hand.

4. Place the knife across the knuckles of the closed right hand (wrist up) so that the blade points towards the thumb. With a quick upward flick of the hand to the left, flip the knife into the ground. Repeat with the left hand.

5. With the tip of the blade held between the right thumb and forefinger, flip the knife and stick it. The knife must rotate once. Do the same move with the left hand. Some call for this move to be repeated seven times in succession.

6. The knife is held by the handle with the point resting on the tip of each finger and thumb and flipped outward to stick. Repeat with the other hand.

7. Hold the knife by the point and flip it from each elbow, each knee, each shoulder, the chest, the nose and each eye.

8. In the same manner, throw it from each ear, with the arms crossed, grasping the free ear with the non-throwing hand.

9. Throw it over the head backwards.

10. Stick the knife in the ground at such an angle that the hand, palm up, can slip under the handle. Flip the knife up and forward so that it comes out of the ground, rotates and sticks again. Be careful not to cut yourself with this move.

Other throws can, of course, be invented if desired.

A mumblety-peg variant, which I suppose we can call "stick-knife," needs a two-bladed jackknife. The knife is opened so that the large blade is at right angles to the handle and the small blade is fully extended. The large blade is stuck into the ground so that the handle is parallel with the ground. The handle is given an upward flick with the fingers to spin the knife. Points are given for how the knife lands: the small blade sticking with the knife vertical is 4 points; if both blades stick, it is 3 points; if the knife ends up in its original position, it is 1 point. If it doesn't stick at all, of course there are no points.

## Prisoner's Base

Prisoner's base is one of the long list of Colonial games that were played by both adults and children. Any number of people divide up into two equal teams and position themselves in opposite lines some twenty or thirty yards apart, extending from a "base" or stake driven into the ground. Each team has a "prison" consisting of a stake or other convenient marker about thirty yards from the base.

The teams line up, holding hands. The game begins when a player from one side leaves his line and runs into the open space between the teams. He is immediately followed by one of his opponents. He is followed by a second player and his opponent and so on alternately until as many are out as choose to run. Each player pursues his opponent and no other. As soon as one of the players tags the other, the tagged player must go to that team's prison while the other player returns home before issuing out to chase another opponent. Once in prison a player must stay there until he is rescued by a member of his team by touching him. Once rescued, both players must make it back to their base before being tagged (Strutt 144-145). The game is over either when one side is all imprisoned or when a player makes it to the opponent's prison without being tagged when it is free of prisoners (Strobell 15).

## Quoits & Horsehoes

Quoits is an ancient game, originally played by throwing iron discs with a hole in the middle from one iron peg, or hob, to another some distance away. The distance is optional but is usually about twenty yards. Two players each throw an equal number of quoits from one hob towards the other "and the nearest of them to the hob are reckoned towards the game" (Strutt 141). Strutt continues:

*If a quoit belonging to A lies nearest to the hob, and a quoit belonging to B the second, A can claim but one towards the game, though all his other quoits lie nearer to the mark than all the other quoits of B; because one quoit of B being the second nearest to the hob cuts out, as it is called, all behind it: if no such quoit had interfered, then A would have reckoned all his as one each.* (141)

Having thrown all their quoits, the players walk to the other hob, count their score and then cast their quoits back towards the first hob. While Strutt says that a player gets a point for each quoit closest to the hob, he doesn't say how many points for getting a quoit over the hob, which is a goal of the game. I would assume that a "ringer" would score 3 points as it does in horseshoes. The game is over when a player reaches

the predetermined number of points, usually 21.

Strutt says that, at least as early as the first part of the eighteenth century, "in the country the rustics, not having the round perforated quoits to play with, used horseshoes..." (142). Because there were always horses around in the military, the game was also the sport of the soldiers, both in the British and American armies (Hickock 286). See Plate 9. The modern scoring for horseshoes—1 point for each shoe that is closer to the stake than either of the opponent's shoes and 3 points for a ringer—can be used. Eighteenth-century scoring apparently counted 2 points for a "leaner," as did we when I played with my grandfather forty years ago. Twenty-one points is usually game.

## Coin Tossing Games

A number of games played by adults and children involve the tossing of coins. The simplest, our "heads or tails," was called "cross and pile" from the ancient English coin that had a cross on the heads side. The game was a favorite of Edward II of England, and the rules haven't changed since his day. One player flips a coin in the air, and while it is in the air, the other player calls "heads" (cross) or "tails" (pile). If he guesses correctly, he wins the coin.

"Pitch and Toss" is a little more complicated, but the basic concept is the same. In this game a group of players stick a knife in the ground, and then from a given distance, each player pitches a coin at the knife. The one getting nearest has the first toss. If there are six players in the "school," or group of players, the winner of the pitch takes a coin from each and tosses them in the air, calling heads or tails before they strike the ground. He keeps every coin that lands as he called it, or he receives a predetermined stake or bet from each player. The player whose coin was next nearest to the knife then takes the remaining coins and tosses them. These winning coins are then removed and so on. When the coins are all taken, the players pitch for the next round (Bell 81.) In modern times this game was a favorite of Fyfeshire miners. The stakes were often a pound for each correct call, and reportedly, "fivers floated around like toilet paper" (Bell 81).

"Hustle cap" or "pitch and hustle" is basically the same game as pitch and toss, except that the coins are placed in a cap, and the first player shakes them up and then inverts the cap on the ground. He keeps as many of the coins as are heads up and passes the cap and the remaining coins to the next player and so on (Strutt 370). There is no calling of heads or tails. It is perhaps of interest that Washington's General Orders of October 3, 1775, forbade officers and soldiers from playing toss-up (cross and pile), pitch and hustle or other games of chance (Carson 89).

John Boydell's "Playing at Quoits" (Carson 181).

# BALL GAMES

The variety of authentic ball games is very great, but for the most part, the reenactor is faced with the problem of obtaining authentic reproductions of the appropriate equipment. Nevertheless, we'll examine a few ancestors of many of our modern ball games.

## Stool Ball

In the 15th century and later, stool ball was a fairly simple game most often played by young ladies (Hickock 153). The game consisted of one player throwing a ball at a stool, which is defended by a second player who protects the stool by batting the ball away with her hand. She scores a point for each time she strikes the ball. She is "out" and has to take her turn as "pitcher" if the first player either strikes the stool with the ball or catches the batted ball. The first player then defends the stool (Strutt 165).

By the early 18th century, the game was being played by both young men and women, a bat was being used in place of the bare hand and more than one stool was used in play. According to Strutt the stools were arranged in a circle with a player before each, with the pitcher in the middle. The pitcher throws at a stool, and if the ball is struck, each of the players "is obliged to alter his situation, running in succession from stool to stool, and if he who threw the ball can regain it in time to strike any of the players [with the ball], before he reaches the stool to which he is running, he takes his place, and the person touched must throw the ball, until he can in like manner return to the circle" (165). Strutt doesn't indicate how this variation is scored, but it probably was similar to his description of the game of "tip cat." The players would receive a score for every stool reached in succession before the player who hit the ball was thrown out. Stool ball does not seem to have been played much after the opening years of the 19th century, and it remained a children's game.

## Trap Ball

Trap ball was played at least from the Middle Ages and like stool ball was a favorite children's game, although by the 18th century it appears to have been played by adults as well, at least in the country. It was a game for two to eight players. In its sophisticated form, it utilized a pivoting ball-holder attached to a raised stand. One end of the pivot was cupped to hold the ball while the other end was straight. Using a flat bat not unlike a cricket bat or a large ping-pong paddle, the batsman struck the end of the pivoting arm, or trap, propelling the ball into the air. He then hit the ball with the bat. This equipment is not necessary, according to Strutt, "boys and the common herd of rustics . . . content themselves with making a round hole in the ground, and by way of a lever, use a . . . flat piece of wood . . . which is placed in a slanting position, one half in the hole with the ball upon it,

and the other half out of it . . ." (177).

Two boundary lines are made at an unspecified distance from the trap, and the struck ball must remain within the boundaries or the batsman is out. He is also out if the ball is caught by a defending player or if the player retrieving the ball throws or rolls it back so that it strikes the trap or comes to rest within a bat's length of the trap (Strutt 177-178). If none of these things happens, the batsman is credited with a point and continues to bat.

Strutt reports a mid-18th century variation played by the "rustics in Essex." Instead of a "broad bat with a flatted face, they use a round cudgel about an inch and a half diameter and three feet in length, and those who have acquired the habit of striking the ball with this instrument rarely miss their blow, but frequently strike [the ball] to an astonishing distance" (178). If the ball remains within the boundaries and isn't caught, the striker estimates how many cudgel lengths from the trap the ball will be when it is thrown back in. If the striker guesses correctly or the ball is even father away than he guessed, he gets a number of points equal to the cudgel lengths he guessed. If the ball is closer than he guessed, he loses his score and is out (178).

## Cricket

The first cricket match was recorded as being played in 1728, and by the time of the Revolution, it was a favorite game both in England and in America. As complicated as cricket seems to Americans used to baseball, it is in essence a simple game: a bowler attempts to hit a wicket with a thrown ball. The wicket is made of three stakes, or "stumps," set in the ground with two crossbars, or "bails," laid across the top. The wicket is 9" wide, with the three stumps 4⅜" apart center-to-center. The stumps are 30½" long with 27" extending above the ground. The bails, which are 4⅜" long, are turned so that they extend only ½" above the top of the stumps (Menke 347). See Figure 7. The bowler bowls from a second wicket 22 yards away. The bowler can make as long a run before pitching the ball as he wishes, but he cannot cross the "crease," an 8'8" line extending through the wicket. In the eighteenth century, the bowler bowled underhand or sidearm with a straight arm, but by 1864, the bowler was allowed to bowl overhand, though still with a straight arm.

219

# FIGURE 7

The layout of a cricket pitch showing the dimensions of the creases and the positions of the bowler, batsman, wicket keeper and wickets.

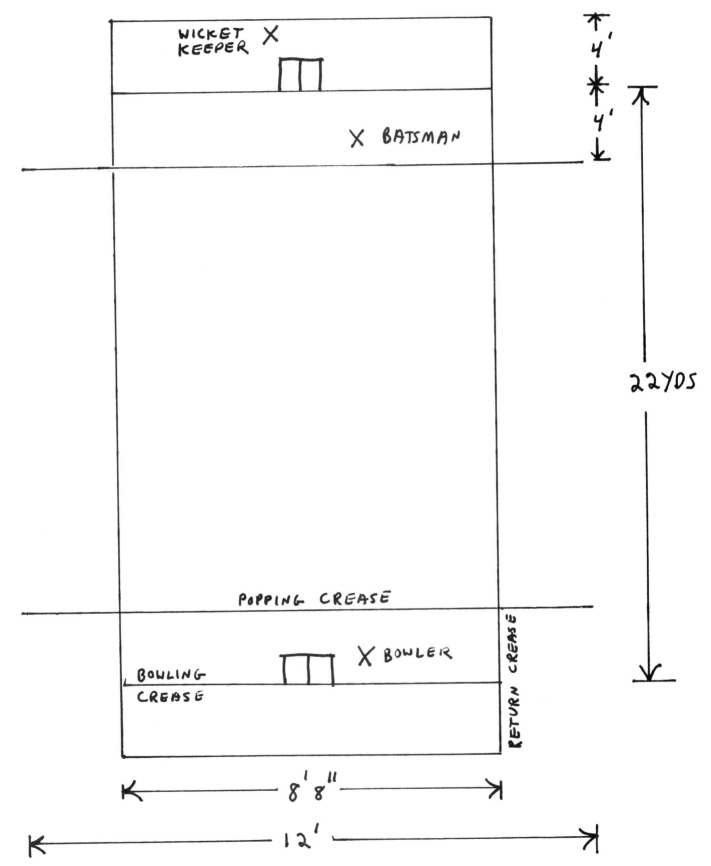

Thomas Henwood's "The Scorer," a late 18th, early century portrait of a cricket scorekeeper. Notice the measuring tape on the table and the cricket bats, ball and wicket under the table.

Francis Hayman's 1743 print of a cricket match. Note the underarm delivery of the bowler, the bouncing ball and the two-stump wicket. The wicket keeper is said to be the artist Hogarth, an avid cricket player (Bailey 8).

The wicket is protected by a batsman who attempts to hit the ball away from the wicket. The batsman must stay behind an 8'8'' line called the "popping crease" four feet in front of the wicket. If the batsman fails and the bowler hits the wicket, the batsman is out. The bowler accomplishes a "hat trick" if he captures three or more wickets in succession, that is, if he gets three or more batsmen out either by hitting the wicket or bowling a fly ball that is caught. Teams used to award a bowler a hat if he did this.

The batsman can strike the ball in any direction—even behind him. If the ball is caught on the fly by an opponent, the batsman is out. If the ball isn't caught, the batsman runs from his wicket to the opposite wicket, thus scoring a run. He can continue scoring runs by running from wicket to wicket, but if a fielder can hit the original wicket with the ball while the batter is out of the crease (in which case he is "run out") or if the wicket keeper (catcher) hits the wicket with the ball while the batsman is out of the crease (in which case the batsman is "stumped"), the batsman is out. He is also out if, while attempting to hit the bowled ball, he hits the wicket with his bat. If he isn't put out he continues to bat, scoring a run every time he runs to the other wicket. If a batsman scores 100 runs or more in a single turn at bat, he has achieved the coveted "century."

When the starting bowler has delivered six "fair balls" from his end, the umpire (there is an umpire at each wicket) calls "over," and a man at the other wicket becomes the bowler, bowling to the opposite batsman, while the starting bowler takes a field position. The fielders change their posi-

tion to conform to the new configuration. After the second bowler has delivered six fair balls, the teams again change positions and the original batsman continues his time at bat. This alternation continues until the game ends.

From the 18th century onward, a team has consisted of eleven players. The team in the field has a bowler at one wicket and a wicket keeper or catcher at the other wicket. The remaining nine players (playing point, cover point, mid off, mid on, short slip, third man, square leg, deep mid off and deep mid on) position themselves around the field, both in front of and behind the batsman. There are also two batsmen, one defending each wicket. When the first hits the ball and runs to the opposite wicket, the second batsman runs to the vacated wicket. When a batsman is put out the next player goes to bat, and this continues until ten men have had a turn at bat (only ten, since the eleventh man doesn't have a partner). This constitutes an "innings" (which is singular, not plural). It is then the other team's turn for its innings. While the usual regulation game is two innings, if the first team to bat still holds a lead after the other team has had its innings, it can compel that team to "follow on" or bat again for another innings. If the second team can't take the lead, the game is over.

The ball and bat have been standardized since 1774. The ball, at 5½ to 5¾ ounces in weight, is a little smaller than a baseball. It has a thicker, harder cover painted red. The willow bat is triangular in cross section, the longest side used as the batting side. It can't be more than 4½ inches wide or 38 inches long. Since 1853, a handle of tightly bound cane has been inserted into a hole in the top (Menke 341).

The first written rules were adopted by the London Cricket Club in 1744, at which time the wicket consisted of just two stumps with a bail across the top, and the bowler

rolled towards the batsman. In mid-century the bowlers began delivering the ball on one bounce. In 1777, a third stump was introduced so that the ball couldn't pass between the stumps without knocking them down and the wicket measured 22'' x 6''. In 1788, the measurements were 24'' x 7'', in 1816 they were increased to 26'' x 7'' and in 1817 they were 27'' x 8'' (Menke 341). Also, in 1817, two bails were made standard. The present dimensions, since 1947, are 27'' x 9''. The rules today are very much like they were in 1817 (Hickock 153). Because of the switching sides after every few bowls, cricket grounds need to be at least 450 x 500 feet, and 525 x 550 is preferable (Menke 346).

Strutt describes a five-man single-wicket game current during the 1770s. In this case there is only one wicket and one bowler, who bowls from a single stump 22 yards away from the wicket. If the batter hits the ball, he runs to the bowler's station, touches the stump with his bat and returns to his wicket to score a run. He is out if the ball is caught on the fly or if the wicket is knocked down by the fielded ball before the batsman can either return home or ground his bat inside the popping crease (175-176).

### One-Old-Cat

A cricket-like game similar in its rules to trap ball, one-old-cat was played in this country from early in the 19th century. Its rules are simple. Two bases are located about 40 feet apart, and the catcher stands behind one and the pitcher behind the other. The batter attempts to hit the pitched ball (probably pitched underhand), run to the other base and return before he is hit by the ball. He is out if he is hit or if his ball is fielded on the fly or on the first bounce. When four boys played there was a batter at each base, and the game was called two-old-cat. This was followed by three-old-cat, a three-base game for six players, and four-old-cat, with four bases and eight players. In four-old-cat there is a batter at each base along with a player who alternates between being a pitcher and a catcher. Every batter runs to another base when the ball is hit, but only the batter who hits the ball can score an additional point (Weaver 96-97). As Weaver points out, "this was very much of an 'individual game,' and each player kept his own score" (97).

### Rounders

Although cricket was extremely popular in the United States—the first international cricket match was played in New York between a London and a New York team in 1751—and was being played in Kentucky and Illinois by 1819—the real American game of the 19th century was baseball. But contrary to myth, the game of baseball didn't spring full-blown from the forehead of Abner Doubleday. Its beginnings can be seen instead in the English game of rounders, sometimes even then called baseball. The first mention of "baseball" is in the denunciation of the sport by a Puritan clergyman in England in 1700, who chided the populace for participating in "Morris dancing, cudgel-playing, baseball and cricketts" on Sunday (Bongartz 44). This English game of rounders/baseball was played here as town ball, goal ball, or baseball.

According to Twombly, rounders was played in

# FIGURE 8

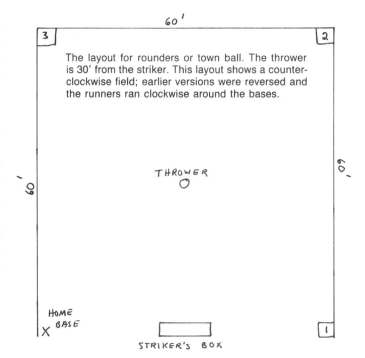

The layout for rounders or town ball. The thrower is 30' from the striker. This layout shows a counter-clockwise field; earlier versions were reversed and the runners ran clockwise around the bases.

America before and during the Revolutionary War (43-44). George Ewing, at Valley Forge with Washington, wrote in his journal for April 7, 1778: "Exercised in the afternoon, in the intervals played at base" (quoted in Bongartz 45). By 1786, at least, the game was being played by Princeton University students. One student recorded in his diary for March 22 of that year: "A fine day, play baste ball in the campus but am beaten for I miss both catching and striking the ball" (quoted in Bongartz 45). But it was not until 1827 that formal rules and a description of the game were published in England in *The Boy's Own Book* (Bongartz 44). In 1834, a book called *The Book of Sports* was published in this country by Robin Carver. In it Carver described the English game of rounders, already known here as town ball, but called it base ball, although the game wasn't yet our modern game (Durant and Bettmann 38).

Rounders (town ball) was played on a square layout with four bases about 60 feet apart (see Figure 8). The bases were either flat stones or upright four foot stakes driven in the ground. The number of players was variable, as were the rules. The equipment included a round or flat bat and a tightly wound string or yarn ball about the size of a modern softball. The pitcher or "feeder," who was positioned usually in the center of the square, pitched the ball underhanded and straight-armed to the batter. The catcher stood well behind the batter and fielded the ball on the bounce. The players in the field, sometimes called "scouts," held to predetermined positions, and none was attached to a particular base. The "three strikes and you're out" rule was in force, and by 1827, hitters were being deliberately walked on four balls (Bongartz 44-45). If the batter hit the ball, he ran the bases clockwise (opposite to the game today), although *The Boy's Book of Sports* published in New Haven in 1839 called for the runner to run counterclockwise (Bongartz 45). The runner was out if his ball was caught on the fly or on one bounce, if he was hit by the ball thrown by a fielder while he was

between bases or if the ball was thrown into a foot wide, 6'' deep hole at home (Weaver 95). A run was scored when a player safely negotiated all the bases back to home base, which was off to the left of the "striker's" or batter's box. Everybody on one team had a chance to bat before the other team was up. The game usually was over when one team reached a predetermined number of runs.

### The New York Game

A variation of town ball was devised in New York in 1842, when the first "Base Ball Diagram" was established (see Figure 9). The batter took his place in the striker's box. From there he ran to first base, 48 feet away, then to second base, 60 feet away, then to third, 72 feet away, and then 72 more feet to fourth base or home, which was still to the left of the batter's box. There were twelve players: two catchers, one thrower or pitcher, four basemen, three regular outfielders, a roving infielder, and a roving outfielder (Menke 59-60). The New York game stayed fairly popular until the Civil War, but after 1846, it was to all intents and purposes supplanted by the new game of baseball.

### Baseball

In 1845, Alexander J. Cartwright (1820-1892), a New York bank teller and a member of the volunteer Knickerbocker Engine Company, and some friends formed the Knickerbocker Base Ball Club. Cartwright presented the group with a new set of rules he had devised for a game of baseball, and in the spring of 1846, they were ready to play. Cartwright's rules established the game of baseball as we

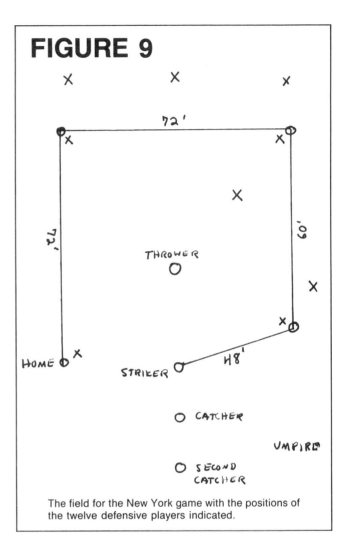

# FIGURE 9

The field for the New York game with the positions of the twelve defensive players indicated.

The Knickerbocker Baseball Club about 1857. Notice the shape of the bats (Durant and Bettmann 38).

224

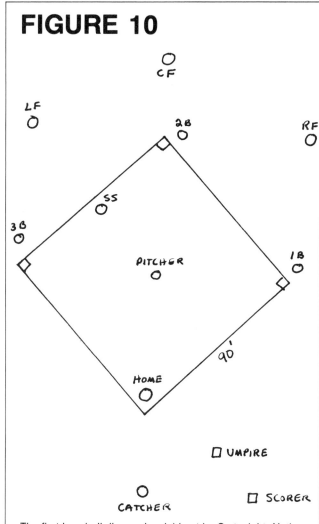

# FIGURE 10

The first baseball diamond as laid out by Cartwright. Notice that the pitcher is only 45' from the batter. Notice also the positions of the shortstop and catcher and that home plate is inside the apex of the first and third base lines.

out between bases or if he was forced out at a base. A balk by the pitcher awarded an extra base, and a ball bounding over the outfield fence awarded an extra base (the ground-rule double). The ball was to ''be pitched and not thrown for the bat,'' but the ball was pitched underhand with a straight arm (Menke 59-60). The ball was to weigh three ounces, and the round, flat, iron home plate was to cover a space equal to one square foot (Menke 69).

In 1854, a new rule established the size of the ball at 2¾ to 3½ inches, and the weight at 5½ to 6 ounces. In 1857, nine innings was established as the limit of play instead of the 21-run rule. The next year the rule that allowed a man to be put out if his ball was caught on the first bounce was abolished. That same year a single umpire was established; previously there had been two umpires, one chosen by each team, plus a tie-breaking referee. In 1859, the size of the bat was set at no greater than 2½ inches in diameter—pitchers were complaining that batters were using huge bats or even cricket bats, which they felt was unfair. By 1860, the base lines were being outlined with whitewash to prevent arguments on whether a ball was fair. In 1862, a new rule declared that the bat must be round, made of wood and no thicker than 2½ inches (length was optional). In 1864, a rule required a base runner to touch every base in making the circuit, and pitcher William A. (Candy) Cummings of the Brooklyn Stars was credited with pitching the first curve ball. In 1865, Eddie Cuthbert of the Philadelphia Keystones invented the stolen base and the slide, and in 1866, Dickey Pearce of the Brooklyn Atlantics laid down the first deliberate bunt (Menke 70).

Cartwright wasn't around to see many of these refinements, since in 1849, he succumbed to gold fever and headed to California. He kept a journal of his trip, which includes this fascinating entry:

*1849—April 23—Monday—Independence, Mo:—During the past week we have passed the time in fixing wagon-covers, stowing property, etc., varied by hunting and fishing and playing baseball.* **It is comical to see the mountain men and Indians playing the new game.** [Emphasis mine] *I have the ball with me that we used back home. (quoted in Menke 61)*

Cartwright never made it back to New York, settling instead in Honolulu.

## *Football*

The football game that eventually evolved into modern soccer is very ancient, perhaps going back to Roman times. It was certainly being played everywhere, particularly in England, in the Middle Ages and continued in popularity, if not respectability, into the 19th century (Menke 817-872). The object was to kick a leather-covered, inflated bladder from one goal to another. The goals were often at opposite ends of the town. Any number of men could play, and it was lawful to trip or kick an opposing player to prevent him from advancing the ball. In fact, anything that kept the ball away from an opponent was permissible (Menke 872). This rather casual, free-form game eventually evolved into soccer in the late 19th century, being played in the United States by the 1870s (Menke 872).

know it today. His playing field (see Figure 10) was essentially the same as we know, with these exceptions: home plate is now at the apex of the first and third base lines; the pitcher is now 60'6'' from home plate instead of Cartwright's 45 feet; the catcher no longer positions himself 15 or 20 feet behind the batter; the shortstop plays behind the base line, not in front of it; and the umpire no longer stands to the side. On the other hand, the bases were 90 feet apart, and the outfielders were placed where they are today (Menke 59).

A game was to consist of 21 runs or ''aces,'' but equal innings were played, so that if the first team up completed its 21 aces in its half of an inning, it would continue to bat until the third out of that inning. Then the other team would have its half of the inning to try to catch up or surpass the score. There were nine men to a team, and three outs to an inning. A ball hit outside the first or third base lines was a foul, and a dropped third strike was a fair ball. A batter was out if he struck out, if his ball was caught on the fly or on the first bounce, if it was thrown to the first baseman before the runner reached the base, if the batter was tagged

"Golfers at St. Andrews, 1847."
Notice that golf bags were
not yet in use, and I'd hate
to play golf in a tail coat and
top hat.

## Golf

Golf is also a very ancient game, and without going into all the attempts to trace it back to Roman times or associate it with an early Dutch game called "Kolf" or a French game called "Choulle," golf was being played in Scotland by at least 1450 (Scharff 1, Hickock 229, Menke 506). It became so popular that laws against playing were being written by 1457, because it was felt that a citizen could make better use of his time practicing his skills with the low bow. The first known organized golf club was the Honourable Company of Edinburgh Golfers founded in 1744. The St. Andrews Society of Golfers (now known as the Royal and Ancient Golf Club of St. Andrews) was founded in 1754 and soon became the trend setter of golf (Scharff 3).

The mid-18th century rules established by St. Andrews included these:

*1. You must tee your ball within a club length of the hole.*

*2. Your tee must be upon the ground.*

*3. You are not to change the ball which you strike off the tee.*

*4. You are not to remove stone, bones, or any break-club for the sake of playing your ball, except upon fair green, and that only within a club length of your ball.*

*5. If your ball come among water or any watery filth, you are at liberty to take out your ball and throw it behind the hazard six yards at least; you may play it with any club, and allow your adversary a stroke for so getting out your ball.*

*6. If your balls be found anywhere touching one another, you are to lift the first ball until you play the last.*

*7. At holing you are to play your ball honestly for the hole, and not to play upon your adversary's ball, not lying in your way to the hole.*

*8. If you should lose your ball...you are to go back to the spot where you struck last and drop another ball and allow your adversary a stroke for the misfortune.*

*9. No man holing his ball is to be allowed to mark his way to the hole with his club or anything else.*

*10. If a ball is stopped by any person, horse, dog, or anything else, the ball so stopped must be played where it lies.*

*11. If you draw your club in order to strike and proceed so far with your stroke as to be bringing down your club, if then your club should break in any way, it is to be accounted a stroke.*

*12. He whose ball lies farthest from the hole is obliged to play first.* (Scarff 3)

Also established at St. Andrews was the practice of playing 18 holes to a round. Until the middle of the 18th century, there was no set number of holes to a round, and even after St. Andrews established a course of 18 holes, it took until the 19th century before 18 holes was accepted as standard everywhere in the world. Holes were anywhere from 80 to 400 yards long.

Golf may have been played in North America in the mid-18th century, having been brought here either by Scottish immigrants or by Scottish regiments during the Revolution, but evidence is not solid. According to Menke, the only supporting evidence is that there were golf clubs established in the United States by the 1780s (507). Charleston, South Carolina, had a golf club by 1786, while golf was played at Harleston Green in 1791 (Scharff 7). The game apparently faded from any popularity after about 1820, not to be revived in any established way until the founding of the Foxburg (Pennsylvania) Golf Club in 1887 (Menke 508).

Until 1848, the standard ball was made of feather-stuffed leather, known as a "feathery." Making such a ball was a long, hard process, and the best ball makers could only produce four to six a day. Alum and water-softened leather was stitched together, leaving a small opening. The cover was turned inside out, and boiled goose feathers were stuffed through the small opening. The ball maker held the ball in a mold in his hand and used a stuffing iron 16 to 20 inches long, which he braced against his chest, to force the wet feathers into the ball. Enough feathers to fill the crown of a hat were eventually stuffed into the ball. The opening was then sewn shut, and as the feathers dried, they expanded further, making a very hard and resilient ball. The ball was

226

finished by being hammered round and coated with three coats of paint (Scharff 201). The best featheries were made by the Gourley family in Leith and Musselburg, Scotland, and a "Gourley" became the most sought-after ball on the market (Scharff 202). Featheries were expensive, seldom truly round, could be cut easily and sometimes exploded in a shower of feathers when hit. Still, they were the only balls available until the introduction of the gutta percha ball in 1848.

Clubs of the 18th and early 19th centuries tended to be long and thin, with whippy shafts and thick grips. One famous club maker made his club heads from hedgethorne which had been planted on the sides of steep banks. The stems grew at an angle to the roots and created a natural bend for the neck. The split-ash shafts were spliced onto the heads (Scarff 206). The heads were elongated and resembled the head of a snake (Hass and Lanzerotti 2). The feathery was swept from the ground with a long, graceful, full swing. There were four classes of clubs: drivers, spoons, irons, and putters. There were "play club" drivers with little loft, which were meant to be used over safe ground or off the tee, and "grasses drivers," which had more loft and served the same function as the modern 2- or 3-wood. There were four spoons—long spoons, middle spoons, short spoons and baffling spoons—which differed only in the degree of loft and which served the same function as modern fairway woods and long irons. There were three irons, driving irons, cleeks and banking irons, the latter two being like today's mid-irons and short irons. There were two putters, a driving putter (much like a chipping iron in function) and a green putter for use on the greens (Scharff 206).

## Bowls

Bowling or lawn bowling is as old as any sport, being traced back to Egypt and Rome 3,500 to 4,000 years ago. The Romans knew it as "boccie," by which name it is still known to Italians today. In England and America, the game was known simply as "bowls." In 1299, the Southampton Town Bowling Club was founded. The club still exists and matches are played on the original 600-year-old green (Menke 693). Bowls, which became known as lawn bowling to distinguish it from the games where a ball was rolled at pins, probably arrived in North America around 1690. Pin bowling apparently was not introduced in this country until about 1800—the first reference to it is in Washington Irving's *Rip Van Winkle* (Menke 694). Bowling was very popular up to the Revolution, when interest or participation ceased, and the game was practically non-existent in this country for the next 100 years.

Today's bowling greens are surfaced much like a golf green, although where grass cannot be easily maintained a sandy-clay combination called marl is used for the bowling surface. Greens are about 120 feet square and are divided into six rinks, each 20 feet wide and 120 feet long. The balls are made of lignum vitae, a very hard, dense wood, and are biased or shaped and weighted so that they will roll in a curved path when bowled. The balls range in size from $4 \frac{13}{16}$ inches to $5\frac{1}{8}$ inches in diameter and weigh from 3 pounds 2 ounces to 3 pounds 8 ounces. Games may be between individuals or teams of two, three or four players (Menke 705).

The game begins by the first player rolling a smaller white ball, called the jack, onto the green. The jack is $2\frac{1}{5}$

An impromptu game of bowls using cannon balls for balls and jacks.

inches in diameter and weighs 10 ounces. He next bowls his two balls, or bowls, at the jack. The object is to get your balls, or your team's balls, closer to the jack than your opponent's ball or balls. It is permissible to knock an opponent's ball away from the jack with your ball. The second man to bowl is the opponent, and if more than two are playing, the bowling alternates between opponents. For each bowl closer to the jack than any of the opponents' bowls, a point is awarded. Game is usually 21.

# CONCLUSION

With such a wide variety of authentic and entertaining games available to the reenactor for his or her own amusement or for the entertainment of spectators, there is no excuse for sitting around camp wondering what to do next. Why split firewood, wash dishes or clean guns when there are so many fun and authentic things to do? The biggest deterrent is, of course, coming up with authentic equipment, but as resourceful as most buckskinners and reenactors are, that shouldn't pose any insurmountable obstacles to a good time.

Finally, there is one sport, which is doubtless the oldest of them all, that is absolutely authentic for any period. An etching by the 18th century English artist Thomas Rowlandson illustrates one version of this sport, and as you can see, it is a sport for which you make up your own rules, establish your own playing field and decide how many players should be on each team. Not only that, but there is never a problem coming up with authentic equipment in this sport. It is usually not considered a spectator sport however, but that shouldn't deter the *dedicated* reenactor from achieving an authentic level of expertise and proficiency.

Thomas Rowlandson's "Country Frolic, or, A Pleasant Way of Making Hay."

## APPENDIX: WORKS CITED

Arts Council of Great Britain. *British Sporting Painting, 1650-1850.* 1974.

Bailey, Trevor. *A History of Cricket.* London: George Allen & Unwin, 1979.

Bell, R. C. *Board and Table Games From Many Civilizations.* Vol. 2. London: Oxford University Press, 1969.

Bongartz, Roy. "Baseball." *Early American Life.* April, 1981.

Carson, Jane. *Colonial Virginians at Play.* Williamsburg, VA: Colonial Williamsburg, 1965.

Cotton, Charles. "The Compleat Gamester."1674. *Games and Gamesters of the Restoration.* Ed. J. Isaacs. London: George Routledge, 1930.

Diagram Group, The. *The Way To Play.* New York: Paddington Press, 1975.

Durant, John and Otto Bettmann. *Pictorial History of American Sports From Colonial Times to the Present.* N.p.: A. S. Barnes, 1952.

Hass, David W. and Bruce Lanzerotti. "Fore! An Expose of the Un-Scottish Game." *N.W.T.A. Courier,* Mar. 1984.

Hickock, Ralph. *New Encyclopedia of Sports.* New York: McGraw-Hill, 1977.

Menke, Frank G. *The Encyclopedia of Sports.* Ed. Peter Palmer. 6th rev. ed. New York: A. S. Barnes, 1978.

Morehead, Albert H. and Geoffrey Mott-Smith. *Hoyle's Rules of Games.* 2nd ed. rev. New York: NAL Penguin, 1983.

Neumann, George C. and Frank J. Kravic. *Collector's Illustrated Encyclopedia of the American Revolution.* Secaucus, NJ: Castle Books, 1977.

Scarne, John. *Scarne on Cards.* Rev. ed. New York: Crown Publishers, 1972.

—.*Scarne on Dice.* 8th rev. ed. New York: Crown Publishers, 1980.

Scharff, Robert, ed. *Golf Magazine's Encyclopedia of Golf.* New York: Harper and Row, 1970.

Strobell, Adah Parker. "Like It Was." *Bicentennial Games 'N Fun.* Washington, D.C.: Acropolis Books, 1975.

Strutt, Joseph. *The Sports and Pastimes of the People of England.* Ed. William Hone. London: Chatto & Windus, 1898.

Twombly, Wells. *200 Years of Sport in America: A Pageant of a Nation at Play.* New York: McGraw-Hill, 1976.

Weaver, Robert B. *Amusements and Sports in American Life.* Chicago: The University of Chicago Press, 1939.

# Pack Saddles & Panniers

## by Bob Schmidt & Tom Bryant

DESCENDED FROM GREAT GRANDPARENTS who journeyed to California in 1865 in a covered wagon via the Oregon Trail, Bob Schmidt was born in San Antonio, Texas, in 1928. He grew up and received his schooling in Oklahoma, then served two years in the Navy. Returning to Oklahoma City, he went to work at a saddle and boot shop where he learned the leather-working trade. A year later he joined the Oklahoma City Fire Department, which allowed him to have every other day off to continue working in the saddle shop.

In 1952, he married Nita Holcomb, and they have three sons and four grandchildren. A move in 1958 to Colorado Springs placed Bob working for the Air Force Academy Fire Department until his retirement in 1978. During those years he continued working the leather trade at different boot shops.

Upon retirement he and his family headed north to settle in Corvallis, Montana, in the Bitterroot Valley. He established the White Buffalo Leather Shop and specialized in custom-made saddles, cowboy boots and other horse tack and equipment. Today, he still operates his shop outside Corvallis where he builds historic saddles and equipment on order. He has been a member of the NMLRA and the NAPR since 1974 and a member of the AMM since 1983.

TOM BRYANT WAS BORN on a farm in south Georgia in 1934 and grew up working with horses and mules. Between days in the fields with his mules and evenings and weekends with his horses, Tom developed a lifelong love affair with animals and the outdoors. "As a kid," he said, "the wild animals and wild places held a special attraction for me. I learned to ride at a very early age, and being on horseback in the backcountry is still the best feeling in the world."

In 1969, he moved to Montana and, in 1970, graduated from the University of Montana with a degree in Health, Physical Education and Recreation. For the next ten years, he was recreation director for the city of Missoula, Montana. In that capacity he wrote a weekly column for the *Missoulian* newspaper on outdoor recreation plus feature stories on hunting, fishing and adventures on horseback.

As a member of the Missoula Backcountry Horsemen, Tom produced for the U.S. Forest Service a slide/tape show on no-impact horse use titled "Go Lightly On The Land." He has been published in numerous magazines dealing with horses and the outdoors and is currently a correspondent and columnist for the *Trail Duster,* the official newspaper of the Great Montana Centennial Cattle Drive.

Tom lives and works in the beautiful Bitterroot Valley of southwestern Montana where he writes, cowboys, trains horses and mules and packs into the backcountry every chance he gets.

WE don't know when, where or how man first domesticated animals and began to use them to assist in his work and play. We do know that the practice of using animals to help man is universal. You will find beasts of burden in almost every culture in almost every segment of the world, and almost every kind of animal that can be domesticated has been used and will continue to work for man's profit and pleasure.

As far back as recorded history goes, paintings and drawings show man using camels, mules, yaks, water buffalo, llamas, ox, reindeer, goats, dogs and horses to push, pull or pack loads of goods and equipment. The horse is probably the newcomer to this scene with the wild ass of the Arabian desert among the first to be used as a work animal.

The ass as a beast of burden is mentioned many times in the Bible, and mules were prized possessions of the early Romans. As early as the 70th Olympiad, 500 years before the Christian era, mules were used to pull chariots in Olympic races.

In 1519, when the Spanish conquistadors landed in Mexico to explore North America, they reintroduced horses to the continent. Two hundred years later the Western plains were well-populated with descendents of these Spanish ponies. The Indians quickly recognized the advantage of being mounted and took to horses like ducks to water.

From the Spanish the Indians learned not only to ride well, but also to use the horse to pack their camp from one site to another. The Spanish brigades used a type of "aparejo" (pronounced "ap-pa-ray-ho") pack saddle, and we'll have more about it later. The design of the aparejo is centuries old. We also do not know who, where, when or how man first used or devised a pack saddle.

Modern pack saddles have evolved through hundreds of years of use, and the surprising thing about the pack saddles we use today is that they are amazingly similar to the ones used in the very earliest of times. The sawbuck pack saddle so often depicted in drawings of the fur traders in North America in the 1800s comes from the same model designed by the Spanish, used by the Mexicans and adopted by the Indians. Variations of the crosstree or sawbuck pack saddle have been observed in almost every European and Asiatic country in the world. The universal appeal of the sawbuck is its simplicity.

230

# PACKING WITH THE SAWBUCK

Just as we don't know when man first domesticated wild animals, no one knows precisely when man started lashing loads on critters' backs and converting the unsuspecting four-legged friend into a beast of burden. The first pack load was probably wood or furs lashed onto a dog or burro by crude ropes made of grass or rawhide.

After the Spanish introduced horses to North America, the American Indians were quick to take advantage of them. The horse transformed the poor, footsore Indian into a proud warrior who could move fast, strike hard and be many miles away the following morning. The same tactics were used by the Arabs, the Moors, the Cossacks and other great warring nations. This warring and conquering was once the primary way new ideas and equipment reached new cultures. It was the way the Arabian horse was introduced to Europe; it was the way the horse and equipment came to America. Warring had its bad side to be sure, but the long-range effects have been beneficial.

The American Indians found that they could build saddles fairly easily. Using the forks of a tree or the branch of antlered animals, the Indians constructed a crude sawbuck pack saddle. They also built a saddle that they could ride, pack and use to pull a travois, and sometimes they used a saddle for all three things at one time.

The sawbuck pack saddle has stood the test of time and hard use. They were used by trappers and traders, by mountain men and miners, by cowboys and Indians, soldiers and civilians. It's hard to beat a good sawbuck for packing a load.

In July, 1988, with seven other people, we rode across the Absaroka-Beartooth wilderness in Montana, some of the most rugged country in the world, on our way to the NMLRA Western Rendezvous. We all used sawbuck pack saddles. Our camps, clothing, food and gear were transported easily and efficiently. There were no wrecks, no lost packs, no spilled supplies. Built correctly and packed right, you can go a hellava long way with a sawbuck.

On our trip to the rendezvous, we used panniers exclusively. Panniers (boxes or baskets) may be constructed from wood, rawhide, tin, canvas, leather or a combination of materials. We have found that the canvas pannier, or canvas reinforced with leather, is just about perfect for packing. Canvas and leather are highly flexible and will conform to your loads.

On many trips today, you may have to pack horse food as well as people food, and the canvas panniers work well for that. We packed grain as well as hay pellets and poured it directly into the bottom of the pannier. This gave the container shape and also served as ballast.

Amigos, balance is THE most important part of packing. If it ain't balanced, it ain't gonna ride. So, if you want a fun trip, free of wrecks and accidents, balance your

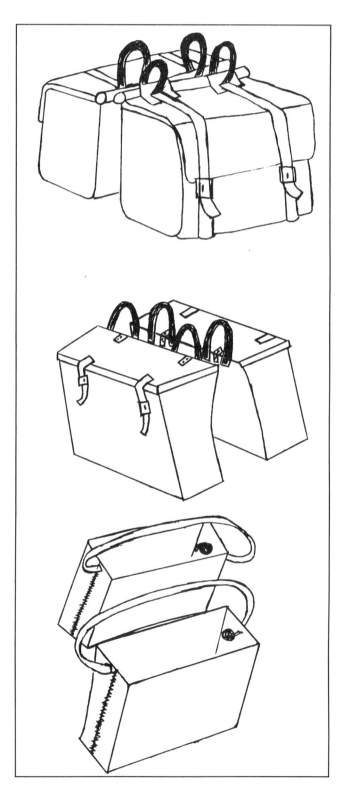

232

loads carefully. Each side should weigh within two or three pounds of the other. Any greater difference will cause you no end of grief and will sore your pack animal and ruin your trip.

In loading your panniers, keep the weight evenly distributed throughout the length of the container. If one end is slightly heavier than the other, place the heavy end forward on the pack animal. You should keep your load and most of the weight just behind the animal's shoulders. A horse or mule packs his body weight with his front legs, so try to help him as much as possible with your packing.

How much weight can your animal pack? They can pack a lot, actually more that we care to pick up and set on their backs. But don't overdo it. Remember, your animal is a living, breathing being. It gets tired and sore just like you do, and it feels discomfort and pain just like you do. Empathize with your animal and look out for its welfare.

The U.S. Army used to figure 250 pounds per mule (Daly 18). Friends, that is the absolute max. Keep in mind that the old brown boot Army was a hard outfit and used up a lot of mules, a *lot* of mules. They packed 30 miles a day on the average. In the mountains 15 miles was considered a good day's pull.

On our ride to the '88 rendezvous, we covered about 18 to 20 miles a day. That made for long hours in the saddle with little time to relax and enjoy the country. We don't recommend that sort of continued travel. As one sage on the trip asked, ''Is this a pleasure trip or a military march?'' And the most frequently asked question was, ''Are we having any fun yet?''

Our loads ranged from 50 to 60 pounds per side with a top pack of another 20 to 30 pounds. So, each animal was packing less than 200 pounds, which is about the way it should be. One hundred and eighty pounds is a heavy load, and two hundred is just about too much.

Plan your loads carefully, thinking about your poor pack animal, and you'll do fine. Your pack animal will do fine too, and you'll have a good trip instead of a busted trip. Just keep in mind that there is no big mystery to packing. It's just proper planning, proper balance and proper placement. Good packing, and good luck.

# MAKING A SAWBUCK
# PACK SADDLE

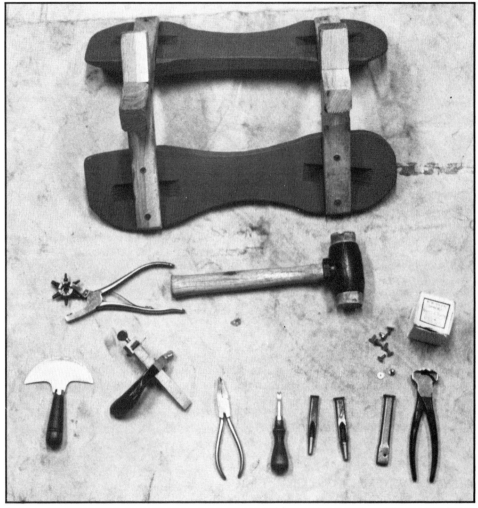

Shown with a Tehama pack saddle tree, the tools needed for making a pack saddle are (clockwise from top left): roller punch, leather mallet, rivet and burrs, nippers, riveting tool, #8 and #9 hole punches, #4 edger, saddlery pliers, draw knife, and round knife.

Fur trappers and traders liked the sawbuck because it was made of wood and leather and could be repaired or rebuilt in the field. If the Indians could build a sawbuck with hatchets and knives and the trappers and traders could repair one just as handy, you can do the same thing.

To make the job of building the pack saddle easier, and we're always looking for the easy way of doing things, you will need a few leather working tools:

| | |
|---|---|
| Round knife | Draw knife |
| Saddlery pliers | #4 edger |
| #8 & 9 round punch | Nippers |
| #9 rivet and burr set | Roller punch |
| Leather mallet | Assortment of #9 rivets and burrs |

The first step in building a pack saddle is to obtain a sawbuck saddle tree. Almost every saddle tree company sells pack saddle trees, just be sure the tree you get is free from defects like splits, cracks, knots or gouges in the bars. We recommend the humane type tree which will fit a horse or mule. Burro saddle trees have shorter bars and will fit only those short-backed animals.

The Tehama tree is the one we use most. The cross bucks on this tree are straight up and down, and we like that better. On the Sierra tree, the bucks are slanted to the front and rear and don't seem to work as well, but this is our opinion. The Tehama tree allows small items to be laid between the bucks, and this offers some advantage in packing.

Next, order a side of leather. Try to get a good heavy

234

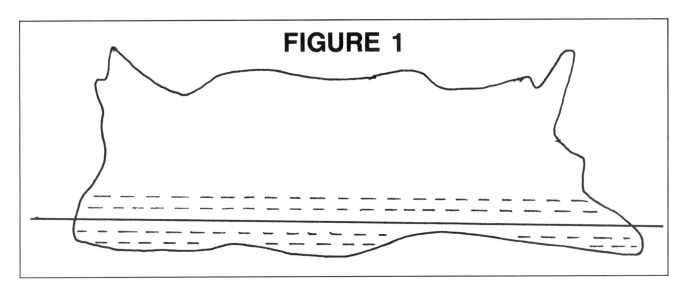

# FIGURE 1

This illustration shows Bob cutting the first strap. Keep one thumb on top of the strap on the draw knife to hold the leather in place.

side of harness leather. Most sides have a brand scar on it unless you order a clean piece. The brand scar makes a weak place in the leather, but you can normally cut around it or use that section in a place that will not be subjected to much stress.

With a wet sponge or sheepskin, saddle soap the smooth side of the leather. Then wet a foot-square piece of canvas, saddle soap it and let it dry. This will be used to put a finish on the leather straps.

To cut your harness side, lay out a straight edge on the leather and mark it with a pencil, as shown in Figure 1. Never use a pen. Cut on the line using your round knife. When using the round or ''head'' knife always work away from your body. Lay the side just off the work table so the knife cuts clean through the leather. Next, use a draw knife to cut 2 full-length straps 1'' wide. These are your quarter straps. Then cut 2 straps 1½'' by 40'' for your rigging leathers. All the rest of the straps will be 1'' wide. Finally, cut the breast collar and the 2 pieces to make the breeching: one piece 4'' by 36'', and one strap 2'' by 42''. There should be enough leather in one large side of harness leather to cut out the rigging for at least three pack saddles. The secret to cutting up a side is to plan ahead and use as much of the leather as possible. You will need 2 pieces of latigo 1¼'' by 6' and two cinches for each pack saddle you make.

All straps should be edged. This keeps sharp edges from cutting into the pack animal or yourself when saddling and unsaddling. Use a #4 edger on both the surface and flesh sides of the straps.

To decorate the straps and to mark a line for sewing, wet each strap by dipping it in water, then wipe it dry. Run a compass point along the edges about ⅛ inch from the edge. With the piece of dry canvas, rub the straps by pulling them through the folded canvas. For further decoration the edges may be dyed a dark brown. Just take a swab dipped in dye and run it along the edges.

Whenever you bend or fold a strap, wet it and tap the fold down with a hammer. This makes the fold lie flat and prevents the leather from cracking. Following this procedure, fold back 3½'' on the end of the rigging straps and punch a triangle of three holes with a #9 punch. The rigging rings can be laced in using these holes, or you can fasten the rings to the straps using rivets and burrs. We like the lacing because it looks better and is easier to repair in the event of a breakdown.

For the lacing strips, use latigo about ½'' wide, making a three-hole knot as shown in Figure 2. Use a punch or Phillips screwdriver to force the ends of the latigo through the holes, then pull tight with a pair of pliers and trim off

# SAWBUCK PACK SADDLE

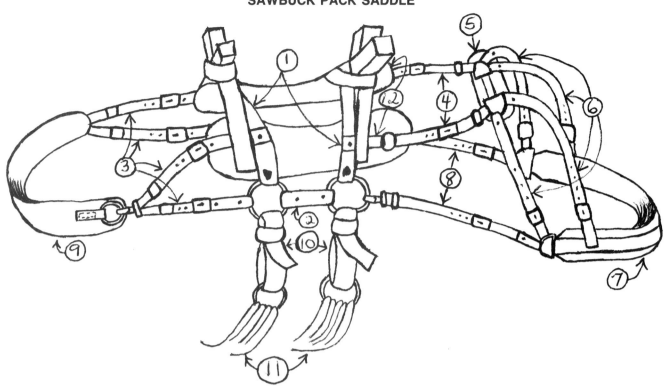

# FIGURE 2

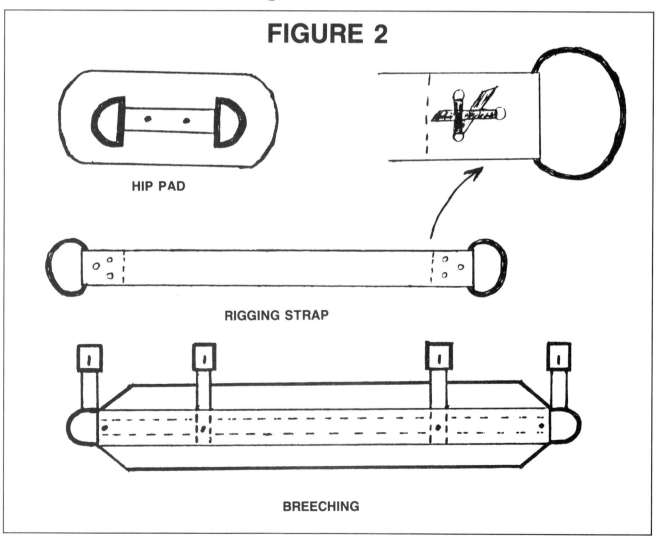

HIP PAD

RIGGING STRAP

BREECHING

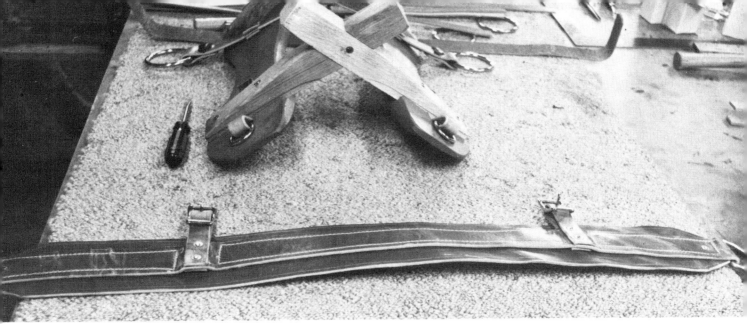

The completed breeching strap.

The rigging straps should circle the cross tree so that the rings hang equal distance down on each side. Anchor the rigging straps with a tack on each side of the tree while you complete the rest of the rigging.

Hardware needed to build a pack saddle includes (clockwise from top left): 1¼" chap snap, 1" chap snap, 3" ring, 2" D-ring, two 1¼" Conway buckles, two 1" Conway buckles, 1¾" roller buckle, 1" roller buckle, and 2" ring.

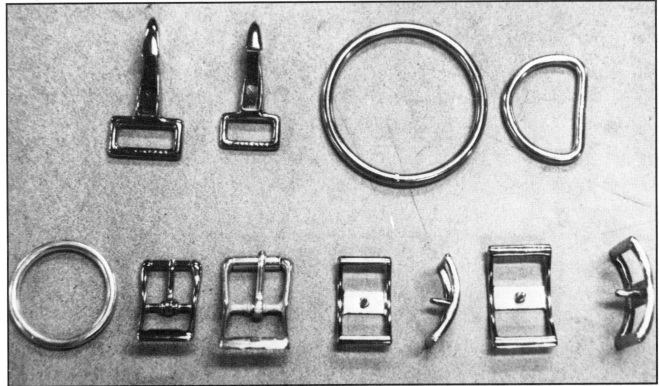

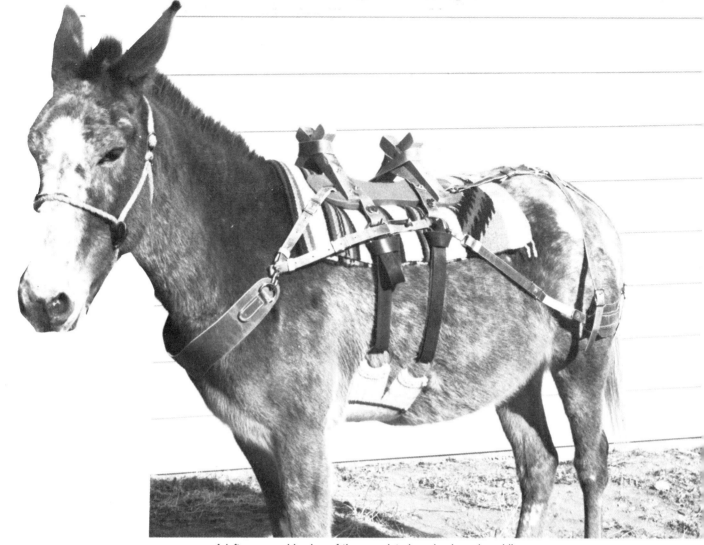

A left or near side view of the completed sawbuck pack saddle.

excess ends. Once the rings are laced or riveted on, lay the strap on a piece of granite or marble and tap the folds flat. If using the latigo lace, make your knot so that the flat side will be against the side of the pack animal. This completes the rigging strap. You need two, however, so repeat the steps above.

Now, circle the cross tree with the rigging strap so that the rings hang equal distance down on each side. Anchor the straps with a tack on each side of the tree. This will hold the strap in place while you are working on the rest of the rigging.

Make two rear keeper straps 1'' x 12'' and edge them as before. Next, double the straps and place 1¼'' rings inside. Push the open ends through the slots under the cross tree in the rear of the saddle. The back straps will be attached to the rings on the keeper straps.

Mark the center of the keeper strap in the slot behind the cross buck and punch a hole in it. This is for the anchor screws. The rigging strap goes between the keeper strap ends, so punch a hole in the rigging strap also and line up the holes in the three pieces of leather. Start a hole in the bar of the tree with a punch, then secure the three straps using a 1'' round-head wood screw with a washer.

The breeching, commonly called the ''britchen,'' may be cut from the belly part of the hide, since it will be rein-forced with a backing strap. Fold under the ends of the backing strap about 2'' on each end and insert a 2'' D-ring in each fold so that they are about at the end of the britchen. Fold double the 1'' x 9'' buckle straps and cut a 1'' slot in the center of the fold so the tongue of the buckle can stick through. After you rivet the two buckle straps about 9'' from the end of the backing strap, sew the backing strap onto the britchen. Finally, rivet 1 buckle strap to each ring.

Proceed by cutting out the 4'' x 8'' hip pad and round-ing out the ends. Also, cut a 2'' x 8'' strap and put a 2'' D-ring on each end. Rivet this strap on top of the hip pad.

Now we begin work on the back, hip and quarter straps. Cut the two 1'' x 26'' back straps, edge them and punch holes about one inch apart for the Conway buckles. Rivet the opposite end to the rings on the rear keeper straps. Cut the four 1'' x 24'' hip straps and rivet one end on the hip pad. On the other end punch holes one inch apart and buckle the straps to the britchen.

Cut the two 1'' x 36'' quarter straps and rivet one to each D-ring on the britchen. Slip on a snap, place leather keepers on the straps along with Conway buckles and snap it to the rigging ring. The ¾'' leather keepers can be made but we get ours ready to use from leather stores. Now, at-tach the back straps with Conway buckles to the rings on the hip pad.

238

The right or off side view of the completed pack saddle.

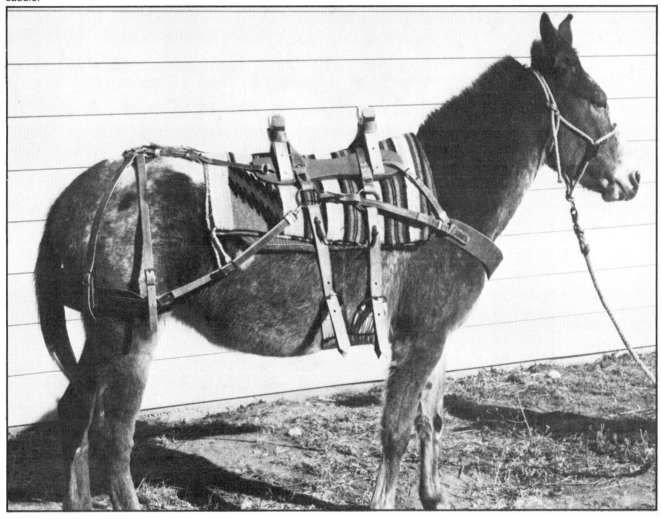

Completing the breast collar and breast straps is the next step in building a pack saddle. Begin by cutting the 3'' x 30'' breast collar out of the belly side of the hide. Put a 2'' ring on both ends.

Cut out the four 1'' x 26'' breast straps. Insert one end of one strap through the slot under the front cross tree the right side. As you did with the rear ring keeper straps, attach this breast strap to the tree by putting a wood screw through the rigging strap and the breast strap. Repeat for the other side of the cross tree.

Punch holes one inch apart for tongue buckles and Conway buckles in the opposite end of these breast straps. Run the strap through the leather keepers and 2'' ring on the right side and back through the keeper to the Conway. The left side breast strap is attached the same way except the end opposite the saddle is attached to a 1'' snap that hooks to the ring of the breast collar.

The bottom breast strap is attached to the rigging ring. Punch holes for tongue and Conway buckles. Run the end of the strap through the keepers and snaps, then back through the keepers to the Conway. Do both bottom breast straps the same. Cut out the 1'' x 10'' keeper strap from either the belly of the hide or latigo leather and round off the ends. Fold it over the cinch rings so that the ends lap each other enough to fasten together. The keeper may be laced together or riveted.

Finally, cut four 1½'' by 6' latigo straps. Edge them and lace the straps to the rigging ring. Attach your cinches, and you're ready to saddle up.

Place the completed saddle on your pack animal and adjust it to fit. You are now ready for packing. Happy trails!

# BUILDING THE HALFBREED BOOT

The U.S. Army found out the hard way what the Spaniards had learned centuries earlier, that unpadded pack saddles cause sores on pack animals. During the heavy-use days of the Indian wars, the Army adopted the aparejo boot to pad the pack saddle and protect the ribs of the pack mules. H.W. Daly wrote in his *Manual Of Pack Transportation* that they experimented with the aparejo boot, filling it with grass to pad the load and making the sides stiff with sticks to protect the mules (19). The halfbreed is a padded case of canvas with side boards to protect the animal

The nickname "halfbreed" is probably an Americanization of the Spanish phrase for harness cover, *sobre-en jalmas*. In time and use, this was shortened and bastardized to sobrejalma, sobre-halma, sovereign hammer and soldier hammer. Because it was a double word with one meaning, *sobre-en jalmas* eventually became known as the half-breed.

The protective boot we use on our pack saddles today is called a halfbreed. It is not entirely necessary for packing, but we highly recommend it. Built correctly and padded

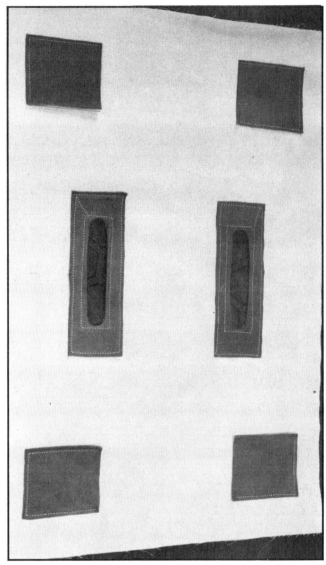

The halfbreed with wear leathers and bar leathers in place.

# FIGURE 3

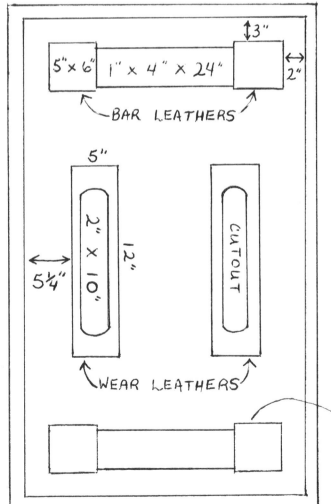

Materials needed:
Two pieces of 26" x 46" canvas
Four pieces of 5" x 6" oil-tanned leather
Four pieces of 5" x 12" oil-tanned leather
Two 1" x 4" x 24" boards
One 2" strip of soft leather for edging

with animal hair, the halfbreed will do a tremendous job of protecting your pack animals' backs. Halfbreeds are also amazingly simple to build.

Figure 3 is a diagram showing the dimensions of the halfbreed. Refer to it as you follow these instructions. Begin by cutting out two 26'' x 46'' pieces of heavy-duty canvas and marking the center crosswise of each piece so the length is divided in half. Come in 5¼'' from each side and mark off 6'' on either side of the center line on both sides. Draw in the 2 rectangles, 5'' x 12'', labeled ''wear leathers'' on the diagram.

From each corner mark out 3'' from the bottom and 2'' from the side. This is where the bar leathers for the side boards will be sewn. Draw and cut out the leather pieces, glue 'em and sew 'em in place. On the left side bar leathers, glue only three sides down. On the right side, glue only two sides. Then you can stick the boards, or bars, in the openings and lace them in place. Bar leathers can also be laced

on or sewn on with a regular household sewing machine.

Cut a 1'' square piece of leather and punch a small hole in it. This goes on the inside corner of the canvas under the bar leather to give the canvas added strength when you lace the bars in place.

In the center of the wear leathers, mark off a 2'' x 10'' hole and cut it out. This will be the opening for the sawbucks. Sew around inside and outside of this opening, or you may sew the two pieces together, then cut the opening out.

Glue the two pieces of canvas together. Do the two short sides and one long side. Also glue a 2'' strap of soft leather edging all around, but leave an opening to insert padding material. Rug padding works well, either the foam rubber kind or the hair pads. Cut the pieces of padding 16'' and 20'', stick them inside the boot and sew the open end down. The halfbreed can also be stuffed with animal hair. Deer hair works especially well, as does hog hair and the mane and tail hair from your horse or mule.

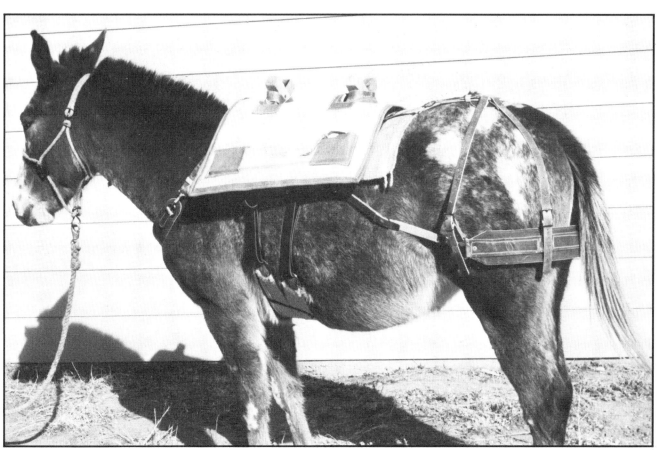

The completed halfbreed over a sawbuck pack saddle.

241

# BUILDING PANNIERS

The simplest way to pack a load on an animal is to use boxes or baskets with a rope or leather strap to hang over the cross trees or "sawbucks" of the pack saddle. This was how packing was done in the earliest of times. Wicker baskets slung on a donkey was a common way to pack water, wood or groceries in the deserts of Africa and in Spain, Mexico and America.

The word pannier, also spelled and pronounced "panyard," comes from the French, meaning basket or pouch. In Spain and Mexico, they are referred to as alforjas. As we said before, panniers, or alforjas, can be made from a variety of materials, but we like and use canvas ones reinforced with leather. These are hard to beat for utility, and they are fairly easy to construct.

Use good, heavy canvas. You'll need two pieces 77" x 36". Lay one of the 77" x 36" pieces of canvas flat on the floor or table and measure out, draw in and cut out two 10" x 36" pieces and a 10" x 26" piece for one pannier.

See Figure 4 for the layout of the squares. Use a sharp pair of scissors or shears and push them through the canvas, but note that cutting with shears leaves jagged edges.

Fold the two 10" x 36" (B) pieces lengthwise, making two 10" x 18" pieces. Glue the ends together with a good fabric glue such as "Tehr Greeze." Just smear it on with your fingers in a one-inch strip along the edges. Firmly press the ends together. These 10" x 18" pieces will be used to make the ends of the panniers. Use the folded edge for the top of the end pieces.

On the 67" x 26" (A) piece, fold the clean edge down one inch and glue it in place as shown in the drawing. Measure 14" up from the end opposite this 1" fold. Place the 10" x 26" (C) piece above this line on the inside of the pannier and glue it in place. This part will be the top piece of the pannier and will serve to reinforce the dowel rod attachment.

Cut two 4" x 8" and six 1" x 3" pieces of oil-tanned

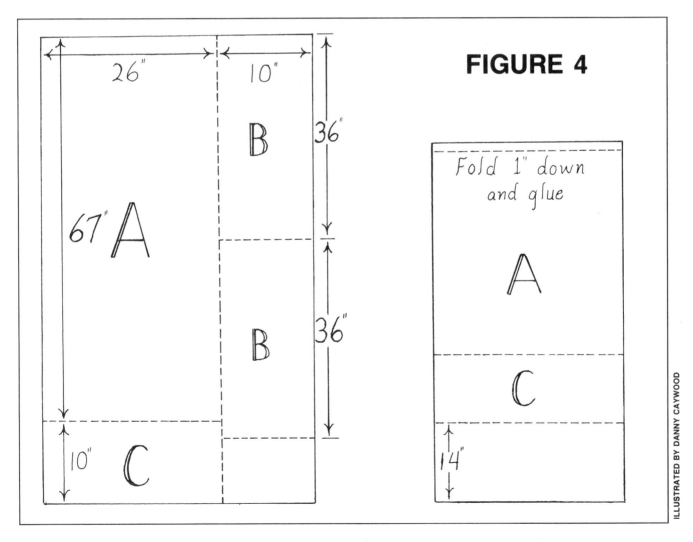

**FIGURE 4**

Fold 1" down and glue

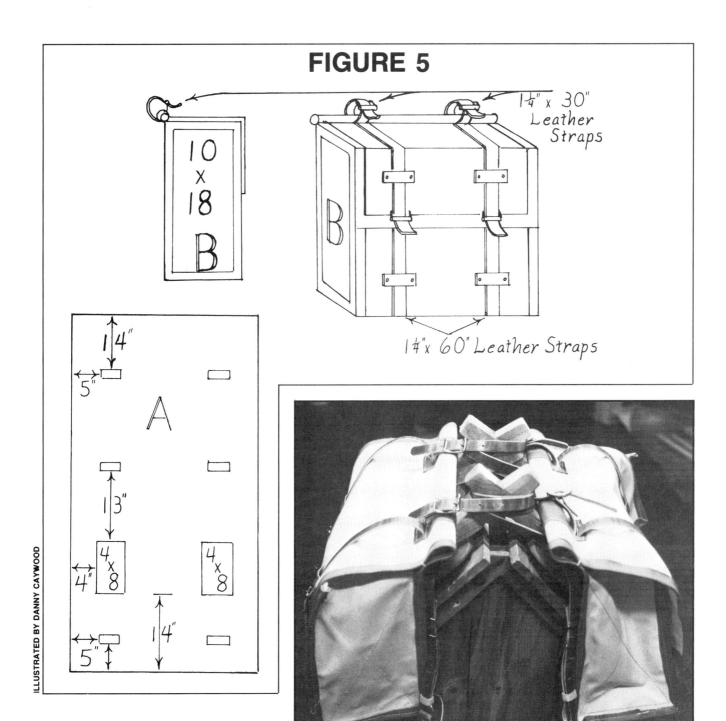

The completed panniers hanging
on the sawbuck pack saddle.

leather. Turn the ''A'' piece right side up and mark the spots for the 4'' x 8'' leathers as shown in Figure 5. Glue these leather pieces in place and sew around the edges now. Punch a hole in each end of the 1'' x 3'' pieces and rivet the leather keepers in place at this time also.

Lay the end pieces (B) in place and glue the three edges down on both ends, one at a time. Cut strips of soft leather two inches wide, fold and glue it over the edges of the ends of the boxes. This leather strip should be sewn on. Your panniers are now ready for placement of the dowels.

Make a sleeve at the top of each pannier by folding the top of the lid over on itself. The fold will be centered on the two 4'' x 8'' pieces of leather. Punch holes in each corner of the 4'' x 8'' pieces and rivet the corners together at

each end. Then cut two 1'' x 24'' wooden dowels and slide them into the sleeves you just made. Now punch a hole through the soft leather strips at the end of the sleeves and tie the sleeves closed with leather thongs. Add the 1¼'' x 60'' leather straps around the outside and you're ready to pack loads in the panniers.

Hanna shows off her packing outfit, including panniers, halfbreed boot and sawbuck pack saddle.

# HOW TO MANTEE A LOAD

Here we go again—back in time. Mantee, also spelled manta and manty, comes from the Spanish word meaning "little cover." Actually, it refers to the handkerchief the ladies used at times to cover their heads. Like so many other Spanish nouns, mantee has become a part of our language, most especially the language of the packer.

Aside from your pack saddle and panniers, one or more good mantees are as important on a pack trip as tobacco and whiskey. Besides wrapping and covering your load, mantees make good ground tarps, bed covers and lean-tos and can be used as a shawl or poncho. A mantee is a handy item on a pack trip. Take two; they're small, portable and practical.

There are many sizes of mantees available, but we recommend an 8' x 8' or no smaller than a 7' x 8'. Once you start packing you'll be forever grateful you went to the larger size. We prefer a medium weight canvas for our mantees, between 12 and 18 ounces. You can get heavier canvas, but it tends to get too stiff to work with when cold and too heavy when wet. However, heavy canvas will shed a lot of water and is more resistant to snags and tears.

Wrapping your gear in a mantee is no different from wrapping a Christmas present. Fold all the corners over and secure it with binding. Usually, the way we pack is to put heavy, hard items in the panniers and top pack soft goods like clothing and bedding. Most packers try to keep that top pack as light and soft as possible. Top packs work best if they're wide and flat. Pack animals, especially horses, wad-

dle when they walk and this causes the top pack to sway. The higher the load, the more the sway, and the more sway in a pack the more likely it is to slip off center and cause a wreck or sore your animal.

That top pack is dead weight, setting squarely on top of the saddle bars. If it gets a little forward, it's gonna sore the animal's withers. If it slips back, it's gonna sore the kidneys. The pack animal's kidneys are very close to the surface, just in front of the hips, and like your kidney area, it is an extremely sensitive region. Use top packs carefully and with much thought about your animal's anatomy and health.

Spread the mantee out flat on the ground and, standing at a corner, lay the load in the center. Take the corner at your feet and fold it up over the load. Take the corner to your right and fold it across the load, then, likewise, the corner to your left. Fold under any excess canvas that tends to stick out. Now take the corner directly in front of you and fold it back toward you, over the load.

The load is now ready for lashing or tying, depending on your preference. Some wrap and tie, some load and lash. Some packers just take their bedroll, lay it out flat across the top of the panniers and snug it down with a diamond hitch, sometimes a double diamond, sometimes a single, depending on the load. We suggest you try both and see what works best for you and your outfit.

To tie up the manteed load, you will need ⅜'' or ⁷⁄₁₆'' rope 30 to 35 feet in length. Manila rope works best. It is

244

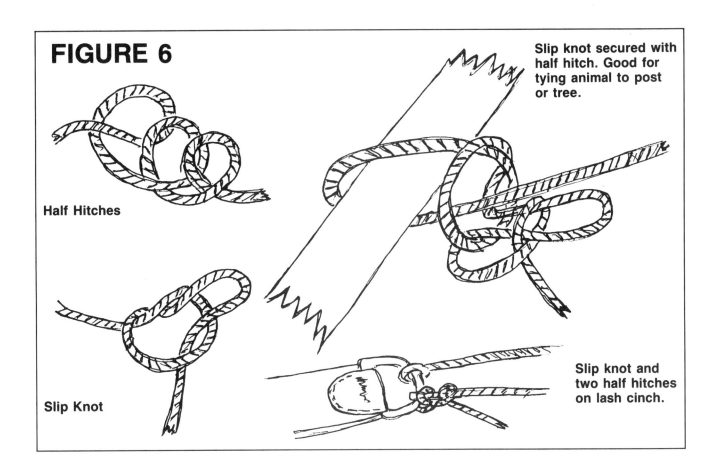

# FIGURE 6

**Half Hitches**

**Slip Knot**

Slip knot secured with half hitch. Good for tying animal to post or tree.

Slip knot and two half hitches on lash cinch.

easy to repair and easy to obtain. It tends to be hard on the hands, however. Use gloves until you get toughened up or the rope is worn smooth. You can smooth the rope by dragging it down a dirt road for a few miles and knocking the burrs off.

Stand at the long end of your manteed load, make a loop in the rope and place the loop lengthwise over the load. Snug the rope tight, keeping the eye, or honda, of the rope near the top ¾ of the load. A good phrase to remember in packing is: once you start pulling on a rope, never let any slack Keep your rope taut and throw a half hitch (see Figure 6) over or near the honda. Pull it down tight and throw another half hitch about halfway down the load and one more at the bottom quarter. Still holding the rope tight, roll the load away from you, encircling it lengthwise with a rope.

Once you reach the honda again, push the rope under the first half hitch, reach in and pull a small loop through. Another packing axiom: keep the loops small. You should now have a small slip knot built over the first half hitch. Snug it down and whip a couple of half hitches around the bow of that slip knot, and that will lock 'er in place. Simply store the rest of the rope under the remaining half hitches, and you're ready to go.

To secure your top pack, you will need a lash cinch. These are made with a band of canvas with an "O" ring on one end and a hook on the other. A 40 to 45 foot long ⅜" or ½" rope completes the outfit. With the lash cinch and rope you can tie down your top pack with several types of hitches, but for this chapter we'll stick with the ones we like and use, the single diamond and the double diamond. Either can be easily thrown and tied by one person, but working with another person is helpful and three people can really do the job right. The army used three men: one to hold the mule, a near side packer, and an off side packer.

Pull about 15 feet of rope through the "O" ring and toss the doubled up end over the top pack. Fasten the end of this loop through the hook under the animal and pull—tight! When you've got 'er good and snug, tie it off at the "O" ring with a small slip knot. This is cheating a little, but, brother, we believe in taking every advantage we can in packing.

Whip a couple of half hitches around the eye of the slip knot and pull tight. Now, reach up on top of the pack (here's where a short-legged critter is a blessing) and twist the two ropes a couple of times (see Figure 7). Fold your lash rope again and poke the doubled up end through the front part of this twist. Run it under the pannier on the other (off) side and repeat this process on the rear of the pack. This will bring you back to the starting point. Snug 'er down tight and tie it off with another slip knot and half hitch. Store the extra rope, and you're ready to hit the trail.

The double diamond is tied practically the same as the single diamond except that instead of one large diamond on top of the pack, you make a small diamond on each side. Figure 8 will show you how it's done.

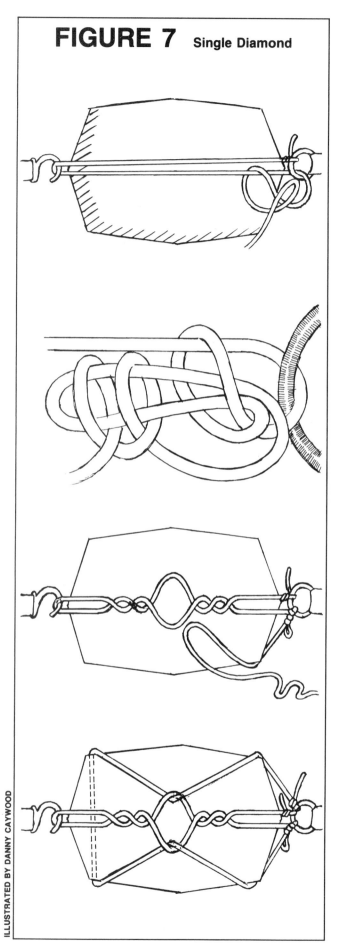

# FIGURE 7  Single Diamond

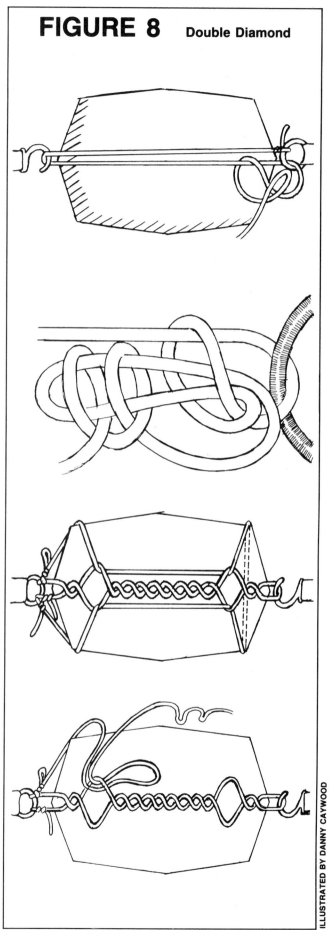

# FIGURE 8  Double Diamond

# THE PACK ANIMAL

As we've said before, almost any animal that you can domesticate can be used as a pack animal. Almost every animal you can think of has at one time or another been used to pack goods for man. Before the American Indians got attached to Spanish horses, they used dogs fairly frequently as pack stock. It was a good arrangement. Dogs were plentiful, self-sufficient and could be eaten when other food was in short supply.

The U.S. Army was into mules for packing, and there is a good reason for this. The mule, while he looks much like a horse, has some very subtle, albeit important, differences from a horse's anatomy. The mule's back is more level than a horse's. Their shoulders and front legs are constructed slightly differently and they have a different way of traveling. A mule picks his feet up, like a moose, and is much more sure-footed, stumbling less than does a horse. Mules are also more resistant to heat and disease and have stronger feet, legs and backs than a horse. So, why don't more folks ride mules? Well, not only does a mule have a stronger back than a horse, he also has a stronger mind. "Stubborn as a mule" is a saying not without firm foundation.

Scientists tell us that animals can't think, that they have no reasoning power. We're not convinced of that. We've seen mules come up to a bog or other obstacle in the trail and stop and mull it over. What they're "thinking" is anybody's guess. But just try to get a mule to cross something

he doesn't "think" is safe, and you'll quickly learn if they have any reasoning power. You can't force a mule into a situation he deems unsafe.

On the other hand, a well-trained horse will do anything you ask him to do. The old horses we ride will go places they really ain't got any business going, simply because they are so trained and will go forward when we give 'em the signal to do so. That's the reason most folks ride horses. Not because the horse is more sure-footed or stronger, but because it is more reliable in a critical situation. When you want to cross a bog, a log or a river, you want to do it now, and most times you have neither the time nor the patience for your trusty steed to stop and "think" about it.

While there were some very good mules, both riding and packing, on our trip, we used horses mostly. There are several reasons for this also. One is that horses are more abundant, therefore more available and, most important probably, more affordable than mules. Horses, in general, are easier to buy, easier to train and in the long run make a better dual purpose animal for riding and/or packing than the average mule.

A mule is a specially bred animal, with an ass, or jack, for a father and a horse (mare) for a mother, and are therefore hybrids. They are sterile but still have the old sex urge. Males have to be castrated, and females, called "mollies," will drive you crazy for the first ten years or so of their lives by falling in love with anything that moves

Clay and Bob Landry top pack Clay's bedroll with a double or two-man diamond hitch.

and some that don't.

So, keep this in mind when selecting a pack animal. Mules are better—but are they really? For the large majority of recreational and occasional packers, a good old solid horse is hard to beat. And mile for mile, on short hauls and moderately difficult terrain, the horse and mule are about equal. It is on the really long trips and the sustained days of use that the mule will outshine and outperform the horse.

There are three things to look for in selecting your pack animal. They are disposition, disposition and disposition. A pack animal has not only got to be sturdy and strong, but partner, they also have to be stable. A pack animal has to endure ropes dangling around its feet, rattling pots, pans and cans, flapping canvas and sagging loads. And that's just the stuff you put on his back. He's also got to contend with birds, bears, backpackers and other strange animals you meet on the trail. In short, your pack animal needs to be quiet and sensible. Leave the packing of colts and broncs to orphans, widowers and suicidal buckskinners. Stick with good, older horses or mules. We like to say, "There are old packers and there are bold packers, but there are no old, bold packers."

After its mind, the next most important part of your pack animal is its back. It is here that your load will ride. Your animal will need a good back, free of blemishes and sores, and should have a good set of withers. Withers, the high, bony projection between the shoulders on the animal, are most important in holding a saddle in place. A round-back or "hog-backed" critter will cause you unlimited grief in the mountains, because the saddle will slip and roll with each dip and turn in the trail. Mules have flatter backs because they have less shoulder and rump than a horse. Mules also tend to have smaller withers. This is why even with riding mules you see folks using full britchen and breast collars, because the mule simply doesn't have the withers to hold a saddle like a horse does. This is not to say that you can't find a mule with decent withers. You can. You'll just have to look longer and harder and, perhaps, part with more money when you do find one.

Your pack animal should have legs that are clean and fairly straight with no bumps and bulges. An animal's legs below the knee or hock should be hard and cold to the touch. A warm, puffy lower leg is an injured leg and needs treatment. From the rear, a mule tends to be a little more cow-hocked than a horse, but don't let that worry you. A mule is just built a little different from a horse, and even some old-time horsefolk are finding out that a horse that is a little cow-hocked tends to give a smoother ride.

The pack animal should also have good feet. By good we mean adequate in proportion to the animal's size and weight. A horse that stands 15 hands tall (60 inches) and weighs around 1,100 pounds, which is about perfect for a good using horse, should have feet that will accommodate a #2 or #1 size shoe with a #0 being the absolute minimum.

For many years in this country, breeders, especially quarter horse breeders, bred for large bones, heavy muscle and small feet. This was a fashion statement; it looked good, but, brother, it ain't fit for mountain travel. That pack animal needs a good foundation under him for the country you're gonna cross. His feet are the number one contact with the ground, and they should support his weight and the load you put on him. The old Cavalry soldiers used to say, "No foot, no horse." They were also fond of this saying: "Without a horse a man's afoot," an extremely unhealthy condition in hostile country.

A mule has a different type of foot than most horses, and it tends to be a little more narrow and lots tougher. Many packers don't even bother to put shoes on their mules unless they plan long trips over very rocky country. On our trip Kirby Werner was packing a young mule with no shoes, and little Taco never put a foot wrong the whole trip. It was only after we reached the rendezvous site, after five days of crossing logs, bogs, rivers and streams that Taco rebelled, refused to cross a small creek, jerked Kirby out of the saddle and kicked him in the belly. But, that's another story. Still believe a mule don't think? They'll work for you for thirty years just to get to kick you once. They're tough, no doubt about it, and you gotta be tough to handle 'em.

Study your potential pack animal carefully and be deliberate. Take your time and get to know the critter. Borrow him if possible and take him on a pack trip if you can before laying down your hard-earned cash. Once you find one that will work for you and suits your needs, marry it and take a vow to keep it through sickness and health. A good pack animal, like a good spouse, is damn hard to find, but it will give you many long years of happy trips. Waugh!

---

# SADDLING YOUR PACK ANIMAL

---

Before you set that saddle on your critter's back, there are a few preliminaries to accomplish. They are small and seemingly insignificant but are actually of critical importance. First, brush the animal and remove all the dirt and loose hair from its back. Brushing the animal is a good time to check it for soundness. Run your thumb and forefinger along the backbone of the animal. There should be no soreness or tender spots. Check the legs and feet of your animal and make sure he has a shoe on each foot and that the shoes fit tightly. Just make a walk-around inspection of the critter and ensure that he is fit and sound and ready to pack.

Next come the saddle pads. We recommend a good thick hair pad over a folded woolen saddle blanket. Use an oversized pad (48'' x 30'') for packing; it'll help prevent the load from digging into the animal's side and causing a sore. Riding pads are 30'' x 30'' and are too small to use with pack saddles.

Set the saddle pad and/or blanket just forward of the animal's shoulders and slide it back until the front of the pad is about even with the front of the animal's front legs. When you set the saddle up, you want about two to three inches of pad in front of the saddle bars.

Most sawbucks are rigged so that the cinch is about in the ¾ position, which we feel is a good place for the cinch

to be. A few old saddles are rigged so that the cinch is full center and comes down about the middle of the animal's belly. This works okay if you've got a pot-gutted critter, but for most animals you'll be better off with that cinch further forward.

We built and used on our trip a sawbuck with adjustable rigging. This worked really well, and we are well pleased with our experiment. The advantages of adjustable rigging are many, but the main one is that each saddle can be custom-fitted for your particular animal. Set it on his back without the pad or cover, and you can see just where that saddle should ride. The front of the bars should fit just behind the shoulder blades of the animal. And there should be some clearance in front of the bars and back of them. In other words, the naked saddle on a naked back should rock a little, forward and backward. If either end of the bars digs into the back, you're sure gonna have a crippled critter.

Cinches for animals, like belts for humans, come in different sizes. You'll need to measure your animal's girth in order to purchase the correct cinch. The thing you want to avoid is a cinch that is too short or too long. Poorly fitted cinches wear holes in hides where the rings rub against the skin. A proper fit will avoid this troublesome problem.

If you carefully study your animal you will see that there are a few flat places on his body. Two of these flat spots are just behind the front legs and along the front of the rib cage. This is where we like to place those cinch rings, both on riding and pack saddles. Any further back and you squeeze the critter's ribs together and restrict his breathing; any fur-

ther forward and the rings rub against the front legs. Old-time packers say this about saddling, "A ring back and a ring up." It means that the cinch ring should be about 3 inches above the "elbow" of the animal and 3 inches behind it. It's a good rule.

When you tighten the cinch, it's best to do it a little at a time. Older, trail-wise critters learn to blow up their lungs when you pull on that latigo. Then you put your load on and find about six inches of slack in the cinch. We like tight cinches. Don't cut the critter in half but pull firmly on the latigo, walk around awhile, maybe saddle your riding horse, then tighten the cinch on the pack animal some more. A little at a time is the way to do 'er.

The breast collar on the pack saddle should fit snugly without interfering with breathing. The britchen should allow the animal to walk a normal stride without rubbing the hair off his hind legs. When going down steep grades, you can tighten up the rear quarter straps in order to hold the saddle where you want it to be.

On some of our pack saddles we use a crupper, just as we do on our riding saddles, and this works well to hold the outfit in place. The crupper is a folded piece of soft leather which loops under a horse's tail and attaches to the back of a saddle. Some old critters learn to use the crupper and will tuck their tails going downhill and help hold the load where it feels best. A word of caution here for first-time crupper users: try it at home in a safe place before trying it on the trail. Some animals go bonkers when a strap gets under their tail. But most learn to accept it quickly and seem to prefer a crupper over a britchen.

# CONCLUSION

One of the most rewarding aspects of buckskinning is building your own clothing and equipment. You read about how it was back in the fur trade period, and you wonder just what it was like to have lived back then. That's what makes buckskinning so interesting; you can build your own piece of history and relive those wonderful days of yesterday.

Buckskinners who are also horse enthusiasts can experience some of the enjoyment and hardships of our forefathers by building their own pack and equipment. Did you ever wonder just how them old trappers and traders made it across the mountains with all the supplies they needed? And have you ever thought about what a job it must have been to pack all that gear? We wondered about this also and read extensively on the subject.

The answer, like the equipment used, is simple. The saddles of the old packers were stout and of simple construction. This combination stood the test of hard use and long years afield. A properly built saddle that is prudently cared for will easily last you a long lifetime.

You can easily build your own pack saddles if you follow our instructions step by step. We hope that you will not be intimidated by the technical jargon and complicated drawings of our instructions. Study the pictures very carefully and go slowly in your work. We have tried to keep the directions simple, but we are aware that what is so familiar to us may be difficult for you to understand at first. Therefore, we stand ready to field your phone calls or answer your let-ters. You can contact us as follows:

Bob Schmidt
1224 N.E. Hamilton Heights Road
Corvallis, Montana 59828
(406) 961-424383

Tom Bryant
1854 Mountain View Orchard Road
Corvallis, Montana 59828
(406) 961-4194

Just take the building process slowly and try not to get in a big hurry. Don't forget: haste makes waste.

For the true beginner and maybe some of you old mossy horns, we plan to put on a few primitive pack trips in the near future. We are also available, at a small fee, to put on primitive packing clinics. Just holler and we'll come a-spurring and a-whipping.

Another beauty of buckskinning is the joy of putting to use equipment into which you have put many long hours of loving labor. The long winter evenings are just about perfect for sitting by the fire, cutting straps, polishing leather and assembling your gear for the coming season. It's a wonderful feeling of accomplishment to pack your gear in panniers of your own construction and hang 'em on a pack saddle that you made by hand. Ain't no feeling better, nowhere, no way.

## APPENDIX A: WORKS CITED

Daly, H.W. *Manual Of Pack Transportation.* Santa Monico, CA: Quail Ranch Books, 1981.

## APPENDIX B: WORKS CONSULTED

Ahhorn, Richard. *Man Made Mobile.* Washington, D.C.: Smithsonian Institution Press, 1980.

Back, Joe. *Horses, Hitches And Rocky Trails.* Boulder, CO: Johnson Publishing, 1959.

Davis, Francis. *Horse Packing In Pictures.* New York: Charles Scribner & Sons, 1975.

Elser, Smoke and Bill Brown. *Packing In On Horses And Mules.* Missoula, MT: Mountain Press Publishing, 1980.

# Fine Publications from Rebel Publishing Company

## THE BOOK OF BUCKSKINNING — $11.95

The Philosophy of Buckskinning, How to Get Started, Rendezvous & Shoots, The Lodge, The Guns, The Clothing, Accoutrements & Equipment, The Skills, Women in Buckskinning and The Crafts.

## THE BOOK OF BUCKSKINNING II — $12.95

Why Buckskinners Create, Working with Leather, 18th Century Clothing, Horseback Travel, Design & Construction of Powder Horns, Firemaking, Traveling Afoot & by Canoe, Making Camp Gear and Gun Tune-Up & Care.

## THE BOOK OF BUCKSKINNING III — $14.95

Historic Guns & Today's Makers, Quillworking, Trade Beads, 18th & 19th Century Cooking, The Hunting Pouch, Beadworking, Techniques for Making Footwear, Period Shelters, plus a Special Color Section.

## THE BOOK OF BUCKSKINNING IV — $14.95

Traditional Blacksmithing, Blankets in Early America, From Raw Hides to Rawhide, Styles of the Southwest, Smoothbores on the Frontier, Trade Silver, Backwoods Knives, Lighting the Primitive Camp and Historic Sites & Museums.

## THE BOOK OF BUCKSKINNING V — $15.95

Trade Goods for Rendezvous, Games, Sports & Other Amusements, Fur Trade Indian Dresses, Tipi Know-How, Engraving & Carving, Old-Time Music & Instruments, Pack Saddles & Panniers, Museums & Historic Sites II, plus a Special Color Section.

## THE BOOK OF BUCKSKINNING VI — $16.95

Horse Gear East & West, The Traditional Hunting Pouch, Making a Wooden Bow, Historic Shooting Matches, Powder Horns, Frontier Trail Foods, Trekking, Finger Weaving, plus a Special Color Section.

## Collector's Illustrated Encyclopedia of the American Revolution by Neumann & Kravic — $16.95 (softcover)

286 pages of photos and descriptions of over 2300 artifacts from the mid to late 1700s. A great resource book for the reenactor, buckskinner, collector or Revolutionary War enthusiast. The life style of the men in the opposing forces becomes a reality.

| Quantity | Description | Price ea. | Total |
|---|---|---|---|
| | | | |
| | | | |
| | | | |
| | | | |
| | | | |

If you need more space, please use a separate piece of paper.

| | |
|---|---|
| Subtotal | |
| Shipping & Handling | |
| Subtotal | |
| Tex. Res. add 6 3/4% sales tax | |
| Total amount of order | |

*Shipping & Handling:*
*$2.00 for 1st book and*
*$1.00 for each additional.*
*Outside U.S. — $3.00 per book.*

**Method of payment:** ❑ **Check**  ❑ **Money Order**  ❑ **MasterCard**  ❑ **Visa**

*For Fastest service call (903) 832-4726 and use your Visa or MasterCard.*  or mail to: **Rebel Publishing Co., Inc., Dept. B6 Rt. 5, Box 347-M, Texarkana, TX 75501**

## OTHER HISTORICAL TITLES AVAILABLE — CALL OR WRITE FOR FREE BROCHURE